SCHOOL OF A DIFFERENT KIND

The story and history of a Hungarian school in postwar Germany during 1947-1951.

Also by Judith Petres Balogh

THIS OLD HOUSE BY THE LAKE

JULIA

BEYOND CONVENTIONS

THE COUNTESS AND HER DAUGHTER

SUNSET

SCHOOL OF A DIFFERENT KIND

The story and history of a Hungarian school in postwar Germany during 1947-1951.

By:
Judith Petres Balogh and *Nóra Hegedűs Sztáray*

and 33 former students,
who generously contributed their memories, letters,
diaries, photos and biographies.

Manuscript editing: Steve Szappanos
Nóra Hegedűs Sztáray
Photo editing and cover design: Zsuzsa Sztáray
Cover drawing (classroom): Katalin Pettendy Stiskal
Kloster Reisach drawing: Toni Melynadasy
Alpenhof drawing: Gabi Csaba

Copyright © 2015 by Judith Petres Balogh & Nóra Hegedűs Sztáray

Copyright © 2007 by Eleonora M. Sztaray

ISBN # 9781507.8566.11

CreateSpace Independent Publishing Platform

North Charleston, SC

All rights reserved. No part of this publication may be reproduced, stored in a retrieval system or transmitted, in any form or by any means, electronic, mechanical, photocopying, recording or otherwise, without the prior permission of the author.

Published by the authors

Printed in the United States of America

This book is the true story of children, made homeless at the conclusion of World War Two, who found a home in an unusual school at an unusual time. It is the story of dedicated teachers, remarkable, supportive parents and spirited youngsters, rapidly growing to adulthood during highly unusual circumstances. The story is about people and about their struggles to overcome the ordeal of witnessing the collapse of the familiar. While facing the loss of home, future, and security, they managed to transmit to their children, or to their students those values and ideals which were the very foundation of their former life. The story is as much part of history as those of the famous battles. It is a tale of time gone by.

Anne Frank, Helga Weiss, and Nobel Prize winner Imre Kertész wrote about Jewish children and youth living or disappearing in the horror of the Holocaust; Esther Hautzig recounted Jewish children deported to the Soviet Union; Helen Szablya and Tibor Fischer wrote about youth surviving in Communist Hungary just after World War Two. The present book fills a gap: it describes, for the first time. the life of the young people, who had to flee their homes toward the end of the war, leaving everything behind. They had to rebuild their life in a country totally foreign to them during bewildering times.

In this respect, the above mentioned books are related to the **SCHOOL OF A DIFFERENT KIND** because it too tells about the true, innocent and unsung victims of a war: children and young adults.

Ha majd az évek elszelelnek
S fehér szint adnak fejednek,
Megrohan majd az emlékek hada.
És öledben ül az első unoka
S esengve kéri, mesélj nagymama!
Jusson eszedbe sok-sok év után
Vidám diákkorod,
Hogy élted napsugaras tavaszán
Együtt töltöttünk sok-sok szép napot.
S mesélni kezdesz.

Istók Ravasz

Interpreted and translated by two former students:

When years have flown away,
Turning to white your youthful hair
The memory will surely return to you.
Your first grandchild will snuggle up to you
Pleading, Grandma, tell us your story.
Remember then after so many years
The cheerful happy student days,
When in the spring of our life
We spent together so much precious time.
And Grandma will start telling the story.

Tony Meynadasy

When many years have blown away
showering silver hues upon your hair,
legions of memories come crowding
around you as your first grandchild snuggles
in your lap pleading:
Grandma! a story, please ...do tell!!
May you remember then:
your joyous student life when in the
shining springtime of the years we shared
so many happy days and may you then
begin to tell your tale.

Dóra Szabó Badzey

So begins one of the poems of Istók Ravasz, son of Dr. Dezső Ravasz as he remembers the times we spent together in Niederaudorf (Germany) at the Hungarian refugee school, established two years after the Second World War ended. He was but a teenager when he wrote the above lines, but he foresaw that after the swiftly passing years, our children and grandchildren would want to hear about a past which to them, living in a happier world, would be more or less incomprehensible.

Istók Ravasz, whose father was our first school principal at the school, lived with his parents and with us in the Pension Alpenhof in Niederaudorf, the first site of our boarding school. In 1948, the family Ravasz moved back to Hungary from Germany, and before Istók turned nineteen, he died of gunshot wounds during the aftermath of the Hungarian Revolution of 1956. His young life, however, was not totally wasted because he too was victim of the grand effort to gain freedom for Hungary from the Russian occupation and from Communism. In addition, he left us his collection of poems, (*Töredékek egy álomról* - Shards of a Dream- published posthumously in 2009) and also a gentle reminder to tell our story.

This we have done.

FOREWORD

I recently hosted an evening book club with 30 women and we talked about our school years. We talked about stern teachers, memorizing multiplication tables, the nuns in Catholic schools, terrible food in the cafeterias, but none of us mentioned going to school in DP camps far from our parents in another, foreign country and having to put up with a scarcity or even total absence of books, maps, or pencils, never mind the lack of food, clothing, heat, activities most school children accept as natural, and the absence of familiar surroundings. This was not mentioned in the cozy comfort of our library because we could not even imagine such things and of course, none of us experienced anything like it.

This book is an eye opener as it moves the reader across the global community and reveals a little known space and time; it shows what was happening in Bavaria (Southern Germany) during and beyond WWII, with special emphasis on school children.

The book market is rich in tales about abused children, but this book does not fit into that category. These children were not abused, unless we consider warfare the greatest of all abusers, and of course, we would not be far from the truth.

Intelligent, inquisitive people crave factual stories and here is one that is rarely told in a narrative but is presented in a well documented format from a personal viewpoint. Reports about people in general during WWII are available, but up to now there was a deep silence over what happened to school children and to young adults during and *after* the war. I suppose this topic is interesting not just to teachers, but to the general reading public as well.

Hearing about the school at Niederaudorf-Reisach from the time of arriving at the Alpenhof, through the programs and hardships at the school to the end of its existence, crowned by a memorial tablet on the a wall of the building where it was housed, was a rare experience. We both read and digested the words with delight. There was so much horror and the poverty was so overwhelming; yet, the children went on doing what had to be done and managed to stay happy while doing it. Students and teachers carved out a small existence for survival and were proud to achieve their goals. At the end of the book, in the highly interesting biographical sketches, we get to know the wonderful people, who emerged from that school.

We loved reading about teachers telling students that God did not cause WWII, nor the death camps, or the vicious treatment of human beings. We loved when they were told that God was there all along at the front lines, in the death camps and everywhere else, suffering with the victims. They were taught that the world cannot live at the level of stupidity and meanness into which it blundered, and that truth and justice are as important as freedom and love. The students were taught to forgive everyone, and they were told that judgment and punishment was not their duty; this burden was God's affair. But in spite of the noble teaching, the students found it impossible to forgive Hitler, even though they could forgive the fighting men of the enemy." What a powerful piece of writing!

The "Show, Not Tell, Writing" also moves the reader to "feel" the lack of food and heat during the times. Mouse droppings in oatmeal are vividly described. Marta brings it to the present by saying she never buys a bag of oatmeal in a shiny Australian supermarket without shaking it first to see whether there are mouse droppings in it – this has become one of our favorite, but totally abhorrent visual images. It builds a bridge to our current comfortable and hygienic life.

The discussions of the "Americans" are so close to home and the very ambivalence of the students about the US military gave us a pause, as both my husband and I worked overseas for the government during the occupation years in Germany. At that time we did not much consider the viewpoint of the other side. Nevertheless, while we were there as part of the effort to prevent Europe from being enveloped by Communism, and be overrun by the Soviet army, there was always the uncomfortable fact that during the war we were allies of the Soviets; yet, very soon thereafter were called upon to prevent their total rule over Western Europe. Reading the students' comments about this we could understand their confusion. Catherine II. of Russia remarked that in politics a capable ruler must be guided by circumstances, conjectures and conjunctions. Perhaps she was right. Fortunately most of us are not called upon to make decisions based on these.

The book brings things to full cycle when the young voices are paired with the voices of the now aging students. It is done in a style and in such a persuasive voice that the reader ends up deeply caring for every individual featured in the interviews. Somehow the story of "School of a different kind" becomes a personal experience even for those, who have never visited Europe and never met a DP!

Every book adds to the strength of our understandings and this book has enriched our library of human stories! Thank you for asking us to read the manuscript and to respond!

Drs. Gene and Debra Knudsen, former U.S. Dept. of Defense educators in Germany, retired volunteers, and adjunct faculty members at Morningside College and Northeast Community College in the greater Siouxland area near Sioux City.

PREFACE

to the original manuscript in Hungarian

Several decades after we left our boarding school and *gimnázium* (academic high school) in the Bavarian Alps, my sister Piroska ran across a book, titled <u>Kastl über Amberg</u>. It gave a historical account of Burg Kastl, an academic high school for Hungarian refugees in Germany. A brief mention was made of our school as one of its predecessors, established after world War II. Out of 13 paragraphs, 12 contained incorrect information. The most disturbing to us was the account of our first principal dying at the end of the first year. Actually, Dr. Dezső Ravasz and his family returned to Hungary in 1948. He was also given the wrong last name: Róka. Both *ravasz* and *róka* have meaning in Hungarian. *Ravasz* means sly or cunning; *róka* means fox. It is easy to see how the connotation of sly and fox confused the writer. We could have laughed, were it not so sad. All the dates and most of the data were incorrect. We were stunned and could not believe that a book was written and published without the slightest effort to do research. We decided to correct this misinformation, and tell our story. At that time we knew of no official records of our school. The source had to be the former schoolmates' input.

After we left the school, and immigrated to the United States, we lost contact with each other. In our rough estimate, close to 200 students were in attendance over the five years of the school's existence. They could have settled anywhere in the world. In the chaos and uncertainty of those times, no one was able to provide a forwarding address. For decades, we were so busy with our own lives, creating a career, raising a family that we weren't even thinking of the possibility of having reunions.

Fortunately, there was a nucleus of 15 former students living in Cleveland, Ohio, home to many Hungarians. In 1983 they held a small party for Márta, one of our schoolmates from Australia. This gave them impetus to organize a world-wide reunion the following year, inviting everyone whose address they could find. Ballusz, (Éva Balla Zahorai) took the lead, searched for addresses, sent out as many as 65 invitations for a reunion to be held in Cleveland in 1984. 28 former students attended from throughout the U.S, Australia and Germany, and those, unable to come, sent letters, telling us of their new life, their family and accomplishments. To our delight, one of the principals, Ferenc Kovács and his wife Erzsébet, also attended the reunion. From then on more than a dozen were held at various locations. Communication has been established.

At the 1986 reunion, held at our first location, the Alpenhof in Niederaudorf, Germany, we passed out questionnaires, and mailed them out to those who weren't able to come. Piroska set up a photo copying machine to make copies of pictures from the albums brought to the reunion. Of the first year and a half of the school's existence, we have no photos. At that time no one had a camera, nor film. The more talented students recorded the world around us by drawing pictures. We are very fortunate that Mari's (Brazil)father, Gábor Buza, took close to a hundred photos at a special occasion in May, 1948. Those and our schoolmate Tony Mélynádasy's (Connecticut) photos, taken between the fall of 1948 and spring of 1951, provide a visual proof of our school's existence. We are grateful to them.

We shared memories, gathered old documents, report cards, letters, other treasures hidden for years in boxes in the attics. We had the habit of dating and signing picture postcards whenever we attended a special event. We kept scrapbooks. Anikó, now living in Australia, sent a page from hers, listing the grade and name of students attending the school in June, 1947. She had actual signatures of the students. We started compiling class rosters. Béla from Michigan shared the postcard, written to him by the principal, asking him to help with the move of the school's properties to the Passau-Waldwerke school. From this we found out that the school actually closed and was moved there on March 29, 1951. Amazingly, we kept all of these little, to others perhaps insignificant treasures. From these and answers to our questionnaires, I was able to put together close to five year history of our school. To verify my findings, I sent out the first draft to more than 30 former participants, asking for corrections. Additional information and material poured in from all parts of the world. A book was in the making. I included repetition of some facts since hearing it from several people made the story more authentic. It was no longer hearsay. The purpose was to correct the misinformation, to tell our story, to shed light on the lives and accomplishments of the former students, and to share our story with the next generation and with everyone else who is interested in this remarkable journey, and finally, to have a "yearbook" of the time we spent together.

By 2002, most of us were retired, had more time to concentrate on finishing the task. At around the same time, we heard from Dr. Lajos Koncz, who was working on a similar project with the former students of another academic high school, authorized by the same School Committee for students living at one of the major refugee camps in Passau-Waldwerke. A parent called his attention to an article about our school, written in 1999 by Dr. Cserháti, editor of "Életünk," published in Munich, Germany. Dr. Cserháti had access to the archives of the Hungarian Catholic Mission in Munich. His article was based on our principals' reports, sent in 1947-1949 to the School Committee. It was a most welcome and valuable find. Finally, we had authentic information, which supported much of our findings.

By 2007 it was ready for publication. At a meeting in Cleveland, Piroska arranged with Dr. Koncz to include our original manuscript in its entirety in his book, "…az írás megmarad; A németországi magyar gimnáziumok története 1945-1956." ("… The Written Word Is Never Lost; The History of Hungarian Academic High Schools in Germany, 1945-1956."), BookSurge, 2008. Dr. Koncz chose the title, based on the classic rule of Roman law: *"Quod non est in actis, non est in mundo"*: that which does not exist in a document, does not exist in the world. It's available for Hungarian readers on amazon.com, at the National Library of Hungary, (*Országos Széchenyi Könyvtár,* Budapest), and at http://mek.oszk.hu/06500/06552/06552.pdf.

A number of our schoolmates wished to have a translation of our story in English. At the 2007 reunion in Cleveland, several volunteered to do that. I divided the manuscript into small sections and passed them out. Very soon, the former students discovered that translation is not an easy task. Only two sections were finished; the rest gave up, saying, it is an impossible job.

We owe a great debt of gratitude to our former schoolmate, Judith Petres Balogh, an accomplished writer of several books, editor of a monthly magazine, for tackling the huge task of translating parts of the original manuscript, preserving the voices of students, and expanding it with background information for the English speaking readers that is of interest not only to our descendants, but also to educators and the general reader. We are forever indebted to her and to more than thirty former students all over the world, who shared their memories and memorabilia.

On behalf of all the Nieder students and descendents, I want to thank my daughter, Zsuzsa Sztáray, for bringing fresh life into the more than sixty year old photos that most of us haven't seen. The new technology is amazing.

Our task is not complete. We are still searching for the original reports of the principals, the records of the School Committee and notes and documents of Pater Fekete, who was there at the inception and at the closing of our school. All of these were transferred to various institutions in Hungary over the past years, and have not been available to us.

Nóra Hegedűs Sztáray

AUTHOR'S PREFACE

Istók's wish was thus partially fulfilled.   But not quite.

In 1945 at the very beginning of the great adventure of life so totally different from the protected, predictable and familiar we knew until then, like most young people, we could not imagine that old age would catch up with us. At that time it seemed even more astounding that at some time in the far future we should be grandparents. Furthermore, in case this incredible event should ever occur, it was beyond us to imagine that our grandchildren would not speak our language. But the truth is that many third generation descendants, even if they speak some Hungarian, are not able to read it, or else it is so difficult for them that soon they give up. So if grandma, (or in some cases grandpa, because after 1948 a few boys also attended the formerly all girls' school) is to tell the story, she (he) must do it in a language the grandchildren understand.

We all agreed that our children's children should certainly know the past. Thinkers, ever since Confucius, have warned: if you don't know your past, you cannot have a future. Although Hungarian is a beautiful and expressive language, despite our personal biases we know that it is definitely not an international language; therefore, the decision was made to translate our book into English, a universal language generally understood even by those descendants, whose parents ended up in South America, or remained in Europe. We also decided to enlarge it with necessary background information and reshape the original into an extended book. This made this version much different from the original.

***

At the end of the war there was a worldwide sense of relief and euphoria that this bloody war, costing millions of lives, was over and a general fantasy of getting on in the spirit of "business as usual" prevailed. However, this was very far from the truth. "School of a Different Kind" offers personal experiences of a group of young girls to show how people lived in those times. It is, of course, as much part of history as are the famous battles or the famous (or infamous) peace settlements.

Discounting scholarly books, few personal memories were written about the post war years, and even the excellent scholarly books tend to concentrate on the later, the Cold War phase of the time period. As we did some research, we found that practically nothing has been written about the large group of refugee children scattered all over Europe.

Because of the German insistence of keeping records, the world knows exactly how many victims were transported to the Death Camps, or concentration Camps, but there are no reliable records about the refugees. Those sources, which mention these masses, only quote a vague approximation of "about hundreds of thousands," but even these do not mention children. We felt that this was an astonishing gap in the history of post-war Europe, and were convinced that our book could add to the pool of information by providing missing facts in a narrative form. This carefully constructed volume, written at a personal level, offers accurate resource material for educators, historians and social scientists. It offers to the reader, regardless of nationality, age or place of residence, a richly varied picture of a remarkable time period, and also offers a glimpse into the educational philosophy of the past. Naturally, it is not possible in a single volume—and after so many years—to write about *all* the children existing homeless and rootless in Europe, but the reader, by becoming familiar with one group of children (in this case teenage girls) is able to form a general picture of the times and situations existing then.

Aside from offering post-war information, it is perhaps also of some interest to Americans and other nations to learn about the refugees or "Displaced Persons" whom they so generously accepted after the war during the middle of the last century, and to whom they offered new homes and a future. From these immigrants, mostly highly educated, skilled, experienced and creative people came a long list of philosophers, doctors, educators, scientists, engineers, artists, authors, who enriched the cultural and scientific life of the USA and other countries.

In this spirit we are now presenting our incredible past to our descendants and to all who are interested in the way difficulties can be overcome in seemingly hopeless situations. The book is a testimony of what people, even children, are capable of achieving; it is a triumph of the indomitable human spirit. It is the story of young girls, reaching adulthood and maturity more rapidly than is usual for young people living in peace and security. It is the account of how these young girls tried to search for truth, justice, love and beauty in a world gone crazy and about to fall apart. In a touchingly inexperienced way, they attempted to tackle the enigma of good and evil, and to find a reason for our existence on the planet. They were learning to have faith, not just in a better future, but in an afterlife as well,—during times when nothing seemed to be fixed, secure or sure any more. And as the girls were groping for a better future, so was an entire continent, which in the bloody horror of the war has lost, among other things, the spirit, which at one time gave birth to western civilization.

The book contains recollections, excerpts from letters, diaries, documents as well as photos. It also contains a selection of short biographies of teachers and of students, describing their life-paths and accomplishments.

But the book is not a dismal list of hardships in evil times and it is not crying out: "Poor, poor me, why was Fate so cruel to me;" rather it is upbeat, and packed with cherished memories. It does not idealize nor vilify the past; it merely tells how it was.

Judith Petres Balogh

TABLE OF CONTENTS

FOREWORD vii

PREFACE ix

AUTHOR'S PREFACE xiii

INTRODUCTION AND CREDITS 1

HISTORICAL BACKGROUND 5

THE BEGINNING - NIEDERAUDORF 13

    How did the students learn about the school? 16

    Arriving at the school 20

ABOUT TEACHERS AND TEACHING 25

RELIGION AT SCHOOL 41

EVERYDAY LIFE 55

    Food, or the lack of it - at the Alpenhof: 61

    Food, or the lack of it - at Reisasch: 69

    Heating, or the lack of it 71

    Keeping clean, health issues, doing tasks - at the Alpenhof: 73

    Keeping clean, health issues, doing tasks - at Reisach: 74

    Recreation and entertainment 76

    Correspondence 91

SCHOOL LITERARY CLUB (Önképzőkör), ... 95

POVERTY, TUITION AND THE BURDEN ON PARENTS 99

SCOUTING AT NIEDERAUDORF AND AT REISACH 109

CONTACT WITH THE WORLD AROUND US 117

GRADUATION 119

OUR FIRST PRINCIPAL IS LEAVING US 125

REISACH 131

    Fun time, exercising, discipline 138

BOYS IN THE GIRLS' SCHOOL 145

MEMORIES FROM REISACH: 149

THE LAST YEARS OF OUR SCHOOL 161

    Voices of students: 162

CONCLUSION 167

BIOGRAPHIES 173

    Students: 173

    Judith Ábrahám – Nagyőszy (Mrs. Nagyőszy-Wolf) 173

    Eva Bonyhay 176

    Magda Hadady 178

    The Hegedűs siblings 178

    Piroska Hegedűs (Mrs. Sándor Zoltán) 181

    Nóra Hegedűs (Mrs. Zoltán Sztáray) 182

    László Hegedűs 188

    Klára Kölcsey (Mrs. Shelton) 190

    Béla Lahner 195

    Dr. Mária Magdolna Markó 197

    Antal (Tony) Mélynádasy 202

    Judith Petres (Mrs. Balogh) 203

    Zsuzsa Petres (Mrs. Szappanos) 214

    Anna Mária (Anikó) Radnay (Mrs. Kent) 220

- Dóra Szabó (Mrs. Badzey) 224
- Éva Tirczka, (Mrs. Piller) 227
- Iván N. Zoltán 232
- Our Teachers: 234
  - Mária Adelsberger 234
  - Mária Bárány 234
  - Kálmán Csia 236
  - Géza Fekete 237
  - Ferenc Kovács 239
  - Dr. Dezső Ravasz 245
- INDEX 249

INTRODUCTION AND CREDITS

This book is a translation from the Hungarian. The original text has been revised, enlarged with information, and reformatted to better address the readers of the English edition.

Most topics are introduced with quotes from the essay of His Excellency Ferenc Cserháti, now auxiliary bishop of Esztergom-Budapest, Bishop of Hungarians abroad. He was a "secondhand" witness to the struggles of our school. Years after the school closed, and before he was appointed to his present elevated position, he had an assignment in München, Germany, where he found the documents and reports sent to the School Committee by the principals. He realized their value, and before these documents would have been lost forever, he incorporated them into an essay, "Iskola a Fogadóban" (School in an Inn). It was published in two installments — in the 1999 September and November issues in the Catholic monthly ÉLETÜNK. His Excellency graciously gave his permission for us to use part of his well documented work.

His Excellency's remarks, as well as the documents, excerpts from letters and diaries of the time are printed in italics. The connecting texts and explanations, not part of the original book, are printed in bold face letters.

Alpenhof, where our school was first located, is often referred to as "*Pension.*" It designates a hotel establishment of a smaller scale. It is somewhat similar, but not identical to the B&B in the U.S (Bed and Breakfast). If a meal, other than breakfast is offered, it is always *table d'hôte:* there is only a set menu without the option of a menu card. The choice of Alpenhof for the boarding school was partially influenced by the fact that having offered meals in happier times, it was equipped with an adequate kitchen and utensils.

About the organization of the school system at that time: the twelve years of schooling were divided into two segments: four years of elementary grades and eight years of further education or some practical training, often the two combined. Niederaudorf was a type of school called *gimnázium* (Gymnasium: the name is taken from the Greek: a place where physical and mental instructions were offered). This type of school offered advanced education for those students, who wished to continue their studies at the university level. It is comparable to the college preparatory schools in the USA. The first year in the *gimnázium* was called "first grade" and graduation was at the 8th grade. In order to avoid confusion, I am using the more familiar 1 to 12 designation for the grade levels.

The Hungarian language uses two distinct types of speaking in conversations. One is the familiar form ("*te*"). It is used among people belonging to the same general group such as age, family, occupation or social standing.

It is also used by adults when speaking to children and young people. It is a more intimate form, such as using first names in English. The formal, polite form ("*Ön*" or "*Maga*") is used with others, and almost always between men and women, even if they belong to the same social group. There are subtle variations even here, but it does not concern the present book. Students of course were expected to use the polite form when speaking to their teachers, but it was most remarkable that teachers used the same formal, polite form when addressing their students. They never used the familiar "*te*" form. It was an expression of mutual respect, deference and courtesy, and it set the tone for the school.

Students were permitted to use the first name of teachers, but always added the honorific "*Néni*" or "*Bácsi*" — aunt or uncle to the name. This of course does not indicate family relationship, but is comparable to Mr. or Ms. or "Ma'am" and "Sir" in English. While we called our first principal "Uncle Ravasz" the second principal, Ferenc Kovács, was younger, and the honorific "Uncle" just did not seem to fit. In Hungarian the word 'school principal' is director'; we simply shortened the word to "*Diri*." Naturally, we would never have dared to address him so, but he knew that behind his back we called him *Diri*.

This book originated as a result of Nóra Hegedűs' work (Mrs. Zoltán Sztáray). Without her dedication in collecting the material, it would never have come into existence. During the translation process and the writing of the connecting texts, Zsuzsa Petres (Mrs. Steve Szappanos) was a constant source of encouragement. Steve Szappanos, not even a former student of our school, shaped the manuscript into book form, and provided valuable advice on several parts of the content. Christina Cantrell not only corrected part of the manuscript, but it was her suggestion to add background information. She pointed out that while to us, former students, the locations and events are well known and require no further explanation, many readers more than a century later and living on another continent, in a different culture, might not be familiar with these. As a result, the connecting text (not part of the Koncz edition) was inserted. My sincere gratitude goes to Gene Knudsen, retired DoDD's Superintendent and his wife, Debra, retired teacher, who from the time they read the first thirty pages of the draft, supported and cheered me on. ("...*both Gene and I think this is a book that has to be published! It is a story never told and the kind we should all read...*" Mrs. Knudsen commented). Many thanks go to Mrs. Zahoray (*Ballusz*), who corresponded throughout the years with the former students and then at the end of each year wrote (and is still writing) a long "Christmas letter" to all of us. In these she reports what she found out about everybody during a given year. This way we keep in touch and always know about each other. *Ballusz* also has a remarkable memory, and contributed a great many details to this book. And of course special thanks go to all those former students who helped by translating their autobiographies into English.

Our school had a peculiar feature: we were amused to find that almost half the girls were named *Éva, Mária* or *Katalin*. There were also three *Judits* and three *Annas*. Either our parents had not much imagination, or else those were the fashionable names around 1930. When someone called "*Éva,*" about half dozen girls responded: "Yes?" In order to avoid such confusion, we immediately started to give pet names or diminutives to those girls who shared the same name.

In the following list, the contributors are listed by their maiden names, followed by their (later) married name in [ ] brackets. The name used in this book is shown in ( ) brackets, and italicized, spelled according to Hungarian rules and accented vowels.

The contributors to this book are:

Judith Ábrahám [Nagyőszy] (*Judit*);
Éva Balla [Zahoray] (*Ballusz*);
Márta Bárány [Draveczky] (*Márta*);
Ákos Barcsay (*Ákos*);
Éva Bonyhay [Magyar] (*Éva*);
Mária Buza [Lajtaváry] (*Mari*);
Klári Csaba [Hidas] (*Csabusz*);
Zsolt Csaba (*Zsolt*);
Anna Dax [Winkler] (*Nusi*);
Lilla Finkey (*Lilla*);
Éva Gruber (*Vica*);
Magda Hadady (*Magda*);
Nóra Hegedűs [Sztáray] (*Nóra*);
Piroska Hegedűs [Zoltán] (*Piri*);
Péter Igo-Kemenes (*Péter*);
Klára Juhász
Ferenc Jautz (*Feri*);
Kati Kozányi [Fodor] (*Koci*);
Katalin Kristó-Nagy (*Katyi*);
Klára Kölcsey [Shelton] (*Klári*);
Béla Lahner (*Béla*);
Éva Mészáros [Katafias] (*Mészárka*);
Antal Mélynádasy [Meynadasy] (*Tóni*);
Katalin Pettendy [Stiskal] (*Kati*);
Mária Magdolna Markó [Gajáry] (*Markóczi*);
Judith Petres [Balogh] (*Jutka*);
Zsuzsanna Petres [Szappanos] (*Zsuzsika, Zsuzsa*);
Anna Radnay [Kent] (*Anikó*);
Dóra Szabó [Badzey], (*Dóra*);
Ági Szkladányi [Vajnek] (*Ági*);
Éva Tirczka [Pillér] (*Tirczka*);
Anna Váczy [Mélynádasy] (*Pancsi*);
Várhelyi Mária [Lajtaváry] (*Dagi*)
Iván Zoltán (*Iván*).

A note to dispel some confusion:
As will be evident from the narrative, the school was first located in the small hotel Alpenhof at Niederaudorf. Later, due to severe financial difficulties, it was moved to the convent at Reisach. When organizing the book, we faced the disturbing reality that some statements about general topics such as food, heating or health were true about life in Niederaudorf and others only about Reisach. Sometimes it was true of both places, but some aspects did not change after the move; these were true of both places. In the end, to avoid needless repetition, we decided against writing two parts, a separate one for each location. Whenever necessary, we added a note to clarify at which location the event took place.

And finally, a word about my personal role in this endeavor. The reader might rightfully ask, how dare I touch a story, which by now is sixty five years old and getting older, just like the students, who once lived at Niederaudorf. I am not a trained historian, only a translator and the author of the connecting texts. But I have excuses to justify my daring attempt.

The first week after the school came into existence, I was already enrolled (at age fourteen) in the sixth grade and stayed there until we immigrated to the USA in 1951, so I too am a personal witness to the struggles and triumphs. In addition, I not only kept a diary, but wrote weekly letters to my mother, who kept them. My parents divorced when I was six years old and my mother insisted that I write weekly letters to my father, then living in another town. Being blindly obedient, I did so; but to be truthful, in the beginning the letters were produced with her generous prompting. (Let's face it: she dictated them). Later, as I advanced in years and school grades, and was more independent in the writing of my weekly *belles-lettres,* she still helped with her suggestions and guidance. I learned how to "pad" my writings to my father with a great many details to satisfy my mother's wish to produce letters long and informative enough. Obviously, writing is skill that can be learned. So by the time I was fourteen and enrolled at Niederaudorf, I was an experienced letter writer. This proved to be invaluable because according to longstanding habit, my letters to my mother from school (and my diary) contained a rich store of details and descriptions, which otherwise would have been lost. A large part of the content of my letters and the diary is incorporated into the connecting text. Both turned out to be good resources when compiling this book. As is well known, memory fades, and even if the past does not sink into total oblivion, the remembered events are sometimes unwittingly incorrect or embellished. All the resources combined: His Excellency's writing, the letters, diaries, documents, interviews, as well as the recollections of the students, ensure an accurate account of the past. Our group of former students is inexorably getting older, and with our passing, this mosaic of a historical time gone would be lost but for this book.

Judith Petres Balogh

HISTORICAL BACKGROUND

In the twenty-first century for those who were not involved in the drama, it is most difficult to visualize the years 1944-46 in Europe. So many years later the horror, chaos, and the total lack of reality seems, even to those of us who lived through it, more like the fiction of a demented author than the real life we faced then. How can one explain to those who have never heard it, that the sudden wailing of the air raid alarm sent a surge of adrenalin through the body screaming "flight" (forget about fight) and why is it that later in a peaceful, happy world it took years until we did not shudder hearing the siren of a police car or of an emergency vehicle? How can one explain that the sound of an airplane, high above in the clear, blue sky flying to some exciting destination with happy people on board was a menacing sound for years? That the Fourth of July firecrackers were scary? That the sight of any sort of uniform caused heart palpitation? That more than a half century later we still can't throw away leftover food? That we refuse to watch movies dealing with war and violence? How could we explain about the nightmares which kept returning for many years? It is over now, and we are thankful that our children, now nearing retirement age, were spared from such a world-class drama.

It was January 1945. My mother, younger sister and I just fled from our town, Székesfehérvár, (Stuhlweissenburg, Hungary) after we endured four weeks of Russian occupation there, which surely qualified as the anteroom of Hell. The Soviet troops were occupying our town from Christmas Eve on, but at the end of January our military drove them out for a short while. This gave the townspeople a chance to hurriedly leave town before the enemy re-entered.

The above sentence is so simple and factual, it is almost banal. It totally lacks the drama which is behind the statement. Even I find it hard to imagine how we lived through it. I marvel at my mother's presence of mind that when escape was possible, she had the strength to make rational decisions about fleeing, and was able to hurriedly pack a few essentials. (How did she know what to pack when she had no idea where we were going, for how long, and under what conditions???) She had one last look at her wonderful, elegant home, the bastion of security, then ushered her two young children out into the unknown. And then the home was no longer. It sank into the murky depth of painful memories. She joined the league of unsung women, who became the protectors of their families, while their husband fought the enemy, God only knows where. A world had disappeared, and naked survival became the issue. How did people do it? How did they function after such a dramatic loss? Not only home, security, and livelihood, but the very future disappeared.

We walked out into the bitter cold night, frightened and having no other plans, except to get away from the fighting line as fast and as far as we could. The snow was falling fitfully and was driven by an icy wind—and the entire improbable scene of the disoriented masses running for their life was illuminated by exploding flares, bombs, grenades, and the fires of burning houses. To the hellish scene, the music was composed of the roar of deep flying planes, the staccato of gunfire aimed at the fleeing masses, and the all too frequent screams when the guns hit home. The world was witnessing an authentic Götterdämmerung (twilight of the gods) as prophesized in the Norse mythology: a war of the gods which brings about the end of the world.

After a long night, which could fill an entire chapter of a book, we arrived somewhere, none of us really knew where. Unknown women bundled up against the brutal cold and surely in line for sainthood, were stationed at the roadside behind makeshift stoves, offering bowls of hot soup to the fleeing masses. Among the three of us we only had one cup, so we took turns standing in line for what I thought was the best meal in the world.

It was my turn to wait in the queue. I was then almost twelve years old, a pale and rather nondescript girl. My hair was cut short the way boys wear it. I still wore the somewhat oversized boy's clothing a neighbor lent me. Both served as disguise in order to escape the lecherous beasts wearing Soviet military uniforms. It did not matter to them if their victim was a child or a very old woman. Everybody tried to hide, or use a disguise.

While waiting for my turn for the soup, I—always very communicative—entertained those standing around me with the horrors we witnessed during the occupation. I was in the middle of describing a particularly terrible scene, which by the way I hardly understood when a Hungarian military officer with the most tired face I ever saw grabbed me by the collar of my borrowed coat and then pushed me, not all too gently, behind the corner of a house where we were out of earshot.

"Listen, you insolent, big-mouthed-poor-excuse-for-a-boy," he hissed at me. I suppose he would have liked to roar, but had no desire to call attention to us. "I order you to keep your damned mouth shut—or else, I'll have you shot right here without losing a single tear over your sorry little ass. Don't you know that spreading rumors during war is severely punished? It is called treason, my boy!"

I was stunned. I did not spread rumors—I only talked about what I saw, which was frightening enough; but it most certainly was not some sort of a made-up, uneasy rumor with an intent of treason. Anyhow, what was treason? War had, among other things, a new and frightening vocabulary. And besides, nobody ever talked to me that way before. I was deeply hurt. It also took me some time to realize that he took me for a boy. I guess my disguise worked better than I imagined.

"But... but I was not lying! I told the truth," I stammered. I was raised never to tell a lie and that was my main concern now. That, and the fear that I might lose out getting my share of the soup. But I did tell it the way it was. Don't call me a liar, or a gossipmonger. And don't use those words at me. Just listening to the words is surely a sin, which I would probably have to confess next time I meet a priest. And say another word and I shall surely cry, betraying my sex.

"I know, son," he responded in a much milder tone. "I know. But look, there are lots of soldiers around here. If they hear your horror tales—and what is more important, they hear these tales from the mouth of a kid—they would immediately know it is the truth and not propaganda, and they would instantly desert. Understand? Nothing could keep them at their posts if they knew what was happening to their families behind the front lines. So go back for your soup, son, but keep your mouth shut. Our country needs fighting soldiers now, more than ever. Don't you see? You have to thank them that you got a chance to escape from your town. You very likely owe your life to them. Don't cause them to desert. This is your assignment in this war. Understand, son? Anyhow, Lord knows, there is not much they could do to save their families in this war of Satan." I guess the last sentence was not meant for me, and perhaps after all he was not such a bad sort. At any rate, he was invoking

God, which was good. His moral standing climbed a few notches, at least the way I saw it. And he made me feel useful and involved; he gave me an important assignment. He made me part of the adult world.

Events blurred after this, and when we thought it could not get any worse, at least the war ended. It was over, but things did not get any better for us. Almost immediately more troubles surfaced. And the war left its indelible mark upon our soul. We would never be the same as we were before.

Two hopeless years followed without any vision of a future. We dared not return back home to occupied Hungary. The rumors seeping out of the country were frightening. After having lived through the Soviet occupation, we believed every word of what was whispered. We could not stay in war-destroyed Germany. There was no future there for us; besides, we were not particularly welcome to stay. That nation had enough of its own burdens and plenty of problems to solve; it had no need for refugees from other countries. Immigration to overseas countries at that time was not an option for us. During the war, Hungary fought against the Soviet Union on the side of the Germans, so for quite some time, even after the uneasy peace settled over the world, we were not considered fit candidates to live in a free, democratic system.

After the war, there were an estimated 7 to 11 million refugees "Displaced Persons" from several eastern European countries, who were seeking refuge, predominantly in Germany, Austria and Italy. The numbers included the barely living concentration camp victims, just freed by the American Occupying Forces. They had no family left who would wait for their return, and they had no physical or psychological strength left to make decisions about their life, so they just stayed, like the rest of us. The D.P.s, regardless of nationality, religion or political beliefs, had nowhere to go, lived in misery but even so, were a burden to the countries where they were staying. President Truman initiated the Act which proposed to allow foreigners the entry into the USA over and above the usual yearly quota. The Displaced Persons Act of 1948 did make this possible, but even then the approval of the applications was restricted. Priority was given to those who applied from resettlement camps, were healthy, or to those who could prove in advance their financial independence after arriving in the USA. This allowed about 200.000 people to enter the USA, but the clause requiring financial independence eliminated most refugees, except those lucky few who had relatives in the USA, willing to provide affidavits of accepting financial responsibility. The would-be immigrants possessed no wealth and all they could offer was their skill, education and the willingness to do work. However, in the years until 1948, even this slight possibility did not exist; the initial wording of the Act did not include Hungarians. It was not until 1950, five difficult years later, when the rules were relaxed and Hungarians were able to enter the USA. By the year 1952 slightly over 400.000 Displaced Persons could enter because of this Act.

I often wondered about our parents who so heroically dealt with the problems and with the kind of poverty they could not previously imagine. We never heard them complain. We did not see tears. We did not understand how they fed us, but they did. They did what had to be done, and preserved their sanity as well as ours. Contrary to the belief held by some that poverty, fear, insecurity and the meanness of a world getting fatally disappointed by its own aberrations cripples the soul—we proved that these conditions do not necessarily deform lives. At least in our case it did not. It is the achievement of our parents that we have not turned out to be neurotic, dysfunctional and useless individuals.

But despite the heroic efforts of our elders, we children were bewildered. Although naked fear was kept from us at bay by our parents, we lived in a state of curious unsettlement, as if we were waiting at some desolate place for a train which never arrived. Nothing much happened, and as weeks turned into months and then into years, we were still living in some sort of temporary limbo. While we did mostly nothing, most of us did not get any schooling either. The adults were more or less paralyzed, or weighted down with the problems of survival. Every day they hoped for some change, for a solution, which did not come. For a while, nobody thought about establishing schools because everybody considered the situation transitory. But as time passed, and the fantasy of transience turned into hardened permanence, the question of schools, or rather the lack of them, acquired urgency.

At most places, especially in the larger towns where the refugee camps were located, German schools could not absorb us, nor did we speak German well enough to be able to attend middle or high school. Establishing an accredited school of our own, which would be accepted by the Hungarian as well as the German Department of Education, and also by the occupying Allied Forces, touched the realm of impossible dreams. Its eventual existence is one of the modern day miracles.

All of the above are, of course, my own experiences; however, these are not unique nor could be considered individual. Every one of us, who landed at Niederaudorf had her own astounding story to tell, matching scene by scene my own, as is obvious in some of the biographies at the end of this book. Anyone else writing this introduction could have started with her own story, but it would be eerily similar to mine. This shared past was perhaps one of the magic ties which bound us together for life: no matter which town, which part of Hungary we came from, we all shared the same loss, the same horrors and the same shocks. Because of the common tribulations of the past, we thought and felt the same way, had the same nightmares and the same hopes for the future. We all experienced the futility of the empty years, the frightening limbo and the realization that life was rapidly passing us by, we had nowhere to go and even schooling was denied us. This forged us together for life, and we consider our group to this day, well into advanced age, as a true sisterhood, as if we are really all members of the same consanguineous family.

The future loomed frighteningly with the recurring questions: what will we do with only a few years of elementary grades to our credit in a world exploding with new ideas and new knowledge in every field? From these concerns, the dedication to our school and to learning was born, which is probably rare among school-age children, who are coming from a predictable, peaceful environment. A child of today would think that a vacation of two or more years must be heaven on earth. She would have a hard time understanding why so many of us found the enforced vacation intolerable, and why it was that later, when finally we did have a school, we were willing to happily give up our summer vacations to stay at school and study in order to catch up the lost years. We were not spoiled by fate. We were constantly hungry and cold, but instead of breaking us, this made us steely, stubborn and goal oriented. Completing our school years became an obsession for all of us.

The result was amazing. Despite the rocky beginnings, every one of the girls from Niederaudorf (and later, as some boys joined us, they too) made a success of life, and raised children who stand out among their contemporaries. This, after all, is not quite so unusual. Some of the greatest works of art were born in abject poverty and misery; creativity. Surprising new ideas abound in difficult times. Severe blows of misfortune appear to tap the secret resources of the human spirit.

To illustrate how this seemingly contradictory statement turns true, it is necessary to relate a reunion meeting of ours, in the course of which we were reminiscing about movies we enjoyed long ago. One of our great thrills was the black and white film *"The Third Man."* During our discussion, Iván reminded us of a remark made in the movie which for some reason stuck in his mind. The remark in the movie was slightly cynical, flippant, insulting, which is why it was probably not forgotten. It attempted to make the point that the good life is not always conducive to creativity. As an example, Italy and Switzerland were compared. In the history of Italy, strife and bloodshed were the way to live for many centuries; yet, they were able to produce Michelangelo, Leonardo da Vinci and the glorious, world-changing Renaissance. On the other hand, Switzerland had long lasting peace, wealth and early democracy, but all they could produce was the cuckoo clock. A lively argument followed because we did not agree with this statement in the movie. Obviously among a great many other things, the Swiss also produce the finest precision instruments, including medical instruments, scales for the sciences, chemicals, pharmaceuticals, not to the mention their heavenly chocolates. And aside from the tourist admired cuckoo clocks, they also make some of the best watches in the world, such as the Omega, which was also chosen by NASA. It was the watch taken to the Moon during the Apollo Missions because of its absolute reliability. (Omega was also worn by J.F. Kennedy, Prince William and James Bond, to mention just three famous men.) The Swiss have the most competitive and powerful economy in the world, and also an amazing and enviable talent for staying out of devastating wars. All these achievements cannot be swept in the category of the cuckoo clock. Of course, we understood perfectly well what the statement tried to convey, and our personal experiences were the proof for it.

Without the insolence of comparing ourselves to giants in arts and the builders of culture, but reducing the above to the small measure of our lifespan and to our limited talents, it could be stated that perhaps the horrors of the war years and the ordeals of the post-war years were the forces which forged us into the enduring personalities and successful individuals we all have become. We did not break, but survived and were stronger for it.

After arriving in the US, many of the boys who attended any of the four Hungarian refugee schools, were immediately drafted and they fought in Korea. Some never returned. As soon as it was possible, the former students enrolled in colleges. Some received generous scholarships from universities across the US; others used the GI bill to finance their education. Still others were able to attend because they secured the cost of tuition and books by working part time, and also by relying on the concerted effort of the family. It was also a great help that our scholastic background was so solid. Almost all applying for college entrance, on presenting their report cards and graduation diplomas earned in the refugee schools, and after completing the entrance tests, received generous college credits from the universities. It was possible for many of the students to start at the sophomore, or even junior level, saving an entire year in tuition and books. In those difficult years of trying to get established in a new country, this was an immense help.

It must be mentioned that in the middle of the last century, relatively fewer girls opted for a career than they did in later years. It is therefore inevitable that the outstanding achievements in science and engineering as well as in other fields were accomplished by the boys, who planned to devote their entire life to their career, as opposed to the girls, who planned for marriage and children. Niederaudorf-Reisach was basically a girl's school, even though during the last school terms some boys too were admitted. At Passau boys outnumbered girls. It follows that the overall achievement of boys seems much higher than those of the girls. Despite this "handicap" (being a girl three quarters of a century ago), all alumnae attended college, or at least some sort of higher education/training. It also must be noted that the girls, opting for marriage and children, raised high achieving and successful children and were generously contributing their time for volunteer services. As a matter of fact, as the third generation of the former DPs is growing up, the same trend for higher education and above average achievements can be observed.

Curiously, during chaotic, critical and dramatic situations, out of the hopelessness leaders emerge, people who are fated to be builders and doers; personalities, who can create order out of chaos, give hope while they personally engage in getting things on the way again. In our case it was a handful of truly dedicated individuals working from their headquarters in München: Mrs. Ordódy, (Hungarian Red Cross) Father Rozsály and Rev. Kálmán Csia, (Catholic and Protestant Services respectively) to mention just a few, and also the members of the CARITAS. Joining in their effort was Dr. Dezső Ravasz a former POW, and his lovely wife, Margit Matolcsy. They had two sons of their own; the younger one was Istók, who wrote the introductory poem. This group of professionals tackled the seemingly impossible.

The school, in our case Niederaudorf-Reisach, was the happy result of dedication and a healthy amount of stubbornness. The task was formidable. They had to find a place not only for operating the school, but also to house the girls. (From the beginning it was evident that because the potential students lived far away, the school could only operate if the students could live in. Because there already existed a coed school (at Passau near a refugee camp), and because of the very limited space at Niederaudorf, it was also decided that it would be a "girls only" school.)

The organizers had to find the right people to help move the project ahead; find the best teachers, round up the students from many dozens of refugee camps and villages (without the benefit of any sort of news media or telephone); overcome objections and concerns. (For example, there were whispered rumors that the school was merely a pretext conceived by the new, Soviet dominated Hungarian Communist government to collect the children of prominent families, high ranking officers, and the aristocracy, then ship them back to Hungary in all secrecy. This would force the parents to return to Hungary in order to find their children. The state then could easily arrest them and mete out the punishment, which they deemed just and deserving—meaning torture, imprisonment and often a death sentence. Fortunately, this particular rumor was totally false.) The organizers had to secure permits; find beds, textbooks, writing paper; working out plans for the instruction as well as the dormitories. But they did it—and did it without committees, without studies, projections, sponsors, telephones, typewriters and even without an exact knowledge where these refugee camps were located. And they did it in an amazingly short time. The establishment of Niederaudorf-Reisach became the miracle of Hungarian school history.

So on another cold January day in 1947, I arrived at the Pension Alpenhof, our future school. This time it was daytime, and the breathtakingly beautiful alpine countryside was not illuminated by fire, but by a brilliant sun, which made the snow cover sparkle. The air was pure and a special sort of beauty seemed to shimmer over the magnificent mountains, which I could not understand or put into words. I was fascinated and could not stop looking because this was the first time I ever saw such high mountains. It was simply unbelievable. The trees and the cozily huddled snow-covered houses presented a picture-perfect fairyland, in the existence of which I no longer believed. I left behind a damp, bug infested former prison cell, which served as my home—and was welcomed here by a friendly principal and was hugged by his motherly wife. The girls, who arrived before me, were already at ease, happy and laughing and surrounded me, the newcomer, with instant sisterly love. I almost choked of happiness. I arrived at a safe place and the world was good once again. Lord God, could it be that two years ago the world was a place of horror—and now we are given all this and more?

And so the story of our unbelievable school years begins…

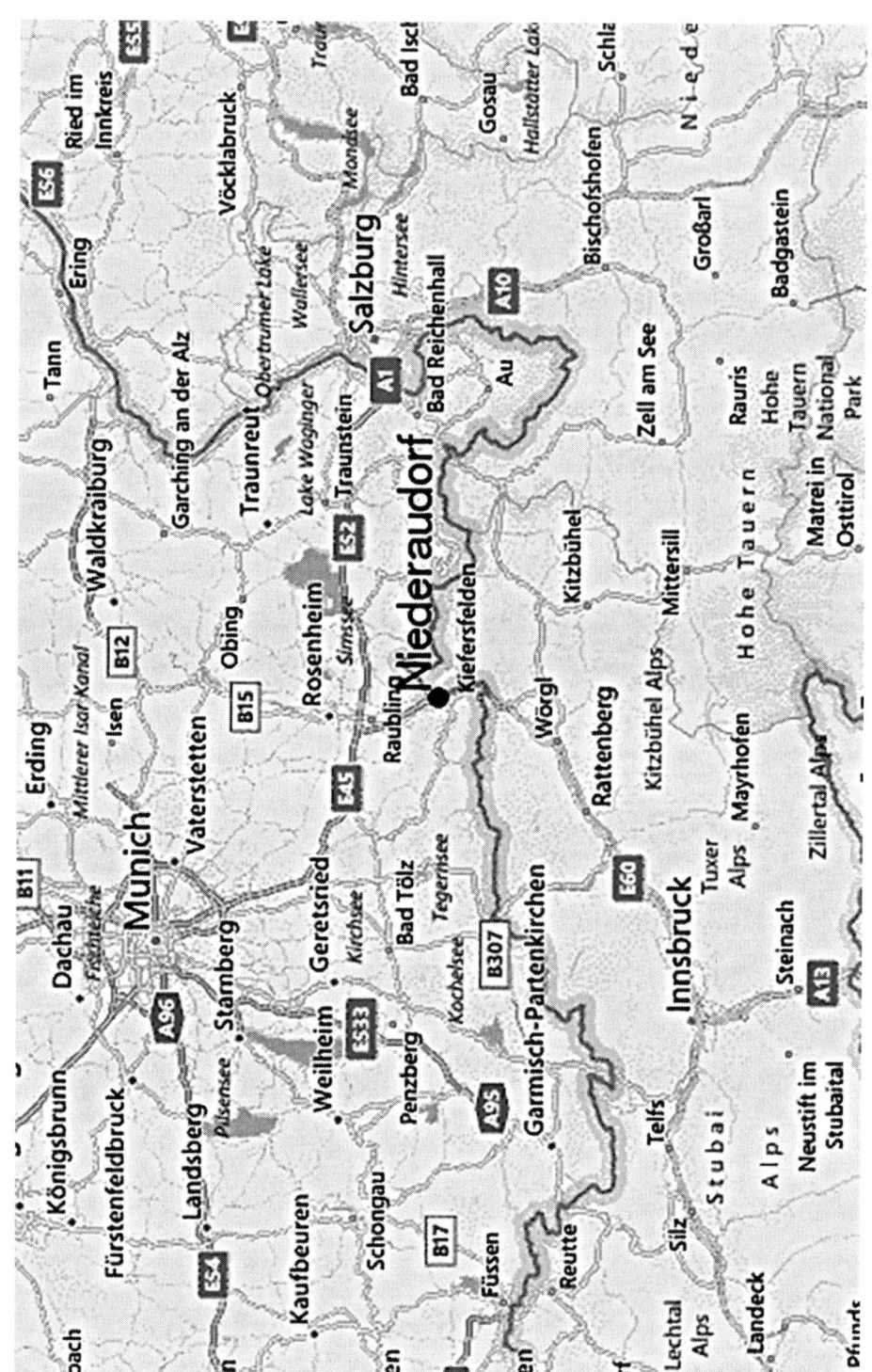

THE BEGINNING - NIEDERAUDORF

From the essay of His Excellency Ferenc Cserháti:

"The Hungarian boarding school at Niederaudorf in Bavaria is certainly the noblest and most inspiring establishment created. Its goal was to educate students in their own language, and to pass on the cultural values of the home country to the children, who with their parents fled their country at the end of the Second World War. The name of the small and not particularly significant village, located near Kufstein, but on the German side of the River Inn, has been forever lovingly etched into the educational history of Hungary, and is part of the fond memories of all those, who benefited by it.

The goal of the school at Niederaudorf was to give an opportunity for Hungarian refugee girls, living then in Germany, to continue their schooling at a time when no local schools could or would accept them.

On December 31, 1946 a contract was signed by Simon Waller, the owner of the Alpenhof pension, and by Dr. Ferenc Rozsály, Piarist clergyman, official representative of Hungarian educational matters in Germany. According to this document, Simon Waller was offering for a set fee his pension to accommodate 40 girls in the planned boarding school, which was to be established on his premises. He agreed to provide tables and chairs and also agreed to offer three meals to the students and to the staff. All other furnishing and needs were to be secured by the Hungarian School Committee.

Students on the Alpenhof balcony. Niederaudorf church in the background. May, 1948.

With the signing of the contract the school became a reality, and on January 2, 1947, the first student arrived at the school.

Priority for admission was given to those girls, who, because of the exodus from Hungary, suffered more than two years of loss. To achieve this goal, during the calendar year of 1947 two grades were completed by the students. The first term started on January 8 and ended on June 20; the second term started on August 22 and ended on December 20. In the year of 1948, again starting in January, there was another short term lasting to June, and thus the loss was almost made up. Starting during the fall of 1948, regular ten-month terms commenced."

The first miracle of Niederaudorf was its very creation, the fact that it existed at all. The second was that somehow the word did reach parents, whose children were not able to attend any sort of school. The refugees lived either in camps, hastily established for them, or anywhere else they could find shelter—some even lived in abandoned freight cars on train tracks no longer used, or in former political prisons such as Dachau or Laufen. In a world which did not have newspapers, television or telephones, the spreading of the news was indeed a miracle. Although radio broadcasting functioned, most refugees had no access to radios that being the last item they found necessary to bring along when they fled their home. The news of the school traveled by word of mouth and it is truly amazing that eventually people did hear about it.

The problem was that they did not hear about it all at once and so during the first six to eight weeks students were trickling in almost daily, until full capacity of the Pension was reached. Any teacher could sympathize with the problems this staggered arrival caused in an already shortened school term.

Sometimes the question is posed why the enrollment was relatively low, when there were so many refugees who had school age children. First of all, it must be noted that elementary instructions were offered in many refugee camps; that was the lesser problem. The burning need was the lack of middle and high schools, and it was for this purpose that eventually the two schools were established. Even so the enrollment numbers were relatively low.

One of the reasons was that almost everybody expected to go back to Hungary as soon as the war was over. The stay in Germany was to be temporary, not exceeding a few months. By the end of 1944 it was quite evident that the war was in its last stage of agony and soon will be over—at the latest by June. The prediction was almost correct; it was missed by barely one month. In the European theatre it ended on May 8, 1945. That year was a time of total bewilderment and chaos, and very few people were able to concentrate on the problem of education.

In the months following the end of the war many of the refugees did return home. For those, who remained in Germany, the issue of schooling was no longer avoidable. Many parents turned to the German schools to enroll their children. In those evil times many were afraid to let their children out of sight, let alone leave them in a boarding school far away, and preferred to keep them as close as they could. German schools were the answer, at least where that was a possibility. In smaller communities, where the number of refugees was less, the German schools could and did accommodate some of the refugee students. But at other, more populated areas this was not an option, as they already operated with overfilled classrooms.

A second reason was that the opportunity to immigrate to South America was offered to Hungarians relatively soon after the end of the war, and great numbers of the more daring sailed with their children to Venezuela, Brazil and Argentina. Another factor was that even before Niederaudorf was established, another Hungarian refugee high school started its operation (at Passau), and students were divided between the two schools. Finally, the ugly but realistic reason was that the school at Niederaudorf was almost totally self-supporting: tuition and board had to be paid in order to keep it operating. Many of the refugees simply did not have the means for it. Combined, this accounts for the relatively small number of students attending the school at Niederaudorf.

The number of school years lost, because of the raging war, was not uniform for all children, and it depended on several factors. Some lost more, others less years. In larger cities, where air raids were almost constant during the day as well as at night, schools had to be closed for obvious reasons. That is, if a school building still existed. Often there was nothing more left of it but a crater, rubble, and ashes. Sometimes the building was requisitioned, as in our town-house a makeshift hospital for the wounded, or to establish military headquarters, or to create temporary shelter for the fighting men, or for the masses of refugees. In a war there are pressing priorities to consider.

Some families moved out from the cities into the country to avoid bombing raids. They found shelter in wine cellars, vacation homes, or rented a room from the farmers. Usually these places had no middle or high schools nearby. Many children did not attend school for many months even before they left Hungary.

Also, people did not flee from Hungary at the same time. Although by the year of 1944 all illusions were gone, and it was evident that the war was going badly, the German forces—in opposition to the Hungarian desire to end the war—insisted on fighting till the end. The deadly and hopeless end-struggle on the eastern front was played out mostly on Hungarian soil, and it was bloody, devastating and relatively slow, and with an enormous loss in human life. Property, agriculture, factories, railroad lines, bridges, public, and private buildings and just about every aspect of life was damaged or destroyed. Someone who witnessed the destruction of Budapest said with tears in his eyes: "This is beyond rebuilding". "We ought to place a funereal wreath somewhere, perhaps at the Parliament building or at one of the remaining pillars of a bridge which used to span the Danube. The message on the ribbon should read, 'Here rests Budapest. May she find peace.' Then go ahead and build a new city 25 miles up or down river." To quote Emerson's opinion of warfare it is: "an epidemic of insanity," or Byron's more specific, albeit gory description: "… a brain-splattering, windpipe-slitting art… the feast of vultures and a waste of life."

To escape the ever-nearing front line of fighting, people chose to leave their homes and take to the roads. The goal was to get away from the fighting as far as possible. The general direction of the exodus started from the eastern part of the country where the Red Army crossed the border. As the war zone moved gradually westward, people in the Transdanubian region, the area west of the Danube extending to the Austrian border, also took to the roads.

By this time it was December 1944, and some students have not been inside a classroom since the beginning of that year. So it happened that by 1947 children from the eastern part of Hungary lost three or more grades, while those from the western part on the average "only" lost two years.

How did the students learn about the school?

Voices of students:

Markóczi: We lived in Mittenwald, which is located at a truly spectacular spot on the transalpine route. Nestled among majestic mountains, the cradle of violin building, the town of lovely buildings and flowers in every window, it is truly a choice location. The trouble with it was that it had no school, not even for the German children. The elementary and high school buildings were first used as hospitals to treat wounded soldiers, then after the war it was made into a makeshift rehabilitation center for the barely living political prisoners and Jews, who were just freed by the American Forces from the concentration camp of Dachau. They were sick, starved, frightened, half crazed by the ill treatment, devastated by the large scale loss of their family members and many were infected by typhus. They needed immediate care, and since the schools were already equipped as hospitals, it was a logical place to transport some of these unfortunate ones there.

A year later, in 1946 a German boarding school was finally opened in nearby Garmisch-Partenkirchen. The initial joy and excitement were soon quenched because, according to the then current barter-oriented economy, only those students were accepted for boarding, who could pay the tuition fee in kind—that is, in amounts of food carefully calculated and determined. Food? What was that? We hardly had enough for our own humble needs and could spare none of the little we had for boarding fees… For a short while commuting to the school was considered, but soon rejected. Trains were unheated, overcrowded and totally unreliable. Sometimes they arrived and sometimes they did not.

Everybody concerned was unhappy about my growing up uneducated. My mother wailed that her daughter would have less education than her servant girls had back home. But life changed during the last years, and we had to face realities. We bartered jewels for food, and keeping servants no longer appeared as one of life's necessities; the practice became totally anachronistic, the comparison became meaningless. My parents had to search for new solutions in our new situation. As a result, a concerted effort was set in motion to further my education. My father taught me mathematics; an uncle staying close by introduced me to physics and Latin; a German nun taught typing; a German friend, who spent years in New York, agreed to teach English. My parents even found a place where I could practice playing the piano. And so the arduous task of my education was taking shape. Of course, all these various teachers lived at opposite ends of Mittenwald, and I got exhausted from running from one teacher to the other. I have never been so tired in my life, but all who cared about me were satisfied that I shall not grow up stupid.

During one of our excursions to Munich with the hopes of being able to trade some of our worldly goods for food, and obtain necessities on the black market, we heard about Niederaudorf. My father was determined to have a look at it. To secure my future according to my own ideas, I made him promise on his word of honor that he wouldn't leave me there. He consented, but I should have noticed that the conviction was sorely missing from his words of promise.

Mari: After an unbelievable run for our life, we ended up in Bavaria, in the village of Bayerbach. Close to where we lived. a Hungarian school was established. I enrolled in the ninth grade; however, the school did not last long as teachers and students soon left for various reasons. In the village, where we lived, there was only an elementary school (for German children), so neither my brother nor I could attend because we were much too old for that.

By 1947 my parents had to gradually accept the fact that we shall never be able to return to Hungary. At this point, they started to look around in nearby towns to find a school with live-in accommodations, either Hungarian or German. However, the German schools were already filled not "to," but well over capacity. "We cannot even accept German students", was the standard reply. We then heard of a Hungarian school operating in Passau, but there was no live-in accommodation for girls. Then we heard about Niederaudorf, and traveled there with new hopes; but we were turned down. The principal, Dr. Ravasz, explained that the school filled up more rapidly than anticipated; therefore, students, who lost two or more years of schooling, and had less than eight years of education, were given priority for admission. The goal was to provide everyone with some education, at least to the 8th grade level. This we had to accept as fair and logical and sadly we left. Later, in November of 1947, when I attended a youth meeting held at the school of Niederaudorf, I again approached the principal with my wish to attend school. He was at that time very uncertain about his and the school's future, and told us to get in touch with him again in January, the following year. My father then wrote to him again and received the disturbing reply that he and his family decided to return to Hungary in the immediate future.

Time passed, and Niederaudorf had a new principal. He found our application among the documents, wrote to my father that in case we are still interested, he can now accommodate me. By February 12, 1948 I was officially enrolled in the school, where I completed simultaneously the ninth and tenth grades. I then enrolled in the eleventh grade; however, I had to leave school in May of 1949 because we needed to move into the camp at Amberg in preparation for our immigration to South America. I could never complete this grade and did not graduate.

Nusi: The German school 'Simmern' in München was converted to a refugee camp, where we found shelter. It so happened that Mrs. Ordódy, director of the Hungarian Red Cross, and her husband also lived there. I knew her well, and one day she approached me with the question, whether I would be interested in attending school at Niederaudorf as a live-in student. If so, she said, she could help me get accepted there, as the school operated under the aegis of the Red Cross. She was as good as her word, and I spent 1947 at the school where I completed two grades simultaneously.

Vica: We lived in Pfaffenberg. My older sister Kató used to travel weekly to Munich to take violin lessons, and there she heard about the school. We applied immediately, and were lucky because at that time the school was not yet filled up. Kató only stayed a short time, just long enough to graduate. After her graduation I took her slot, and was enrolled in the eleventh grade.

Ági: Dr. Ferenc Rozsály, an ordained priest of the Piarist order, (also known as the order of Scolopi, or Escolapios) worked at the Hungarian CARITAS in München. My older sister also worked at the CARITAS. She heard from Father Rozsály the news about the new school. And this is how I ended up in Niederaudorf.

The newly created boarding school was ready to receive the students, who at this time did not quite know what was awaiting them. School was a cherished dream come true, but in those unrealistic postwar years the only reality, the only security was the family. Letting go of the safe anchor was traumatic, to say the least. The students also knew that serious studying awaited them if they wanted to make up the lost years. After being absent from schoolrooms for two or three years, they were not sure how they would fit in again. And when they received the daily schedule, all illusions were gone.
    Some remember it:
    The plan seemed military and austere; this was the moment of truth, and we almost balked then. After years of freedom this schedule was unbelievable. Wake-up call came far too early, followed by physical exercises, a very quick wash, which in the freezing temperatures was probably something of a blessing. A sparse breakfast followed: mostly a cup of back coffee-substitute and a piece of bread. By 8:00 we were seated at the tables in the two former dining rooms of the pension, which now served as classrooms for all of us.
    At 1 P.M. our main meal was served. It was light and sparse enough to qualify as lunch, but the next meal, after seven in the evening, was even lighter. Post-war economy took care of our weight problems. After dinner we had half an hour of free time.
    We mostly used this time to compare notes scribbled hastily during classes. We had almost no textbooks, and the few we had, had to be shared. It was necessary to make notes during the instructions, but nobody had any expertise in this; therefore, we shared our notes—which by noon we ourselves could barely read. But we

needed somehow to decipher them, and if possible, complement them from the notes of others, or from what we recalled. In the end, we did construct something vaguely resembling a textbook, from which we then could study.

After this frantic editorial conference we took a short walk, and then severe silence followed while we studied and did homework. At four, we had a snack—provided our principal could acquire a donation of something, often it was just another piece of bread. Then back to studying again. After the evening meal we had an hour of free time, which we could use for anything we wanted, but mostly we did our wash, mended our belongings, which were so worn they were kept together in one piece by pious prayers only, by the long-standing habit of the material, and by our feeble attempts at mending. Since we were expected to clean our rooms, the bathrooms, wash our dishes, we had several chores to do. After this period of doing household tasks, there was a time not quite of total silence as in the afternoon, but definitely subdued vocalization was expected until lights were out.

No, this certainly was not what dreams were made of, but then nobody promised roses. Tears and hard work perhaps, but not roses. However, this is what we wanted, and we were not going to complain or back out. Looking at the bleak, forbidding schedule, we did not yet understand that it was just a frame, which we would gradually enrich and fill out with discoveries, knowledge, music, fun, laughter, caring for each other, and a giddy sense of accomplishment.

Even before the week was over, we discovered the sunny side of our existence. For one thing, we adored our principal Dr. Ravasz and his wife, and the entire teaching staff. Dr. Ravasz was a man not only of visions, and having a sense of responsibility for people other than his immediate family, but he was also an understanding, loving father-figure to all of us. Many of us had absent fathers—killed in combat, or held as war prisoners, or simply were still searching somewhere for their families lost in the great exodus. Dr. Ravasz could and did substitute the missing fathers. He also helped us ease back into the routine of studying without bewildering us, and the program he designed was sound and thorough, despite the fast pace we had to follow, and despite all the handicaps.

We loved the teaching staff, who spent a great amount of time with us—not because they were control freaks, or terribly strict, but being with us in the combined dining/living/ room, heated by one small stove, was still warmer than their rooms in the pension, or in the village.

In the foreground: the small stove, the only source of heat for the entire first floor.

Arriving at the school

Voices of students:

Anikó: I was the very first student of the school, arriving on Jan. 2, 1947. I think it took two more days until the second candidate arrived... I was pretty lost and lonely for a while, but the principal and the teachers made me feel welcome. I recall a really funny incident right at the beginning. One day a young man arrived, seeking a job as a teacher. Our principal, whom we always lovingly called "Uncle Dezső" let the extremely good looking fellow stay for two days to get to know him, but then in the end did not hire him. Actually, the affair had a bad start because the young man's last name was Sarolta, (Charlotte), and when he sent in his application, Uncle Dezső assumed that the future teacher is a woman. At the end, his parting words to the would-be teacher were, "You are too young, too good-looking and too single to be near so many young and beautiful girls."

Markóczi: We arrived at the Oberaudorf train station where we discovered that Magda, a girl my age and her mother were heading in the same direction, down the road to the next village to the school. We borrowed a hand-pulled wagon at the station for our luggage, and seeing them piled on the wagon I had the sinking feeling that my father did not mean to keep his word of honor when he said that we would only look at the place, but he would not leave me there. I knew enough about the required number of things for overnight stays, and my luggage was far too bulky for such a short time. If it would not have been for Magda, I would have burst out in tears. I could not disintegrate emotionally while she was calmly watching. In brilliant sunshine, but with the January snow crunching under our shoes, Magda and I pulled the wagon, while our parents, walking behind us, discussed the options. Magda was optimistic, and tried to convince me that all would be well. She told me that certainly it would be a gorgeous place with Persian rugs on the floor. I don't know where she got her (mis)information; but, we rapidly discovered that the Alpenhof was by far not a place of mindboggling luxury. By that time we couldn't do anything about it, all objections were swept aside as Dr. Ravasz and his wife greeted us not just kindly, but with genuine love.

Magda and I were not the first arrivals, there were already six or seven girls present, but every day more arrived, and they were kind and friendly to us. And truly, after a few days at this school, it did not matter to us that there were rough sacks filled with straw in the bunk beds to substitute mattresses, that there was only one room for all of us to study, eat, and live in, that there was only a very small iron stove to give just enough heat to make the room's temperature tolerable but no way comfortable, and that we would be expected to gather wood for it daily in the snow covered forests. I no longer wished to go home.

Kati: I arrived at the school with my friend, Klára, in January, 1947. We were accompanied by our mothers. Together we piled our belongings on a sled and pulled it on the long way from the Oberaudorf train station to the next village, Niederaudorf. The accommodations shocked me. I have never lived in a boarding-school before, but heard a great deal about them, and I had different expectations. What awaited us was a real dump, already overcrowded, and the furnishing looked like genuine secondhand rejects. My friend and I were assigned to the "lower bedroom," so called because it was a former dining room on the ground floor. We found that we would share the place with a delightful, fun-loving group and this compensated us for the poor accommodations and the straw sacks. We were only worried about the close proximity of Mária Adelsberger's room. She appeared to be a strict and forbidding teacher. At the end, it turned out that she was neither; she was a thoroughly kind person with a great sense of dry humor.

Márta: From the Oberaudorf train station carrying the small suitcase which held my very few belongings we started the long walk to the next village, Niederaudorf. The Pension Alpenhof was surrounded by picturesque snow mounds piled high and glittering in the cold sunshine, but as we entered the building, we discovered with dismay that it was not much warmer inside, but definitely less picturesque. On the other hand, the welcome extended to us was genuinely warm, which was a compensation of some sort.

I have not been in school for more than two years and I missed it terribly; I believe all the students already there felt the same way.

One of my first and cherished non-scholastic experiences was to see a few beautiful white ermines run around the wood pile in the back of the building. I have never seen these pretty animals, which seemed to be friendly, tame, and at home, and not much bothered by the presence of people.

However, it did not remain a "non-scholastic experience" for long because our teachers, seeing our interest in the beautiful animals, immediately decided to expand our knowledge. They told us that the ermine with the melodious Hungarian name of "hermelin" belongs to the weasel or stoat family. (What a disappointment for them to have such lowly relatives! And because we considered weasels with about the same disdain as we looked upon rats, we too had second thoughts about them. I guess in the animal kingdom the rule is no different from that of humans: you cannot choose your relatives. So we decided to ignore their family connections.) Sári néni told us that the ermine wears his beautiful white coat with the black-tipped tail only during the winter as a camouflage in the snow, and that this winter coat is the most expensive fur in the world, mostly used as trimmings for coronation gowns or similar official garments of kings, the clergy, and some Very Important People, like judges in high courts. (At this information the value index of the ermine rose in our eyes.) Erzsi *Néni*, who taught literature and art, told us that Leonardo da Vinci painted the famous portrait of Cecilia Gallerani, young mistress of Lodovico Sforza, and titled the painting "Lady with an Ermine." As we later discovered Sári *Néni*, who taught mathematics and physics, was less romantic, had a much sharper tongue than her sister Erzsi *Néni*, and although never malicious, she did have a definite streak of irony. When she was displeased about something, she put on a haughty facial expression as if she were exposed to a very unpleasant smell. Her one eyebrow, like the top curve of a delicately drawn question mark, shot up high (I could never figure out how she did it) and a remark followed, which was never lethal, but sharp enough to be felt by the victim. Now in her true Sáriesque style and haughty posture she remarked, "It only shows Leonardo's sense of humor. The ermine was always a symbol of purity and virtue. He himself wrote in his notebook that the ermine, out of moderation never eats but once a day, and it would rather let itself be captured than take refuge in a dirty place for fear of staining its purity. So why on earth would he portray a mistress—a mistress!—with the symbol of purity? I appreciate the chuckles he must have had while painting." We were fascinated and intrigued. Nobody talked to us before about mistresses, stains on purity and such. We were quite pleased to be a little shocked. What an unusual start for a school year! However, soon the woodpile was used up, the ermines took off looking for a more congenial playground and we were left there in the cold without fire wood and without our charming friends.

Dr. Dezső Ravasz was prisoner of war of the United States Military Forces. He was released in January of 1946 and immediately thereafter started to teach refugee children in an abandoned railway wagon in the town of Rosenheim. When the accommodations were no longer tolerable, the school at Niederaudorf was established and he was appointed principal. This was the first boarding school in Germany for Hungarian refugee students. Dr. Ravasz sent regular official reports to the School Committee located at Munich, and these documents too are incorporated into the present writing about the school. At the completion of the first short term of the new school on June 21, 1947, he sent the following summary, which Dr. Ferenc Cserháti quoted in his essay:

"The short history of the school is simple and to the point: members of several refugee organizations located at München, such as the CARITAS, the RED CROSS, the Office for Hungarian Affairs and the Offices of the Catholic and Reformed Churches were deeply concerned about the Hungarian refugee children, who year after year were growing up without education. It is the result of their relentless work that finally the first two official schools were established: one at Passau and the other at Niederaudorf. This is not the place to discuss their tremendous efforts, but I feel obligated to mention with gratitude the names of Mrs. Sándor Ordódy, Dr. Ferenc Rozsály and Rev. Kálmán Csia, whose untiring efforts made it possible that on January 7, 1947 we were able to receive the first students at the new school in Niederaudorf.

The initial difficulties foreshadowed the future problems and tribulations, and from the beginning it was obvious that students and teacher alike were embarking on a difficult road. It was also clear that the extraordinary situation in which history had swept us, required an extraordinary measure of will power, perseverance, patience, endurance, and the willingness to work far above what would normally be expected. It also meant that teachers and students needed to evaluate, and then accept this situation, which is truly unique in the field of education.

The first, physical impression of Niederaudorf is lovely and alluring. The home for our school is a smallish, modern pension, and outside, as far as we can see, the alpine surrounding is totally enchanting, picture-perfect. The air is clear, healthy and invigorating. On the other hand, the interior and the furnishing of the place are not only depressing, but grossly inadequate.

At the pension ours to use are three dining rooms downstairs, one of which is actually only a glassed-in, poorly insulated former terrace, unusable in the cold winter months. The smaller of the two other dining rooms is used as a bedroom for fourteen girls with bunk beds. The largest of the dining rooms is used as school room, dining room, living room and school office. (In the coldest month we squeeze all forty girls into this one room.) Upstairs there are two hotel rooms for the rest of the girls, and a very small room, set aside for sick students. This is the total accommodation for the forty girls currently enrolled at our school. In addition, there are two more bedrooms: one for teachers, and the larger one for me, my wife who is the acting housemother, our two sons and my father-in-law.

Although we were able to secure enough military bunk beds from München, we had no mattresses. There were no acceptable sleeping places for the arriving students. It was truly touching to witness how the housemother borrowed a small cart, then gathered the girls, and in the bitter cold visited farm after farm in the countryside where they begged for handfuls of straw, until they had enough. They piled their booty on the hand cart, and over snow covered roads lugged it back to the pension, over and over again. Later, they stuffed the precious straw into sacks just obtained, to serve as mattresses. We did not have a single cabinet. These, and other odds and ends necessary for our daily life, were begged for at the farms. Again, the girls, barely more than children, brought these back to the pension, and dragged the cabinets and such upstairs to the bedrooms.

Just when we finally had almost everything we needed, we almost used up all the coal for heating. January in the Alps can be brutally cold and we had to consider the closing of the school at a time when it barely began. But the students wanted to study and would not hear of going home. It was their insistence which finally led us to the solution: our entire big family, teachers and students, would sleep in unheated bedrooms. What little fuel we saved in this manner, would be used for the one large dining room, where a little stove was hastily installed in the middle of the room. During their afternoon walks the girls regularly gathered twigs and pinecones to feed our stove in addition to the little coal we had. We moved all the tables from the terrace dining room into this bigger room and squeezed all forty students into this one room, each two grades seated together, but at a different table. All classes were held here, and this is where we all ate and lived; the school office was also located here. The amazing aspect was that our students lived in harmony, were considerate to each other and learned to talk softly to reduce some of the noise generated by all of us in that cramped place. The love and care for each other was touching, and to watch their enthusiasm for reaching their goal was enough to break the heart. Fortunately by April the weather was mild enough and we could move some of the classes back to the terrace dining room.

Added to this keen discomfort of cold is the problem of the food served us, which the girls truly hate. Sadly, even the disliked food is rationed, and the portions are extremely small. It wrenches the heart to see hungry children, and to know that nothing can be done for them. The Hungarian social services in München, as well as the Catholic and Protestant churches attempt to help, but they have very little to share, and although we are grateful for the little we receive, it is never enough. The heroism of the hungry children ought to be preserved in some sort of a grand national epic poem.

Equally difficult was the organizing of the educational program. In order to make up the lost years, the calendar year is currently divided into two terms. In this way the students can absolve one grade in a shortened term of less than six month. This is difficult enough, but two grades simul-

taneously taught by the same teacher, at the same table, serving as the classroom for both grades, is a difficult situation for both students and teachers. There is, of course, no centrally worked out school program, nor such basic items as textbooks, teaching aids, blackboard, chalk, maps, notebooks or even pencils. There are no separate classrooms for the grades. Until April, all grades from the fifth to the twelfth were *taught in the same room as only that could be heated. Moving half the students to the outer dining room in the spring offered only a mild relief.*

And yet, the greatest problem was not even the necessity of note taking, or the lack of teaching aids, but the fact that all students missed more than two years of school, and what they once knew was completely erased from their mind. We had to face the fact that even the most basic information was gone, and at times we did not know just how far back we needed to go to jog their memory.

Another initial difficulty the teachers had to overcome was that not all students arrived at the same time, but staggered in over a period of weeks because they did not hear about the existence of the school at the same time. It actually took almost two months, or one third of the planned shortened school term, by the time we reached our full capacity. But somehow that too was mastered.

The instruction and education is divided between the principal, three teachers, and the house mother, all certified for teaching secondary school. In addition, Ferenc Kovács visits the school weekly to teach philosophy for the upper grades. Géza Fekete, ordained Catholic priest and Kálmán Csia, Protestant pastor, spend three hours each on Saturdays at the school, instructing students in religion and moral philosophy…"

ABOUT TEACHERS AND TEACHING

Ferenc Cserháti:
"The instruction plan of the school was based, more or less, on the program developed by Count Pál Teleki, in 1936. History was taught according to the requirement of the Bavarian Ministry of Education with special emphasis on European history. Teaching and learning this material was by no means a simple task, especially during the first short term of the school "year." Some of the students, who enrolled late, had to learn the material designed for nine months in about four month. For some grade levels and for some subjects there were no textbooks at all. The few available textbooks were not enough to go around. An added difficulty was that in the very coldest months all students were moved into the warmer of the two rooms, where all students were instructed in the same room at the same time. Only when the weather turned warmer could some of the groups be moved back into the outer, badly insulated dining room.

Necessity dictated that instruction be given to combined grades. Thus the second short term in the fall of 1947 was arranged as follows: the sixth and seventh grades constituted one group; the eighth and ninth the second group; and the third group consisted of the tenth, eleventh and twelfth grades. During this term there were no fifth graders enrolled. The program for the combined classes was excellently designed, the students took their work seriously and by the end of the second school term in December all required subjects were covered. 39 students passed their examinations with outstanding results."

In a report to München Dr. Ravasz wrote the Mission Statement: (Also from Ferenc Cserháti's notes):
"The existence of the school is largely determined by the extremely difficult circumstances and needs of the Hungarian refugees, more specifically families with school age children. It is also clear that financially the school cannot expect more than the absolute minimal contribution from the parents, and this amount just barely covers the cost for room and board.

A School Committee was established, which includes the Vatican Mission, the Protestant Church Services, the Hungarian Red Cross, the Office for Hungarian Affairs and the CARITAS. This Committee is now the maintainer or sponsor of the school, but it is riddled with two grave problems. First, refugees in Germany have almost no judicial standing; even the Committee's right to enter into contract with Mr. Waller, a German citizen and owner of the Alpenhof, was doubtful. Thus the Committee is not a legal institution and cannot act as one.

The second great problem is that it has no financial resources. It cannot promise to accept such responsibilities for the school, which it cannot fulfill; its help is most often only expressed in unfailing, intangible moral support, which of course is greatly appreciated. The involvement of these well known and esteemed institutions in the School Committee gives credibility to and acceptance for our fledgling school.

It is also true that the Committee does everything in its power, using different contacts and resources, to provide some material goods as well. These are mostly in the form of food or clothing from charity donations given by individuals or institutions. The girls have little in the way of personal items, and as they are still growing and outgrowing their dresses and shoes, the gifts are truly appreciated. At times the Committee can even transfer to us some much needed money. But it is obvious how difficult it is to build a solid structure on the foundation of unpredictable help and occasional donations. This unstable situation causes a constant state of stress for the teaching staff; I am sure the students too sense some of this.

The American Occupying Forces are involved, and were so especially during the very early stage of the establishment of the school. We can count on their help, but the support given to us is semi-legal and does not offer financial help or security. The relation between the School and the German officialdom, as well as the relation of the Committee and the German owner of the Alpenhof is based not on legality, but more or less on good will, and sometimes just on polite indifference. The Committee's true powers are non-existent.

The staff is fully aware of the situation; I clearly outlined all the problems at the very beginning. When the educators accepted the positions of teaching in the school at Niederaudorf they knew that there is no solid, legal backing which would consider their individual, social or financial rights and needs. They knew that they will have to work with extreme limitations on a dangerously insecure foundation. They knew from the start that often they will have to work even without their minimal pay while they are building the future of their charges.

But yes, we are all willing to accept uncomplainingly the cold, the hunger, the discomfort, the total lack of privacy, the mostly hostile environment around us. We accept poverty and legal insecurity, the constant threat of insolvency which would be the end of the school. But we gladly devote our energies and talents to do an outstanding job ahead of us. We have to prepare our students for all the hardships and injustices of the world, which surely awaits them. They are all facing a very rough future and they must be strong enough to be able to survive it without damaging their souls and their characters. We have to do this by constantly showing the example of how to love and to care for each other; how to work; how to suffer and to endure without complaining; how to fight hard to reach a goal in order to triumph. They have to learn to survive and then build a better future..."

Faculty, from January, 1947- January, 1948

Our principal, Dr. Dezső Ravasz, and his wife Margit *Néni*, our housemother. From the year he was our principal, we have no photos. It's fortunate that the picture on the right was found on a webpage of Makó's secondary school, where he was principal in the 1930's.

Standing: Erzsébet Takács;
Sitting: Mária Bárány and Sarolta Takács.
All three were our teachers until spring 1949, when the Takács sisters immigrated to England, and Mária *néni* found a new home with her mother in California.

Páter Fekete, chopping wood, assisted by students Péter Igó-Kemenes, Feri Jautz, Béla Láhner and Tóni Mélynádasy. Páter Fekete was one of the founders of the school and remained its supporter until it closed in 1951. Photo was taken in 1950 in Reisach.

Ferenc Kovács, teacher in 1947, principal from February 1948 until Fall, 1949. Here with his wife Erzsébet, also our teacher and their daughter Erzsike.

Faculty with students graduating in June, 1948

First row: Rev Ernő Nagy, Erzsébet Takács, Ferenc Kovács, Principal, Sarolta Takács, Páter Fekete.
Back: Zsuzsa Császár, Erzsébet Kovács, Magi Renkey, Mária Bárány, Éva Bonyhai.

Voices of students:

Jutka: Our school operated without even the basic equipment. We had no textbooks, or just very few of them. Notebooks and pencils were rare treasures. Maps, let alone teaching aids for biology or physics were nonexistent. But the parents of students tried to help in every way they could. For example, the father of one of the students had a job in a large office. Actually he was a member of the cleaning crew. Their job was to empty the cabinets and to burn the useless documents. He noticed that only one side of these papers was covered with writing, the backsides were blank. He realized that these could be used for notebooks. He collected all the papers and shipped them to our school. Thus, for quite some time, we were well provided. What a joy that was! Somebody, lucky enough to have fled earlier during the war, was able to take along more than the bare necessities. He sent us his slight collection of books. We were happy with this rare treasure and read the books over and over again. My uncle, an ordained priest serving in a large parish and also teaching Church Law at the University of Pécs, (Hungary) understood our problem. Using the thinnest air-mail stationary he could find, he typed the Latin grammar lessons for our grade, also the speeches and poetry of the Romans, and segments of Greek and Hungarian history and literature. These he mailed to us weekly from Hungary. Doing this he took serious risks. In those times correspondence with people in western countries, on the other side of the Iron Curtain, was suspiciously watched. Letters were almost always censored. Whatever the censors found objectionable was simply erased from the letter, or else the entire letter was destroyed. The offending writer was henceforth closely watched by the secret police. For anyone, especially for a priest, to be engaged in any sort of activity with a western institution, be it ever so innocent such as providing our school with teaching material, was invariable labeled spying as in "collaborating with, or spying for the West." It meant certain imprisonment, torture and most often death. He was extremely fortunate that nobody noticed his amazing amount of correspondence, or else some postal official decided to look the other way.

Because of these unusual circumstances, our instruction and our learning were very different from other school programs. Since we had no books and no strictly defined school plans, we learned mostly by discussing general ideas, by being trained "to look at the big picture." Of course, some facts by necessity had to be learned and remembered; it is hardly satisfactory to merely see the "big picture" in chemistry, or for that matter in the multiplication table. We also had to memorize an impressive number of poems in three languages. But in general, we were shown (especially in history, ethnography and geography) a universal, general picture of the world and its institutions. Today I couldn't name without hesitation the third largest lake in Canada (that country has so many large lakes!) and I have no idea about lakes and rivers in Australia or New Zealand, but I can talk up a storm about the social and economic changes caused by the bubonic plague, or about the dramatic climate changes in the fourteenth century. We enjoyed the instructions and discussions then, but after our life was once again organized and civilized, and we enrolled in universities, did it first dawn on us what an excellent education we received at Niederaudorf. It was nothing less than the ability to think and to see the connections, consequences, results. It was during our college career when we truly appreciated the teaching and training given us. While we generally did well on all examinations, we always showed our best side on essay tests. I am sure this was the result of the way we were taught and made to think.

Márta: Although there were very few textbooks for the grades, the teaching staff guided by our principal Dr.Ravasz, constructed programs for each of the grades. The teachers made notes of their combined pool of knowledge, and taught from these notes. From their notes and from their teaching we made daily notes and then used these as textbooks.

Katyi: We spent weeks reading and translating the erratic meanderings of Odysseus. He was the enigma of my young life, which by his best intention Homer could not explain to me. How could it be that a supposedly excellent sailor couldn't find his way home in a more direct route? I mean, he had excuses galore, including the story that he was actually looking for a new home. But the fact remains that it took him twenty years or so to reach his home from Troy. I mean Troy was not located in another galaxy. The time it took him to get home surely is a world record. In my youth I witnessed the coming home of soldiers after a lost war. They couldn't be fast enough to reach their families.

It also seemed to me that Odysseus rather enjoyed his diversions and I could never understand his wife's patient faithfulness. Didn't she hear on the grapevine about Circe? Was gossip nonexistent in the ancient world? Is it a new invention? Or was she so naive that she did not believe the rumors? But then how did she explain his long absence?

Maybe he had no desire to return home to his wife—or at least not in a hurry. She was so very pathetic in her powerless bungling. She was unable to control the rampage of the suitors in her husband's home, or the behavior of her servants, and certainly did not take good care of the home while her husband was gone. She was a totally demoralized woman, incapable of organizing her life. She was sufficiently dramatic to play the role of a quasi-widow, and sad enough to arouse in others something close to pity or at least a rush of anemic sentimentality; but she lacked the real stuff which makes a woman great. What a pushover! Nothing but a sorry failure in comparison to any of our mothers! But Mária Adelsberger would not let me bad-mouth either Odysseus or Penelope. She told us that his story is a warning to us to always have a clear goal, (some sixty years later they call it "mission statement") and for us to remember to diligently work toward achieving the goal without sidetracking. We could have argued this quite effectively because he was the one who sidetracked several times. But Adelsberger would not have been impressed, let alone convinced, and she concluded her defense speech: "On the other hand, Penelope is a shining example of loyalty and patience. And now ladies, let us proceed with the translation…." I did not argue with her. One never argued with Mária Adelsberger. But I noticed that she slid pretty fast over Circe and spent a great deal of time on the tribulations of the poor sailor. I was still not convinced. I could think of a dozen women, without straining my brain, who, when it came to loyalty and patience, would have outshined Penelope in broad daylight. Speak of the weaker sex! And, as a bonus, the stories of these women were not written in Latin.

Mészárka: And then in our fast paced studies we moved a few centuries forward leaving Greece behind, and arrived in the middle of the flowering Roman Empire. We studied the brilliant legal system they created, their architecture, their wars, customs and debaucheries. We learned about the Roman roads, which connected the far reaching military posts with Rome, also about the limes, or boundary defense lines of the Empire, some of which ran through Germany, not exactly at the doorstep of the Alpenhof, but some of us have actually seen reconstructions of some watch towers. History was close by. We were thrilled and shuddering while listening to the drama of Mt. Vesuvius. But we were also getting tremendously confused. It seemed that the Romans were eminently practical and were intellectually brilliant. If they were pushed a little, they could probably have built the first airplane, the computer, or could have sent a toga-clad Latin-speaking warrior to the moon. But they did not. I think they failed in this because they apparently lacked imagination and the joy of playing with the absurd, with the unthinkable. These are absolute requirements when wanting to achieve great things or invent astounding gadgets. Spiritually and emotionally they were apparently comatose and so they were incapable to invent even their own religion or their own gods.

From the Olympic Mountain they borrowed the entire company of Greek gods with all their attributes, quirks, marital problems, jealousies and dramatic malice, renamed them and landed them all at the River Tevere. This was to the great chagrin of students twenty centuries later because Zeus became Jupiter, Hera turned into Juno, Aphrodite into Venus and so on. Poor students henceforth were never totally sure, which was a Roman name and which was a Greek one, and who belonged to which century and to which civilization. This lack of the Roman imagination even made crossword puzzles difficult to solve. When a four letter word for the god of love is asked, the problem always presents itself: which one? It could be either Eros or Amor. It was inevitable that Odysseus should also turn up in Rome, this time as Aeneas. Or at least to me they seemed dangerously alike. This gentleman too bungled his way through many adventures, but several hundred years after Homer, Virgil in his epic poem arranged for different scenarios and a less satisfactory, abrupt ending. If nothing else, this poem certainly proves that a spark of imagination was after all part of the military and intellectual genius of the Romans, or at least in some of them. Unfortunately for us students it was an added difficulty to keep our minds from being tied into knots by the dangerous similarities while we learned both names for the same deities and same or similar heroes.

And if you should think that my intellectual discourse on classical poetry is an attempt to show off my educational excellence, I hasten to correct this totally wrong impression. The truth of the matter is that I messed up my final examination on this topic so badly that I all but flunked. I was to write about Virgil's epic poem. Acutely suffering from my usual fright during examinations, I found myself in a state of excited bewilderment, and as a result I married Aeneas to Penelope and from then on committed one blunder after the other. Shortly before I was about to conclude my essay, (and ten minutes before the examination time was up), I suddenly discovered that I was about eight hundred years off, bungling about in the wrong civilization and coupled the wrong people, leaving poor Lavinia completely out of the story.

At this realization the palpitation of my heart could be heard four villages down the road and my hands were so wet I could barely hold my pen. I was paralyzed for precious moments which I should have used to make some corrections. In the remaining few minutes I tried damage control of sorts by crossing out names and writing new names over the crossed out ones, but not very successfully. My written work was a total disaster and I just barely passed. This was so much more humiliating as I really knew both Homer and Virgil. And I didn't just know the material by inspiration or by approximation; I actually studied hard for the test. To this day I do not know what sort of special devil took hold of me on that fateful day to compose all that nonsense on my test. It was certainly the worst experience I had at that school.

Markóczi: Studying was hard work, but it was doable. We helped each other. Some subjects were easier, some very difficult. Our teachers, whether they taught Hungarian, German, English or Latin, demanded a great deal of memoriter work. They believed that committing poetry to memory improves the ability to remember, and in general refines thinking skills and ennobles our speech. Did this method work? I haven't a clue. If I make an effort, I can remember my phone number or the numbers on my license plate, and can figure my way out of most problems; but so can millions of people who were never confronted with "Arma virumque cano, Troiae qui primus ab oris..." Do I speak better than others? I am still waiting for my Nobel Prize in literature...

Anyhow I remember many frustrated afternoons when I tried to memorize segments of Vergil's Aeneas, or the beginning of the Toldi Trilogy, but could not advance beyond the first few lines. I was sure I shall be expelled from school because I am too stupid to remember a simple and basically clear and beautiful text. I felt that I was not college material, and I should vacate my place for a more worthy student. It made no difference whether I had to memorize Vergil in Latin, Arany in Hungarian, or Goethe in German— my fully developed mental block appeared in all cases and all three languages. Fortunately Tirczka, our creative schoolmate, was also a talented musician, played the piano well and was always helpful. She composed music for the Latin text and choreographed a dance to go with it. We sang and danced the lines, and to our astonishment, the mental blocks disappeared and the words stuck. I suppose, thanks to this unique learning method, sixty years later I can still recite long segments of the Aeneas.

My friend Éva was also totally demoralized. She could deal with Toldi and Vergil, but for some reason botany was a tribulation for her. She was hopelessly lost between the terms of phylum, class, order, family, genus and species. "I can't remember which is which, and I don't care," she wailed. We sat on the lowest step in the hallway, crying copiously and trying to console each other, but with very little success. Éva also had difficulties with math, but at least I could help her with that. For some reason I was immune to Sári *Néni*'s teaching, perhaps because we disliked each other. She thought I was spoiled and I often bristled because of her cutting irony. But my father was a great help in this subject. First of all when with the help of various volunteer teachers I studied doing "marathon runs" at Mittenwald, he was my math teacher and gave me a solid foundation in this subject. This foundation was clear, reliable and it delighted me with its beauty and seamless logic. Later, when he visited me at the school and I complained to him about the impenetrable fog descending on me, he explained the mystery, and as a result, the chaos suddenly cleared and I understood the workings of the math problem. The truth is that I liked the subject. I liked it very much. I helped Éva not only to study, but during testing I passed her crib notes.

Naturally, Sari *Néni* caught us immediately and did not really appreciate my cheat sheets. She coldly ignored our basic philosophy that a friend in need is a friend who must be helped. When my father was informed about my moral slip, he merely shrugged his shoulders. He did not think women ought to be particularly smart in math. He considered it unfeminine and thought it was OK to give Éva the help she needed so she could move on.

He was more concerned about his daughter being so proficient in the subject that she could actually help others. He believed that math is definitely not for women, and of course for a woman to teach math is nothing but Nature's sorry aberration. On top of it he was convinced that teaching in general is a most difficult and thankless job and ought to be avoided at all costs. Understandably he was becoming uneasy about his daughter giving remedial teaching in math. Heaven help us, he moaned, she might be gravitating toward teaching! Teaching math at that! He now pointed out that the Romans, a thoroughly rational and practical folk, left teaching to be done by their Greek slaves because it was considered a nasty, lowly job, fit only for slaves. He never mentioned the exceptions, and was presumably so worried about my unnatural interest in the subject that he tried with every means to discourage me from too much mathematics. He did not dissuade me with an open attack; he knew better than that. I am stubborn, which together with my love of math I inherited from him. A straight attack would have the opposite result. But with obvious intent he described the tragic fate of Hypatia, brilliant mathematician, who also taught philosophy, astronomy and was the last librarian of the Library of Alexandria. Perhaps he hoped that hearing how she was dragged naked over the streets of Alexandria until she died, would make it clear to me that math and the teaching of it could be deadly. (Nature's quirky sense of humor arranged it so that I earned my living for 27 years, teaching mathematics. He never quite recovered from the shock of it.)

Vica: I remember most Mária Adelsberger because she was so different from anyone else I knew. She was tall, gaunt, pale, had a halo of pale hair, her paleness was emphasized with almost colorless eyebrows and very light blue eyes, which could see through brick walls and could freeze a volcano. She was brisk and strict and virginal. I imagined this is how an ascetic abbess must have looked and behaved during the high Renaissance. She taught Latin with the conviction that no person could achieve intellectual accomplishments or moral refinements, unless she was able to fluently translate Cicero's orations against Lucius Catilina. She was a stickler for details. Her favorite saying was that the devil is always lurking in the neglected detail. She warned us from being negligent, and asked us if we could imagine what would happen if an engineer, while planning to build a bridge, would forget or misplace a decimal point. We could, and henceforth respected the decimal point as well as all bridges. Then she elaborated the point in her own field, Latin, and warned us about the importance of the comma. As an example she told us about the sentence fragment, well-known to students of Latin: *"Ibis redibis nunquam, per bella peribis."* (You leave and will not return—that is you will perish in the war) Or: *"Ibis redibis, nunquam per bella peribis."* (You leave and will return,—that is you will never be lost or perished in the war.) The difference in the meaning merely depends where we put the comma. At this we started to respect, beside the decimal point, the comma as well, and even to this day I hesitate where to put or not to put one. I still feel Adelsberger's disapproving gaze at me for the sin of creating ambiguity.

We left her class thoroughly warned and frightened about this important fact, until somebody, I forgot who it was, made us laugh by relating an old joke about the student who was not sure about the Latin word *"porta"* (gate). He thought he heard the word before, but could not remember in what context. Sometimes before he was in the sorry situation of trying to deliver the translation to his Latin teacher in front of the entire class, he formed a nodding acquaintance with the preposition "ante," (in front of, or before) but in his grievous need even that knowledge eluded him.

Now put on the spot, he was desperately searching for some sense of the phrase he was to translate, while he was hopelessly lost between the mysterious word and the preposition in front of it. All he could remember were the times he and his family stayed at hotels, and the *porter* took their luggage to their rooms. *"Porter"* and *"porta"* seemed pretty much the same to him. The phrase to be translated was: *"Hannibal ante portas"*: Hannibal is before— in front of—the gate (of the city), but he came up with the baffling translation: "Hannibal used to be a porter before." Every old joke is new to a young person, and we laughed with relief. However, despite her strictness and sometimes downright mysterious eccentricity, we truly loved Mária Adelsberger.

Lilla: I most remember Mária Adelsberger, who taught Latin and German, and was very, very strict. She, like the Ravasz family, also returned to Hungary, and rumor had it that she became a nun. I often wonder what happened to her because by 1950 in a wave of antireligious fervor, the Communists closed all the convents in Hungary, and the nuns were sent on their uncertain way. I hope that our Mária Adelsberger had a place to go and did not fare badly. I do not know if she had any family. She never talked about her private life.

Jutka: It was strange to learn about geography without a map. We learned about the fascinating places of the world, but it was most difficult to locate or to place them in our mind., especially for us in the the lower grades, who were never before introduced to a map or a globe. The upper grades were more fortunate because at least for a few years, while they attended schools in Hungary with well equipped teaching aids, they were exposed to visual learning as well. They have seen a map; we never did, or if we did, we certainly no longer remembered anything about it. We had to rely on the sketches our teacher attempted to make of the world.

In general, some of the material by necessity was rather abstract for us. I recall my amazement bordering on awe, when after arriving in the US, I first saw a Thesaurus. Of course we knew about it because our teachers saw to it that we should have some idea about the tools of literature and of library science, but we have never been personally introduced to them. I was so impressed by the wonder of the Thesaurus that it was the very first book I ever bought in my new home.

Éva: I found math exceptionally difficult and not at all amusing. When I tearfully complained to Sári *Néni*, our math teacher, that I'll flunk and I shall never in a million years understand the algebric equations, she put on her impenetrable facial expression, raised her one eyebrow, and merely quoted Queen Victoria: "We are not interested in the possibility of defeat." With this all future arguments were pointless. Unperturbed she continued the impossible task to make me understand and like math. Having just read the Queen's biography, I could have responded with her majesty's other well known remark: "We are not amused," but thought the better of it. Sári *Néni* didn't care for impertinent responses, even if the quote came from such formidable person as Queen Victoria.

Nusi: Our entire class had at the most one textbook in most subjects. Sometimes there were no textbooks at all and we had to take notes. Our handwriting deteriorated terribly.

Judith: Someone gave me for safekeeping a few documents concerning the school. From these it is evident that Mária Barany, teacher and housemother received a salary of 300 RM up to July 1948. Following the money reform her salary was 80 DM per month. (Roughly 40 EURO or around 30 some dollars, depending how the erratic stock market moves.) It is not clear from the notes, but it can be assumed that she did not have to pay for room and board.

Jutka: (excerpt from a letter written from Reisach to her mother in 1948, during the first ten-month school term.) *"…Zsuzsika (the younger sister, just enrolled in 1948) enjoys school more than I can tell you. Every day she is full of the news how she was praised by the teachers. We are a very small school at the present: in the fifth grade only she and Dora are enrolled. There is no sixth grade at this time, and there are only two students in the seventh grade. The grade with the largest enrollment is the eleventh grade. But our principal tells us, that soon more girls will arrive.*

I truly enjoy the new, leisurely pace. We don't have to cram as before, and studying is so much more enjoyable this way. Imagine, the upper graders are studying philosophy, and when we, in the lower grades, happen to have a free hour during their instruction time, are permitted to "sit-in." It is ever so wonderful because in this way we can learn a lot, without the stress of having to do tests, homework, or be asked to answer impossible questions. We have the joy of learning but none of the horror of bad notes or awful examinations. I hate tests, and am always mortally afraid of them. If I could design schools, this is how all instructions would be. So we are immersed in learning, and we find out things so strange that I cannot imagine what sort of people can come up with ideas like these. For example, we learned that the romantic writers, whether prosaic or poetic, believe that Nature and God are the same. We read during our German literature class what Hölderlin, the lyric poet, had to say about it: „Eines zu sein, mit allem was lebt, das ist das Leben der Gottheit, das ist die Erlösung der Menschen." As we translated it, it means that to be united with everything which lives, to be one with Nature, is the life and the essence of God, and this total identification with it is the salvation and self-fulfillment of Mankind.

Well, one can spend some time in contemplating this romantic statement, while also attempting to improve the so far miserable writing style we have in the German language. And of course, never losing sight of the important fact: one must attempt to earn a passable grade from the difficult task of translation. This is not all that easy because our teacher believes we should speak the German language better than our own. This view is rather natural, as he is teaching German. His wife, who is teaching Hungarian grammar and literature, has a totally different bias.

In connection with poetry, we learn a lot of fascinating ideas. For example we alternately discuss — (in pitifully fractured German) with Kovács Diri, and (in fluent Hungarian) with his wife, what constitutes beauty. Unfortunately I forgot whose theory we discussed, and I sincerely hope that this little detail won't be on the test. Otherwise it will be a sorry grade on the report card and much crying and gnashing of the teeth. (And to prove to you how well I pay attention on Saturdays during the religious instructions, may I add my new knowledge here: "mene, tekel, upharsin". If I remember correctly it means something like 'numbered, weighted and found wanting.' Because I am not quite sure about the translation, hopefully this won't be on the test either.)

Anyhow, the dialog went something like this: painting is mute poetry; poetry is vocalized painting. We get the message, or meaning most readily from a painting, as most people are predominantly visual types. In other words, when someone is reading a book, in his mind it is immediately transformed into pictures, and he can "see" it, as if he were watching a movie. This is why so often people are disappointed when they see a movie version of their favorite book. Their mental images do not agree with what they now see on the screen, and invariable they feel disappointed, even cheated. Their images were better. Then the discussion turned to music, which is the most abstract and the purest form of artistic expression. And to continue the description of our class discussion: architecture is frozen music. Both are art, but only if they express true emotions, true ideas. Art must always be true and genuine. However, one finds the most intense drama in sculpture. This is what our instructors covered in both languages. But then where does dance belong? When I posed the question, our teacher, Mr. Kovács was not impressed. I guess he does not get enthusiastic about any form of dancing. I could not really come up with a valid argument, as I have never seen artistic dancing performed on a stage, so I did not have too much to say in defense of my question, which appeared superfluous to him. He won that one.

In history we are bravely stumbling in mankind's various conflicts up to 1492. The difficulty is that we are required (per request of the German Ministry of Education) to remember most of the rulers of Europe, or at least those, who sat on their throne at least a year or so. It is a lucky break for us that some of them have really hysterically funny sobriquets, such as Leopold the Accursed; William the Bastard; Louis the Pious; Wenceslaus the Drunkard; Pippin the Hunchback; Richard the Lionhearted; or Isabella the She-Wolf of France. A little color in the confusing world of world history."

Markóczi: Having no history book for our grade level Dr. Ravasz taught us ad lib. "Ad lib" is not quite the correct word because the term indicates that someone speaks on the spur of the moment, without preparation, without notes. Dr. Ravasz certainly was prepared, but not in the conventional way. He didn't teach it in the usual manner, but talked about the events of history as if he were a participant. He made it come alive, made it sound immediate. At the same time instead of concentrating on details and dates, he presented the entire picture, and showed how one event connected to something else within the same time period. He effectively demonstrated that history is not a petrified set of events, which has nothing to do with later generations, but rather a flowing, interacting fate of mankind, where every event has its consequence, the past mirrors in the presence and influences the future. It was a wonderful way of getting to know the past of our world. But still, we did make notes because it was one thing to listen to a fascinating story, and quite another to be examined on the same topic.

At one time, one of the stores in Oberaudorf sold green sheets of paper. I think we bought the entire stock, and then sewed together the sheets to form notebooks. Every bit of paper was a great treasure for us. Later, after the "Währungsreform," the shops had real notebooks, but by that time most of us had no money to buy these wonderful items.

Ballusz: We had no books, even the teachers lacked them. As we hurriedly fled our homes and packed the absolute necessities, school books were not a priority. Our bags were so packed that every one of us should be able to carry his/her bag even when walking great distances. Everything that was heavy, such as books, was left behind. So after school started, having no books, we had to make notes. When classes were over, we corrected and expanded these. Very soon it was obvious that our group had "specialists." We could always rely on Mari for math, Kati for Hungarian literature and grammar, Éva for English, or on Markóczi, who always knew everything. In the end with their combined help our notes were fairly good and usable.

Koci: Poor Sári *Néni* did her best to teach us math, but with me she had no outstanding results. She failed, or I failed, or both of us did. Once she spent half an hour trying to make me comprehend Pythagoras. When she thought she said it all, she asked. "Now, do you understand?" "No," I answered truthfully. "Well then I must assume that you are some sort of an anti-talent," she said in her unadorned way. From then on, I was careful not to expose my ignorance to her. Instead, I approached Diri, and he could explain it in such a manner and so patiently and in so many different ways that even I could understand it. I never learned to like it, but understood it enough to help me achieve a fairly good grade.

Márta: The administration of our school consisted of one person: the principal, Dr. Ravasz, who also did much of the teaching. He had a wonderful wife, Margit Matolcsy, formerly a famous singer; she was our housemother. They had two sons; the older one, also named Dezső, was the heartbeat of almost all the girls. The younger one, who considered himself a "roughneck," was Istók, who tragically died before his nineteenth birthday. He probably was not at all that rough, but this is how he liked to sign himself in the keep-sake books.

Dezső Ravasz, Jr.　　　　　　　　　　　István (Istók) Ravasz

Jutka: - from a letter: "*We are having so much fun laughing at everything and nothing. We also have a new teacher for Latin and he is a riot. He is only 35 years old, but his hair is gray, he always wears gray suits and has the manners of a very old bachelor, if you know what I mean. He is formal and fussy, calm and speaks softly, just like Uncle Iván used to. He would never understand a joke. Everything has to be just so and no other way. He has an orderly method even in* *the way he places his pad and pencil on the table. Because he is so gray, we of course call him Mr. Gray, although his name is Ferenc Strada."*

Zsuzsa: I remember that the years 1948-1949 were very difficult and hard. I was a late-comer to the school and could not take advantage of the short term school years offered earlier. In order to catch up the lost years, I completed two school years in a ten month period. It was very hard. The other reason for the difficulty was that there were hardly any textbooks and the teachers dictated the material for us to write down. What we managed to write down was the text from which we studied. We wrote as fast as we could because whatever was left out, could not be replaced. Needless to say, due to this daily speedwriting our handwriting suffered greatly.

In those days there was a great emphasis to learn Hungarian history, literature, geography and also folk songs because, of course, we all thought that soon we shall return home again. Our teachers also insisted on a strict religious and moral upbringing, regardless of the individual student's religious denomination. They tried hard to implant their considerable knowledge into us. All in all, studying was very hard; however, they were understanding and helpful in a way that I never experienced again in my high school years in the States. I'll never forget one particular oral test of which I was mortally afraid. My teacher, Takáts Sári *Néni* knew that I did my very best in preparing for this test. I can still see her face as she tried to prompt me through my horrible "stage fright." With her encouragement I got my self-assurance back and to my own surprise, I passed the test with a very good note.

Ballusz: I truly loved Dr. Ravasz and his wife Margit *Néni;* yet, when we parted, it was not in the best of spirits. It was my fault, of course. It so happened that my brother came to visit me, and I could hardly wait to see him, but my request for permission to meet him at the train station at Oberaudorf was denied. I am not sure why. Apparently, there was some sort of a drama being played out among the staff, and as a result, they became rigid and very unlike their true character. At any rate, it was decided that Dezsőke, the son of Dr. Ravasz is to meet my brother, instead of me. I was bitterly disappointed, and knew that my brother would be too. Hastily I wrote a short letter to him and explained in it why I could not meet him. I asked Dezsőke to give the letter to my brother when they meet at the station. I was bitter, and in my anger I called the staff names. I didn't spare anyone. I was especially angry at Margit *Néni* because it seemed to me that she was the one who orchestrated the situation. If I recall correctly, in my letter I called her an "enraged rooster." Well, that fink Dezsőke, whom I trusted, did not give the letter to my brother; instead he gave it to his parents. Well, I need not describe the trouble this caused me, nor the tone and content of the lecture given to me about honoring my elders, and so on. That was the end of our friendship, which hurt me then, and the memory of it is still painful. It should never have happened.

The keepsake book was our most treasured possession. We made this booklet ourselves by stitching together sheets of paper to look like a book, and then asked students and teachers to write something permanent and uplifting in it for us, so we

would always remember them, and at the same time have a trusty guide in our future, a philosophical advice on how to live a happy and full life—much like the messages we are now daily receiving in our e-mails. Of course everybody made her own entry elaborate with drawings, quotes from favorite poems, or special compliments and reassurances of everlasting friendship to the owner of the booklet.

Drawings of the Alpenhof by Gabi Csaba (1947) and Kloster Reisach by Tóni Mélynádasy from Nóra's keepsake book. It was a treasure since the first year and a half no pictures were taken.

In 1947, Kati Pettendy captured with her drawing the spirit of silencium, the compulsory study time. Twenty-five of us, grades 7-12, were crowded in the Alpenhof's dining room/class room. This drawing on the book's cover appropriately represents the School of a Different Kind.

RELIGION AT SCHOOL

Ferenc Cserháti: I am quoting from the report of Dr. Dezső Ravasz, sent to München in the fall of 1947: *"...Our students come from homes, where religion is very important, and the school operates accordingly. Despite the initial difficulties of obtaining qualified instructors in religion, the problem has been successfully solved for both Catholics and Protestants.*

The Catholic students attend services every Sunday and on all holidays at the church of Kloster Reisach. On these occasions they have the permission from the Prior to sing several Hungarian songs in the church. They walk the distance with teachers, and they also participate regularly in the sacraments of Confession and of Holy Communion. Although it is not required, many opt to get up early in the morning each first Friday of the month and walk over to Reisach to participate in the Holy Mass. In May and June they attended the evening prayers and litanies at the small Niederaudorf church. Confirmation took place in May. The quiet but continuous and dignified religious participation won the respect of the German villagers for the students of the school.

3

Niederaudorf Church in foreground. Kloster Reisach center right, Austria in background. The river Inn flows between the two countries.

The non-Catholic students of the school are regularly visited by pastors of their own denomination to conduct religious services, and Bible studies. Dr. Lajos Segesváry, Ernő Nagy, Kálmán Csia, and Margit Kovács, Sándor Zoltán are to be mentioned.

Instructions in religion are given on Saturdays in two hour time frames, separately for the Catholic and the Protestant group. In addition, on Saturdays, all students, regardless of their religion, receive instruction in moral philosophy, taught by Ferenc Kovács. The instruction is divided into the abstract as well as into practical applications. Because the Protestant ministers live far away from the school and have far too many obligations elsewhere in the refugee camps, at times they cannot make it on Saturdays to conduct their lessons. In such a case, the Catholic priest, Father Fekete, out of consideration for the non-Catholics, changes his plan of instruction and instead of the Catholic liturgy in his plans, he invites the various classes to discuss questions of ethics.

Religion is practiced in true ecumenical spirit. All students pray together in the morning and in the evening, before and after the instructions, and at the meals. There is great understanding and harmony between the ministers of different faiths, and between them and the school staff. Religious differences have never been a problem among the students. Many of the non-Catholic students opt to walk along with the others to the Catholic services."

Voices of students:

Markóczi: (excerpt from her diary) *May 4, 1948." Every evening we walk to the little church of Niederaudorf to pray the Litany of Loreto. These evenings are lovely and intimate. We are the only ones in the church and we sing Hungarian church songs and say the litany in Hungarian. We are then one big family, safe and loving, and we feel as if for a short while we are back home in Hungary. It is a wonderful but emotional experience. In general, everything is so very good here at school, and I like being here as much as I love being at home. Our teachers couldn't be kinder or more understanding and helpful. I have to laugh at myself when I think about how forcefully I fought against being enrolled."*

The Niederaudorf Church where the Confirmation was held on May 27, 1948.

Rev. Kótay held confirmation for the Catholic students at the Niederaudorf church. From left to right: Éva Mészáros, Marica Renkey, Vera Hadanich, Gabi Csaba, Jutka Petres, Rev. Zoltán Kótay, Éva Hochenburger, Margit Oltfalvy, Kati Jászberényi, Ági Szkladányi.

Kati: During our ethics-religion classes Mr. Kovács, who later was appointed principal of the school, repeatedly admonished us about the necessity of "being well bred." He explained: "Your parents taught you the basics, and we at the school are continuing their work. Our common goal is to help you become accomplished in the highest tone of human feelings and conduct. In you we hope to see the combined components of a refined person; one, who can lead and build, and who can make a difference in the world. Intelligence and beauty are a gift of God and of a lucky combination of your genes. We can't add to that. But there are areas, such as virtue, morality, wit, an educated mind, graceful manners, love of beauty and truth, courage and elegance, which can be acquired. Having all that, you will be well equipped for life, and will always be an unquestionable member of the spiritual aristocracy—even without the money or power your families once had." I would add self-reliance to this list, and then call it all by a common name: integrity. These were lofty ideals and I wonder just how much could we actually acquire of these goals, and how short did we fall from the expectations—despite our and their best efforts.

Markóczi, from her diary: "I find Saturdays to be the most stimulating and exciting days of the week. On these days we have instructions in religion, moral philosophy and theodicy (the proving of the existence of God, and how good and evil can exist side by side in a world created by an absolute just and good God. The theory and method was first introduced by the German philosopher Leibniz.). Last week we had a written test. We had to discuss the difference between *"cultus latriae"* (the honoring of God) and *"cultus duliae"* (the honoring of saints) in connection with Jesus. The second question was the continuation of the first, and had to do with *"obiectum materiale and formale,"* and finally we had to discuss *"cultus absolutes"* and *"cultus relatives"* (Honoring God, but also honoring people living among us here on earth, who live a saintly, exemplary and creative life.) Once we got over figuring out the meanings of the Latin terms, we went ahead and wrote about the themes, hoping that we did not commit too many instances of sacrilege or heresy.

Ballusz: Saturday was dedicated to religion and moral philosophy. Protestant Ernő *Bácsi* taught religion to the Protestants; Father Fekete taught the Catholics in the lower grades and Ferenc Kovács, even before he was appointed principal of the school, taught the upper grades. Usually there was an hour of discussions about dogma (the established belief or doctrine held by a religion; the primary belief in a religion), apologetics, (the discipline of defending a religious position through the systematic use of information) and philosophy to all the upper grades, regardless of their denomination. For the ethics sessions, (moral philosophy, concepts about right and wrong) the lower grades also joined in. Father Fekete then taught liturgy to the Catholics. At one time Zoltán Kótay, the papal delegate, visited the school.

After witnessing our Saturday program, he asked our principal: "What is your goal with these girls? Are you planning to raise female priests and pastors?"

Nóra: The religious instruction for the Protestants, although carefully planned, was not always on a regular basis. The pastors and teachers were living and working quite some distances away from our school—as a matter of fact Ernő Nagy commuted all the way from Austria. They had to rely on the capricious schedule of trains which most often did not operate as expected. The pastors also had a great many other obligations and duties in the many refugee camps of the Hungarians. Bavaria being predominantly, almost exclusively a Catholic region, there were no Protestant churches anywhere close by. We attend the ethics classes on Saturday. On Sundays we went to church with the Catholics at Reisach. Eventually we organized a Bible Study hour and connected with the Soli Deo Gloria group in München.

Quote from a letter written by Nóra to a friend on March 21, 1949: *"...Now we have Bible study hours every Sunday at school, while the Catholics attend church services at Reisach. In the beginning the leaders were selected from the upper grades, but gradually the younger ones are also involved. The very first session was led by Tibor Diószeghy, and he was so good that we all got very enthusiastic and are now working hard to match his excellent presentation when our turn comes and to make the Bible Hour meaningful. Last week it was my turn, and I had a very bad case of stage fright, but hope to be braver next time. You wouldn't believe how much we are learning this way, and how our self-confidence grows after each session."*

Nóra, some 60 years later continues her reminiscences: By 1949 a Hungarian Protestant youth organization, the Soli Deo Gloria, was reactivated in München, under the leadership of Dr. Géza Soós. They organized a four-day Palm Sunday conference, held in the resort town Prien on the shores of Chiemsee. We, four students from Niederaudorf, felt honored that we were invited. We also felt lucky that our principal Kovács Diri gave us permission to attend it all by ourselves. He trusted us. An entirely new world opened up to us. The new connection strengthened our faith and we were grateful for the support promised for our weekly Bible studies. Now we were part of a larger group, which was deeply concerned not only with the development of our religious life and our spiritual growth, but which also had on its agenda the future of Hungary and the present problems of existence. They were actively seeking solutions to the many problems: physical, emotional and spiritual.

With Dr. Soós: Piroska Hegedűs, Éva Király, Éva Csia, and Nóra Hegedűs at the Palm Sunday Conference, Prien, April, 1949.

Dr. Soós kept his promise. Over the following years we had regular Bible study leaders, coming from Munich, guiding us in our religious education. It didn't hurt that several of them were young university students who caused some severe heart palpitations...

Hillary Rodham Clinton gave a most meaningful title to her book written about child raising: *"It Takes a Village."* And indeed, it takes the family, the school, the Church and the whole village to raise a child successfully. Remove, or weaken any of the four elements, and failure looms on the horizon. Child-raising has often been compared to a wagon and these four elements to the four wheels. Remove or merely damage one, and see how far the vehicle will go. In Hungary, all youth organizations, devoted to caring for children and youth, always were considered important factors by State and by the school system. For this reason every congregation or organization, be it scouting, literary club, sports club, or Bible Studies, always enjoyed the full support of the entire nation. The work done in connection with them was taken most seriously. It is also true that during Communism, lasting 40 long years after the War, all religious organizations and eventually even scouting, were banned. Soli Deo Gloria is one example of these organizations which thrived, and then was banned.

Soli Deo Gloria was established in 1921 by the Reformed Church of Hungary. At that time the country went through tremendously traumatic experiences: the double devastating effects of World War I and of the Treaty of Trianon resulted in the loss of 1/3 of its population and 2/3 of its territory. Some of the borders were arbitrarily drawn along railroad lines, rivers, or even across homesteads. Families, organizations, the whole structure of Hungarian life was torn apart.

The Reformed Church looked for ways to revitalize the despondent population. One of its attempts was reaching out by caring and strengthening the spiritual life of the youth, destined to grow up in very difficult times. For that purpose the Church created the organization "Soli Deo Gloria"— only to the glory of God. They organized daily and weekly Bible studies and conveyed Calvin's fundamental message: the Bible, supported by faith and knowledge, can and should be incorporated into the daily life of Christians. With this help and guidance, it is possible to overcome all the difficulties life offers. The motto was and still is: If God is with us, who can be against us?

This message spread like wildfire. Starting with the first 50 theologians, who were the initial planners, the Soli Deo Gloria became a countrywide organization in the following years, reaching out to the youth in the remotest corners of the land. The group leaders were, of course, connected to local churches and received guidance from there. They held Bible studies, offered regional summer camps and statewide Palm Sunday conferences. These were attended by several thousand Protestants, both young and old. In addition to strengthening the youngster's spiritual life, they also addressed the great need for the physical well-being of the student population, who were attending seminaries and high schools away from home, at central locations. The organization provided boarding facilities and canteens where accommodation and food was available and affordable. They organized tutoring, created traveling libraries, encouraged and supported international studies, and provided free health care for needy students. They connected families in the congregation with the students, who needed help and care. Eventually they did outreach to all segments of society, especially during the difficult years of World War II. Although he was a lay person, a lawyer, during most of his life Dr. Géza Soós was the mover and shaker of Soli Deo Gloria. He was a devoted member and organizer of the movement ever since the time he was a teenager. At age 24, in

1935, he was elected president and headed the organization until it was disbanded in 1946 in Hungary.

Dr. Soós made many international contacts in the role of a delegate to ecumenical and international conferences in various countries. In the 1940's he held a high position in the Hungarian government, in the department of "Ministry of Foreign Affairs," and was responsible for maintaining contacts with Switzerland, Sweden and Finland. In addition, he was also appointed to look after the political refugees from other countries, who sought and found refuge in Hungary. He was in such key position that he had opportunities to save many lives; persecution was practiced at every turn in those years. He worked closely with the Swedish diplomat Raoul Wallenberg. Dr. Soós was also a key player in the Hungarian Resistance (or Independence) Movement, established in response to the German occupation of Hungary in March, 1944. He was once sent on a secret and ultimately failed mission to Italy at the end of 1944 in a desperate effort to bring about the end of the war and so lessen the loss of human lives. For all of his activities, he was diligently sought both by the Gestapo and later by the Secret Service of the Soviets, the GPU. After the end of the war, in 1945, he joined his family in Geneva, where he completed his studies and earned a degree in ministry. Dr. Soós continued his service among the refugees in Germany during the last half of the 1940's and finally moved with his family to the U.S. in 1951.

During the Soviet Communist years Soli Deo Gloria went underground, but resurfaced in 1989 after the fall of Communism. It continues to do the much needed work today, offering support and help. However, during these "dormant years," the organization was actively operating abroad, offering help to the youth of Hungary in exile.

Voices of students

Nóra: I was confirmed in Berchtesgaden by the Lutheran minister Rev. Gyula Asbóth. It was a beautiful, a never-to-be-forgotten experience, but also in a way sad. Back home in Hungary, this would have been a huge, joyous family celebration, but here I was glad enough that at least my mother could make it to Berchtesgaden. There was no money for the train fare for the rest of my family.

Koci: Going to church was always a wonderful experience. We loved to sing there, and did it very well because Diri took care of that. We sang the songs in harmony of 3 or 4, which was not always easy because he was upstairs in the loft of the huge church playing the organ (where we could not go), and we had no conductor to guide us below in the church. But with enough practice we were able to do it.

Our non-Catholic classmates always sang with great enthusiasm with us in church, making our singing fuller and richer. As a return favor, we sang with them during their services. It was a most wonderful way of learning to respect the religion of others. This was years before the great churches of the world made their first attempts to accept and respect each other, but we were already raised that way. It was only many years later when we realized that not all the world thought the way we did, and how wonderful it was to grow up without prejudices and biases. At the end of the church services we always sang the Hungarian national anthem, which is really a prayer.

Kloster Reisach

Vica: On Sundays we went to church at Reisach. Diri played the organ and we sang Hungarian church songs, which the German congregation always appreciated. In May and June we went to Niederaudorf to say the Litany. Diri played the organ and I was elected to tread the bellows which supplied air to the organ pipes. (I could not perform this duty at Reisach, as the organ loft could only be reached through a part of the convent called "*clausura*", closed to females. I suppose one of the brothers performed this task there. When Tony was enrolled in our school, he was honored with the job of pumping the bellows of the organ.) I was also the "*pre-orator*", the one who started the prayers and called out the sentences to which the girls responded. I was pretty happy with this assignment, at least until the day when someone made a half-humorous remark about my strong Transdanubian accent. I was ashamed and hurt, and gave up the pre-oratory position to someone who was not handicapped by an accent.

Piri: The school arranged for religious instructions for us, Protestants. Rev. Kálmán Csia prepared us for Confirmation, which took place in 1947 at Pentecost. Fourteen girls were confirmed on that day in a beautiful and uplifting ceremony at Alpenhof. Our Catholic classmate, Mészárka, played the piano to accompany our singing of the Psalms. (No pictures were available for events in 1947.)

Béla: I am a Protestant. But the character, gentleness and teaching of the Catholic Father Fekete, and his absolute, unconditional love for all mankind influenced my entire life.

Anikó: We were avid church-goers and prayed and sang a great deal. Diri's organ playing enchanted our romantic, young souls, and made it easy to sink into meditations. In Niederaudorf-Reisach we built the foundation of a deeply spiritual life, which helped us through the difficult years then, and for the rest of our life.

Jutka: (from a letter) *"...Nowadays we walk to Niederaudorf for evening prayers and the Litany, but I have serious problems about the result. I wonder if our spiritual high is profane or is it truly God oriented. The setting is soothing and mysterious: the church is dark with the exception of a few candles; we, from the school, are the only people present, and then Diri, a gifted artist, starts to present an organ concert to make us shiver from the center of our soul. I must admit that all I do is listen, drink in the sounds and not a word of prayer leaves my lips. I hope God won't be too disappointed that my mind and emotions are straying elsewhere. But then, if He created everything, than this wonderful music must also be His doing. He cannot be but happy that we love His world, and everything in it, including Diri's tempestuous organ recital. God's gifts are so unspeakably manifold and wonderful ..."*

Markóczi: (excerpt from her diary) 1948, October. *"We shall start our chapter of Congregatio Máriana!* (A religious movement to strengthen the religious upbringing of youth, introduced to Hungary in the year 1580). *Diri told me to start enlisting members. I have already talked to Ballusz and to Kati. Diri told me he expects lots of enthusiasm from the girls. He will get that, to be sure. Our first meeting was scheduled for last Saturday. I was appointed prefecta, or president. In our first meeting as a festive opening Jutka was supposed to recite a poem, but she was hopeless. Half way through we had to prompt every line, but she could barely get through it. After that, it was my turn to speak about the congregation and its goals. At the end Diri told me that my speech was good because the thoughts expressed were sound and clear, but unfortunately it was not a speech. I have no voice, he told me, and the conviction did not come through as I whispered my way through the prepared text. And I was not speaking, he continued, but merely reading aloud what I wrote before—and did that in a barely audible tone. This man is hard to please. Well, perhaps next time it will go better."*

Jutka: from a letter *"...Yesterday at the first session of the Congregation, I had to recite a poem, which Markóczi handed me the last minute. I am glad you were not here Mother because you would have been deeply ashamed of my performance. It was a cultural scandal. I had no time to memorize the poem, and should have refused to present it. But as the Bible says, 'Pride goeth before destruction and a haughty spirit before the fall'. I too was proud, excessively conceited, haughty and self-assured. I thought I am smart enough to be able to memorize it overnight. Wrong! I was fine until the middle of the poem, but then I blanked out and could not remember a word. Klára, bless her soul, was steadfastly prompting me by whispering the next phrase: 'the recurring springs' ... But that was not my problem. I did know the 'spring' part and was pretty sure that the lovely season would continue to reappear, but had no idea what followed, what wonderfully deep thoughts I was supposed to transmit to my captive audience. As a matter of fact, I could not remember a single word from 'spring' on. I probably could not even remember my own name at that point.*

So what does one do, when standing in front of a large group of people, and is in the middle of proving to the world that she is stupid, ill prepared and stuck? I don't know what other people do when they are embarrassed; I, for my part, started to laugh. Not because I was happy, but because I was so ashamed. I was standing there, hopelessly lost in the middle of nowhere in a poem I was to render with conviction and emotion, laughing like one bereft of mind. It did not improve things. Indeed it was a sorry performance, and I swore, 'never again'."

Nusi: Although the Saturday religion and ethics classes were compulsory, nobody ever forced us to attend church. Yet, we never missed the services, not even in the worst cold spell in the winter when the long walk to Reisach was a true hardship. We went to church because we liked being there.

Kati: One of the Saturday classes ended with the remark by Diri: "On this planet our race can only be saved from self-destruction and from absolute disaster, by learning to practice a high degree of virtue, practiced, of course, not just by a few, but by every single individual living in the world. Can you imagine what would happen if for some time period, as short as perhaps five years, everybody without exception would be virtuous? No greed, no sloth, no hatred, no violence, no envy and no pride, nor the rest of the evils mankind seems to cherish…"

In the little dramatic silence that followed, Dagi—because she was Dagi, who was never able to control her mouth—answered: "We'd find that we woke up from the dream." Her voice sort of rose at the end of the sentence, so it was not really a statement, but rather a timid, innocent question of a confused child. It was absolutely hysterical and we acknowledged her remark with bursts of laughter. When the merriment subsided, Diri calmly said, "I was thinking about a real possibility. I propose that at the end of such an unbelievable five years we would have peace on earth, unprecedented plenty, happiness, contentment and growth in every area, such as we have not seen since the Fall of Man." "Paradise returned, Milton would have said. Just five years of such paradisiacal good and virtuous life might cause man to reject the current state of total depravity it pleases to call civilization and give a totally new content to life on earth." And of course Dagi again couldn't help herself and as a conclusion whispered barely audibly: "As I said before: at the end of five years we'd wake up and find the old planet in its former mess, complete with every depravity and warfare, albeit with improved weapons."

In the beginning, just after arriving at the school, we were overwhelmed by our new life. We had to get used to being away from our parents, and were engrossed daily in the excitement of making new friends. We were fascinated by the wealth of knowledge offered to us and although our young body's demand for food and warmth did not leave us—that would have been too good to be true—but somehow it appeared less unbearable, as time passed. Life lost its rough edges and was far better than it has been for the past two years.

Concerns with abstractions and of trying to make sense of the mindboggling wickedness to which we were witnesses came later, and even then very haltingly at first. We saw too much of the ugly side of life, and our first reaction, fueled by self-preservation, was to bury the experiences and to hide them from the pain of inquiry. Before arriving at the Alpenhof, many of us found ourselves staring into the face of concentrated, incomprehensible evil. We saw soldiers and civilians maimed almost beyond recognition. We met women half-crazed from being victim of gang rapes

committed by enemy soldiers. We saw the barely living humans freed from the concentration camps. After a while the horror would no longer stay safely packed away in artificial oblivion, the questions, or rather the desperate cries for help and for answers surfaced.

Our teachers and religious leaders tried to aid us in our search for answers the best they could. It must have been extremely difficult for them. The world in its new, nefarious reality was probably as strange to them as it was to us. They certainly had no previous experience of hearing the agonizing questions from the lips of young girls; the questions, asked by hundreds of thousands: how could it be? Where was God? How could He allow it? Our teachers and pastors told us, what teachers and pastors always tell in similar situations: God did not cause it. It is all the result of free will, which is a given condition of the Universe. Because Man and the angels are endowed with the gift of thinking and were given total freedom of choice, the option to choose between good and evil was always present and will always be the fact of life on the planet, they said. And some of the created, whether angel or human, can and will choose power, greed, and so victimize the rest of mankind. They will always live with the proud conviction that Man can create his own world and won't consider the cost of their choices.

Diri told us that "...once a sin or an infraction is committed it never disappears completely. Toward the end of a person's days the memories, the joys and the good deeds fade. What was once important will have little meaning. The self-congratulatory virtues evaporate and not much of it is remembered. But the sins, the failings, the missed chances still torment the soul. A merciful God forgives the sins of those who are contrite—but self-forgiving or forgetting is very difficult. All saints from St. Theresa of Avila to St. Augustine knew this. But if we truly believe that we are redeemed, then we can heal from the agony of our sins. This is the very part that concerns us because each of us is fully responsible for our own soul, for our own salvation. Of course, there are plenty of evil-doers, destroyers, monsters around us. We don't understand them and we need not judge them. God takes care of that. That is His responsibility"

Did this explanation resolve our fears and our questions? Perhaps momentarily. But still, what we saw and what we experienced, was too monstrous, too unacceptable. How could those soldiers, who committed those horrors, ever return to their families and continue a normal life after what they have done, what they have condoned? How could a man's bestiality turn again into peaceful benevolence, once the dust settled and the bloody fog dissipated? How could the soldier, SS or Soviet, ever find joy with his children, how could he ever hug them with love, after he has done the unspeakable to other people's children?

We understood that diseases, often horrible ones, natural disasters and death are part of the human condition, and must be accepted. What we found so unacceptable was the monstrosity of what was willfully done to others; such deeds, which were not necessary and could have been avoided. The awful realization that we were witnessing not the human condition of predictable and unavoidable events, but the wickedness of Man and his capability to hurt his fellowman in ways worthy of Satan, frightened us. People with smooth, benign faces, perfect social behavior, often with brilliant education, who enjoyed art and felt spiritually uplifted while listening to classical music, could and did sit down at a polished conference table to make decisions about actions one usually associates with totally demented minds. Other individuals—and not just a few, but hundreds and thousands—who were known to be sober, hardworking men at other times and in other conditions, turned bestial without the slightest thought about decency, morals, feelings.

Of what frightening material is the soul of Man made? "Perhaps all of it was just a fatal and monstrous misinterpretation," mused one of the former students from the wisdom of eighty-some years. "When the Lord said 'Let (Man) have domain over the fish in the sea, and so on', He wanted man to be a good master, not a tyrant, who tortures animals and causes the extinction of many species."

He failed to understand what the Lord meant under the term "rule," and instead chose to subjugate the world because he did believe that he was better than the rest of creation and he was free to do as he wished. He found nothing objectionable in bear-baiting, bull fights, training animals for circus tricks, caging others and mistreating them, overworking them on his fields. Finally, the horrors culminated in the industrialized and inexcusably horrible animal farming for food.

After he convinced himself of his superiority and decided for himself what the Lord meant when He said "rule", it did not take a quantum leap for him to decide that some other humans, less powerful than he, are no better than animals and that he has the God-given right to rule over these too, to use and misuse them as he saw fit. And when he elected himself to be the Übermensch, there was no stopping him in his decision as to who shall live and who shall die."

And then Father Fekete said something, which made an awful lot of painful sense. He explained that the concept of the Original Sin is nothing but the turning away from the will and love of God, of trying to build a different, personal universe, excluding God. In a very true sense, the so-called "Original sin" is not just an isolated sin committed eons ago by the First Couple. If it were so, it would be easy to say that it has nothing to do with us, and even easier to complain about an unforgiving God for punishing us, "innocents," across countless generations. This, however, is not the case at all, he explained. The truth is that every one of us is guilty of committing the very same original sin every time we turn away and plan to go our own way, alone, without God. But this solo walk cannot be done. Adam and Eve failed in this, and eventually so did mankind. Which is why we have this tragic, hopeless, tortured world. God did not create war, nor concentration camps, Father Fekete told us. God never left the world, never turned from the suffering of man. He was there all along on the bloody frontlines, in prisons, in hospitals, in the concentration camps, under the ruins of collapsed buildings, crying with the dying and the injured. But remember, He also gave mankind two of His most precious gifts: intellect and freedom of choice. Whenever the two gifts are used for evil purposes, Man has to take responsibility for it. You see, once freedom of choice is given, it cannot be taken back from anyone. It is the same way as with the gravitational force. Once it had become the law, by which the Universe works, it cannot be taken back, cannot be made retroactive. To change the world in order to fit individual situations would lead to total chaos and the ultimate collapse of the world created according to a higher order. A child falling out of a sixth story window is an unspeakable tragedy, but the gravitational force at that particular space cannot be changed in order to eliminate that particular tragedy. The world was pretty well made up in the first place, we shouldn't try to tinker with it. Instead it is entirely up to us to get rid of evil, starting in our very own souls. And one way of starting this is to pray for those who perished, and also for those, who committed the atrocities.

- Why for them?

- So that sometimes, before it is not too late to escape everlasting hell, they would realize what they have done and be deeply, sincerely repentant. And because Jesus taught us to forgive.

This was a hard one to swallow. Pray for Hitler? Pray for those who occupied our country and did those horrible things? Father Fekete must be joking, or else he must think we are apprentices for sainthood. But we were not. Far from it. Whenever we prayed "... as we forgive those, who sinned against us," we always felt like adding the clause "except..."

After a while the demons went to sleep again. Perhaps we were young, and that helped. Young people are wondrously resilient. We had so much catching up to do, so much to look forward to. Life was good and we were immersed in all that laughter and bubbling life force. Demons had no place there. Or at least not all the time. There were of course times when they would crawl out of their hideout, but it was no longer a constant agony. They would never be totally banned; they had too much power. But they were successfully controlled, and perhaps even made to serve us—this is perhaps the reason why for the rest of our lives we all tried in our personal, limited way to work against their ever again taking the upper hand in the affairs of Man. Did we make a measurable difference? Who can tell?

More than a half century ago someone wrote in my keepsake book a sentimental thought, which, nevertheless, like most worn sentiments, has some truth in it, worth for more than just a passing consideration: 'If every person on earth would plant at least one single tree in his life, the world would turn into a Garden of Eden; if every person would make another person thoroughly happy, and would fully forgive just one person who did a bad turn for him, the earth would turn into heaven.' One does not necessarily need to do stunningly big deeds, the ones recorded in history books. Some small works of love and creativity might be enough to achieve the miracle—but the emphasis is on the two words "every person." It would only work if everyone participated.

EVERYDAY LIFE

Voices of students:

Markóczi: School started and we lived with a rather rigid schedule. After a very early wake-up call, a brief wash-up in the icy water, a breakfast of bread and a mug of coffee substitute, the instructions began. We had a short break at ten in the morning, then back to hard work. After the noon meal we had a short period when we could let off steam, a walk in the woods, and then a period of silence followed, the much disliked *silencium*. It was our responsibility to be prepared for the next day. When, after doing our homework we had some time left, we could do anything we wanted as long as we did it soundlessly. Some read, some drew, and some wrote letters. We always had adults with us—no wonder; where else could they go in that unheated building? We were used to their presence and they did not intimidate us. Our room at least was more or less warm, or at any rate warmer than anywhere else. After our evening meal, Margit *Néni,* the wife of Dr. Ravasz, who was a professional singer in Hungary, entertained us by singing Hungarian folksongs, which was her specialty. Erzsi *Néni,* a former opera singer, introduced us to the wonderful world of opera, sang us selected arias, explained the plots, or told us amusing stories which happened behind the stage. On the weekends we climbed mountains and when the weather turned warm, we went swimming regularly. Every day we took a walk, even on the coldest winter days.

Lilla: The local boys were endlessly and excessively fascinated by our presence in the village. I don't know about the other people around us, but the boys certainly knew about existence, and gave us a hard time. The "lower bedroom" was their favorite target. It was formerly a dining room with an oversized window, which was almost a glass wall and had not the luxury of curtains. It practically offered itself for those who wanted to peek in, and the boys most certainly wanted to. At one time, one of the students was doing her evening wash-up and she was half naked. Just then a group of boys arrived at the window. She screamed, the boys giggled, and we were outraged. From then on while the girls did their daily toilette, a few of us hid outside in an old cabinet which was conveniently placed under our window. We armed ourselves with brooms and sticks and were determined to beat them until the doctor came in case the unwelcome visitors would again appear. They must have gotten wind of our plan, or else were taught better by their elders, but did not show up again. We were endlessly amused by their being scared off by—girls. These boys now are our own age, or older, perhaps by now have several grandchildren, are respected pillars of society in Niederaudorf. I am often wondering: do they remember us? Do they think back about those silly raids which at that time caused so much excitement on both sides?

Ballusz: I was assigned to the "lower" bedroom, so called because it was a former smallish dining room on the ground floor. There were seven bunk beds there for the fourteen of us—and the room was full. A washbasin in one of the corners was the only other item in the cramped room. There were no ladders to the top of the bunk beds, those who slept on top, had to find a foothold on something and swing their way up; except for me. I lived next to the washbasin and could not find anything to support my ascent, except the washbasin, but I was afraid to step on it. All things being equal, the minute I would have put some weight on it, it would have come crashing to the floor. I would probably have been expelled because of the damage I caused. Not that it would have made much difference to anyone—the water was frozen in the pipes most of the winter and we could not use the basin until spring finally came and melted the ice. I don't know why the pipes never burst from the ice. It was probably luck. I have no idea what principle guided the staff when they made the bedroom assignments, but it worked excellently. Rather than dividing the girls according to age or grade levels, each of the bedrooms had a mixture of all ages, grades, temperaments and inclinations. Soon we learned to take care of each other; the younger ones enjoyed having an "older sister," and the older ones enjoyed their mothering role.

Our joy (and sometimes frustration) was the huge window in our room, looking out directly at the Brünnstein, our favorite mountain. The drawback of the window was that we were never safe from the German boys trying to peek in. Its advantage was that we in our turn, could observe, especially after lights were out, the exciting happenings going on outside, of which the most fascinating was the development of a torrid love affair. The Wallers engaged a girl, Betty, to help in the kitchen, and she met her sweetheart near the woodpile where the ermines used to play. Some of us from our beds could well see the enamored couple, but those at the back of the room missed the romantic drama. Mészárka, residing in the upper bunk right next to the window, supplied a kiss-by-kiss report. It was great entertainment, although we could not hear their whispered sweet nothings, or the promises for everlasting love. We wished them the best, but do not know if they ever married.

One upper class girl, who was usually a very serious young lady with impeccable manners, had an affliction: she could not stop laughing once she started. Naturally this was infectious, mostly because we were supposed to be silent after we entered the bedroom. It is an unavoidable fact of life: one always has the most passionate urge to laugh when it is forbidden. In a short while we were almost choking with laughter. Mária Adelsberger's room was next to ours, and she could hear us through the thin wall. First she called to us through the wall to be quiet; then she was knocking on the wall. She first did it gently, almost pleadingly and then with increasing irritation using her fist, or her shoes, and finally she tried to outshout our laughing fit, and threatened us with all sorts of awful consequences. In the end, she marched into our bedroom—but by the time she completed the trip to our door, deadly silence awaited her, punctuated with an occasional gentle snore. And of course, as soon as she left, the laughing started all over again, although we did try to muffle the sound into our pillows.

The winter was cold and the quality of air in our crowded bedroom was getting quite ripe, not to say putrid. We discussed the possibility of keeping the window open for the night. Magda made the final decision with water tight and unquestionable logic: "Many have died because of cold, but there is not a single case of death recorded on account of foul smells. I suggest we leave the window closed." And that was that. The edict was especially hard on the girls who slept around Magda, as she used to rub her hair with an onion and then bundle her head in a towel for the night. She heard somewhere that this is a magic cure for thin hair. I am not convinced that it worked, but I shall never forget the smell.

Magda: Ballusz, Ballusz, you are not really objective when you complain about my onion soaked head—which by the way was tightly covered with a towel in order to give me the greatest benefit and it assured for you girls to get the least amount of the sulfuric compounds released from my beauty aid. But have you considered the smell of the fourteen straw sacks, which after a year should have been refilled with fresh straw? Those were not sources of heavenly perfume either. And fourteen girls don't exactly exhale rose-scented air either. But I still insist that if we had slept with the window open in those temperatures and with those ridiculously inadequate, thin counterpanes we had, we would have been frozen stiff by the time the wake-up call came in the morning. Kindly remember, you have me to thank that you are alive today. I rest my case.

Lilla: In 1947 I completed the 7th and 8th grades at Niederaudorf. I remember how terribly cold it was and at one point it was discussed whether the school ought to be closed altogether. In September 1948 Germany's monetary unit changed from the RM (Reichsmark) to DM (Deutschmark) with the result that overnight our savings became totally worthless, and my parents could no longer afford the fee for the school. I had to leave.

Ági: Katyi, one of our classmates with an exceptional talent taught us to embroider. She had good "seeing" eyes and a gifted hand, so anything she drew was really excellent, but her specialty were the decorative and rich motives which were stitched on clothing, painted on walls, and pottery, woven into linen, carved into wood in Hungary's various regions. She first showed us patiently how to draw  the designs, and then made us compare our drawings to her own until we got it right. She explained that each region rigidly adheres to its individual motive, and that there is never any deviation, not in design and not in the choice of colors. Later when we were able to get pieces of cloth and yarn, we attempted to stitch the motives onto cloth. I remember how many times she made us undo the work if it was not right. She insisted that the stitches had to be so neatly done that one should not be able to tell which is the top and which the underside. She decorated our keepsake books with some of these regional motives, which we could later use in our work.

Lilla: One late evening after lights were out, we told hair raising ghost stories in whispers. After we were thoroughly frightened, somebody suggested that we ought to conjure up some spirits. On silent feet we tiptoed out to the backyard and sat in a circle concentrating really hard. We had a definite goal: we wanted to know whether Hitler is really in hell, roasting to a well deserved crispness. But no matter how hard we tried, his spirit refused to appear, and we were getting cold. Just about when we were about to give up the experiment and return to bed, Dagi appeared, sheeted in white, giving out unearthly sounds. We of course screamed for fear that Hitler came back, and the screams brought out the teachers to the scene of spirit conjuring. They were not happy. We were ushered back into our rooms, admonished how sinful spirit conjuring is, and how unladylike our behavior was. We never found out how Hitler fared in the afterlife, but we hoped that he got what he deserved. We prayed daily that "forgive us our sins, as we forgive those who sinned against us," but the forgiving, stopped at Hitler. No pastor and no priest could change our conviction about this. He belonged in hell and we all wanted to be sure that he has arrived there and that he did not find a garden party with lampions and champagne.

Kati: The Wallers owned a little wagon. It was a simple enough conveyance, made of wood, with wooden wheels. It was pulled by hand. This wagon was an important and cherished part of our life. At times it served as an ambulance. When Olivia twisted her ankle and could not walk, when Markóczi was too ill to walk, or when Klári Juhász had to be taken to the hospital for surgery, we pulled the patients seated in the wagon to Oberaudorf. At other times, we used it to haul wood from the forest. But the best part was to see it at the train station at Oberaudorf, when friends came to pick us up at the beginning of school. What a relief and joy it was when we could pile our luggage on the wagon and did not have to carry it all the way to the next village! As I grew older I was marveling at the craftsmanship of the people, who built such things way back. They made objects carefully, with love and skill to last and last. We have used this wagon almost constantly, putting lots of weight on it and dragged it on all sorts of expeditions and roads, including the steep sides of mountains when we were gathering fire wood—but it did not show the wear. We appreciated it and took excellent care of it. No one can say that we were a generation of a throw-away society.

Now I am living in Australia and recently visited an antique shop where a similar wagon was on display. It might sound strange, but suddenly I felt a keen sense of homesickness, as the memories of the past rushed at me. I had to keep my emotions at bay. It would have been a rare spectacle to see an elderly lady looking at an old hand pulled wagon while surreptitiously wiping away silly telltale tears.

Dining/Classroom – upper grades

Éva Tirczka, Marika Markó, Mari Buza; Inci Tóth, Mara Szűcs, Magda Hadady, Mari, Anikó Almay.

Across, with their back: Éva Hochenburger, Inci Tóth, Piri Hegedűs; Magda and Kati Czihy.
Below: Éva Balla, Katyi Kristó-Nagy, Mária Berlányi, Kati Pettendy;
Kati, Munci Váczy, Éva Bonyhay, Magi and Lacika Renkey; next to Magi, Éva Gruber.

Dining/Classroom – lower grades

From left,
around the table:
Nóra Hegedűs,
Marica Renkey,
Ági Szkladányi,
Lilla Finkey,
Éva Mészáros,
Dagi Várhelyi,
Vilma Eördögh,
Anikó Radnay,
Gabi Csaba.

From left:
Dagi, Éva Király, Zsuzsa Szűcs,
Gabi Kovács (behind vase)
Pancsi Váczy   "
Nusi Dax,
Leila Spöttle
Kati Jászberényi
Panni Szabó,
Gabi Csaba
Picu Mayer
Anikó
Vilma
Nóra
Marica

Upper grades room:

From left:
Mária Berlányi
Éva Bonyhay
Lacika Renkey (visiting)
Éva Gruber
Ferenc Kovács and a
guest. (not identified)
Rev. Zoltán Kótay, on
the occasion of the
celebration of the Confirmation of nine students, May 27th, 1948.

Photos by Gábor Buza, 1948.

Food or the lack of it - at the Alpenhof:

All was not a bed of roses; often all we had were the thorns, but we did learn to live with them and while they were unpleasant (who likes to be pricked by thorns?) we never considered them particularly tragic.

There were two recurring themes in our life which we could not sweep aside: one was the constant and numbing cold, and the other the equally constant, painful hunger. We were not only growing children needing food, but the wonderful alpine air, praised as the ultimate for healthy living, made us ravenous. The food we received was really terrible, but we were so hungry that most of us ate it—and could have eaten more of it, but the portions were very small. We usually got up from the table almost as hungry as we sat down. We tried to still our hunger the best we could. Our parents managed to send us packages from time to time and it was always with great joy when we discovered that the packages also contained edibles. In the winter as we passed orchards during our walks, we could sometimes dig from under the snow frozen apples left on the ground after the fall harvest. In the warm months when we went swimming in a nearby lake we discovered with glee that there were small crabs in the water. We caught as many as we could, cooked them in salt water and pretended that we were treated to something exotic and wonderful. It was our personal tragedy that these crabs had so very little meat on them.

At one time our class picked up a crow on the roadside, shot by passing American soldiers, and we cooked a soup from it. This was before we knew what the daily menu of the crow was. Some girls from the other grades—less lucky because they didn't find a crow—questioned the quality of the bird and also our culinary skills. The objections were quickly swept aside because it was quite obvious to us: pure jealousy prompted the remarks. We had the crow; they did not.

The question of which parts of the bird to include in the soup and which to discard was more imminent. We thought that heart and liver were OK, but what about the intestines?

"We could pretend that it is just noodles in the soup," suggested somebody. But the opposition jeered saying, "You could also pretend that it is a long worm, the kind that crawls on the roads after a good rain." At the image of that the more sensitive ones suddenly lost all appetite. But we cooked it anyhow, omitting the intestines, and although not really a true Sunday dinner, it was edible.

At one time in the basement, where we did our washing, we discovered a small room, and in it a large barrel of sauerkraut. We stood around it seriously debating and badly tempted, our hands only about four inches away from sin. The Wallers, the owners of the pension and of the kraut, knew what they were doing, no doubt about that. The cabbage retained its snowy white color, and a tantalizing fragrance rose as we lifted the cover.

- Would it be stealing?, someone formed the timid question.
- Is the snow white?, was the rebuff.
- I know that. But the question is: which falls into the category of sin: taking the cabbage, or eating it? (This timid person would probably make a pretty good lawyer in the far future).
- Because one of us could take the cabbage out of the barrel, confess the sin on Saturday to either the Prior or to Father Fekete. "Nothing to it," the would be lawyer calmly continued. "After the act of contrition, an expiatory prayer, consisting of a couple of Pater Nosters, should do. But listen, my point is: if eating the cabbage

is not a sin, we are free. One of us would steal it, then share it and then all of us would have a feast. One sin and six full bellies. One sinner, who steals it, and five innocents."

- You are such a cynic. It hurts my ears to listen to you!

- I am not a cynic. I am a hungry Christian. And my logic is perfect and water-tight, wouldn't you agree?

- Perhaps. It is definitely kraut-tight. And of course, after we take the cabbage, we could fluff up the top a bit, and nobody would be the wiser for it.

- True, and there is so much of it. If the Wallers would eat cabbage every day until August, the barrel would still be half filled. They could not possibly eat this much. And they would never miss it.

- Maybe they are saving it for us for a special meal.

- Of course. And water is flowing upstream and we have snow storms in July.

- Or maybe it is used for something else. Like maybe they make booze from it.

- Well?

- Well what?

- Are we or are we not going to have the feast?

- I have seen how sauerkraut is made, announced the one who was the best in every subject, and always knew the answers. The cabbage is shredded, salted and then it is put into a big vat. Then the family removes the shoes and stomps on the cabbage, the same as they stomp on grapes to make wine.

- You are jesting, of course.

- No, I am not. I saw it being done. And I vote that we stay virtuous, and abstain from the feast.

To eat a crow was OK, but to eat stolen cabbage, trampled by unknown bare feet was not. Of course we decided against the plan. And of course we did not really trust each other, and engaged in regular, but highly secret patrols to check the cabbage-level in the barrel. It never changed, and slowly we started to believe in the integrity of our sisters and stopped looking.

Our parents from time to time were able to somehow scrape together some basic ingredients, probably heavily relying on the black market contacts they had, and baked cookies for us. These were not the kind we used to eat in Hungary; nevertheless, they were unbelievably good. It was our habit to share the contents of the packages with all classmates at our grade level. Nobody would think of eating the goodies alone. These packages were mailed to us through the erratic and not always rapid postal route, and sometimes the content was moldy by the time we received them. We appreciated it nevertheless, thanked our parents profusely, scraped off the mold and enjoyed the treat, but in our letters we never mentioned the fungus, and none of us ever wrote home about hunger or cold. We knew that our parents did their utmost to keep us in school, and we also knew that they had next to nothing for themselves, so instinctively we felt that complaining was not acceptable.

We also suffered from something which we labeled specific hunger: had we received more than we could eat from the usual food, we would still feel hunger, a keenly demanding hunger for special foods. The memory of vegetables and fruits, of milk and freshly baked bread was maddening. Thinking about a bowl of boiled potatoes with parsley and butter seemed a magnificent delight of another world. We doubted that such things existed any more. Perhaps these disappeared in the war, together with our homes, relatives, warm rooms, and shoes that fit.

One of our terrible pastimes, which almost equaled choice Chinese torture methods, was to talk about food. We recalled every favorite dish, every holiday meal we ever had, until we all but drove each other mad talking about Lucullian feasts. The memories bordered on being sensual, and talking about such keenly felt physical memories probably bordered on sin. In the Middle Ages this could have been reason enough to send the hungry, but sensuously desiring sinner to the next convenient pyre. People were punished for less (but probably did more on the sly.)

- "And do you remember those fried chicken thighs?" moaned somebody in the dark. This was after we went to bed, bundled up in every piece of clothing we could find, including our knitted caps and gloves.

- Oh, yes, with crisp, crisp coating … But I really would want my mother's apple pie now… came the comment from the other corner.

- Lord, yes… and do you remember the fragrance of the buttery dough and the apples with cinnamon as the pie baked? The kitchen then was heaven. This comment came from somewhere near the washbasin, and the sigh accompanying it sounded as if she were just about to take the first bite from the magical pie.

- You are waxing poetic!

- What *is* poetic? Hunger or a full belly?

- It depends on the food you put into your belly. Yesterday's "Italian soup" does not qualify, was the opinion of the philosopher, living nearest the window in our bedroom.

- I think it was made of grass.

- Nor did the one potato, sprinkled with poppy seeds, we had at noon.

- Those weren't poppy seeds and you know it. I would rather not analyze what it was. We had poppy seed cakes at Christmas back home…

- So did we. It was good, but I would rather have the apple pie right now. I could eat half of that pie.

- And ice cream… lemon…no, chocolate…no, strawberry… or better, all three…

- OK, let us then have apple pie with ice cream.

- But first the fried chicken… was the practical solution.

- If they don't have chocolate cakes in heaven, I don't want to die and go there…

- Why? Just how much of it do you get here on earth? Now this was logic, the kind Mr. Ferenc Kovács could praise in his next philosophy class, but then it was well known that Marika was a born philosopher.

- Stuffed cabbage with sausages and smoked meat… This was a painful moan rather than a rational statement.

This was only the start. With ever more passion we listed every delightful food we could think of, until Ms. Mária Adelsberger, the strictest of our teachers, stormed into our room in her faded flannel nightgown to put an end to it. Her room was next to ours and perhaps she heard the listing of the decadent foods through the thin wall. As she too was hungry, she probably could not stand the agony of listening to it any longer. Indeed, she wanted us to sleep. At least, during sleep, one does not feel hunger. But sleep did not come because then we got the giggles. It was so funny to see the severe teacher of Latin conjugations and German irregular verbs in a nightgown. A teacher in a nightgown! It was hysterically funny because everybody knows that teachers have no private lives, no nightgowns, nor hunger, or indigestion. We all but choked laughing.

And how we could laugh! We laughed so that dozens of muscles and the tear sacks were activated; no wonder this is sometimes called a belly laugh. This laughter bubbles up from the depths of a secret inner place where life force, hope and unlimited energy are housed; the laughter is the very affirmation of life itself. It is a heady feeling, a precious gift of Hebe, the goddess of youth; a benediction given to youth only. We laughed not because something was particularly funny or witty, but because we were young and enjoyed the world no matter what it offered. We acknowledged and accepted its adverse conditions, but it did not influence our love of life. Other than recurring homesickness and occasional tears because we could not master a particularly difficult segment of the program, we were never unhappy.

As the years pass we forget how to laugh in this way, almost without self-control, overtaken by ever returning spasms of merriment. In our dignified old age we gaze uncomprehendingly at the laughing youth of today and are tempted to call them silly. When was the last time we laughed so heartily at nothing in particular? We haven't because we forgot how. Or perhaps we are afraid of the possibility of a padded cell. Or else, we unlearned this laughter because the source, the spring, which is youth itself, dried up. Nowadays we merely produce smiles, sometimes because we are content and sometimes because we are polite, or we use it as a tool to avert having to speak about something we would rather not discuss. Old age starts when this kind of hearty laughter stops and becomes alien to us.

Voices of students:

Vica: We were always hungry. At least I was. We watched carefully what was portioned out to us; we even considered the size of the potatoes put on our plate. My sister's recollection concerning food is funny, although at the time she was mortally embarrassed. It so happened that one day Mrs. Waller invited her into the kitchen and gave her the huge pot, in which our oatmeal was cooked. She was given the rare delight to lick it out. As her head practically disappeared in the large pot, a team of inspectors entered the kitchen. She removed her head from the pot, and there she stood, face smeared with oatmeal and while the men stared at her in disbelief, she all but died of embarrassment. After all she was not a child, but close to being a young lady, supposedly with refined manners.

Lilla: We were poor and often hungry, but we were a happy group, full of joy and always ready for fun. We joked about the food, such as the "mush": oatmeal cooked in water and nothing added to it to make it palatable. We laughed about the potato sprinkled with a tiny amount of blood sausage. The potato looked as if it were sprinkled with poppy seeds, so we always called it the "poppy seed potatoes."

When we started to write our memories about the school, I called up some of the alumnae. They too remembered the story of the crow, shot by Americans and eaten as a soup by some of the students. It made me happy that I was not the only one remembering it because for a while I truly questioned my memory, fearing that that ugly man, Herr Alzheimer, was lurking around the corner and made me confused. It was reassuring to know that everyone recalled it and I did not make it up. Betty let the girls with the crow into the kitchen, which was her personal domain, to cook it. She generously donated some noodles to put into the soup. The principal was also invited to taste it. (A good principal would do almost anything to make his students happy!) He accepted a small ladle of it, but then asked for black pepper and sprinkled it liberally. I don't think he gagged; he was too much of a gentleman to do that. I seem to remember that it had a bitter after taste, but we were hungry, and ate it anyway.

The blood sausage or black pudding was invented in many parts of the world hundreds of years ago when no part of the animal was to be wasted. This sausage is made from a generous amount of blood mixed with pieces of inferior "fall off" meat and with innards such as lungs, viscera and so on. A filler is added in the form of rice, or bread, barley, or oatmeal. Onions are added, then the mixture is cooked until it thickens. It is generally seasoned with salt, pepper, and a variety of herbs, then filled into casings. Before serving, it is baked until the casing is crisp. Blood sausage is still a favorite food in many parts of the world, especially in Germany, where it is called Blutwurst. Our sausage had no seasonings, and in general it was perhaps fortunate that we just got a little bit of it. It is not everybody's dish.

Márta: Despite the numbing cold and the truly miserable food, none of us ever considered quitting and going home. We ate what was served us and tried to joke about it. The German cuisine was never world famous but in the war years it sank to its absolute lowest level, which is no wonder because food stuff was very limited. Rationed amount of beans, soy beans, oatmeal, potatoes and sometimes some root vegetables were all that was available. What was allotted on the ration cards was so little that it was ridiculous by any standard. To give an example, at times a person received for an entire month two eggs, four ounces of margarine and one pound of meat. Also many of the foods we could buy were made from some secret elements which probably had no close relation with any sort of known organic matter. These were probably manufactured by the weapons industry and were labeled "ersatz" or "substitute." We had ersatz honey, ersatz jam, ersatz dried tomatoes, ersatz milk and ersatz coffee. They all had a peculiar taste, the kind a sane person would rather not put into his mouth if he wanted live to his next birthday. Nowadays they would probably be banned from the market as carcinogens. We get upset about gene manipulated grains and vegetables, and worry what these would do to us, but it is perhaps a good thing we did not know what we ate then.

All food, including vegetables and the mundane potato was rationed. Everyone was allotted a minimal amount of (brown) sugar each month. Since the Wallers did not bake and so did not need the sugar, this was portioned out to us at the beginning of each month to use in our ersatz coffee, or to put it on our mush. But since the amount was so little, we learned to drink our ersatz bitter, eat the mush in its natural horror, and instead, most of us sprinkled it on the (brown) bread and pretended that it was a cookie.

We never figured out why the bread was so awfully dark brown, a totally alien color in the world of breads, but perhaps it was another good thing that we did not know what went into it. Probably ersatz grains. I remember eating bread, which apparently was first baked to feed the army during the war; the date of preparation was stamped on the bottom of the bread. Unbelievable, but according to the date, this bread was several years old! Talk about expiration date! It was rock hard, slightly bitter, but for some reason not moldy, and all in all it was edible when dipped into some liquid.

The most memorable meals at the Alpenhof were the so-called "Eintopf" concoctions—this was an entire meal consisting of one dish. In case someone is interested in the recipe, this is how it was made: Betty, the kitchen help, put a big pot of water on the stove and then searched the premises and put everything into it that she could find in and around the kitchen. Naturally each day this had a different taste, depending on what Betty could find. Unfortunately for us, she most often could find nothing but turnips or rutabagas. The dish, although pretty horrible, had undeniable variety.

When the condition of the girls, very near starvation, was repeatedly explained in München at the CARITAS, we finally did receive help, mostly in the form of great quantities of oatmeal, soy beans and lentils. I don't know where this generous gift was found for us, but it was obvious that the area of origin had a lively community of mice. I remember many an evening when a few of us sat in a corner with Kálmán *Bácsi*, the principal's father-in-law, and while we listened to his fabulous stories we tried to separate Cinderella-fashion the oat flakes from the mouse droppings. At times it seemed there were more droppings than oatmeal, and more tares than lentils. As we contemplated the sacks of gift, all of which needed to be picked over, it seemed an endless, hopeless job. There was nowhere a fairy godmother with the magic birds, who would help us in this impossible task. When we reached the totally unhappy stage of hopelessness and thought that we shall never finish separating the darnel or the mouse droppings from our would-be dinner, Kálmán *Bácsi* in his lovely, slow and reassuring voice quoted the words from the Bible:

"Another parable put He forth unto them, saying, The kingdom of heaven is likened unto a man which sowed good seed in his field: But while the men slept, his enemy came and sowed tares among the wheat. But when the blade was sprung up, and brought forth fruit, then appeared the tares also. So the servants of the householder came and said unto him, Sir, didst not thou sow good seed in thy field? From whence then hath it tares? He said unto them, An enemy hath done this. The servants said unto him, Wilt thou then that we go and gather them up? Nay; lest while ye gather up the tares, ye root up also the wheat with them. Let both grow together until the harvest: and in the time of harvest I will say to the reapers, Gather ye together first the tares, and bind them in bundles to burn them: but gather the wheat into my barn."
—Matthew 13:24-30,

The words, or his voice soothed us and we continued our hopeless, endless job. We grumbled only *sotto voce* about the reapers who neglected to first burn the weeds. Unfortunately Kálmán *Bácsi* had no parable for us about mouse droppings... To this day, when in a shining Australian supermarket I am buying for my family beautifully and hygienically packaged oatmeal in see-through bags, I cannot keep myself from shaking the bag a bit just to see if I could detect some mouse droppings in it. Such is the result of early conditioning.

We always appreciated the packages our parents sent us. These did not always contain what we hoped for, but we were happy nonetheless. We always shared what we received and as we put a single sardine for each girl on the dry (brown) bread, we felt lucky indeed. Also quite rich because in our poverty we were still able to give something to each other.

Mészárka: Oh yes, the hunger! It was always with us, both as a physical pain and as a question of survival. But is hunger really a pain? We often tried to analyze it. It does not hurt like a cut or a burn does, but once it appears, it takes over and rules all emotions and thoughts. After a while nothing is left, only the hunger. We needed food to still the pain—or whatever it was—and we needed it to survive. Matthew's verse (6:25) never made more sense to us than it did then. "Therefore I tell you do not worry about your life, what you will eat or drink…Look at the birds of the air. They do not sow or reap or store away in barns and yet your heavenly Father feeds them."

During our afternoon walks, just like the birds of the air we also took to the fields and searched for the promised food our heavenly Father might have in store for us. And the things we found during the summer and fall! We became quite adept in our ancient yet modern role as gatherers, which is only natural. After all, during most of his existence on Earth Man was used to that kind of life: all our ancestors were foragers. A bit short of two million years ago, Homo Erectus had to find his food where he could if he wanted to survive. That poor, badly equipped man couldn't even hunt! The gathering mode of life lasted through the ages of the Earth up to about 12.000 years ago. In Niederaudorf we, the late descendants of Homo Sapiens, simply fell back to a life style quite natural to our ancestors. We did not find it particularly surprising that until the end of summer the afternoon walks were devoted to finding food—and during the winter to finding wood for our stove.

We gathered orach, a kind of wild spinach; nettles; fiddleheads; burdock roots; wild onions; mushrooms; the berries of the blackberry, blueberry and raspberry bushes and also of hawthorn (this was not a particular treasure as the berries had huge, hard stones and very little fruit to go with it); rosehips; small wild apples; spicy green leaves growing at the banks of a small river. Not even Sári Néni knew its name, but it did not matter because it tasted good and we did not get sick from it.

With the same sense of victory the Stone Age man must have felt as he returned to his cave and to his hungry family, we carried our bounty home where Betty, our angel in disguise, helped us to make the greens into salads, or she cooked them into side dishes to enliven the sad situation of mush or dried beans.

In late fall, our group landed on the harvested fields, transforming Jean–Francois Millet's painting "The Gleaners" into an authentic tableau vivant. Our hand-me-down jackets and sweaters in their hopeless drabness were appropriate and in perfect harmony with the painting; the gathering mist of the afternoon just had the right dose of gloom to fit the mood of deep poverty expressed in the painting. We were bending over to find edibles, just like the peasants for as long as memory goes back had done, gathering the leftover corns of wheat or oats. We then happily chewed the tiny corns we found. That year the field mice went to their holes quite hungry because we were the first on the fields.

Anikó: I cannot say much about the food, as there was very little of it. But I do remember that somebody acquired a bag of dried beans. I do not remember any more whose idea it was that beans, when cooked long enough and mashed up, would taste like chestnut puree, our all time favorite. The original is a feathery light concoction fragrant with vanilla and is smothered with whipped cream. I assume it is the staple food of angels; it is definitely a heavenly dessert, which our cooked beans were not.

Ballusz: Toward the end of the last year we spent at the Alpenhof, the German authorities were getting concerned about the continuous malnourishment of children both native and refugee, and under the name "*Schulspeisung*" allotted somewhat more food to schools. We never really knew what additions were made, but we started to get strange gourmet offerings. Apparently at one time a certain quantity of raisins was allotted. The Wallers forced it through a meat grinder and applied a thin coat of it on our afternoon (brown) bread. What can I say about it? It was perfectly awful. Perhaps it was ersatz raisins, made from heaven only knows what. Mészárka guessed that they were fish eyes before they landed in the Wallers' kitchen. The following month the official addition was a generous amount of dates. Aside from the fact that we have not seen dates for many years and were delighted at getting such an exotic delicacy, the added virtue of the date is that it has a large, hard stone. Fortunately the Wallers, (or Betty,) found it too much bother to remove the stones, and so the dates were not ground up for a bread spread, nor chopped up to sprinkle on our lonely potato, but were given to us in their natural, unadulterated form. What a happy a day that was!

Tirczka: The food (or the lack of it) at Niederaudorf is a vivid memory for me. Right after the war, food was very scarce in Germany, and we ate at the school what they could procure, which was not much. At one o'clock, the serving window from the kitchen was opened and we were treated to some choice horrors, such as barley soup, or the terrible blood sausage with the potato. (The singular mode of the potato is not a grammatical error on my part because we only got one single potato, and a very small one at that.) To this day I get sick just thinking about that particular dish. The inadequate food did have its advantages though: we had no problems staying slim. As I looked at the photos of the reunion of 2007, it seems that since Niederaudorf none of us went hungry, and it shows.

The mother of Mari, our classmate, was able to buy a few eggs somewhere and at one of her visits she brought them for her daughter. Another girl had white sugar, and we went to work. We stirred the yolks with the sugar until it was smooth and pale, and then very carefully added the whipped whites. We divided the concoction among us. We closed our eyes and ate it slowly, sinking into a state of delight only known to the gods on Olympus. Mari had enough eggs to repeat the feast a few times, Kati had sugar and I had nothing but a wonderful appetite. Markóczi had chocolates, so they say.

Markóczi: You are absolutely wrong about this. We only dreamt about chocolates. I have not seen any since 1943.

Mészárka: When we prayed '...and give us this daily bread...' the words were not time-worn and meaningless, but a real supplication for real bread. And when as a miracle we got enough of it, we changed the plea in the prayer to '...and this day we give thanks for our daily bread.'

Ballusz: One night we were so hungry, we just couldn't fall asleep. Mészárka informed us that she had a can of sardines, which she was saving for emergencies. Mari had saved her bread from breakfast, and a fourth girl had a can opener. "This sounds like a meal," Mészárka whispered. We dared not eat it in the bedroom, which was forbidden in the first place, and also it was very dark there. "So dark indeed, that we won't find our mouth," Mari said.

So very quietly we slipped out to the toilette and squeezed ourselves into the tiny place. The bread was divided, the can opened and Mészárka placed a single fish on the small piece of bread. "This is almost Biblical," Mari remarked. "I mean the miracle of fish and the bread." "It would be, wouldn't it, if only bread and fish would miraculously multiply," said the owner of the can-opener, who gulped down her portion without chewing it, while the rest of us delayed the delight of eating by taking very small and very slow bites to make it last longer. At Mari's remark we, of course, started to laugh because it was so daringly delightful to say something so scandalously irreligious. Needless to say, Mária Adelsberger heard us. She was amazing; I swear she could hear a butterfly's hiccups. In no time she appeared at the toilette door towering over us in her majestic height, looking like the wrath of God. "And what exactly are you doing here, young ladies?" she demanded to know. The three of us froze, Mari quickly swallowed the last bit of her food to hide the evidence. But Mészárka was not intimated. She looked at the Judge and smiled her sweetest smile and said, "Please forgive us. We are only eating." And then something unbelievable happened. Mária Adelsberger laughed! She placed her hands on the door frame and laughed as hard as any human being ever laughed.

It was there in the toilette, close to midnight, in the gloomy month of November, when her rigor and otherworldliness melted away and we learned to love her.

Food or the lack of it - at Reisach:

"At the Alpenhof the cooking was done by the Wallers, but at Reisach the mother of our housemother took care of the job."

"In the evening we helped our cook by peeling potatoes and chopping vegetables, while singing enthusiastically. I must add that this was the very first time in my life that I peeled potatoes or any other thing growing in or above the soil."

"Most of the time we had bean soup, or lentils, often "paprika potatoes," which is prepared like a goulash, (original spelling: gulyás) but instead of meat, potatoes are added to the onions and paprika. We also had polenta quite often. It was still poor fare, but what a difference in taste! I do not know how she did it, but our wonderful cook had a trick of flavoring the simple fare with herbs and whatever was available so that it actually tasted good. We enjoyed our meals and there was always quite enough of it. And no more gruel soups and blood sausages and similar horrors!"

"Just before Christmas we tried to concoct '*szaloncukor*' from odds and ends sent from home. We had something called artificial honey, and heaven only knows (or maybe not) what its secret ingredients were. It is safe to say that it was never in touch with bees or flowers. Anyhow, we tried to heat it on our little stove to make the *szaloncukor*, but it boiled over in no time, and the classroom was engulfed in black smoke and we all but choked in it."

"*Szaloncukor*" is a fondant, a creamy confection which originated around the end of the fourteenth century in France. It was used to decorate elaborate cakes or to sculpt pastries. It is somewhat similar to cake icing. In its simplest form sugar (or honey) and water are cooked to the soft ball consistency, cooled slightly, flavors added, and then stirred or beaten until it becomes an opaque and creamy mass.

In the nineteenth century the fame of the fondant reached Hungary through Germany, bearing the German name "*Salonzuckerl.*" (Mór Jókai, the most read Hungarian author called it "*szalonczukkedli*" in his writings). In Hungary it was cooked longer than in France in order to form a harder mass. The mass was cut and shaped into candy squares, and then wrapped elaborately and individually into tissue paper. First the two opposing sides of fine, white tissue paper squares several times longer than the candy, were cut to form fine fringes. The candy was placed in the middle of the rectangle, rolled up, and then the tissue was twisted at both ends to secure the candy. As a final touch, the middle section, hiding the candy, was covered with silver foil. Someone thought of decorating his Christmas tree with this wrapped candy. Many copied his idea and since then it became tradition to hang a couple of pounds of it on the festive tree. Hungarians cannot imagine their Christmas tree without the sight of the *szaloncukor*. And indeed, it is a magical sight. The slightest movement of air makes the delicate fringes flutter and the candle lights reflect on the silver foil. It is truly wonderful, and it was part of our childhood. As far as I know, no other nation has this custom, so it could be called a true Hungaricum. But slowly this magic too is going down the sad road of mass production, or else, is changing in order to please the taste of the masses. Lately, the store-bought variety no longer has the fine fringe at the ends of the tissue paper, which was the essence of the candy. The new, thickly cut fringe of the no longer snow white paper is hopelessly ugly, the paper is cheap and thick, and has no longer any magic. A windstorm of hurricane force couldn't make it flutter, and it looks like so many ugly scraps of paper on the tree. The traditional and elegant silver was exchanged for foil in primary colors. It hurts one's sense of esthetics. The more adventurous home-makers (and those who have the time for it) buy the candy because at least it is still good—but rewrap them in homemade paper, according to the old standards.

Most children have learned early how to filch the candy from the wrapping, and then how to rewrap it so that nobody was the wiser for it. Only when dismantling the tree on the sixth of January was it detected that all the candy from the tree was gone, or at least at the level of a child's reach. The faked surprise, when discovering the missing candy, is a repeatedly performed family game.

Because of sheer nostalgia, we tried to create the illusion of bygone Christmases by attempting to make the candy, but our efforts went up in smoke. Literally. Apparently, fourteenth century confectioners had more skill, or better ingredients than we had. And perhaps ersatz honey is not really the preferred basic ingredient for a fondant.

Jutka: from a letter sent from Reisach, the new school site *"…To put your mind at ease, Mother, our bedroom is not at all cold. Late afternoon we start a fire in the stove, and by the time we go to bed, the room, despite its huge size, is comfortable and quite warm. In our individual "cells" or the rooms belonging only to one grade level, where we spend almost all of our time, the fire is going all day. These are all decent stoves and they never smoke up the rooms as the one did at the Alpenhof. And they do not engage in other tricks most ill-mannered stoves like to play on people, such as a stubborn refusal to get going in the morning.*

The food, I can tell you, is quite good. I don't know what our new cook Miss Mária Bárány's mother does with it, but she makes everything tasty. She does magic with onions, some bacon and herbs she procures somewhere to enliven the beans and lentils or the polenta, and so is able to put something on our table that has a heavenly, exciting fragrance, and is really good. The bread is rationed out in the morning for the entire day. For our afternoon snack we get a tablespoon of honey, or dates, and sometimes an apple. We landed in the fairyland of good food…"

Heating, or the lack of it

Ferenc Cserháti:

In November 1947 Dr. Ravasz wrote in his report to the CARITAS in München that: *"…feeding the students and heating the school are ongoing problems. The straw in the sacks for the beds needs to be exchanged, but none can be procured. The lack of basic school material is still not solved. There are also some secondary problems, which might appear less important; however, the solving of these requires time and effort. One of these problems was for example the lack of a typewriter. The increased amount of administrative work made it necessary to have one. Unfortunately the München office could not help in this matter as they are having the same problem. Eventually Mr. László Irányi, a Hungarian refugee (from Szeged, resident at Reisach at that time,) donated his own, thereby providing enormous help for our school…"*

Notes of Students:

Márta: Two dining rooms of the Alpenhof were used as classrooms, but in the coldest months all classes were moved into the bigger of the two, which was heated by a small wood burning iron stove. The brave little stove (photo p.19) tried hard enough, but was not really able to heat the room adequately. Instruction was regularly interrupted every forty-five minutes, so we could move about, playing children's games or dancing around in order to warm up. This was most difficult because the room was already so very crowded; we could only move by temporarily placing the chairs on top of the tables. It was terribly cold. The bedrooms were not heated at all, and each morning the faucets were frozen. We slept in hats, mittens and socks. During our afternoon walks we gathered wood and carried it back to the pension to feed our little stove in the big room. But in the end we had some good luck. A former student of Dr. Ravasz visited the school during the Christmas Holiday of 1947. He was by that time a well-known painter. While he was staying at Niederaudorf, he painted the portraits of a coal handler and his wife. As a form of gratuity, the coal handler provided the school with a nice shipment of coal which got us through the first month of 1948.

Nusi: Yes indeed, we were cold. But there were some kind people around, who helped. Once trees were felled on a mountain side. The wood cutters permitted us to gather the branches. This was very good because these were much thicker than the twigs we usually found. We pulled up our little hand wagon on the steep mountain side, piled the treasure on it, and pulled it back into the village to our pension. It was a tricky job because rolling down the hill our wagon had its own will and plan. Instead of pulling it, we had to hold it back with all our strength to prevent it from crashing down the steep path. We made several trips, and we were cold and dead tired, but it was worth it. We had a warm room, and one of our classmates, who stayed back in the pension in sick bay, baked bread for us while we were hauling the wood. How delightful that fresh, wonderful bread was! I can still recollect the taste of it. We were so excited about the bread, we forgot to ask where and how she got the white flour for it. On that day, instead of Pythagoras and Cicero, we learned all about wood cutting and hauling.

Ballusz: In the late fall of 1947 we had absolutely no fuel, although the cold temperatures come early in the Alps. One morning we decided, with the blessing of our principal, to spend the day in the woods, gathering twigs. This would not have been bad, we had done it before. But meanwhile the rain started to fall, and then to pour. Of course, the forested areas are all on the steep sides of mountains, and as the soil softened, we kept slipping and sliding, and were covered with mud. It was difficult to keep up our spirits. But we were in for a big surprise: around noon the girls who stayed home because of illness, packed our noon meal on the hand cart and brought our food to the forest. It was a real treat, but it is a mystery how they knew where we were. After all, we were surrounded by forests, and how did they divine in which to find us?

Koci: It was 1948 and as usually, the wood for our stove was all gone. We received permission from the village council to cut down some trees, which they marked for us beforehand. The school did not have money to hire a wood cutter, so we did it on our own. The principal cut down the marked trees and we chopped off the branches, and then sawed them and the trunks into proper sizes. It was unbelievably difficult. Our fingers were numb, our nose was dripping and despite the cold temperatures, we were sweating as is proper for real woodcutters. But if we did not want to freeze, it had to be done. After it was all done, we wallowed in the glory of accomplishment! What a heavenly feeling that was! We even made up a song about our triumph, which went something like this: "We did it! We did it! We went out and did it! We chopped and we sawed, and we sweat and we ached, we hauled and we cried, but we did it, we did it." We sang it in giddy and triumphant happiness as we hauled our treasure all the way to the pension and returned again to the forest for another load, several times during the day. Yes, we did it on our own, without any help; we alone made sure that there was heat in our room. All right, I know the song is not Grammy material, but then our accommodations were hardly of Hollywood standard either. But that did not diminish our insane sense of joy and accomplishment and the joy of having a warm room to stay in—at least for a while.

Keeping clean, health issues, doing tasks - at the Alpenhof:

Several tubs and basins were installed for our use. Once a week the boiler was fired up and we could take a bath, wash our hair and also do our laundry, using our bathwater for it in order to save the precious warm water in the boiler for the next girl in line. Other than this we only had cold water all week.

Anikó: Surprisingly and considering our situation, we were not very often sick. The worst case I can remember was diphtheria. The father of the girl who got it was a doctor, and he arrived at the school as soon as he was notified of her illness. He stayed with her until she was well again. Mária Adelsberger gave up her room for the two of them. I do not remember where she stayed during this time. Thankfully, nobody else was infected, but the fear was great. We lived in a terribly crowded environment, were undernourished and in any case medicaments were almost impossible to get in case somebody got really sick. But we were lucky, or else Somebody was watching over us.

Lilla: One of the girls in our bedroom developed tuberculosis and she had to leave. We prayed a lot for her recovery, but we never heard of her since. I had fever every night, and it turned out that it was caused by my inflamed tonsils. During the school vacation they were removed and I was never ill after that.

Ballusz: One day the doctor from the village, Dr. Arnold, came to the school and he planned to give us shots, but I do not know for what. Everybody was brave enough, except Klári, who fled to the woods to avoid Dr. Arnold. The principal and his son were running all over the village, and searched our favorite spots in the woods to find her, but she did not show up while Dr. Arnold was in the pension. She really was a disgrace to her father, who was a physician. However, eventually she was somehow persuaded to submit to it, and next day she was displaying her arm rather proudly as she announced that she too got her shot.

Jutka: The basement at the Alpenhof was our delight and our luxury. We lived in such confined spaces that in comparison the proverbial sardines in the can enjoyed extravagant spaciousness; therefore, the basement appeared to us like a true labyrinth and the room where we performed our luxurious bath appeared royal because of its generous size. This room was ours once a week for bathing, showering, washing our hair and doing our laundry. Considering that the rest of the week we only had icy water, this was heaven. At one time this room with its concrete floor was probably designed for the pension's large-scale laundry needs and was perhaps also used by the personnel to take showers. At any rate, more tubs and basins were added for us, and once a week the huge boiler was fired up. We had the wonder of hot water for an entire evening. Twenty-first century real estate agents would not hesitate to call it a "Wellness Oasis," which to us it really was. We laughed, and talked, and splashed, slid and slipped on all the water on the floor; it is amazing how quickly 40 girls can turn an ordinary basement room into a vast sea of soapy water. Water, water everywhere! Or as Robert Bridges phrased it more poetically:

"Above my head the heaven,
the sea beneath my feet."

A good thing that the floor had a good-sized drain. I don't know why they didn't stagger the bathing days, but it was fine with us as it was. Right after the evening meal, until lights-out, it was our absolute delight and our fun time although hazardous too, as I found out soon enough. The wet, slippery floor sent me flying against the opposite wall where I fell, and as it later turned out, broke my smallest toe. It hurt, but in those times the unwritten rule was, especially for refugees: don't seek medical help unless there is massive bleeding, third degree burn, obvious big bone fracture or signs of myocardial infarction. Anything less would heal by itself; anything worse would kill the patient anyhow, so why bother a doctor? So my toe healed on its own, albeit somewhat crookedly. This is not really a problem, unless I am longing for an exceptionally stylish pair of shoes. But from then on, slightly limping, I was very, very careful of my steps. Whenever I happened to start my own water rituals toward the end of the bathing evening, after my schoolmates already transformed the wash room into a sea of water below, and a cloud of mist above, I was ungrateful enough to forget how much I loved this day, and "benefits forgot" I dared to agree with the Bard: "Now I would give a thousand furlongs of sea for an acre of barren ground." Or a dry floor.

Keeping clean, health issues, doing tasks - at Reisach:

Anna: It was a terrible ordeal to carry the cold water from one end of the long, cold hallway into our bedroom on the opposite end. There was a narrow bench there and we placed the washbasins on it to do our morning wash. Since forty of us slept in the bedroom, there was usually a monumental traffic jam at the washbasins, and ocean-sized puddles on the floor.

Ballusz: Most of the time we stood in line with our washbasins to get a spot at the bench. When we finished washing ourselves, there was another long run back to the other end of the hallway to spill the water from our basins and to brush our teeth. Wednesday was our washday, for which the cook donated warm water from the kitchen. We hung our wash all over the bedroom.

Judit: I suppose keeping clean was the only point in which Alpenhof was a better place. There we had a big basement room with tubs and the opportunity to have once a week a full bath or a luxurious hot shower, and enough warm water to wash our hair and do our laundry. Although with the periodically frozen faucets, the rest of the week at the Alpenhof was not all that luxurious either. Interestingly, none of us can recall how we kept our bed sheets clean. Perhaps we mailed the dirty sheets to our parents? Or did the Wallers do it? We could not have laundered them ourselves because we just did not have the accommodations to wash such large pieces, let alone dry them. We did launder our pillowcases and towels, but as far as I remember, that was it. After the money reform, laundromats opened in many places, and what is more, even public baths were created where people could soak in a tub. It was just a question of money, and we had none of it. Luxury never has been the lot of have-nots.

Koci: In the Alpenhof we only had to clean the bedrooms the toilettes and scrub the big cooking pots. The rest of the cleaning was done by the Wallers. When we moved over to Reisach, Kovács Diri called a meeting and posed the question: should he hire a cleaning woman, or would we prefer to save the money and spend it on a radio and loudspeakers so we could have music piped into the bedroom and the classrooms. We voted for the music, and henceforth spent our Saturday afternoons cleaning and scrubbing. With music.

Jutka: from a letter *"Now I must finish my letter because I am running out of paper. From the writing paper which is left I need to fashion an envelope. But one more thing I must add: our soap is all gone. Would it be possible for you to somehow get at least one bar for us? Zsuzsika and I used up the last little bit washing our hair and our stockings. Perhaps we are washing ourselves too often and this is the reason that the soap does not last. Also I think that our towels are terribly dirty, although everybody says they are not all that bad. I don't know. They look pretty bad to me, but as long as we use the edges, they might serve us until we get some soap to launder them. The edges are not as dirty as the middle. And thank you for the shoes and the stockings you sent me. I am terribly careful with them. I wear them only on Sundays to church and in the bedroom. No harm can come to them that way..."*

Ballusz: The daily plan called for an afternoon nap right after the midday meal. We were not going to have any of it, so finally the housemother was satisfied if we just rested for an hour quietly on our bed. During this time, those who were on duty that week, washed the dishes, swept and aired the rooms. Once a week we had to scrub the hardwood floors in the classrooms, the bedroom and the hallway. It was not one of our favorite pastimes.

Mari: One of the really unpleasant tasks was to scrub the floors of the classrooms, bedroom and the hallway. There were altogether too many square miles of hardwood and stone floors. We only had cold water for the task, and the detergent was very harsh so that, together with the dirt from the floor, the skin of our hands also came off...

Markóczi: I was quite ill in 1949. The girls helped me into our little hand cart and in it they pulled me to the doctor's office in Oberaudorf. His diagnosis was hunger, or nutritional deficiency. It took me a long time to recover.

Klári: Sometime during this period my Dad, a physician, was assigned to accompany the trains transporting DPs to Italy to board ships to Australia and South America. The trains he accompanied went right past our school building at Kloster Reisach. On several occasions, he had thrown packages for us from the moving train. We knew, when the train would pass, and we were waiting for it by the tracks. These packages were for all of us, and contained medications and other rare stuff such as vitamins and soap. I was reminded of it in the 1948 Mikulás poems (which made fun of everyone) with the lines: "Klári, with the shots" (of vitamin B, etc.).

Klári's granddaughters visiting Reisach in 2009

Recreation and entertainment

On weekends our principal organized fascinating outings (every possibility was considered as long as it did not cost money—or at least not much.) Without him we probably would never have experienced the heady feeling of standing on top of a mountain. I am sure that on my own volition I would never have conceived the unusual and exhausting, altogether irrational plan to climb a mountain. I was not the only one bewildered by it—some of us returned dead tired and half crippled from such outings. As we finally hit the straw sacks, we were sure that within minutes we'll meet our Maker.

Mountain climbing forced us also to rethink the morality lessons pounded in to our heads, which more or less carried the message that it is very, very easy to rapidly slide down from the peak of accomplishments. Wrong! Unanimously we came to the conclusion that it was terribly difficult to climb a mountain—but oh, it was ever more so difficult to come down from the peak, and there was no easy sliding down as was prophesized. In a way, of course, the descent threatened to be fast, much faster than we planned; but that is not what our parents meant, and it certainly was not what we expected.

On the way down, we grasped quickly enough the golden rule of physics: a moving body will continue to move with uniform speed in a straight line, unless it is acted upon by a force. We learned that lesson well enough in class, but when facing the reality of the law, two things were also quite clear: one that no force will act upon our moving body to stop it; and two: the straight movement would quickly accelerate by the gravitational pull on the steep mountain side, as would the slick rolling stones under our shoes. And of course there would be absolutely nothing to stop this body helplessly speeding downward. Clearly the immediate task was to prevent acceleration, which was a most difficult affair, this being the understatement of Alpine mountaineering. We had to consider and evaluate every step while overcoming the considerable force of the gravitational pull. We also discovered the joy of a cane (actually just a sturdy branch of a tree we were lucky enough to find) to support us in the descent, which every minute threatened to turn into a free fall. We had pain in muscles we did not even know we had. We grew blisters upon blisters.

Some of us even tried to slip off the shoes and attempted the last stretch of the trek in socks only. Well, that was just another experiment which failed, and it failed spectacularly. So to recover and do whatever damage control was possible, we sat down and tried to put the shoes back on, only to discover two more truths. One was that under no circumstances should anybody sit down during mountain climbing (or descending) because there is a good chance that she won't be able to get up again. Ever. Also learned: one should not remove the shoes because in a very short time they will no longer fit. The attempt to put them back is not only incredibly painful, but almost impossible. During the last few miles, those crippled because of a most sensitive skin (or the worst fitting shoes), were actually carried down by their friends, who acted temporarily as Good Samaritans. Needless to say, when the next opportunity came to climb yet another mountain, we would not miss it for the best (and biggest) meal in the world. We turned into enthusiastic mountain climbers.

Much later, when I myself was teaching, I was often wondering about the laxity of the staff. Nobody asked our parents for permission slips to climb mountains in the Alps, or to make fieldtrips into potentially dangerous places. Nobody thought it unusual that once two girls were left for the night on top of one of the mountains all alone in an empty hut because they were too tired and their feet hurt too much to risk the descent. Everybody accepted that it was the right decision. Even more amazing, we always told our parents about our excursions and adventures, but none of them ever attacked the staff for letting us take risks. We were growing up and had to learn living on our own. They trusted us to choose; and trusted us to know our limits. And they were actually happy because of our adventures. Also, despite the war which raged just a few years ago across the Continent, it was a much safer place than it is today. It was a very different world.

Voices of students:

Tirczka: From our bedroom window we could see the mountain Brünnstein (1619 meters) which we climbed several times. Once we took the cog-wheel train to Wendelstein; however both were baby mountains in comparison to the others. We were endlessly fascinated by the range of the Kaiser Mountains. The formidable steep sides were not for us; expertise and long training were necessary for that. (Also shoes that fit and a guide, who had to be paid.)

Jutka: excerpt from a letter: *"We climbed yet another, mountain, the Brünnstein. The view from there was breathtaking. From below it looks like a solitary mountain, but from up there you know that you are mistaken in this. It is surprising but true: right behind it is a long range of mountains, one peak after the other; there is just no end to them, but from our valley you cannot see them and have no idea that they are there. We love this mountain, the Brünnstein, almost more than the others. For one thing, its foot is practically in our backyard. It lives with us and probably knows the irregular verbs better than we do. For another thing, each morning we know by just looking out the window what the weather will be like. At times the Brünnstein is so enveloped in clouds, mist or fog that the mountain simply isn't even there. Then we know that it will be cold and damp all day and our stove will probably smoke. It is a funny mountain: instead of a peak, it ends in a long and narrow line on top. We can (and do) sit at some part of this mountain top so that one of our legs hangs down one side of the mountain and the other leg on the opposite side, as if we were horseback riding. We joked about mountainback riding. It was a dizzying experience, even for those who do not suffer from acrophobia."*

Zsuzsa: As hard as school was we had a lot of fun too. When weather permitted, we went on a lot of outings, and to swim. All of this was free, truly God's gift to us. We were extremely blessed that our school was located in a lovely country with spectacular mountains.

Jutka: excerpt from a letter in 1948. *"...We had a spectacular night which I'll never forget. I am so fortunate that I could witness it. With the last tests school ended yesterday by noon, but fortunately we decided to stay at school overnight and go home the following day; otherwise we would have missed it. It was June 21, the date of the summer solstice, which is when the day is the longest and the night the shortest in the year. Men from dozens of villages climbed the mountains all around us, and camped high up at different points. At midnight they lit huge bonfires and sounded their alphorns. It was magical. Dozens of great fires burned at once at different points up in the* *mountains. They were big enough so they could be well seen from the valley. The people were out in the streets celebrating and singing. Erzsi Néni told us that the custom of celebrating the sun goes back about thirty thousand years, when cavemen lived. That information was interesting, but we pretended that it was a celebration put up just for us to celebrate the successful completion of the school year.*

And the alphorns are something else! The men showed them to us the day before they climbed the mountains. I have never seen an instrument like it. It looks like an extra long pipe, longer than a man is tall, something that would fit a giant if he wished to have an afternoon smoke. They blow into it at one end. The other end, because it is so very long and probably heavy, rests on the ground. Really funny. It has a haunting, melancholy tone, unlike any other sound. Very fitting to such a heathen midnight festivity."

Márta: The river Inn at the Kaiser Mountain region divides Austria and Bavaria. The Bavarian region was occupied by the American forces, and the Austrian region by the French. Our school at Niederaudorf was located on the "American" side of the border. Across the river is the town of Kufstein, then under French occupation. Its forbidding fortification was built on a tall rock about 300 feet above the town. One part of it, the circular Kaiserturm, was an infamous prison operated by the Austrians during the Austro-Hungarian regime. It is a forbidding place, which chills the visitor to the bone. Its walls are guarding the memory of immense suffering and a tragic chapter of Hungary's history.

After the Revolution of 1848 against the Austrian repressive policies, over 90 Hungarians were held prisoner there in extremely harsh conditions. The inmates were mostly members of the aristocracy, such as Lady Blanka Teleki, educator, especially concerned with the higher education of girls; her helper Klára Leowey, also a teacher; Miklós Wesselényi and others. But there were also authors, poets, preachers, bishops, noblemen and educators, and even a Robin Hood type person, the "betyár" (highwayman) Sándor Rózsa, who also fought for the country's freedom along with the others. Their sentences were anywhere from five to ten years.

Our most sincere wish was to be able to walk across the bridge to Austria and to place flowers at the cell doors of those suffering so much pain, deprivations and indignities many years ago. But the French would not grant us permit to cross the border. However, we climbed the 3600 feet high Schwarzberg nearby, and from the peak we could see Kufstein across the border. There we said a silent prayer for those who suffered for the freedom of Hungary.

Ballusz: It was great news when the movie house in Oberaudorf started operating again, featuring American films with German subtitles. The movie house was small and there were not enough seats. We enjoyed the films standing up in the back. The first movie we saw was „Sun Valley Serenade." It was the first time we ever heard jazz, and we loved it. As we were standing, we could beat the rhythm with our feet.

I always hated any sort of exercise, but once the girls talked me into climbing the Brünnstein. It was a strange experience when in July, clad in our summer dresses, we had a wild snowball fight up there. There is a little chapel on top of this mountain and we wrote our name on its door frame under all the other names of people who were there before us. It was great, but I never repeated the feat and deeply admired those, who climbed it several times as easily as if they just ran to buy something at the corner grocery store. My chief exercise consisted of swinging my way up and down my bunk bed.

When somebody had a birthday, we celebrated it happily, although there were no cakes or presents. When our principal's wife had her birthday, we collected immense amounts of wild flowers in the meadows. Their window opened to the terrace and our plan was to tiptoe past their door, go out to the terrace, and serenade her at their window. We wrote the words to the tune of The Blue Danube, and planned to give her all the flowers. Although we walked on tiptoes and talked in whispers, apparently the forty of us made quite a lot of noise. Naturally the principal heard us and appeared at their door quite angry, obviously expecting to catch us in a world class mischief. When he realized what we planned, his anger disappeared and only said what he always said when he did not know what to do with us, "Girls, girls!"

The principal's wife Margit Matolcsy was a renowned and celebrated singer in Hungary, specializing in Hungarian folksongs. She and Erzsi *Néni*, an opera singer, introduced music into our life. We loved to listen to their tales of a world gone by, loved to hear the wonderful songs, which they accompanied on the old piano. Margit *Néni* had several roles simultaneously: she was a reassuring mother-figure, a glamorous diva, a wonderful teacher as well as a powerfully upbeat presence. When we were severely afflicted with homesickness, she was there to smooth away the pain. When we were half sick because of the cold, she would sit down at the piano, play fiery songs, and order us to dance. We did this enthusiastically, and in a while we were actually enjoying the warmth generated by our dancing. Polka and csárdás were preferred, as these two dances provided the most heat to our shivering bodies. This pleasant and useful diversion had its drawback too: while dancing, we often took the male, or leading role (especially the taller girls did) and years later, when we no longer danced to avoid freezing, but danced for pleasure at the elegant Hungarian balls at the Hilton, Sheraton, Intercontinental or Ritz-Carlton, the husbands of these "girls" never stopped complaining. Their wives were difficult dance partners, they claimed, because they assumed the leading position, which often lead to covert struggles or hissed admonitions about who is to lead whom. Even the most devoted husbands were critical about this aspect of the "girls." (To this day the former students are still referred to as "the girls" —although the youngest is older than three quarters of a century. And we no longer dance.

Lilla: There was a movie house in Oberaudorf and the price of tickets was reasonable, even for us. The only problem was that according to the rule of the movie house, we could only go with adult supervision. Our teachers did not always have the time or the inclination to visit the movie house, so we organized our outings the best we could, persuading any willing adult to come with us. At one time we managed to talk my visiting father into accompanying us. He did not mind it too much, not even when the girls insisted calling him "Uncle Lilla."

There was some sort of an American air base not too far from us. The soldiers heard about us and often donated some food to the school. As a sign of gratitude, we invited them to attend a special show we put up for them. One of the girls already spoke passable English and she was the announcer. We treated the military men to songs, dances and short scenes from our school life. I do not know whether they really enjoyed it or not, but they claimed that they appreciated our efforts and had a good time at our school.

I remember that we sang and danced a great deal. When weather permitted we danced on the wide upstairs terrace. The music was furnished on the accordion by one of our talented classmates. We had some favorite songs which we sang often, and the German boys, always lurking nearby, learned these. Later they serenaded us and sang our Hungarian songs for us. It was so sweet of them. I wonder whether in their advanced age they still remember that once a very long time ago, when we were all so young, they could sing in Hungarian?

We danced to the music of Katyi, playing the accordion.

Anikó: I enjoyed the evenings when we danced. I just loved to dance. Although I was the youngest, I was also one of the tallest, so I always took the lead part. I was a good dancer; therefore, even the girls from the upper grades did not mind to dance with me although I was just a kid in comparison to the almost fully accomplished ladies. Those were the years when a few years of age difference meant serious social limitations.

We danced while singing the "Horsy, horsy, hop, hop, hop..." on the front yard of the Alpenhof, now the hotels' parking lot. Kloster Reisach in background.

Nusi: Each morning we had physical exercises on the wide and open upstairs terrace or in front of the school. One teacher supervised our exercises while another patrolled the rooms to make sure that none of us missed this invigorating event in the freezing cold. The villagers were rather awed by this spectacle, and the German boys watched eagerly. Naturally, we pretended not to notice the attention…

We lined up in the front yard of the Alpenhof to say farewell to our guests.

On our daily walks we were always accompanied by our teachers.

Jutka -Excerpt from letter (1948) "... *we got a bit wet during our outing to München, but we did not mind it, or at least not much. The rain did not bother us because it always rains when we plan an outing and there is nothing that can be done about it. First we went into the Botanical Garden—and it was very difficult to leave it. I was spellbound, rain or no rain. The guide told us that it is the biggest botanical garden and arboretum in Europe. I believe him. There are acres and acres of plants and lots of glasshouses. One houses plants from hot and humid regions, the other from hot and arid regions, and in one there are hundreds, perhaps even thousands of orchids. This is the first time I saw orchids in my life. They are wonderful and so delicate. It surprised me that despite their fragile beauty, they have no fragrance. I expected to be intoxicated by an exotic perfume. I got nothing. The orchids are totally boring in this respect, and I think a flower that has no fragrance is somehow a mistake of creation. But what I remember most—and this will surprise you—is the wonderful fragrance of roses in the rose garden. No mistake was made there. I would like to live in a house which smells all the time like this. The Garden is a most wonderful place. Then we went over to the opulent Nymphenburg palace, which I did not like half as much. Then we went to see an art gallery, which was fantastic. And I mean fantastic in the sense that it was unbelievable. We saw paintings which, instead of giving pleasure, baffled us. Imagine something that is not a thing and it is impossible to describe what it is: lines, dots, shapeless forms, splotches, unbelievable chaos. I tried to see what we learned from Kovács Diri: painting is mute poetry, but I was not able to see a single line of poetry anywhere. It is art, Diri said, but ever so strange. I had the funny feeling that the artists were lurking somewhere behind a door and laughing at us, as in all seriousness we contemplated their jokes on us. I bought the guidebook paying 3 RM for it just to show you. It has photos of these paintings so that you too can see it and be properly scandalized. Another day we climbed the Giessenbachklamm. It is of course not in the class of Mt. Blanc, but we almost died reaching the top. But it was worth it.*"

Koci: I loved our outings and trips. Often we just walked somewhere, or climbed a smaller mountain, but once we traveled to München and visited a museum of fine arts. Diri took us and he introduced the paintings to us. We loved it. Once we took a cog wheel train to a planetarium on a mountain top. We were terribly excited about it and in order to be ready for the great experience, we were studying astronomy with special enthusiasm. However, halfway through our ascent we got into a big snowstorm, and had to return without being enlightened about the stars. A very great disappointment. On the other hand it was truly exciting to travel in that funny little conveyance which is half train and half elevator, and be totally enveloped in the white fury of a huge snowstorm. It was scary and exciting, but I think we were all relieved when finally we made it down safely.

Lilla: Naturally we all remember the American Air Force, stationed at the nearby Brandenburg base, which provided us with great romantic adventures. In the afternoons, weather permitting, we used to study in our swimsuit outside on the lawn, or on the terrace. The young men, flying in their small planes over our school, noticed us and waved. Naturally, we thought this was the greatest thing that could happen to young girls, and waved back enthusiastically At one time we were inside and worked in the severest of all silences when we heard the planes. Our friends were coming for their daily visit, but we were kept inside! But then we looked at each other and reached a wordless agreement. All of us rushed out to wave and to cheer. Dezső *Bácsi* was totally powerless, and could only resort to his usual grumbling, "Girls, girls…"

Mari: Of course I remember that incident with the American pilots, our aerial friends! We even included the story in the long song we composed for our end-of-the-school-year celebration!

Kati: At times we were confused by the Americans. Technically we should have disliked them. They were allied to the Soviet Union, hence in a way also supporting Communism—and Hungarians are genetically programmed to hate both. American planes darkened our skies and bombed the hell out of our cities. Yet the ones we knew were lovable and ever so helpful. It was very confusing and we tried to sort out what is right and wrong, good and evil. If all "enemies" would be like the Americans were to us at Niederaudorf, then the part in the Lord's Prayer—"forgive our sins and we forgive those who have sinned against us…" and forgive and love your enemies—would be truly easy.

Jutka: I know what you mean; it boggles the mind. I was eleven years old and visiting my grandparents in the summer of 1944 at Lake Balaton. It was the most peaceful place on this war-torn continent, even during the worst bombings and fighting. I wore a bright red and white polka-dotted dress and was out in the vineyard with my grandfather. We were investigating the health of the growing grapes. A low flying plane came out of nowhere and fired at me. I didn't get hurt, but the supporting stake of the grapevine next to me exploded in splinters. I was totally scared, absolutely immobilized and did not even hear my grandfather's yelling, "Down, get down on the ground." I just stood there paralyzed. However, the plane took off just as fast as it came and I was safe again. It all happened so fast that a few hours later I was wondering whether perhaps it was all just a dream. But it wasn't. The splintered stake and my grandfather were my witnesses. I, of course, did not know whether the plane was Soviet, British or American. It could have been any of the three. However, if the gunner in the plane had a better aim… I guess it would not have made much difference to me or my parents, what nationality the man who pulled the trigger was. Yet, at the end of the war we, as thousands of others, were willing to walk, to hang on to overcrowded trains, beg for a ride on the roadside—do anything just so that we could move on as fast as we could into the region, which according to our calculation should fall under American occupation. We were so convinced that we would be safer there. Go figure.

I once read a tour guide book, (and I read so many of them during my travels that I no longer remember which book it was) and in it a tour guide with halting English and a preference for the word "usually" was mentioned. He was pointing out some ancient ruins to the travelers and said something to the effect, "During the wars these were *usually* destroyed, and then were *usually* built up again." Of course, archeologists have always known this. As they dig down at their sites, they keep discovering layers upon layers of once built, then destroyed, and then rebuilt cities.

There you have it: man is such a baffling creature. First a Continent is bombed out of shape and then totally rebuilt with the generous help of those, who destroyed it in the first place.

And then they helped so much. The guys from the nearby airfield sent us food. American girl scouts and others of unknown organizations, or driven by private initiative clothed us, and some did more. Once I received a package with a dozen pencils, half dozen pens and three books: "Gone with the Wind," "A Tree Grows in Brooklyn" and "The Keys of the Kingdom." Using the basic English I learned at school and a rather limited dictionary, I embarked on reading them—and so learned the English language. Never mind the pronunciation. To this day I hesitate to use some words I know very well, but am not sure about the pronunciation to the great delight of my American-born children, who like to make fun of their well-read mother because she cannot talk properly.

Ballusz: At one time we took the train to Rosenheim to see the play "Jedermann." There were only a few of us because not everybody had enough money for the tickets. It was performed by amateur actors, and what they lacked in expertise they made up in enthusiasm. When Death was calling for Jedermann on the darkened stage we shivered from sheer excitement and terror. I noticed then that Kovács Diri was smiling to himself. I suppose he was amused by our violent reaction to the play. However, the play did not enjoy great box office success, and the following week, free tickets were given to anyone who was interested, so we went again, this time the entire school participated.

(Jedermann, or "Everyman" in English, is a morality play, an allegorical drama dating back to 1400 A.D. and is still enjoying considerable popularity in Europe. Everyman is a typical human being who neglects his spiritual life, but in the end when confronted with Death, he panics. His friends, acquaintances, family and servants abandon him, and he struggles with allegorical figures representing hope, charity, empathy, sloth, greed, pride, passion, revenge, love and all the other virtues or failings of mankind. At the end, Everyman realizes that his only salvation is an absolute belief in God, and that whatever deeds he performed during his life, it will accompany him into the afterlife. While its theme is religious, it is not a dry morality lesson, but in the tradition of the Renaissance, it is quite earthy, at times coarse and funnily ribald.)

Anikó: There were two trips I shall never forget. One was to the Chiemsee to see King Ludwig's palace, the other to Oberammergau to see the Passion Play.

Chiemsee is the largest lake in Bavaria. On its largest island called the Herreninsel, King Ludwig II. of Bavaria built a reproduction of the Palais Versailles. The palace is as opulent as the original, but smaller. This strange, artistic, controversial, misunderstood, lonely and lavishly spending young king, cousin of Elizabeth, Empress and Queen of Austro-Hungary, had two models who greatly influenced his life: Richard Wagner and Louis XIV, the Sun King of France. Influenced by Wagner's music, he built the famous Neuschwanstein castle, which again inspired the design

of the hallmark building of Disney World. The other palace, on the Herreninsel in the Chiemsee, reflects his admiration for the Sun King. Ludwig II. was declared insane (without the benefit of a medical examination), forced to abdicate, and banned into a sort of house arrest. He died young, under very suspicious circumstances, drowning in the shallow part of a lake. (He was an excellent swimmer.) The irony of it is that today one of Bavaria's most important income is derived from tourists, who visit the two famous palaces he built by the hundreds of thousands each summer.

Jutka: Fate loves to play games with us. Thirty-five years later, in 1986, I was again in Germany, but this time as a teacher on the US Military Air Force Base at Rhein-Main. (DoDDS: Department of Defense Dependents Schools). Very likely driven in some degree by my long ago memories, I took my class of fourth graders on two field trips: to Neuschwanstein and in the spring to the Herreninsel on the Chiemsee. (Insel is 'island' in English.)

These children were just as wide-eyed as we have been way back, as they listened to the story of Ludwig, about his loneliness, his frenzied rides during the night on horseback or in an ornate sleigh, his fascination with birds and flowers and music. There was a hushed silence as we reached the end of the story when Ludwig drowned in the lake. It was obvious that the romantic streak did not wither in the younger generation. They were as fascinated by him and by his story as we have been. On returning to school, they wrote about their experiences, and two of my students decided to express their impressions in poetry. Because these were the writings of children not even ten years old, I was touched and kept them through my many moves since:

"Ludwig the Second was made king at eighteen.
He took midnight rides in a golden sleigh.
He lived in splendor, but had no one to share
some of his midnight rides on a mare.
His favorite birds were the peacock and the swans,
He kept them on his green, flower-bordered lawns."   Loranna Kearsley, 4th grade

****

"Ludwig the Second
was a lover of arts.
He loved music and beauty,
palaces and graceful birds.
He was born in a golden place of grace
and died mysteriously, alone in a lake.
The only thing left
of the great Ludwig
are the tourists who every day
walk in his palaces,
snapping pictures everywhere.
He is sadly looking down,
right now thinking aloud
where did I go so absolutely wrong?"   Tyler Cole, 4th grade.

Oberammergau, Passion Play. During the Thirty Year War in 1633 there was a major epidemic outbreak of the bubonic plague across Europe. The craftsmen of Oberammergau were well known for their superior woodcarvings, and men from the town traveled widely, delivering the goods to churches and palaces. They were richly paid for the carvings, but apparently on returning they also brought home the plague. In a short time about one hundred people died in the relatively small village, and panic broke out. The townspeople prayed to God and made a vow: if they would be spared from further tragedies caused by the plague, they would perform on stage once every ten years the last five days of Christ. The plague suddenly disappeared; there were no new cases and no deaths. The town was spared. Keeping their promise, the first performance was already staged in 1634, played by the townspeople.

It is a formidable performance of eleven acts, lasting seven hours with a three hour intermission, and is repeatedly presented during a five month period. It is a carefully constructed and deeply moving blend of Biblical texts, music and tableaux vivants. There are over 2000 people involved, actors, musicians, technicians; all residents of Oberammergau, none of them professional actors or producers. Tickets are sold out months, even years before the performance.

During the centuries it has grown in scope and in popularity and has undergone many changes, improvements and modifications. The greatest impact on the Play was the accusation after WWII of alleged anti-Semitism. As a result changes were made in text, dress, speech, and roles in the Tableaux vivants were modified. The prayer over the wine at the Last Supper is now said in Hebrew, and at several points in the performance Jesus speaks fragments of Hebrew. The text from Matthew 27.25 ("Behold the Man...") was omitted to make the story of Jesus politically correct. Compromises were made and mutual understanding reached. Hopefully this is the end of this painful conflict. It was cancelled only twice in its almost four hundred years of history: once in 1770 because it was considered too worldly and not reverent enough. The second cancellation was in 1940 because of the World War.

One of the changes made a century after its inception was the date of performance, which was especially important for us at our school. Formerly, the Play was always performed in the year ending with 4, but this has changed in 1770. From then on it is always presented in the last year of the decade, in the years ending with a zero. It just so happened that the first performance since 1930 was in 1950, and we were fortunate enough to be right then in Germany and fairly close to Oberammergau. A group of us had the unique opportunity to see the Play. This was a rare gift, which few of our contemporaries were fortunate enough to receive. During the long intermission we had a chance to walk around in Oberammergau, where every second store offers wood carvings of incredible quality and astronomical prices.

After the national catastrophe of Hitler's reign, Germany was eager to show the world its other, noble face and its commitment to Christianity, so the Play of 1950 was enthusiastically awaited after a twenty-year pause. 480,000 people attended and instead of the originally planned 33 performances, 87 were presented, and even so many went away disappointed because there were not enough tickets to go around. On the opening day such dignitaries were present as German Federal President Theodor Heuss; Chancellor Konrad Adenauer; Bavarian Governor Erhard Höchster; and Dwight D. Eisenhower, who represented the Allied Forces. The high number of visitors was astounding because 1950 was still a very difficult year in Europe both financially and emotionally. It borders on a miracle that our group was able to obtain tickets.

Jutka: In the calendar year 1947 we completed two school years and had a very short summer vacation. Most girls went home to their parents, but I had nowhere to go. My sister, once again ill, spent a large part of that year in Tyrol, where my father was physician in a hospital for Polish refugee children. My mother, also ill, was hospitalized at the time of my vacation. I do not know who arranged it, but at the end of the school term I was accepted in a summer camp in the neighboring village of Kiefersfelden. The camp was sponsored and conducted by some American organization. Contrary to my expectations, we did not live in wigwams, but in a rather lovely hotel. The food was out of this world and I wondered how difficult it will be to go back to gruel soup and the poppy seed potato. As soon as I arrived, I was put into a group of girls the same age as I was, and from then on we were offered regular entertainment, non-stop. From morning exercises to bed time every moment was filled out. We had arts and crafts, treasure hunts, cooking classes, group singing, excursions, and all sorts of games, including baseball. This seemed to me at the time a very odd game. There was so much waiting and doing nothing, and I was so puzzled when a girl was running from corner to corner as the rest of us watched her idly. Even our regular swimming was organized into competing groups. Every minute was filled out with activities, and by the third day it seemed to me a bit too much of the good thing. Thankfully, one day we woke to torrential rains. I had visions of a lazy day, finding a quiet corner for reading, or meeting the girls for a chat, or finding out if any of the other girls from the Alpenhof were also present, but put into another group, and so we didn't meet yet. I guessed that on this rainy day our devoted American camp leaders would come up at the most with arts and crafts, but all outdoor activities would be cancelled. Wonderful, I naively thought, we can finally rest up from all the frenzied activities, the condensed fun and for a change do nothing much.

I was right about the art project, which took up most of the morning, but right after lunch we were ushered into the ballroom of the hotel and were shown a movie. It was a wild tale about cowboys and Indians chasing each other. They were hanging from cliffs, stepping on snakes, ambushed and shot at with arrows or guns. I no longer remember the issue between the two groups, but finally the Indians got the upper hand and were able to capture a few of the cowboys, who were then dragged on top of a wood pile and tied to a stake. The plan was obvious. I don't remember the final outcome because at that point I and several others got violently ill and we had to leave the room in a hurry. The camp leaders were terribly upset. Later officials arrived in big American cars to examine the kitchen and the leftover food because food poisoning was presumed. But it was not that. Our American leaders, coming from peace and security, did not realize that we were all damaged. Violence was not entertainment for us. We experienced it firsthand. Our body rejected it as violently as it would have opposed the poisoned food.

Commemorating the 1848 Revolution.

Buza Mari is reciting Petőfi Sándor's famous poem, the "Talpra Magyar"

Tirczka Éva is performing the very popular herdsman's dance

Csaba Klári and Balla Éva dance the csárdás.

Correspondence
Voices of students:

Kati: **(excerpt from her diary.** 1947. *"We lived in Durach, and my brother accompanied me to the school. I arrived at the end of September, more than a month late, and as it happened right during snack time. The principal used this time to give a very pointed lecture to the girls. He said that among the mail there are far too many letters from boys. This is against the rule established by the school, and so they will not be delivered to the girls. Then he turned to me, and said that although I just arrived, I already have one of these forbidden letters addressed to me. He showed me the letter from a distance and then tore it up. All I could rescue was the envelope so that I could save the address. It was from Laci Hefty.*

October 1. Laci wrote a letter as if he were my brother, and I did receive this one.

October 20. There was a workshop organized for scout leaders in Guttenburg. I too received an invitation. At the same time Laci wrote that he too will participate in the workshop. Cautiously he signed his letter as María Buza, a name he made up.

October 28. Arrived at Guttenburg. The boy scouts were waiting for me at the train station. I soon met a girl and after the introduction it turned out that her name was María Buza. I told her that I know her because she wrote me a letter! She was confused until I explained about our trick so that Laci could write to me at school. We had such a good laugh."

Koci: The letters we wrote home were first read by someone on the staff. Most of them by the House-mother

Mészárka: I remember the kind old mailman to whom I confided the letter situation at school. From then on, he delivered my letters from Karl, my future husband, to a German family in the village, and I could pick them up from there.

Jutka: excerpt from a letter to her mother: *"... Remember my girlfriend, Erzsi Madocsay, in Hungary? I miss her so much and do not know what happened to her and her family. So I wrote a postcard to her and hoped against hope that maybe, perhaps, my note will reach her and we can get in touch. I discussed my plan with Dezső Bácsi and he had no objections, but suggested that for the 'sender' I write your name and address instead that of the school's. He did not think it would be a good idea (and perhaps not safe for her) if I advertise the existence of our school. The postcard, on which we agreed, showed the castle of Kufstein in Austria across the River Inn. Ten days later the card came back to the Pension with the remark'. The amazing part is that it did not go back to you, as was clearly written on the open postcard as the sender's address. Nor was it delivered somewhere in Austria—but was sent back straight to Bavaria, to our school. This was a shock— apparently whatever powers are in charge know all about our school, otherwise we cannot find an explanation why it was delivered here, instead of to you. Perhaps the stamping on the postcard told them my whereabouts, but even that is strange, for I walked to the next village to post it. Yet, they knew exactly where to send it back. Dezső Bácsi too was disturbed about it and he said 'Big Brother is watching.' And I am sad because now I shall never know what happened to Erzsi and know that we shall never meet again."*

Zsuzsa: In our letters back home we never complained. Anyhow, all our letters coming and going were read by the housemother. When it was letter-writing time, they practically told us what to write, which was probably a good policy. We all knew that we could only stay at school at the cost of enormous sacrifices our parents made. It was fair that we should not burden them with complaints which at any rate they could not alleviate for us. We never wrote home that we were hungry; on the contrary! We knew, if we would complain, they would send us even the little they needed to stay alive. If we ever asked for anything, it was always something we needed really desperately for the school, such as writing paper or a pencil.

Ballusz: Our letters were censored, and correspondence with boys was strictly forbidden. Our morals were most carefully watched over. But the postman of Oberaudorf had a tender and romantic heart and understood the love pangs of young people. He always found a way to smuggle to the girls the forbidden letters.

Later in Reisach, when boys were also enrolled in our school, our teachers were quite uneasy. They took great precautions and we were never alone with "our boys." Our instructors watched us with the diligence of the all-seeing Argus with the hundred eyes, but still they could not prevent that eventually and inevitably pairs have formed. If the young lovers wanted to talk privately, then the girl would go to the bedroom window (upstairs) and he would be standing under the window at our make-shift volley ball court. In the short pause between two trains barreling down the tracks almost by the window, they could shout to each other their sweet nothings in Romeo and Julia fashion. Diri of course knew about this arrangement, and called these pairs the "geraniums," ostensibly because the girl at the window reminded him of the pots of geraniums blooming on the windowsills of every house in Bavaria.

Jutka: We had enough money for stamps, especially before the "Währungsreform." Our problem was not that, but rather the lack of writing paper and envelopes. Very inventive, we soon learned to fold a sheet of paper so that it turned into a handy envelope. If paper supplies happened to be scant, we wrote our letter only on one side of the paper leaving wide margins, then folded up our letter and wrote the address on the blank side. Betty was good to us; if we asked her, she provided a teaspoon of flour, which, when mixed with the proper amount of water, turned into a passable glue to seal the makeshift envelopes.

Fifty-three years later I met the flour paste once again, this time in Romania. We were at Temesvár (Timisoara) in 2000 to attend the premiere of my husband's new play at the theater. Wanting to send some postcards to our children, we visited the post office. Amazingly, in the middle of the room there was a long, high table with little pots of flour paste. People stood around the table and used the trusty paste to affix their stamps and to seal their envelopes. No self-sealing stationary there, nor flavored sealers! I knew instantly what was happening, but my usually knowledgeable husband was quite taken aback until I explained to him this tricky technology.

Jutka: from a letter: *"...and now for the great news of today! You will never, not in a million years guess who wrote to me on April 19, 1948! To me, to a little Nobody in the 8th grade of the Niederaudorf refugee school! Not less of a person than his Serene Highness nagybányai Horthy Miklós, the regent of Hungary himself!* **(Miklós Horthy de Nagybánya was regent, head of state in the post war (First World War) kingless kingdom of Hungary from 1920 to October 1944. His political views, especially toward the end of the Second World War greatly differed from that of Germany, and for this reason he was ousted from his position after the German occupation of Hungary.)** *You can imagine the excitement this caused among the girls! Now you are surely going to wonder how this happened. I must admit, he did not initiate the correspondence. I did. He only answered the letter I wrote him, but still it is a wonderful thing, don't you agree? I knew that he was living with his family in Bavaria, and knew that he must be very sad and disappointed. He lost so much more than we did. I wanted to make him feel better, so I wrote to him about our school, what our goals are and told him how our parents found all sorts of different ways to make money in order to keep us in school. I never thought that he would get my letter, let alone answer it because I only knew the name of the town where he lived, but nothing more. The German postal service is terrific and it found him despite the inadequate address! And he did answer! And this is what he wrote:*

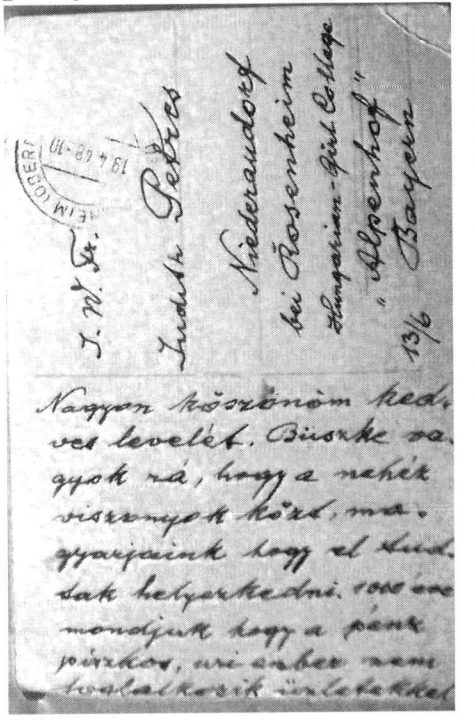

'Thank you for your lovely letter. I am very proud that despite the difficult circumstances our Hungarian people are finding ways to survive and to preserve and transmit our culture to the young people. Throughout 1000 years we have claimed that a gentleman does not involve himself with business affairs—and now they proved that they can do even that. Give my regards to the teaching staff and to the girls, and my message to them is to hold on, and to bravely keep on doing what they are already doing—until we can all return home! H.M.'

Is this not a wonderful thing? Our work and your sacrifices are appreciated by the top man of Hungary! And he is telling us that we shall go home again. I miss Grandmamma and Grandpapa so very much. Will we ever see them again?"

SCHOOL PHOTO - MAY, 1948.

Names are given as in Hungarian: last name first, with proper accent marks.

Front: Szkladányi Ági, Jászberényi Kató, Dax Nusi, Szűcs Zsuzsa, Kristó Nagy Kati, Szűcs Mariann, Finkey Lilla, Csaba Klári, Renkey Marica, Spöttle Leila, Király Éva, Kozányi Kati, Gruber Vica.
Children in front: Kovács Erzsike and Renkey Magi's and Marica's brother Lacika.

2. row: Váczy Munci, Bonyhay Éva, Hadanich Vera, Váczy Pancsi, Kováts Gabi, Mayer Picu, Tirczka Éva, Markó Marika, Buza Marika, Hadady Magda, Császár Zsuzsa.

3. row: Czihy Kati, Petres Judit, Mészáros Éva
Back row: Kotai Zoltán, Papal delegate, Kovács Ferenc principal, Kovács Erzsi Néni, Várhelyi Marika, Oltfalvi Margit, Csaba Gabi, Csia Éva, Hegedűs Nóri, Radnay Anikó, Hegedűs Piri, Balla Éva, Hochenburger Éva, Tóth Inci, Renkey Margit, Berlányi Mária, Pettendy Kati, Bárány Mária néni, Eördögh Vilma, Almay Anikó.

SCHOOL LITERARY CLUB (Önképzőkör),

SINGING AND POETRY

In prewar Hungary almost all schools sponsored and maintained clubs (önképzőkör) which were similar to the US literary and debate clubs. The basic difference was that in the US these clubs operate at higher grade levels, (many at the college level), and the emphasis is on debate. In Hungary, it was moved down to the middle and high schools, and the emphasis was on the deeper understanding of literature, the cultivation of better thinking, learning the skill of effective oral presentation and learning to make constructive evaluation of the material presented. Eventually, the clubs expanded to include other subjects besides literature. Some even specialized, where the discussions and presentations were limited to one area only, such as mathematics, physics, music, astronomy or art. The clubs met after school, were open to everyone, but attendance was not required. The meetings were usually attended by one or more teachers, and often an invited guest, who was a specialist in the field being discussed is. The establishment of such clubs was perhaps an early attempt to offer advanced education to those with special interest, before the term "gifted and talented" was invented. At Niederaudorf-Reisach, the club centered on Hungarian literature, but included other subjects as well. For example, in one of Jutka's letter there is a reference to a male student who offered a presentation about the atom, and it was received with great interest. His presentation was part of a regular club meeting.

Nóra: (fragments from letter) *"...Our last session was exceptionally good. Tibor Diószeghy introduced the program by explaining the goals of the club. Back home in Hungary, he was president of such a club operating in his school, so having had some experience in this area, he could speak with authority. His introduction was followed by Kati's discussion of one of Ferenc Móra's books. The third presentation was delivered by Iván about the atom; then again Tibor spoke about how an author's personality and world philosophy can be recognized in his prose and poetry. The last presentation was done by Vica about the life of Mozart. The preparatory work was quite difficult for these students because almost all the resource information was in German, even that of the Hungarian author, Móra. First, the gathered information had to be translated by them into Hungarian before they could work it into a presentation of a notably high standard."*

Nóra adds years later:
Years later the son of Ferenc Kovács found the minutes of the club among his father's documents and sent them to Éva Balla, who was formerly the president of the Club at Niederaudorf. Samples of the minutes:
"First meeting was on October 31, 1948. Coordinating teacher Erzsébet Kovács introduced the goals of the Club and she outlined the format of presentations. She explained that during these sessions we shall be exposed to topics which are not usually presented in the classroom. At other times, we shall hear about familiar topics, but in more detail. She told us that we shall learn poise and self-assurance through our presentations. The first few sessions will be presented by the

higher grade because those students were exposed to the club's activities in Hungary, and are able to demonstrate what is required.

She informed us that expressing creative critique is a skill, which must be learned. For this purpose, the following process will be established: after each presentation two students, appointed by the coordinating teacher, will express their evaluation. The coordinating teacher will then critique the presentation and the two student's evaluations. The principal will close the session by evaluating the program. After the opening remarks, Éva Balla was elected president and Kati Czihy secretary. Following this introduction, readings from literature were presented. The theme of the selections was autumn and the passing of time.

Second session, November 28, 1948. Topic: The History, Life and Character of the Hungarian Peasant. Presentation was done by the 11th grade.

Third session: February 13, 1949. The 9th and 10th grades presented László Mécs, the Priest-poet."

Sample of evaluation of the meeting above by the principal, Ferenc Kovács:
"…It is the merit of the participants of this session that their presentation did not consist of reciting poems and reading selections of the author's work only, but they composed music to some of the poems, making it more interesting and enjoyable. It was also a clever idea to include choral speaking, which would have been even more impressive had the group been larger. Even combined, the two classes did not number enough speakers to make the choral representation completely effective. Perhaps they could have invited members of another class to increase the number of speaking voices.

The presentation was excellent and as a literary genre it was rich, creative, and surpassed the presentation of the month before. For this reason I suggest that the minutes include a special mention of excellence."

Anna Váczy recording secretary voiced the following critique about one of the sessions. It appeared on page 29 in the minutes:
"…The entire program was outstanding, but the most remarkable of all was the presentation of Iván Zoltán (The Atom). His essay was the most difficult because it was the most abstract and the least familiar to the students. It was a difficult task to make the greatly unfamiliar easily understandable to the audience. He achieved this beautifully.

Marika Markó (Markóczi) incorporated her own knowledge of the subject in her critique. Her evaluation in comparison to those we heard before was far more outstanding and she deserves praise.

Tibor Diószeghy defended a contributing member, who was accused of expressing generalizations in her poetry. He argued with the evaluating Principal: 'Sir, a poet often exaggerates and generalizes, and therefore we cannot judge it as a great fault of the present author. In my opinion a far greater blemish in her poetry is the ugliness of non-Hungarian stylistic elements, which by the way is the fault of most of the presentations so far. Greater care should be taken to avoid the dominantly Germanic elements in our speech and writing.' At the same time, Tibor questioned some of the definitions mentioned by Iván in his presentation and asked for clarification. Iván clarified, and to support him, Sarolta Takáts, mathematics and physics teacher, gave more information on the topic. I found the dialogue thus evolving of great merit, and it shows the interest and the involvement of all concerned."

Tibor, born in 1926, was the oldest student in our school. He attended after boys too were admitted. During the war at age 18, before completing his high school studies, he volunteered to join the army. He was sent to the front and captured by the Russians. He escaped, returned to his unit, was wounded and then was shipped back to Hungary for treatments. Seeking to complete his schooling, he enrolled at Niederaudorf-Reisach. When that school closed, he moved on to the still existing school at Passau. He achieved outstandingly in literature and poetry, harvesting awards almost yearly. He died young.

Ballusz: Poetry and singing were important part of our curriculum. We had no song books, no records or other teaching aids for music, and the old piano was out of tune. But we were unbelievably fortunate because we had two teachers who compensated us for all the things we did not have. The principal's wife, Margit *Néni (Matolcsy)* introduced us to Hungarian folk music, and Erzsi *Néni*, (Takáts) who taught literature and art, was a former opera singer, and she could sing *a cappella* everything that was ever composed for a soprano. She introduced us to the world of opera and we were fascinated. This was the first time I heard Cio-Cio San's aria from "Madame Butterfly" and as many times as I heard it later under rather more glamorous circumstances, I always thought that nothing compared to Erzsi *Néni*'s performance. She was so convincing, so full of barely repressed excitement as she sang "Un bel di, vedremo—levarsi in fil di fumo,—sull'estremo confin del mare…" We could actually see the strand of smoke, then the ship appearing at the horizon, and finally Pinkerton climbing the hill to Cio-Cio San's house. Pinkerton, the man hardly worth her love, let alone her life. I had tears in my eyes. Still do.

Jutka: We loved to sing and used every occasion for it. Poetry reciting was also part of our life; we especially enjoyed choral speaking. We were carefully trained in that, and as a result, the meaning, the message always came through clearly. Also, when speaking together as a group, the inevitable stage fright of solo performance was gone and we could thoroughly enjoy the performance.

Koci: I forgot the exact occasion, but our school was hosting important guests. The Prior from the Kloster of Reisach and the mayor of Oberaudorf came. American guests were invited, who on many occasions gave us wonderful gifts of food and clothing and several delegates from the Hungarian organizations in München arrived. We were very excited about performing for this elect group, and wanted to give them a special treat, and if possible to impress them. Mrs. Kovács (Diri's wife) coached us with angelic patience in a song, which we sang in harmony. The unusual feature of this production was that it was made up of four totally unrelated Hungarian folksongs, each with a different text and different melody, each starting at staggered intervals. The melodies and the voices chased each other, the words blended, but at the end it all worked out to be an unbelievably harmonious and lovely choral work, as if all along a composer had just this very outcome in mind—although of course, folksongs have no known composers. It was the idea of Mrs. Kovács alone.

It wasn't quite Bruckner to be sure, but we loved it and felt that we managed to impress our audience. It earned us so much applause and praise so that we almost lost our demure, ladylike demeanor, which Mrs. Kovács expected from us.

Anikó: I remember when Maggie won first prize in a contest of poetry recital. She was terrific. I can still hear her voice heavy with emotions as she said the lines, translated not quite professionally into English: "On silent wings I wish to fly high above, but am chained to earth by sorrows and am shedding silent tears over my shattered dreams." On many occasions in my life I realized over and over again how true the words are.

Jutka: (from a letter to her mother) "*...Next week we shall have a poetry reciting contest, and I am taking part in it. I chose for my presentation that awfully long poem when an exiled man is speaking to God, alternately crying, questioning, complaining, accusing and in the end accepting. Remember? When I was last home I read it to you and you found it to be beautiful and appropriate. You said it made you shiver. I thought that I could not have made a better choice than this poem. I hope its length won't be the stumbling block, and I shall be able to memorize all of it and won't make again a fool of myself.*"

POVERTY, TUITION AND THE BURDEN ON PARENTS

Nusi: Summer 1947, Dr. Ravasz attempted to solve the financial problems of the school by offering young children a chance for vacationing between the two school terms. At the same time, he also provided room, board and instructional help during this short period for those who were either preparing for graduation, or were "home study" pupils. I stayed at the school during the short summer break in 1947 after the others left because I planned to absolve two grade levels in one school term and needed the time to study intensively. There were a lot of little kids vacationing at the Alpenhof at that time. They were sweet and boisterous, but they hated the meals of gruel made of soy meal, or other horror concoction as much as we did. Katyi (Kristó) also stayed at the school, and utilizing her knowledge, gained at the leadership workshops for scouts, she supervised the kids and organized games and excursions for them. In this way she earned part of her tuition for the following year.

Markóczi: Because we were young and because we were girls we spent time in worrying about our clothing—or the lack of it. We all admired, (and perhaps even envied a bit) Magda's magnificent penny loafers, sent to her by her American relatives. In our eyes, it was the height of elegance and desirability.

In those times, despite the difficulties the mothers contrived to clothe their children—more or less. Second hand dresses were often available on the black market, and with a little bit of luck, could be successfully altered. Shoes were the real problem. Shoes have the abominable habit of being worn out so they cannot be re-sold, not even to refugees, and cannot be altered like old clothing. Yet children's feet kept growing regardless of the market situation. No wonder, Magda's new and well fitting soft leather loafers caused so much excitement.

I owned three pairs of shoes. One was a pair of black patent leather sandals, which used to belong to my grandmother. Not a very practical wear in the alpine winter wonderland, nor were they fit for mountain climbing. I also had a pair of black and white patent leather spectator type high laced shoes, which before the war was the ultimate fashion for very young children. (It shows how impractical the fashion trends can be. I wonder, who came up with the idea to put patent leather shoes on kids, and what is even more amazing: in black and white! Or perhaps kids played differently 75 years ago, so they could wear such finicky shoes. My own child would have totally destroyed them before the morning was half gone.) At any rate, I was too old for it and was ashamed to wear them. My third pair of shoes was a new acquisition. From time to time it was possible to obtain a special "ration card" for children's shoes, and we were fortunate enough to get one. My mother, seeing how quickly I grew and how tall I already was, expected me to keep on growing. She also knew that she won't get another ration card any time soon, so she carefully chose a practical type of shoe, a few sizes larger than my feet. She assured me that at the rate I was growing, the shoes would soon fit me perfectly. I could barely walk in them, even if I wore several socks. In a perverted way of Nature I never grew another inch and my feet also remained the same size. I took the pair of shoes with me when we immigrated to the US, but I never grew into them.

We all agreed that Vera had the nicest dresses. Her mother was a real artist and she also studied high fashion design before the war. As a result, she could fashion wonderful things out of all sort of rags. My mother also tried her hands at dressmaking and stitching, but it was with limited success. First a nun had to instruct her how to let down the hems of my skirts, but it was rough going for her. She gave me one of her dresses, a wine-red beauty, which was my holiday pride. Later, as I outgrew my winter coat, she gave me hers. Only as an adult did I realize that in doing so, she was left without one. But the poor thing ended in a bad way. Once, when we returned from our winter walk and shivering with cold, still in my inherited coat, I leaned against the tiled stove to warm up. The damage was done before I could smell it: the back of my coat burned, and an ugly brown area testified to the world how efficient our stove was. I had no other choice; I had to keep wearing it. Nobody made fun of me or my coat at the school. Refugees in their bottomless poverty had a lot of understanding for the troubles of others. But on arriving home in Mittenwald the little kids on the street ran after me and taunted me.

From time to time we received bundles of used clothing from the CARITAS. Margit *Néni* divided the content among us according to need, or made her decisions on a more practical consideration, such as who would fit into the dresses.

Jutka: We received a CARE package from Italy and among the items we found a lovely story book for little children, written in Italian. Of course, we gave the book to young Erzsike, Diri's daughter, who at four could not read in any language. Immediately she started to beg us to read her the story in the beautiful new book. Relying on our familiarity with Latin, and also on the colorful pictures, we translated the story for her as best as we could. We didn't know anybody who spoke Italian so to this day we have no idea whether our translation was correct, or whether we made up an entirely new story. However, Erzsike wanted to hear the story over and over again, and approached different students with her request. Like all children, she too insisted that the story be told exactly as she heard it the first time. But because we all made up the story individually, we all told it a bit differently, and in her four year old mind she must have decided that none of us could read correctly. It was quite funny as she corrected us when we made a "mistake," imitating Mária Adelsberger in her unbending strictness.

Anikó: In the summer of 1947 an American scouting troop somehow heard about us and sent us a huge package with clothing and shoes. From this generous gift I received a pair of shoes and also a great friendship, which lasts to this day, even though I live in Australia and my friend Kathy in the USA. The shoes were a real treasure, and I was extremely grateful and thanked the unknown Girl Scout, who sent it to me. She answered and a very active correspondence followed; although, in the beginning, I did require some help to write my English letters. I only saw her once. Some years ago I was visiting friends in Cleveland and from there I was able to drive to her home where I spent an unforgettable week with Kathy and her husband.

Pancsi: My parents ran out of money. After the money reform it was increasingly more difficult to sell some of our belongings. Paying my tuition posed grave problems. I remember while at Reisach, once we paid with high quality ground red pepper (paprika) in lieu of money. My grandfather in Hungary developed smuggling to an art: he cut out the pages between the hard covers of a book and filled the hole with paprika and mailed it as "library material." Although every piece of mail was censored coming or going, for some reason nobody caught it, and he was able to send us several times this most valuable treasure, priced very high on the black market. Mária *Néni*'s mother used it well; our meals were made very tasty with this added spice.

Nóra: After the war the German money (Reichsmark, or RM) was worth absolutely nothing, with one exception: the stores had to accept it in exchange for goods bought on ration cards. The rationed amount of food was so minimal that it was not nearly enough to live on and it was imperative to procure additional food either by bartering or on the black market. Life was ridiculously difficult. A few short excerpts from letters written by my mother to my sister Piroska (Piri) and me during this time gives an adequate picture of the life then:

"*March 13, 1947. Piroska what is the situation with your glasses? Could Dezső fix it for you? I mailed you my own because you need it more than I do. Now I am left without one, and it is difficult because I can barely see. For this reason I am asking that from now on you write with large letters, and if possible with a dark pencil, so I can read your letters.*

March 17, 1947: I fear that you go hungry, and I can't do much about it. But then you expected this much, didn't you?

May 27. Lacika (my young brother) will get a noon meal at the German school, but we have to wait another fourteen days until it goes into effect. Now he is busily collecting June bugs into a jar then delivers the bugs to Fanny down the road. Because she doesn't have enough chicken feed she is glad for the bugs; she feeds her chickens with them. Lacika so far earned one egg for his labors and he is very proud of his salary.

September 27, 1947. At this time I am only able to send you some cookies and a few apples and pears, which I have been saving for almost two weeks. I could not send it earlier because I had nothing in which to pack them. Finally Frau Mittelmeier down the road kindly lent a box, but I need to return it to her. So please, be very careful with it so that it does not rip or get damaged in any way.

February 22, 1948. This month we were allotted four eggs on the ration card. I was so glad because now I am able to bake a birthday cake for Lacika, which requires two eggs.

May 1, 1949. I'm sorry about the paper on which I am writing this letter, but this is all I could find. Real stationary has appeared in the stores, but buying it would be an inexcusable luxury which we can ill afford. I hope you are able to read it despite the abominable quality of the paper."

Jutka: Women have always been very inventive and creative when it came to be dressed properly. Cinderella found a way to appear beautifully attired at the court ball, and Scarlett O'Hara made a bewitching dress from the curtains of Tara. Refugees altered old, outgrown dresses, or created something new and almost fashionable from rags they found at the second hand markets. They made passable coats from army blankets. But shoes belong to a totally different class in the general attire. They are totally resistant to alterations or renewals. Once their life span is over, it is over and done with. Shoes in those years were by far the greatest problem, at least as far as our attire was concerned. It was especially difficult for the youngest ones, since children's feet grew regardless of the economic situation, so new shoes were no longer a question of fashion but a case of dire need. There were times in our life when we only had one pair of good shoes among the three of us. It was fortunate that my mother had delicate, small feet, and at the same time my sister and I underwent a growth spurt, so our shoe sizes were almost the same. At least we did not have to attend church barefooted, but could take turns. Fortunately the church at Laufen had several masses every Sunday. When my mother prepared me for Niederaudorf, she contacted every person she knew on the black market, and in exchange for some jewelry, I was provided with shoes. It was the time in my life when I could honestly say that I walked on gold.

Nóra: In our family there were three of us children aged 6, 11 and 13, when unexpectedly we had to leave our home in Hungary in the middle of the night. In spite of the very short time to get ready, my mother packed carefully everything that we might need. But when the temporary exile turned into months and years, we outgrew everything we had. During the first years after the war, the stores were totally empty and closed. Many children wore their outgrown shoes by having the front part at the toes cut away to fit the growing feet. This of course did not work well in the winter. During one of these difficult years my sister and I shared a single pair of winter shoes.

My sister and I were already enrolled at Niederaudorf when my mother was able to obtain some yards of material at the black market. She then found a seamstress who according to the standards of the time was willing to fashion dresses for us in terms of the barter economy. If she asked one bushel of potatoes for making one of the dresses, my mother would have to trade something she owned to get the potatoes to pay for the dressmaking. Finally the terms were agreed upon and the seamstress did make the dresses, albeit without ever seeing us or without a single fitting. Now all my mother had to do was search the second hand stores or the black markets to obtain a box and strings in which to mail the two dresses, and then entrust it to the whimsical schedule of the trains, and hope that the box would eventually find its destination to Niederaudorf before we outgrew the garments.

Vica: We all wanted to look if not elegant, but at least a little festive during our graduation examinations. Piri lent me her beautiful dark blue skirt and so I could appear properly garbed for the tests.

Zsuzsa in a letter to her mother: *".... could you please find for me somewhere a little piece of green material for a tie? I am a girl scout now, and would like to have such a tie—actually it is more like a scarf. But if you can't find any, it is OK too. I can be a Girl Scout without a tie. Also, could you get us a little piece of some sort of a rag? We need it to scrub out our washbasin.*

And today my requests have no end. Could you please send me a table cloth? Remember the one we found in our house after the Russians left, that blue one? That would do nicely, but only if you have no need for it. We now have our own dayroom at Reisach and it is quite friendly the way we fixed it up, but we have no tablecloth. And if you can find any sort of school books or notes, could you please send these also? Nünü arrived at school yesterday and brought for me your letter, the sugar and the doll. Thank you so much for them, these made me so happy."

    Zsuzsa was twelve years old, when she wrote this and apparently still at the stage when a doll made her happy…

    The reference to the table cloth the Soviet soldiers left needs some explanation. During the entire time of the four week long occupation it was their habit to go from house to house and take (loot) whatever they fancied. However at times, already loaded up with "goods," they more often than not found in a given house something they liked better than what they already had in their hands or baskets from another house. They simply dropped, what they have taken somewhere else, and took the item they valued more. They considered the entire town a giant bazaar with the added benefit of not having to pay for what they took. After they left town and we returned to our ravaged home from the air raid shelter we found more items which originally belonged to others than what were our own belongings.

    Zsuzsi's mother promptly responded and sent the items she asked for. She not only padded the postal package with cookies, a bar of soap and a loaf of homemade bread but gave her an astounding piece of advice: *"…I tried to get scouring powder for your washbasin at the store, but I might as well have asked for a star out of heaven. However, take a little wood ash from the fire place and use that to scrub. It also works on pots and pans, at least in a fashion. Whenever you walk near the river, get a little scoop of sand and mix that with the ashes, and then it works even better…"* As far as Zsuzsa knew her mother never so much as touched a piece of firewood back home in Hungary, let alone ashes; there were people in the household for that. It was a puzzlement where she picked up this unusual information.

    Nóra remembers:

Parents who lived far from the school visited seldom, or not at all because not only was the train fare an unthinkable expense, but to stay overnight was not an option in those times. Those parents, who lived closer and were able to return home on the same day, visited more often, but even that was difficult as the letter from my father proves: *"My Dearest Ones, I plan to visit you this coming Saturday, but it will be a short one. I can leave my job at Augsburg only at noon and would arrive at Oberaudorf at six in the evening. However, I must take the next train back home, which leaves at 7.15. Please be at the railway station Saturday evening so we can see each other and talk a while. I am very happy about this prospect, but at the same time I must warn you that there is always a possibility that they won't let me leave at noon. Should this happen, I'll try to notify you in time. But if I can't get the word to you then please forgive me if you have to wait in vain at the station. However, if they keep me over on Saturday, I will get compensated with an alternate half day off the following week; then on that day I'll travel to Oberaudorf for sure."*

    Reading this so many years later, I still get emotional about my father, who after working an eight hour shift, was willing to travel twelve hours to see us for an hour and fifteen minutes.

Letter written by Ferenc Kovács to parents at the end of the summer in 1948:

"...We are constantly working on solutions to save our school from closing. Grievous problems have to be faced and solved and little hope is left; yet, with an almost irrational confidence we hope that we shall be able to open the gates of the school for the returning students... As soon as your circumstances permit, please send the 18.00 RMs to the pension's owner, Mr. Waller. This amount is your contribution to your child's room and board for September; the balance is financed from other sources. To this date only 1/3 of the parents were able to pay, and Mr. Waller has complained that the school, as well as the parents are apparently insolvent and he will not be able to renew our contract under these circumstances..."

Jutka: from a letter: *"And one more visitor came by, a lady who has a PhD. in applied arts. I learn something new every day, for I had no idea that PhDs are handed out for such things as pottery, weaving or embroidery. Now I know. She gave every girl a blue kerchief, printed with Hungarian motives. We are supposed to embroider them, and then wear them on our heads. It will be quite a sight as we march through the village in our uni-babushkas. But it was really sweet and thoughtful of her. And then who knows, I might master the skill and eventually earn a doctor's degree in babushka embroidery. Won't you be proud of me?"*

Markóczi: My parents sent me an allowance every month, or at least they have done so before the money reform. They also sent me packages, which contained food: sugar, bacon, milk powder or whatever they could find on the black market. I also had clothes to wear. My mother bartered something for a few kitchen curtains, and she made summer skirts out of it. Once she was able to "buy" a Russian parachute. It was big enough to yield material for whatever we needed, but my favorite dress was made out of a colorful bed sheet. I had everything, and never felt that we actually lived in abject poverty.

One of the students actually embroidered one.

Zsuzsa: The Catholic and the Protestant organizations sent us packages from time to time. The contents of these were quite varied, depending on what they were able to get, what they were given. We always shared everything equally, no matter whether it came from the Catholics, the Protestants or the Americans. Also the barter trade was operating better and more efficiently in our school than the Stock Exchange did in Frankfurt. We were always able to trade for things we needed, which we far preferred to asking our parents for things.

Ballusz: Our life quality was slowly improving at Reisach. Diri bought us water jugs, so the girls on kitchen duty did not have to run to the end of the hallway during meal times to provide drinking water, two cups at a time. At the same time, he hired a general help, and this freed us from hours of housekeeping. She was the mother of one of our classmates, and to tell the truth we felt pretty uncomfortable watching her scrub the floors, while we sat comfortably in our classroom and studied the mysteries of astronomy. Having been on the "scrubbing squad" more times than

I care to remember, I knew very well what a miserable and hard job it is. She was a frail little person and did not last long in her position as our cleaning angel. We were back with the buckets and the miles of floors.

Diri, devoted to music as he was, naturally owned a radio. Whenever there was an especially wonderful piece of classical music, he invited us to their room to listen. The latecomers, who did not fit in the room, listened to it less comfortably in the hallway through the open door. One morning we woke in our bedroom to wonderful music. Our housemother stood in the doorway waiting to witness our delight and surprise. It so happened that after the cleaning lady left, Diri asked us whether he should hire somebody else to fill her place, or whether we would be willing to clean again. If we are willing to scrub, he said, he could use the money so saved on loudspeakers. Nothing else was said, and we forgot about it. He did not. In all secrecy he bought the loudspeakers and while we studied in the afternoon and then took our walk, he installed them into the bedroom and into our dayrooms. From then on, instead of being woken by the nasty sound of a cheap cow bell, wonderful music was our wake-up call. Is it a wonder that we adored such a man?"

Zsolt: We had to apply to the authorities to get a special pass for reduced fares on trains issued for students. First the application had to be obtained, filled out and signed by the principal. Then we had to mail it to our parents for their signature. On getting it back from them, it was directed back to the authorities whereupon our pass was finally sent to us. Presenting it at the ticket window, we could finally purchase the ticket at the reduced price. I have done every step required, but the process sagged somewhere. All the students have already left for the Christmas vacation, but I was still waiting for my pass. I saved up the money for my ticket home, but it was only enough if I could buy it at the reduced rate. The boys, naturally, did not live in the school; we lived in the village at various homes of the locals. I lived in a very cold room at Frau B's house, and all my food for the week was a loaf of bread, and some lard. I was so cold that I barely left my bed, and I was miserable. I sent a post card to my parents to explain the trouble, and told them not to worry; they could not have helped the situation anyhow. Of course, I could have walked over to Reisach and told Diri what happened (who by the way could not even guess that I did not leave with the others and that I was still in the village), but I wouldn't even consider that option. After all, I was sixteen years old, no longer a kid, and I figured it was my responsibility to solve or to endure the situation. I was not about crying for help like a little kid. As far as Frau B. was concerned, I don't think she gave a rat's whiskers what was happening in her attic room as long as she received the monthly *obulus* on time. I had no choice but to wait a full week until the magic pass finally completed its erratic roaming and was delivered to me. I arrived home on Christmas Eve.

After Christmas when we returned to school, I told my good friend Tibor about my adventure and my nourishment of the week consisting of a single loaf of bread. He being a poetic soul quoted Omar Khayyam, not quite without a hint of bantering malice: "A loaf of bread, a jug of wine and thou…" The fool! What wine? I would have given a lot of things in exchange for a cup of hot tea. And as far as "thou" was concerned, I only had one person in mind: the mailman with the pass in his hands, and was immune at the time to any other "thou." But in order to have the last word, I answered him, quoting Robert Frost: "Forgive me my nonsense as I also forgive the nonsense of those that think they talk sense." That shut him up, at least for a while.

Jutka: Amazingly on one of my excursions to Oberaudorf in one of the stores I was able to buy two pretty headscarves. I was delighted and could not believe my good luck. In my excitement, I practically ran the few miles back to school where I immediately fabricated a summer blouse for my sister from the two scarves. Having no experience in sewing, I decided to forget about sleeves, buttons, buttonholes and such unnecessary details, and simply stitched together the two pieces, which she then could slip over her head poncho style. The corners of the scarf-turned-blouse were hanging down in front and in the back in uneven elegance; it would have been very fashionable at the beginning of the twenty-first century, the ragged look then favored. Unfortunately this style was not at all that common in 1948, or I should say it was rather unusual, perhaps even bewildering. However, Zsuzsa of the angelic patience never complained about the unusual haute couture her big sister made for her, and she was even grateful because the blouse was light, and the weather turned suddenly quite warm. She loved its airiness, as she told me later. Or perhaps she was astute enough to realize that the truly great artists, in this case her sister, usually are decades ahead of the rest of the pack. It is so true that geniuses are not understood and appreciated in their own time; they are invariably spirits of the future. However, sad to say, the world lost a great fashion designer, as I ultimately chose teaching instead.

Markóczi: After my mother's death, I found an amazing book among her personal papers. Apparently she was a very conscientious book-keeper. She marked down every expense from the time she married and when they bought their furniture. She carefully noted how much was paid the midwife at my birth, how much was paid for groceries or vacations. Every little thing was neatly entered and dated. This book was so important for her that she packed it among the few possessions we took along when fleeing Hungary. Reading through it was like seeing my life in a different dimension, in a new language, presented in a totally new number-context.

From his book I learned that the monthly expense of my schooling, including tuition, room and board was 75 RM (Reichsmark). The amount varied slightly every month: apparently it was figured on a daily base. In months with only 30 days the fee was less, and in June when school ended, she entered only 30 RMs.

The money reform of 1948 changed everybody's life. I returned to school in September and stayed until May, but she only entered a single expense: 5 RM for enrollment fee. Apparently she could not pay anything from then on. I do not know how I was entered into the school's bookkeeping and do not know how I could stay in school from September to May without paying the fee. No wonder that the school eventually went bankrupt! My parents could no longer send me an allowance, or food packets, and they could not visit me anymore. They were only able to somehow scrape together enough money for me to travel home for Christmas.

Koci: My parents just could not afford the fee for the school anymore, so half way through the 12th grade I had to leave. I tried to study at home in order to be able to graduate, but even that seemed hopeless. But then—miracle of miracles—Katyi, (Kristó) a former schoolmate at Niederaudorf and a good friend of mine helped me out in a wondrous way. Katyi already immigrated to Venezuela and she mailed me ten pounds of coffee! We sold this rare treasure on the black market, and this made it possible for me to return to school and to graduate.

Ballusz: The summer of 1948 was a long one and I could hardly wait to return to school. However, the money reform made it impossible. I wrote to Diri how sorry I was, but it just cannot be done. With return mail he answered, not to worry and to get on the first train. He will somehow get me a stipend to cover the cost.

Nusi: My parents were able to finance one year at the school, but then all the money was gone. I was heartbroken because I loved being at Niederaudorf. I loved everything about it; the school was my second home. The daily walks had a special charm for me. It is hard to explain what it was. Perhaps the spectacular countryside, perhaps the happy laughter, the conversations or the shared joy of bodily motion—whatever. I knew I would miss it terribly. But then a kind and anonymous person took it upon himself to finance my last year in school. Whoever he is and where ever he is, may God bless him here on earth, or in all eternity because he probably is no longer with us.

Vica: I wanted to return to Niederaudorf to complete the 12th grade in the fall of 1948 and then to start studying for the graduation, but because of what the money reform did to us, I could not. We had no money. But a few days before Christmas, Diri wrote to me that he found someone who would sponsor my tuition, room and board. I was able to graduate in 1949. I will forever be grateful to Diri and the kind priest in America, who sent the funds for my tuition and room and board.

Vica kept the note, copied below, in which Kovács Diri informs her on December 19, 1948, that she can return to school on January 7th, 1949, to finish her studies. She would need to pay only 5 DMark each month to defray the cost for health insurance and Schulspeisung.

The 200 DM stipend or scholarship was being provided by a Hungarian priest living in America. In Diri's words: "I am happy to inform you that little Jesus is bringing you a 200 DMark scholarship directly from America, from a Hungarian priest…" The mention of little Jesus bringing the money refers to a Hungarian custom. Children received gifts at Christmas from child Jesus and not from Santa Claus..

This must have been a wonderful news at Christmastime in 1948 for the family; Vica was able to graduate at the end of the school year. She actually saved this note and sent it to Nóra fifty years later when she was gathering information about the school.

Magyar Leánykollégium
Ungarisches ... ...legium
Hungarian ... College
Niederaudorf
226/1948-49. BAYERN

Reisach, 1948. 84. 19.-én

Kedves Vica!

Örömmel értesítem, hogy a Zsmola Marcsi Néginek egyenesen Amerikából egy magyar paptól 200 DM-s ösztöndíjat, [kapott], amelynek alapján jan. 7-én bevonulhat az intézetbe, hogy tanulmányait befejezze. Csupán ösztöndíj + Schulgeistung amely havi 5'-DM-et fizetnie.

Amikor nevetetlel gratulálok ehhez, kérem, legyenek szíves mielőbb magyar kórosztoblevelet írni a köv. Cimmel: P. Dengl Miklós O.F.M., Cleveland. Ezt én
továbbítás végett a Consnanak küldöm-meg.

Kedves Istvánnak és Katinak kézcsókom küldve
a Kellemes karácsonyi [ünnepet] kívánva

[aláírás]
nch. ig.

SCOUTING AT NIEDERAUDORF AND AT REISACH

The scouting organization was conceived around the turn of the last century by Lord Robert Baden-Powell, affectionately called B-P. His book about the warfare in South Africa: "Aids to Scouting" was an enormous success. The enthusiasm of the readers, especially of boys, inspired him to form an organization of scouting for young people between the ages of 12-18. Schools at that time were only concerned with the development of young intellects. Lord Baden-Powell's aim was to develop, in addition, character, citizenship and physical fitness. He carefully listed the goals in the promise, or oath of the scouts, and in the laws. He was very clear about expectations in such areas as self-reliance, courage, initiative, helpfulness, love of nature, integrity, outdoor activities and resourcefulness. He expected scouts to understand their society and heritage and to always respect the rights of others. He wanted his scouts to be God-respecting, regardless of their religion. To test his ideas, he organized an experimental camping event in 1907, and this date is recognized as the beginning of scouting, which caught up very quickly worldwide. Today it is the largest youth organization in the world. His care and dedication to scouting is beautifully illustrated in his farewell message to the scouts for publication after his death:

"Dear Scouts - If you have ever seen the play 'Peter Pan,' you will remember how the pirate chief was always busy preparing his farewell speech because he was afraid that possibly when the time came for him to die, he might not have time to get it off his chest. It is much the same with me, and so, although I am not at this moment dying, I shall be doing so one of these days and I want to send you a parting word of good-bye.

Remember, it is the last time you will ever hear from me, so think it over.

I have had a most happy life and I want each one of you to have as happy a life too.

I believe that God put us in this jolly world to be happy and enjoy life. Happiness doesn't come from being rich, nor merely from being successful in your career, nor by self-indulgence. One step towards happiness is to make yourself healthy and strong while you are a boy, so that you can be useful and so you can enjoy life when you are a man.

Nature study will show you how full of beautiful and wonderful things God has made the world for you to enjoy. Be contented with what you have got and make the best of it. Look on the bright side of things instead of the gloomy one.

But the real way to get happiness is by giving out happiness to other people. Try and leave this world a little better than you found it and when your turn comes to die, you can die happy in feeling that at any rate you have not wasted your time but have done your best. 'Be Prepared' in this way, to live happy and to die happy—stick to your Scout Promise always when you have ceased to be a boy—and God help you to do it.

Your friend, Robert Baden-Powell"

A teacher in Hungary, László Králik, read B-P's handbook and proceeded to publish an article about it, ending with the suggestion that Hungary too could benefit from such an organization. The idea was enthusiastically embraced, and already by 1910 there were several active chapters, or troops in Hungary. Count Paul Teleki, later Prime Minister of Hungary, was especially engaged, and soon occupied the rank of Chief Scout of Hungary.

After the First World War during the brief Communist rule scouting was prohibited, but as soon as that regime was displaced, the organization again started to operate with new vigor. During the international jamboree of 1929 in the UK, Hungarian scouts won first place in the sporting events, and this offered the privilege to host the jamboree of 1933 in Hungary. It was held at Gödöllő, the royal retreat of Elizabeth Empress and Queen of Austro-Hungary. It was attended by 30,000 scouts from 46 countries, and thousands of guests. Lord Baden-Powell, Chief Scout of the World was present and to the delight of all he inspected the camp sites riding a magnificent charger. Also present were Miklós Horthy de nagybányai, regent of Hungary, and of course Count Paul Teleki.

After the Second World War, when Hungary was under Soviet occupation, and once more under Communist rule, the scouting organization again was attacked. Its ideals did not fit the concept Communism planned for young people. The emphasis on God, patriotism, citizenship and heritage was especially onerous to them.

However, young people are incredibly conservative; therefore, it was not easy to completely eliminate it. Youngsters don't tolerate changes easily and insist keeping what they value, be it scouting, or Santa Claus, whom the Communist tried in vain to change into Father Winter. A good example for this stubborn conservatism is Brueghel's painting, "Children at Play," dated 1560. On this large canvas, he depicts over 200 children participating in eighty games, and amazingly these can all be recognized in the XXI century, and are still played by modern children today—at least by those, who are still playing. It is remarkable that children did not eliminate, modify or change their games, nor the rules of the games through the centuries. Brueghel's painted encyclopedia of games was probably not contemporary; very likely the same games were played long before the painting was done.

Knowing this resistance of young people to any sort of change, scouting was not immediately put on the Black List, but was gradually changed and united with new, Communist approved organizations (Uttörők) until its character designed by Lord Baden-Powell was effectively choked out. Scouting was eventually prohibited and could not exist in Hungary for forty years, but it came to life and flourished in the Hungarian refugee camps in Germany. Two years after the end of the war, there were active chapters, one of them established at Niederaudorf by the Chief Scout in Exile, Gábor Bodnár. As immigration to various countries were commencing, the love of scouting travelled with the Hungarians into their new homes. Today, wherever larger groups of Hungarians are living, one can be sure to find an active scout life, enjoyed by Hungarian youngster.

Some prominent Hungarian scouts were: Count Paul Teleki, prime minister; László Almássy, researcher of Africa; Miklós Jancsó, film producer and regisseur; Imre Sinkovits, actor; Antal Szerb, author.

OATH OF THE HUNGARIAN SCOUTS:

I, ... promise that I will do my duties to God, my Country, my fellow people and my Hungarian identity loyally. I will do my best to help others. I know the Scout Law and will keep it always.

THE HUNGARIAN SCOUT LAW:

1. A Scout is upright and always tells the truth.
2. A Scout does his/her duties to God, his/her Country and his/her fellow people.
3. A Scout helps whenever he/she can.
4. A Scout is a brother/sister to all Scouts.
5. A Scout is gentle with others, but strict to him/herself.
6. A Scout loves nature, is kind to animals and takes care of plants.
7. A Scout obeys his superiors willingly and wholeheartedly.
8. A Scout is cheerful and considerate.
9. A Scout is thrifty.
10. A Scout is clean in body and soul.

OUTDOOR CODE

I will do my best to
- Be clean in my outdoor manners.
- Be careful with fire.
- Be considerate in the outdoors, and
- Be conservation minded.

MOTTO: Be Prepared!   **SLOGAN:** Do a good turn daily!

Notes of students:

Tirczka: The objective of the scout work is incorporated into four points: serving God, homeland, fellowman and service to the Hungarian causes.

Scouting started at Niederaudorf in July of 1947. Kristó Katyi (student, and an active Girl Scout even before she enrolled at Niederaudorf) and Mrs. Ravasz composed a pamphlet about scouting, and every student returning for the second school term received a copy.

When school started, three scouts from the *"Hontalan Sas"* troop: Gábor Bodnár, Lajos Kővári, and Tamás Rónay came to the school to "recruit." After some spirited campaign speeches, they wished Katyi (Kristó Nagy) in scout fashion plenty of good luck and work to be successfully done and announced that from then on she was to be in charge, and that they are putting their full trust into her hands. Everyone was quite touched and the three guys left with the feeling of "work successfully done." Without wasting time, Katyi started the "No.32 Cecily Éva" Girl Scout troop and as long as she stayed in school, she was a devoted and enthusiastic leader.

By the end of October of 1947, several girls from Niederaudorf took part in the advanced leader training camp at Guttenberg: Marika Markó, Kati Pettendy, Marika Szűcs, and Katyi Kristó Nagy. They also took part in a Teleki Memorial Day at Landshut, accompanied by Kovács "Diri" the new director of the school, and by Mari Buza, who completed her junior officer training at Irlsbach.

Our girls attending one of the early training camps in 1947. Kati Kristó-Nagy, Éva Tirczka, Mara Szűcs on the right. This is where Hungarian scouting in exile started.

On Kristó Katyi's suggestion, we produced a *"Plakátujság"* called *"Mákvirág"* or Poppy Seed. It was a wall newspaper, similar to a poster. It was made of a large (30"x 38") sheet of brown wrapping paper. At first Katyi illustrated it. She drew beautifully! She had an incredible hand. It was she, who illustrated the first Girl Scout handbook, which was published in 1962, in Garfield, New Jersey. After she left school, Mari Buza continued the role of leadership and the illustrations of our newspaper. The rest of us donated cute little commentaries, which were sometimes serious, sometimes less serious, or downright witty.

It was towards the end of 1947 when we first engaged in serious scout work, namely we had to harvest firewood for the winter months. The city had cleared a large patch on the side of a mountain, and we assume d the task of cleaning up the branches and twigs left there. It was very hard work. The branches were long, heavy and abrasive, constantly getting all tangled up and stuck together. We worked very hard for hours, perspiring, panting, but in the end brought everything down to the road from where we carted the fruit of our labor back to the school. Winter could come; we were well prepared for it.

Another scout activity came on June 13, 1948 when we attended the *"Tag der Jugend"* in Rosenheim, which was a Youth Day with lots of German youth groups present. There were discussions, meetings and performances We were the only "foreigners" performing. Of course we did not possess scout uniforms. I wore a white blouse, long pants and a green scout neckerchief and danced a solo called *"kanásztánc."* (*Kanász* was a very proud swineherd!). Besides my number, there were other solo dances, also pairs dancing *csárdás*, the formal *palotás* (Hungarian court dance) and we presented Hungarian songs. We really performed our best and were a total hit; as a matter of fact we were rewarded with an electric iron which in those days was a huge treasure!

Our performance at the „Tag der Jugend" in Rosenheim. June 13, 1948.

Éva Tirczka is performing the *kanásztánc*; Klári Csaba and Éva Balla are dancing a *csárdás*.

Wir rufen die Jugend!

Am SONNTAG, den 13. Juni in Rosenheim ASV.-Platz
bei Regenwetter Markthalle Rosenheim

TAG DER JUGEND

Die Jugend des Kreises singt und spielt!

In friedlichem Wettbewerb will sie ihren Eltern und Freunden, besonders aber auch der Jugend die außerhalb den Gruppen steht, von ihrer Arbeit und ihrem Tun ein Bild geben.

Alle Jugend, Eltern und Freunde der Jugend
sind herzlich eingeladen, den ersten „Tag der Jugend" des Stadt- und Landkreises Rosenheim mitzufeiern und mitzuerleben.

Zum Ausbau unserer Jugendarbeit erbitten wir einen Unkostenbeitrag von RM 1.—. Freiwilligen Zulagen nach oben, die der örtlichen Jugendgruppe zugute kommen, sind keine Grenzen gesetzt.

Jugend komm — sing mit!
Freunde der Jugend, werdet einen Tag jung — feiert mit!

Kreis-Jugend-Ring-Rosenheim
Stadt und Land.

Obb. Druckerei G.m.b.H., R'heim, Rathausstr. 4

Was wir mitsammen gestalten wollen:

- 8.00 Abholen der Jugendgruppen vom Bahnhof;
- 8.45 Begrüßung auf dem ASV-Sportplatz;
- 9.00 Kathol. Jugendgottesdienst auf dem Sportplatz;
- 9.00 Evangel. Gottesdienst in der evangel. Kirche;
- 10.15 Fußballwettkampf der Schülermannschaften ASV-Jugend Kiefersfelden gegen Rosenheim, 1. Halbzeit;
- 10.30 Staffellauf der ASV-Jugend Rosenheim;
- 10.45 Fußballwettkampf, zweite Halbzeit;
- 11.00 Leichtathletikwettkämpfe, in mehreren Gruppen gleichzeitig:
  ASV-Jugend, Kiefersfelden,
  ASV-Jugend, Rosenheim
  Sportbund-Jugend, Rosenheim
  Sportclubjugend, Schloßberg.
- 11.45 Gemeinsames Singen;
- 12.00 Gruppenweise Ausgabe des Eintopfes;
  Während der Mittagspause:
  Vorführungen des Jugend-Rot-Kreuzes,
  der Bergwacht-Jugend,
  der Wasserwacht-Jugend;
  Besichtigung von Zeltbau und Zelteinrichtung: Pfadfinder Rosenheim;
- 13.30 Gemeinsames Lied;
  Begrüßung durch Herrn Oberbürgermeister u. Herrn Landrat;
- 13.45 Katholische Jugend Pfraundorf — Lieder —
- 14.00 Falken-Jugend, Rosenheim — Reigen —
- 14.15 Katholische Jugend Endorf — Lieder —
- 14.30 Katholische Jugend Prutting — Flöten —
- 14.45 Katholische Jugend Kiefersfelden — Spiel —
- 15.10 Katholische Jugend Oberaudorf — Jodler —
- 15.15 Ungar. Mädchenlyzeum — Tanz und Lied.
- 15.30 MTV-Jugendgruppe — Gymnastik
- 15.40 evangel. Jugend Rosenheim — Lied
- 15.45 Katholische Jugend Kastenau — Spiel —
- 16.00 Katholische Jugend Rosenheim — Lieder —
- 16.20 Preisverteilung;
- 16.45 Schlußwort und Schlußlied;
- 17.00 Ende.

Mari: I was a scout even before I came to Niederaudorf. It was on August 20, 1947 during the Altötting pilgrimage when we met Gábor Bodnár and the boy scouts from Pfarrkirchen. My brother joined right away and I joined soon after. I was really devoted to the organization. After Katyi Kristó Nagy immigrated to Venezuela at the end of the school year of 1948, I took over the leadership of the "No.32 Cecey Éva" Girl Scout troop. By that time we have already moved from the Alpenhof to Kloster Reisach. There were about thirty members in the troop divided into four patrols (*őrs*).

We conducted at times special troop meetings when we discussed the scout rules and decided to dwell on self-discipline. We also kept correcting each others' faults. It was at one of those meetings when I found out from my loving friends that I was a despicable glutton and an obvious eager beaver or "strobe". I tried to correct this.

Working nightly in the kitchen at Reisach was a scout project. Putting our best forward, we sang during potato peeling and the cleaning of beans, or when chopping vegetables.

Zsuzsa: Of course, we had no uniforms. At a time when we hardly had any decent clothing to call our own, but this did not particularly bother us. We were pretty much used to not having things. But the question of uniforms was different. We thought it must be the world's most wonderful gift to own one. We dreamt about it and felt that we were not real scouts in our everyday dresses. At a general meeting Katyi (Kristó Nagy) told us (and we blindly believed her) that the spirit of scouting has nothing to do with outward attributes. Special attires only show the world to which groups we belong; they sort of identify us. We know a policeman, a fireman, a soldier, a doctor or a chimneysweep by what each wears. But it does not show who they are, only what they do. She told us that we should shine in our deeds and in our behavior, regardless what we are wearing. Nevertheless most of us were able to find a piece of green material from which we fabricated a tie or kerchief, which scouts all over the world wear. We felt that our good deeds and our behavior could shine much better when we performed them while our neck was decorated with the precious green kerchief.

It was more disappointing that we had not the means to camp outdoors. Most of us heard or read about those wonderful camping days in tents, but that was another thing we could not have. Instead, we climbed mountains, but with a few exceptions we returned to the school on the same day, so it was hardly a proper camping event. Later, when we gained some experience (and endurance) in mountain climbing, we tackled higher ones and a few times we overnighted in the tourist huts kept open for such a purpose.

The existence of these huts was an interesting arrangement, and I don't know if such an accommodation is available anywhere else in the world, or indeed whether these are still operating in the Alps today. These huts were built of wood on stone foundation, somewhat similar to log cabins, and were charming and inviting. Most consisted of a very large living room with tables, benches and a huge stone fireplace built so that part of it accommodated cooking. There were also some cooking utensils and tableware next to the fireplace. Above the large room was a loft filled with fresh fragrant hay and straw, where we could sleep. There was no charge, nobody tended it, although I suppose from time to time someone did check on it, and perhaps exchanged the hay and straw and filled up the wood pile with something better than just twigs with which we replaced what we used, but it stood completely empty, awaiting tired tourists. The place was always open; all that was asked of the overnighters that they leave the place the way they found it. The room had to be swept, dishes washed and replaced, and if any wood used, it would have to be replaced by gathering fallen limbs and twigs around the cottage. It was a charming, cozy place high up in the mountain, offering shelter and warmth. Even in the summer months the temperatures are very low at such high altitudes and it was wonderful to sit around the fireplace, sip hot herbal tea and sing. It compensated us for not being able to participate in real camps and in real tents.

Feri: I was an active scout while at Reisach, and I really loved it. One of the hardest and most remarkable assignment was given to us boys: we had to climb the Brünnstein (*nota bene*—it is 1916 meters high, or about 6000 feet, give or take some inches) and had to lug up two buckets of white paint to paint the little chapel on top of the mountain. What a glorious accomplishment that was!

Anikó: Among my fond memories is scouting. Not so much the mountain climbing of which there was plenty. However, believe it or not, I really enjoyed going out into the forest to chop fire wood for heating.

Lilla: I can still remember taking the scout oath. I felt very special and morally elevated.

Márta: The biggest event of the second half of the 1947 school year was the organization of scouting. The Scout Movement, prohibited in Hungary, came to life in the refugee camps. Katyi Kristó Nagy completed the scout leadership course and with the help of others organized scouting at our school. We followed her guidance with a lot of idealism and happiness as members of the Cecey Éva troop. One of the important founding rules of scouting is the importance to love another and the fact that everyone can be loved and should be embraced in friendship.

Jutka: from a letter to her mother: "...*scouting is now raging with full force. They hit upon several ideas which are amiable and proper and sometimes even entertaining. Since we have become scout nominees we don't amble along on the road when going somewhere, but march nicely, which looks good and creates a great impression on the German villagers, who are devoted to marching as it is. It is less uplifting privately because when we are very tired, as after gathering wood for a few hours, we grumble because of the pace of marching dictated by our physically fit group leader, Tirczka. She has little empathy for tired feet and only barks: 'Shush, Anya' (a favorite nickname used by all girls towards each other). 'All this whining cannot be endured by people of sound mind... Lock your mouth, smile and march! One...two...three...' I suppose she is the one who has the sound mind. But then what have we? And is this being polite? And imagine, yesterday we had our first campfire! It was so beautiful! We started the fire at about 8:30 and we sat around it in a circle. It was pretty late by then, and all those sparks were just flying in the dark. We made the fire out of our own firewood reserve. Unfortunately, we cannot often afford such luxury of burning wood for just the pleasure of it. Sadly, our self-gathered firewood pile is finite, and we can afford such extravagances only once in a while. And you do know, don't you, who has to get more wood once this is all gone!*"

Zsuzsa: From a letter a long time ago I had written to my Mother, I can see that I was already a scout by the age of 12. I wrote to my Mom: "I belong to the Geranium family." Of course where Mari Buza was, there was no way out of it. Everyone was "scouted" by gentle and sometimes not so gentle persuasion. And to tell the truth, we really enjoyed it.

CONTACT WITH THE WORLD AROUND US

Ferenc Cserháti:
"The school experienced marked indifference from the German officials; the 'Schulrat' of Rosenheim was especially outstanding in its deeply rooted disinterest. Although the Hungarian school at Niederaudorf was not only officially accepted and registered by the American Occupying Forces but by 1948 was placed under the aegis of the Schulrat (School Council) of Rosenheim. Nevertheless, Niederaudorf might not even have existed as far as they were concerned."

However there were exceptions, as is obvious from the report of Dr. Ravasz:
"...We cannot be thankful enough for the truly wonderful support of M. Ostermann, the director of the 'Jugendausschuss' organization at Rosenheim. He offers loving-kindness and continuing help such as we have not experienced in Bavaria yet. His good will and unselfish caring are unique. He not only donated note books, paper and writing material, which made our work so much easier, but he follows our struggles carefully and is always here with help. He donated various items to the school to make the household chores easier and when once during a storm the window broke in the schoolroom he arranged to have it replaced. He arranged for us to participate in the 'Tag der Jugend' (Day for the Youth) in Rosenheim, which was quite an event. On Dec. 6th, 1947, he appeared with a few German boys from his organization and brought gifts for the girls, and also for the school. The girls each received a ceramic cup filled with candy, notebooks and also individually wrapped gifts of all sorts. For the school 'Santa Claus' brought maps, games, books, sewing material, rulers, and compasses. We were touched and grateful for so much caring and love..."

Lilla: During the German Jugendtag, (Youth Day) our school was invited to Rosenheim. We marched through the city singing together with the German kids. There were also Ukrainian scouts present and they marched besides us, all boys! They sang beautifully. We were not even close in volume to their strong voices. We all marched into the sport arena where several events were already in progress. We performed our dances and also sang, naturally in Hungarian. We wanted to outfit the girls, who danced the parts of the boys, with proper boys' pants, but we could not manage this because, with the exception of Éva, who was so skinny that the pants actually slid down on her, the rest of the girls did not fit into any of the pants we borrowed. I don't remember who gave us the pants.

There was a huge applause from the many Germans present, but of course the scout never applauds; therefore, the Ukrainian boys just shouted huj-huj, hajrá! (Kind of a battle cheer). After the show, we were treated to lunch, but we did not have any canteens or implements and thought that we would have to leave hungry. But the Ukrainians came to our help. When they finished their lunch, they lent us their canteens and tableware!

Ballusz: During one of our walks, we discovered a rivulet, probably a tributary of the Inn. At one point the river widened and there was a diving board. Obviously this part of the river was arranged for swimming. It was hot and the water was irresistible. Near or far not a soul was visible. Some of the girls took off their shoes and waded into the water; others, more daring, shed most of their clothing and actually swam for a while. The following day the German boys of Niederaudorf appeared en masse at the Alpenhof, singing and marching, and on a long stick they carried their flag: one of the unmentionables of a girl, who in her hurry to get dressed, left it at the river. Naturally no one would admit ownership of the delicate piece of underwear, so the boys marched off again flourishing their unusual flag and very likely scandalizing the poor villagers. Public moral probably has not been the same ever since.

Kati: December 6 and the traditional St. Nicholas day was approaching. We were busy and excited as we were preparing a festive program. The German youth leader Herr Osterman was our guest of honor. The program was to be the expression of our gratitude for his ongoing kindness and for the much appreciated help he gave us whenever he was able to procure something for us. But it turned out the other way around: instead of giving him a pleasant hour as a gift, he was the one, who surprised us. As soon as he arrived, we were all sent to our bedrooms to wait, and when we were called back to the school room the tables were set with white paper in lieu of tablecloths. At each place there were gifts: everyone received a pretty ceramic cup filled with hard candy, and also various other gifts, which he collected for us, heaven only knows how, and from where. We were touched and delighted. As soon as our surprise and pleasure subsided we presented our program to him, and then the moment the guest of honor left, the Great Barter Session commenced.

One of my gifts was a German story book for children. This I traded for an ashtray, which Magda received. I don't know why she wanted the book, but I was delighted because the ashtray would be a great Christmas gift for my father. Earlier my mother sent me some sugar, which I have saved up. Now I traded this for hard candy, then I traded all the hard candy for three more of the ceramic cups we just received, and for a cigarette case. Now I had four cups altogether, a perfect gift for my mother. My brother would be pleased with the cigarette case. I was elated about my successful trading on the Barter Market, and knew that I had truly great gifts for those I love. I could think about little else but the coming of Christmas.

GRADUATION

Cserháti Ferenc:

"In June 1947 and again in December of the same year written and oral graduation examinations were offered at Niederaudorf. The procedure was conducted according the specified rules used in Hungary. Rev. Nándor Kálózdy from the high school at Passau and Dr. Dezső Ravasz, Principal of Niederaudorf, presided. Later, the Bavarian Ministry of Education did not accept the diplomas awarded because there was no German supervisor present. The candidates were later required to repeat the examinations. In order to avoid this problem in 1948, the German Ministry of Education nominated Dr. Karl Lang, Director of School Commissioners, to act as supervisor. A year later, Dr. Anton Keller, high school teacher at Rosenheim, was replacing Dr. Lang. Both supervisors were impressed by the knowledge of the students. The written tests of the candidates, covering six subjects were translated for the German supervisors; the oral examinations were conducted partially in German, and partially in Hungarian. When needed, translation was provided by the officials for the German supervisors. The evaluation of the Hungarian teachers matched those of the both Hungarian and German supervisors and again praise was given for the high quality of teaching and the impressive amount of acquired knowledge by the candidates. The report cards were signed by both Hungarian and German supervisors, by all the teachers, then were sent to the German Department of Education, where it was approved and with an official seal, were sent back to the graduates."

Graduation from high school in Hungary, and in most European countries, has been (and still is) undergoing countless changes and modifications, and every change is predictably accompanied by passionate arguments among professionals and among members of the government.

High school graduation was first introduced by the Prussian government in 1788, but it was soon accepted by most European school systems. The hidden agenda then was to control the number of students admitted to higher learning. In 1849 Count Leo von Thun-Hohenstein was appointed minister (secretary) of education and religion of the Austro-Hungarian Empire. He immediately started reforming the school system. His plan, "Organisationsentwurf," is still a guideline; it was introduced to Hungary in 1855 under the shortened title "Entwurf." Basically the plan increased the years of high school, and required high school teachers to have a special certification in the field they were teaching and made the tests more difficult in order to minimize college entrances. He removed some subjects from the college level and introduced them into the high school curriculum, and regulated the process of graduation. After considerable resistance by Hungarian educators as well as by the Hungarian government, the plan was finally accepted, albeit with considerable modifications. The resistance of the opponents to the plan was growing out of a real concern because the plan attempted to germanize Hungarian students: it openly eliminated the Hungarian elements from the school curriculum and replaced them with German ones.

Some important facts about the graduation.

The purpose of the graduation is threefold: it is a closing examination to measure the proficiency of a student (and a guide to determine in which field the student would be most successful in life); it serves as entrance examination to university studies; and is a requirement for civil service and office work. It consists of written and oral examinations from at least five subjects. The tests are extremely difficult and the students generally consider it as the most stressful period of the school years. The tests and testing are strictly regulated by law, and are carried out in the presence of an appointed committee. It is not mandatory. Candidates may apply for examination months before the date, but applications are only accepted from those students who maintained a high grade average and tested well in two foreign languages. After successful graduation the student receives a „Certificate of Maturity" (Reifezeugniss) and may enter college, civil service, or participate in military officer training after which he becomes a reserve officer (similar to the US ROTC program). An interesting fact is that in the years of 1978-1979 Hungarian history was eliminated from the required list of tests, presumably as not important enough. Just as the Austrians tried to germanize Hungarian students by first eliminating Hungarian history and then literature, so hundred and twenty-five years later another attempt was made to eliminate the nation's past, but again it failed.

June 1948 graduates

Magi Renkey
Zsuzsa Császár
Éva Bonyhay

Jutka from a letter, summer 1948 "... *At the third graduation in our school all our seven candidates made it; all of them passed the graduation examinations and great was our rejoicing. We organized a proper farewell for them. First Manci recited a poem, then it was my turn to speak the farewell words, after which I handed each of the seven a red rose. Next in the program was Diri, who of course spoke from his heart, as did Gyurka Olgyay, one of the graduates. After the tears dried we walked to church. The seven in black, then the teachers and the rest of us. Lehel, one of the boys who just graduated, is especially precious. He is as skinny and frail as Lilla, but has a huge sense of humor and wherever he appears, laughter is sure to follow. At the church service we sang enthusiastically, and the resident priests and brothers illuminated the church magnificently, just for us. In other words it was very touching and emotional. Returning back to the Pension, a festive supper was served, but the mood was definitely subdued because we knew that we shall never again see our newly matured, suddenly adult friends. Nobody was in the mood for conversation, we ate silently; you could only hear the discreet sound of spoons and forks hitting the plates. Only toward the end of the meal was the mood lifted a bit, perhaps because wonder of wonders, wine was then served to the graduates and the upper grades, for the first time in their life! Carefully of course, more like a ritual than for enjoyment, portioned out drop by drop,— but it was wine nevertheless, and we all felt quite adult at that point. But even so, you could not say that we were bursting with happiness or hilarity. Soon the sleepiest ones retired, but I made some coffee and Gyurka woke up a local merchant from his well-deserved sleep, asking for another bottle of wine. Gradually we started to sing, and even to dance. Diri wanted to end the festivity then, but we talked him into coming with us to the house in the village where two of our favorite teachers lived. And what else? We, of course, serenaded them. On returning back to the Pension, Diri sent the boys home and locked the doors, but somehow they found their way back into the building and we then serenaded together Diri, his wife, and the housemother. The stars were already dimming when we said good bye once again to our pals, and attempted to go to bed. But then again we heard them singing under our bedroom window. They sang the favorite song of each of the girls, and of course we giggled in the darkened bedroom. After the last song we finally went to bed, but first of course we had to discuss the happenings of the evening. And then we realized that it was morning and all the rest of the girls, who went to bed on time, were getting up... Where did the night go? And we did not sleep a wink!"*

Summer 1948 graduates with German Supervisor dr. Lange at the center.

Front row: Erzsébet Takács, Ili Kührner, Erzsike, Váczy Margit, Kató Vereczkey, Lehel ?
Back row: Ferenc Kovács, Principal, Mária Bárány, Erzsébet Kovács, Éva Gruber, Dr. Lange, Sarolta Takács, Rev. Ernő Nagy, Erzsébet Császár, Páter Fekete.
Not in picture: György Olgyay, taking the photo.

June 1949 graduates with German supervisor Dr. Anton Keller.

Front row: Kati Pettendy, Dr. Anton Keller, Iván Zoltán, Vica Gruber, Endre Román
Back row: Mária Bárány, Dr. Otto Daniel, Molnár Sándor, ?, Béla Csikesz,
Ferenc Kovács, Erzsébet Kovács.

Voices of students:

Vica: I was ever so happy and relieved after the last day of the oral examination of which I was mortally afraid. I did not mind so much the six written tests, but to be cross examined for hours by experts was something else. I shivered and my teeth chattered—I was that scared. To this day, I am convinced that our Principal hypnotized me into calmness, and this was the reason I was able to give correct answers. Almost sixty-five years later I still remember that I pulled Vörösmarty, the poet, in Hungarian literature. When I realized that in Hungarian history I was expected to discuss any given period, chosen by the examiners, from the Conquest (**roughly about 900 A.D.**) to the end of World War Two, I all but fainted. However, I was lucky because the period chosen by the examiners was not the unbelievably confusing time after the death of the first king, St. István, so it went well. From world history I had to show my knowledge about the long and involved political and diplomatic connections of Hungary with Imperial Germany and the Austrian Empire. In German I got Goethe. How lucky can one get! But I passed, and passed with good grades and lots of praise.

My sister Kato's graduation was more complicated. She was among the first students enrolled at Niederaudorf and completed the 12th grade during the first short term, after which she graduated. She was always an outstanding student, so it was natural that she graduated with high notes. We were expecting her return to our home with great excitement. My mother even baked a cake for her. This was an unheard of luxury, but we wanted to celebrate the great day properly. It was a great shock when a few months later we received a letter from the German Ministry of Culture (Department of Education in the US) informing Kató that her graduation examination was unacceptable by the ministry because no German official supervised it. In December she had to travel to Passau, and repeat the examinations, which of course lasted again for several days. She was tense because she had very little time to go over the material before the tests, but she made a success of it. At Passau the German officials were just as impressed by the knowledge of the candidates as they were at Niederaudorf, and claimed that their level of knowlge, especially in Latin and mathematics, surpassed that of German graduates. We were happy the second time around, and Dr. Ravasz was bursting with pride when told about the brilliant results and all the praise.

Kati: (from a letter, dated July 9th, 1949)

"All three of us (Kati Pettendy, Iván Zoltán and Vica Gruber) graduated successfully, and now would be ready for matriculation if there would be a university somewhere, which would accept us. Imagine! Vica stayed up daily up to two A.M. to study. Let me tell you, there was plenty

of material to catch up. At times we felt the things we did not know were more than the things we were expected to know. We did not yet receive our Certificates of Maturity because they were first sent to the German Ministry of Education for something or another. Perhaps to decide whether indeed we were mature enough... But fortunately our teachers saw the grades we received from the delegates, and they assured us that these are the same as the ones we received at the closing examination of the twelfth grade. This, at any rate, is good news.

Now let me tell you about the examination. We started on Monday with the written exam of Hungarian literature, and this lasted from 8 A.M. to noon. We had a choice of three topics:

1. The advent of popular tendency in poetry.
2. Will my country ever have a future, the argument being based on past literature.
3. Széchenyi and Kossuth as seen from a literary point of view.

Vica and Iván chose the third topic, I chose the second one. The written examination of religion in the afternoon lasted from 3 P.M. to 5 P.M. We again were offered three topics from which we could choose one to write about. Tuesday morning we suffered through the German exam, which was conducted by the German supervisor. He started by dictating a text for half an hour, which we were supposed to write down more or less free of errors… Then he read a section (naturally in German) about Socrates, and we were then asked to paraphrase in writing what he read to us. (Again, naturally in German. And need I tell you, besides the German language he also tested our capacity for remembering….) Fortunately there was nothing scheduled for that afternoon and we had some time left to go over the remaining subjects once more. On Wednesday morning Vica and Iván were asked to show their knowledge in Latin. During this time I was writing my chemistry essay about this and that, more specifically about the wonders of the carbohydrates.

In the afternoon we had no choice about the topic; we all wrote about the atom. This examination not only went easily, but our essays greatly surprised the supervisors. We attribute this success to Iván, who, during one of our club meetings, regaled us with lots of information, not really found in the usual text books. (And don't ask me where he gathered his impressive knowledge.) It is also a fact that the dropping of the atomic bomb on Japan was still very much on our mind, so we were fairly well informed about the atom, and keenly interested in its workings. No wonder that we had a great deal to say about it.

Thursday morning was started with the math examination, which was a truly eclectic plate, consisting of such delights as trigonometry, analogues of Pythagoras and Heron, interpolation, auxiliary and equivalent problems, and for good measure, a little bit of mathematical history thrown in—name it, and we had it.

Friday morning English was on the program. Just like in German, we started out by writing what was dictated, then again, a section from a book was read to us in English and we were expected to write it down, paraphrasing. The last part was translation of a text from Hungarian into English. Monday the required oral examinations followed: Hungarian and German literature and history. Vica was terrific, she knew everything. The German examination was naturally conducted in German by the German supervisor. You can imagine the scene—Iván the All-around – Brain talked fluently, but as far as I was concerned, I merely groaned my way through it.

Here I must remark that twelfth grade English was taught by a German teacher, and for some reason, known only to him, he objected to our participating in the graduation examination. However, at the end he relented, and everything came out right."

OUR FIRST PRINCIPAL IS LEAVING US

Cserháti Ferenc,
"In January of 1948 Dr. Dezső Ravasz resigned, as he planned to return to Hungary. On January 15, 1948 Ferenc Kovács was appointed as interim principal of the school, and on March 12 of the same year his permanent assignment was approved in München. The principal's wife was designated to teach history and literature. Mária Bárány, a new-comer, was appointed as housemother, teaching Hungarian language arts and social studies, and was also the appointed homeroom teacher for the lower grades. The third (shortened) school year started with a festive 'Veni Sancte' for the Catholic students, and a separate service for the Protestant students. The enrollment rose to forty-five, and of course there was a lack of sleeping place for the five additional student. Military field beds were set up in the classroom, to accommodate the extra students during the nights."

Ballusz: When we returned to school in January 1948 after the Christmas vacation, we were informed that the Ravasz family is returning to Hungary. Uncle Dezső wrote a nice, individual letter to every one of us, and it was signed by his wife and by his father-in-law. Most of us cried as we read it.

Nóra: Before Dr. Ravasz left, he wrote a personal letter of farewell to our parents, and then individually to each of the forty-five girls. His letters are testimony of his love for us; he considered us to be his daughters. The love was totally reciprocal, and we cherished his letter and kept it through our many moves. The letters are telling about his love, his ideals, but also about the pain and insecurity concerning his decision about returning to Hungary. At that time he did not know that before eight years will have passed, he would lose his wonderful young son because of this decision.

Anikó: I kept Uncle Dezső's farewell letter to this day:
"Dear Anikó! I believe you will for the rest of your life remember the common room and our dining table in it where together we tried to eat more or less politely and without too much complaining about the food served us. And you will probably also remember the geography lessons where at times I made you so very unhappy with difficult questions. What you did not know then is that the tears welling up in your eyes hurt me just as much as it hurt you, and I would have liked to wipe them away, were it not that to make you secure, and your world hale again would have taken more than a simple physical gesture or the offering of a handkerchief.

Dear little Anikó, comparing us in centimeters, you were not much shorter than I am, but as far as age, you were the youngest and most vulnerable of all the girls. My wife and I always tried to look out for you.

Now it is time to say farewell. We are returning to Hungary. Our decision gave us a great amount of joy and happy anticipation, but we are also worried, anxious and sorrowful. The most painful among the many reasons for our sadness is the parting from you—from the student body. We loved you, and love always has a hard time accepting partings. But we also feel that the love we created here in our poor little, struggling school is not the kind that lives for the moment like a soap bubble, or the quick flame of burning straw, but is permanent and it will continue to live, despite the terrifying distances. I believe it is safe to say that this love and all the memories we hoarded at Niederaudorf will accompany us to the end of our life. And so I say my farewell with the certain knowledge that something wonderful happened to us: a magical bond between teachers and students, and between students and students, a bond, which is permanent and precious.

On January 21 we'll start our journey from Piding to Hungary. We are leaving a large part of our soul with you lovely girls, at the Alpenhof. Take care of it, keep loving it, and then one day bring it back for us into our beloved home, Hungary where we shall build the destroyed homes anew. Peace, happiness and harmony will rule in our much suffering country.

With cordial greetings to your parents and to you, we are saying farewell with all of our love your Uncle Dezső, Margit *Néni* and Kálmán *Bácsi."*

Klára Juhász: sharing her letter from Dr. Ravasz:
"…A few months ago you told me it is so easy and joyful to welcome a loved person; now I could tell you how painful it is to say farewell to those closest to our heart. We are commencing our trip back home to Hungary from the collecting camp of Piding on January 21.

You might ask, why. Why have we decided so? We have asked the same question of ourselves many times. Perhaps homesickness drives us, the realization that we cannot survive being transplanted into new soil. We are too old for that. Or perhaps the longing to be reunited with our extended family was the reason. The pull of the home is most powerful. Or maybe we no longer can tolerate the hopelessness of the present situation. So many reasons, so many questions unanswered. We lined up all the pros for staying against the reasons for returning, and after plenty of agonizing we decided that the force pulling us back home is stronger than the considerations of staying in Bavaria. So we are leaving with high hopes and also with fear and sadness, but nevertheless, we are leaving. Indeed this parting is painful. We have formed such a tight bond, such a close relationship at the Alpenhof that we no longer were a unit of teachers and students, but we were living as in a large, loving family. This was unique, and I believe it cannot ever be replicated anywhere else on earth. To achieve it we had to be bound by all our ridiculous difficulties and our common goals. And of course by love, which I believe will be enduring."

Nori's and Piri's letter:
"…The Alpenhof was always much, much more than a mere boarding school. We always felt that the girls living and studying there were in a way our very own children, and that in those difficult times we were fortunate to be blessed with the gift of becoming substitute parents to them.

Now that we are going on a new, somewhat frightening path leaving behind what we built up and cherished, we find the parting to be very painful. Yet, a rich compensation was given us. On our journey home we are taking along spiritual provisions: the memory of your love, honesty, goodness of heart, your hard work and happy laughter—your very own lovely self. May God grant that you'll never change, but instead keep developing in the same wonderful direction as you started. And let us hope that we shall meet again…"

Jutka (from a letter to her mother in 1948)
"…I received a sweet letter from Uncle Dezső today. They loved us as much as we loved them. I know that he wrote to you too, but am enclosing his letter for you to see what a lovely man

he is. We are already missing him so much. School is not the same without them, and we sort of feel lost and bereaved because they took a part of our soul with them. Meanwhile we received a postcard from him, mailed from Hungary. They arrived safely home, and after a lot of running around and knocking on doors, he was appointed to be principal at Salgótarján at a high school. It seems like they made a good choice."

After the Ravasz family left, Ferenc Kovács was appointed interim principal and in March he was approved as permanent principal. His wife Erzsi *Néni*, also a teacher, carried a full load of classes, and Mária Bárány, despite her young age was appointed housemother. Students in all grades instantly accepted and loved the two women, but it took a little more time to open their heart to Kovács. The upper grades knew him from the philosophy classes he taught earlier, and were delighted with his appointment. The younger students did not know him and were somewhat bewildered in the beginning.

He was definitely not a father figure. Some thought, especially when comparing him to Dezső *Bácsi*, that our new principal was cold and aloof. At that time none of us realized the enormous problems he faced due to the school's hopeless financial situation. He wasn't cool or aloof. He was worried sick. His struggles to keep us at the Alpenhof against all odds were heroic and must have cost him many a sleepless night while he tried to figure out ways to save the school. He did not want to alarm us and only shared his troubles with his wife and the staff.

In the end after a little more than half a year of fighting against all odds he lost the battle. He had the choice of closing the school, or finding new accommodations at a lower cost, but this seemed quite hopeless. He had nobody to help him in this dire situation, and had to find a solution on his own—and do it fast. Not until we were finally moved to Reisach could he find some respite from his worries and dedicate his time to what he most loved to do: teaching. Very soon he became our cherished "Diri."

Perhaps the best way to introduce Ferenc Kovács (Dr. Francis Kovach) our new principal would be by starting at the end, sharing one of the eulogies written after his death.

Here some explanations are necessary. First the different spelling of his name might be confusing. He appears in this book as "Ferenc Kovács" but later it has been changed to "Kovach." Many Hungarians upon arriving to the USA changed the spelling of their name partly for easier pronunciation, but also with the hope that the new spelling would approximate the original sound of their name.

In the book the PhD title is not used because he earned it later at Cologne, after he left Niederaudorf. And here is one of the eulogies:

"Dr. Francis J. Kovach had dozens of articles published in scholarly journals, had many more addresses to philosophical conventions along with numerous books ('Scholastic Challenges' was his most recent volume) and was a featured keynote speaker at dozens of philosophical congresses in the U.S. and abroad. Kovach was listed among the 'Who's Who in America' many times over and was cited among the notables in '2000 Men of Achievement.' Feature stories and interviews were done about Dr. Kovach by publications including Time-Life and by the television and radio media as well. He died from complications after an extended hospitalization for triple-bypass heart surgery. Dr. Kovach was 84.

More than a great thinker, Dr. Kovach was also an acknowledged artist and was a gifted and award winning musician as well. During his life he supported numerous charities, and his family recalls how he secretly helped feed Jews during the Nazi occupation of Hungary. The fact that

Kovach had the will to study Hebrew during those dark days under Hitler's occupation of Hungary speaks of his courage and character.

Francis Kovach had 7 children, two of whom died toward the end of WWII. This took place as he and his family crossed the German lines heading west toward the Allied Forces sector in 1945, fleeing as the Soviet troops were bringing decades of Communism in their wake to Eastern Europe. Kovach spent years in a refugee camp in Germany he helped to organize and run a school with his wife, Elizabeth. He and his wife, before he was able to come to America with his family in the early 1950s, also headed a high school for two years for Hungarian refugee students in Niederaudorf, Germany. Like so many immigrants, the family came to the U.S. with a single trunk holding all they owned. Though a highly respected teacher in Europe, and with a PhD he humbly toiled for some time in the cold winters of Minnesota—inside and out—at various jobs like shoveling snow and being an orderly until he would finally get the opportunity to teach once again.

Dr. Francis Joseph Kovach was born in Budapest, Hungary July 19, 1918 to Anna Roch and Joseph Kovács. He completed his undergraduate and graduate studies at Pázmány Péter University of Budapest, Hungary. He was the first student to graduate summa cum laude at the Albertus Magnus University of Cologne, West Germany where he was awarded the PhD in Philosophy. Dr. Kovach taught at three American Catholic Colleges from 1953-1964, including Villanova University before he came to the University of Oklahoma and taught there for 24 years until his retirement in 1988.

When the Catholic Church was going through the gut-wrenching challenges of the post Vatican II. era, Dr. Kovach and his wife stood for orthodoxy, publicly and privately. His powerful voice filled classrooms at O.U. and elsewhere. He was known for being able to address hundreds of students clearly without a microphone. He taught thousands of students in various Catholic colleges and the University of Oklahoma during his teaching career, many of whom have since gone on and had fine careers as philosophers in their own right.

Kovach's areas of specialty were mediaeval metaphysics, philosophy of beauty and art, philosophy of science and ethics. He was an internationally respected expert on St. Thomas Aquinas. He was fluent in 9 languages, including ancient Greek, Latin and Hebrew, as well as English, German, French, Italian, Portuguese, and his native Hungarian.

Like all men, Kovach had his faults and weaknesses. But as his son L. A. Tony said, "That he struggled heroically against the wounds of his soul in cooperating with God's grace is what allowed him to do so much with his life—it is what made my father a treasure in clay.'

Among his many accomplishments, he won an award in a national contest in 1958 for his original composition of an 'Ave Mária.' He was an accomplished artist; his works are displayed in the National Museum in Hungary. He enjoyed writing music, listening to classical music, playing chess, drawing and travel in the U.S. and abroad.

He married Elizabeth Thököly in 1941 in Hungary. In 1951 he came to the United States with his wife and their two children. He was proud to become a naturalized citizen in 1957.

At the time of his death, he had five children, ten grandchildren and seven great-grand children.

A sample comment from one of his colleagues...

"Francis Kovach was a respected colleague (he was always a colleague, even after he retired) and, more important, a treasured friend for nearly forty years. His passing is a sharp grief to me. Dr. Laura [Schleschinger] says that we don't need more smart people; we need more good people.

Francis Kovach demonstrated by his life—in the most convincing way possible—that being smart and being good are not mutually exclusive: he was both. He knew what he believed, and he was fearless in declaring and defending his beliefs. Within the past three weeks, I described him to one of my newer colleagues this way: No one ever accused Francis Kovach of temporizing or equivocating."
Dr. Kenneth Merrill, PhD

Group photo: 1948-49 school year.

Names are given as in Hungarian: last name first, with proper accent marks.

First row: Hegedűs Nóra, Király Judit, Csaba Gabi, Csaba Zsolt, Petres Zsuzsa, Hajtsár Györgyi, Kölcsey Klári, Váczy Pancsi, Kozányi Kati, Szkladányi Ági, Balla Éva.

Back row: Bárány Mária néni, Király Éva, Takáts Erzsi néni, Zoltán Iván, Renkey Marica, Hochenburger Éva, Csaba Klári, behind her Hernády Miklós, Ábrahám Jutka, Takáts Sári néni, behind her (hidden) Hegedűs Piri, Markó Marika, Petres Judit, behind her Gaál Béla, Mélynádasy Tóni, Balla Marika, Pettendy Kati, Gruber Vica, Hadanich Vera, Kováts Gabi, Oltfalvy Margit

Group photos from 1949-1950 School Year
Fall, 1949

Names are given as in Hungarian: last name first, with proper accent marks.

Foreground: Vígh Gyuszi. Behind Gyuszi: Gyulay Eszter?, Román Kati, Mayer Teréz, Budai Mária, Liska Éva. Back row: Nagyőszy Judit, Csaba Klári, Csia Éva, Petres Judit, Hegedűs Piroska, Oláh Béláné Anci néni, Király Éva, Kettenstock Trúdi, Hegedűs Nóra. Missing: Hegedűs Laci, Mélynádasy Tóni, Balázs Hedvig, Balázs Gertrud, Csaba Gabi, Hadanich Vera, Kováts Gabi, Balázs Gertrud, Csaba Zsolt, Égi Éva, Hajtsár Györgyi, Lakatos Mária, Balla Marika, Király Judit, Petres Zsuzsa, Csaba Jenő.

Winter, 1949-50

First row: Budai Mária, Gyulai Eszter?, Kettenstock Gertrud, Király Judit, Mayer Teréz Liska Éva. Center:: Égi Éva,? Back row: Mélynádasy Tóni, Hegedűs Piri, Balázs Hedvig, Vígh Gyula, Seidl Erzsi, Csaba Gabi, Oláh Béláné Anci néni, Kováts Gabi, Balázs Gertrud, Király Éva, Hegedűs Nóra, (?) boy, Kardos Éva. Missing: Csaba Zsolt, Hegedűs Laci, Scheuer Erzsi, Csaba Jenő, Lakatos Mária, Jautz Feri.

REISACH
September 1948—March 1951

Ferenc Cserháti:
"Because of the monetary reform of June 1948, the school became totally insolvent, and the parents were not much better off. This was another hard blow for the school which was just completing its third successful term. It appeared that the noble and brave beginning had no future because the difficulty seemed unsolvable. The School Committee was just able to cover part of the expenses of the school up to June, but at the same time declared that despite its willingness and best intentions, it is not able to help cover the school's expenses in the future.

The situation was even more difficult because the school was in serious arrears with its payments to the owner of the Pension, Mr. Simon Waller. His lawyer informed Ferenc Rozsály at the CARITAS that because of non-payment, Mr. Waller intends to break the contract with the school on September 30, 1948. Dr. Gabor Stoll, the director of CARITAS, appealed. On July 17 in his answer to the appeal Mr. Waller agreed to extend the contract to December 31, but only on condition that CARITAS assures him of payments. Despite the best intentions, this was not a possibility. Because of the changed financial situation, the school was not able to pay the required amount for room and board at the Pension, and there was no place to go, there were no financial resources it could tap. The boarding school at Niederaudorf was facing the end of its short history and was at the point of giving up its home.

Finally the Kolping Foundation in München extended a helping hand and solved the problem by offering the school that wing of the convent at Reisach, which was under the Foundation's management. The convent is just a mile away from the Alpenhof. The entire spacious upstairs area was offered to the school for a monthly rent of 150 DMarks. It was gratefully accepted because the rent was so low that it was affordable—more or less. The school moved in October to its new site.

Once again the beginning was very difficult. In order to sustain the school it was calculated that 35-40 students were necessary, each paying 55.00 D-Marks per month for room, board and tuition. Many parents simply could not afford this, especially if they had more than one child in the school. The school started with only twenty students enrolled. Fortunately with time more students arrived and the enrollment did rise to 40. Meals were now the responsibility of the school, and were prepared by a cook hired by the school administration. It appeared that the school was saved, despite the fact that it had to self-support its operation: pay the rent, the utilities, the salary of the teachers, the cost of the meals, and all other incidental expenses. The only reliable income came from the tuition the students paid; the school could not hope for substantial help from anywhere."

After the Ravasz family left, the new principal, Ferenc Kovács, and his wife Erzsi *Néni*, (also a teacher), took over the financially troubled school. And it was troubled all right, even to the point that the school owed rent to the owners of the Pension—which it simply could not pay.

The reason for the sudden poverty was the financial master stroke, the "Währungsreform" (money reform) which the Allied Forces and the operating German government introduced in order to put a stop to the unbearable economic condition of the country. In the post-war years, the German economy was just a hair breadth away from total collapse. Banks were in debt, business concerns all but paralyzed, black market thriving, infrastructure and factories destroyed, stores totally empty, services not available and money was regarded with suspicion, even contempt, worth almost nothing. People resorted to bartering and black marketing.

At the same time the United States government was concerned about the spread of Soviet Communism in the devastated countries. Extreme poverty is always receptive to the solutions promised by Communism. To avoid the dangerous swing to the left, it seemed imperative to rebuild Europe. The initiative to give monetary support to the devastated countries for recovery was named after George Marshall, then Secretary of State of the USA. The Marshall Plan (in Europe called ERP: European Recovery Act) went into effect in April 1948, when billions of dollars were poured into rebuilding what has been destroyed. This was the foundation on which the wealth of western Europe was built; or seen another way, it was the starter, the ignition of the engine.

One of the solutions of putting the economy back on track, and the consequence were felt immediately by everybody, was to eliminate overnight all the old money, (RM) and replace it with a very limited amount of newly printed money (DM), thus making money rare. This drastic change was called "Währungsreform" and it worked like a miracle. According to the time tested rule of economy because money was now rare, suddenly it was desirable and in demand. While the reform itself was a sophisticated and complicated procedure, especially for the banks and business concerns, and had to be worked out with considerable political and diplomatic finesse, for the man on the street it basically meant that on Sunday morning, June 20, 1948 his old R-Marks became worthless and ceased to be a legal tender. He was given 60 D-Marks in two installments of 40 and 20 DMs to tide him over until his next paycheck. He could build a bonfire with all his old RM paper money.

For the first time in years there was a valuable monetary unit in circulation, and what is more, people actually could buy goods with this money. As if by magic the stores filled up almost overnight with spectacular goods not seen in many years, mostly imports from the USA. Consequently, the black market and barter economy disappeared, the country's economy, which was at a standstill, started working again. Factories and the infrastructure were rebuilt with the aid and grants offered by the USA. The spectacular rise of Germany was initiated. The Marshall Plan and "Währungsreform" resulted in Germany's unprecedented growth and prosperity. This "Wirtschaftswunder," or miracle of economy, was truly considered with awe as a true miracle of the twentieth century, lavishly provided by Mammon, god of money; or to be specific and fair: by the United States.

It was also a fact that together with the new and tremendous upswing, prices were rising too at an almost alarming rate. The reform was unbelievably beneficial to the country, and to all who had jobs, that is to all German citizens. Most Hungarians and other refugees did not have jobs, or at the most they were hired for insignificant, badly paid and usually temporary work only. After the initial 60 DMs were gone, refugees had no other resources.

Until the Reform most Hungarians relied on the money they brought with them to Germany when they fled their home. They also sold what they brought with them, most often jewelry, later anything they had, including bed sheets and clothing, in order to buy food.

Many tried various schemes to earn some much needed money, and almost everyone was involved in black marketing. They were also rather creative in their enterprises. They learned alteration work for dresses; unraveled old sweaters and then knitted new ones from the wool; "manufactured" cloth slippers, rag dolls, or wooden toys, sandals from old car tires. Some fabricated hand-pulled carts made of wood, something vaguely reminiscent of the "little red wagon" in the USA. These however were not toys, but very important means for transporting goods, and were cherished about as much as the cars would be years later.

Examples are my mother's activities in those times. Genetically programmed to always have Plan B ready, she had two specialties at the same time. First, she not only taught herself how to make worn dresses fashionable again, and could fabricate a new, larger dress from two outgrown ones. The stores were empty and services non-operational, but children's bodies had the discouraging habit of growing even when it was impossible to obtain new clothing, so her skills were in demand. She had enough work to keep her up half the nights because having no sewing machine, she hand stitched everything.

Her second specialty was to manufacture shoulder pads. The pinnacle of fashion at that time was to look like a football player, and for this look, shoulder pads were essential. Out of a mysterious material, which heaven only knows where she obtained, she cut equilateral triangles of ever decreasing size. These gradually rising triangles she layered and stitched together so that when the finished product was inserted into the garment, the one angle pointing to the neck would be almost flat, while the line connecting the other two angles and resting on the tip of the shoulders would reach a dizzy height of an inch and a half, or sometimes even more. She then would deliver her finished pads to dressmakers who then covered the basic constructions with the material of the dress they were sewing. Thus the female shoulder, so lavishly painted by Rubens, Rembrandt or Tintoretto was converted into a predictable geometric shape, not unlike an engineer's drawing and was admired and envied by all. It was not the pleasantest occupation to stitch through thick layers of materials, or fashion something acceptable from worn rags, but it helped to keep her two children in school.

All our parents were tremendously inventive and creative, which was even more admirable because they had no previous training or experience in any of the outlandish enterprises they attempted. But they did it in order to feed their families and to ensure their children's education. But none of these jobs was permanent, or well paid even while they were in high demand.

Then the monetary reform happened. On the morning of June twentieth our parents found that they had nothing. Their money worthless, they were suddenly penniless, or in our case using German currency: Groschenless. At the same time the stores were suddenly full of goods, and the primitive attempts of these entrepreneurs were no longer in demand, the black market disappeared overnight. Many did not know how they would put food on the table when the 60 DMs (Deutschmark) were gone. The "Wirtschaftswunder" worked excellently, but not for the many thousands of refugees who were closed out of the happy community of employed and well paid German citizens.

After this German monetary reform (Währungsreform), parents found it difficult to scrape together the money for the tuition, and the school itself was in serious difficulties and was unable to pay for the "room and board" on time, and in full because, of course, the prices were higher than before. Herr Waller, our landlord, was not happy, but then neither was anybody else, who was involved in the situation.

We students knew almost nothing of the financial world, or about the desperate negotiations among the owners of the hotel, their lawyer, the CARITAS and the new principal. We did not know about the imminently pending eviction, set for September 1948. Just as during the war our parents kept the raw truth from us, now the teaching staff did the same. Not until we were ready to move over to Reisach to the convent did we realize the full truth

Our school found a new home in "Kloster Reisach" within walking distance of Niederaudorf.

It is necessary to explain the term "*Kloster*" ("convent" in English,) to dispel a misunderstanding, which is bound to come up. As is commonly known, in modern English a convent is the place where religious sisters, or nuns are living. Religious brothers, or monks reside in monasteries. In larger monasteries, the Abbot heads the religious community while in smaller monasteries, the Prior is the leading person. Since part of the huge building complex at Reisach was still occupied by brothers when we moved in, it would be more correct to call it a monastery, (or priory, or friary); however, to this day its official name is "*Kloster,*" or convent.

There are several reasons for it. First of all a few hundred years ago, when the place was founded, the term "convent" was used interchangeably, without the modern clear distinction indicating whether sisters or brothers are residing in it. In the case of Reisach the name "*Kloster*" stuck to the building complex, and to this day it is registered as such.

Second, even today a building, even if religious men live in part of it, is sometimes called a convent as long as it is also used by the public, as Reisach is and always has been. The word "convene" comes from the Latin meaning to come together, to assemble. Lay people, both men and women, have always come, and are still coming to the convent (are still convening), for special purposes such as retreats or conferences, hence the term is not incorrect.

Third, when we moved in it was easier for us to refer to it by its commonly accepted name "*Kloster*" (convent), than to explain to baffled people the anomaly verging on the scandalous, why an all girls' high school is located in a monastery.

The "*Kloster*" was founded in 1731; its construction completed in 1747, and was named "Kloster Urfahrn." It not only consists of the church and the housing for the brothers, but it has a totally separate huge wing, which was historically used for retreats for lay people, or for youth conferences. After the dedication of the building in 1747, Carmelite brothers from München moved into one part of the complex. In the year 1802, as a result of the secularization of church properties in Bavaria, the building became state-owned (and is to this date). Its doors were closed and it seemed that it would just crumble away. However, in 1836-37 the Bavarian King Ludwig, cousin of Elizabeth Empress and Queen of Austro-Hungary, reinstated the building. It is since then functioning as it did before, only the name was changed from Urfahrn to Reisach. At the time of this writing four Carmelite priests live in the vast complex, but is open to those who seek a quiet retreat for meditation. Because it is state owned and part of it is administered by the Kolping Foundation, we were able to move in. It was an added bonus that the rent was very reasonable.

Adolph Kolping (1813-1865) was a German Catholic pastor, social reformer and publicist. He came from a very poor family and at age 13 was apprenticed to a shoemaker. After having mastered his trade, he became a journeyman, moved to Cologne and traveled widely as part of his responsibilities. He was appalled by the living condition of most people living then in Cologne and was shocked at the treatment the apprentices had to endure.

At age 23 he decided to make a total change in his life and in due time he was ordained as a Catholic priest. From here on, he was a dedicated reformer. His goal was to change the life of apprentices, journeymen and in general the life of all tradesmen. He organized the Association of Journeymen and through it he offered physical, social and spiritual help never before experienced by these young people. As time passed, his work became more involved and reached out to ever more young people. The change he envisioned was already quite obvious during his lifetime. Due to his untiring efforts and organizational skills, not to speak of his talent for getting the financial support for his projects, soon schools, homes, clubs, and even recreational facilities for families grew everywhere like mushrooms after a good rain. Today the Kolping institutions, modeled on his ideas and supported by the Kolping Foundation, are found all over the world, and the benefits of these cannot be praised enough. In 1991 Father Kolping was beatified.

So in a very short time interval we had a new principal and a new home for our school—and we considered both with trepidation. It was equally painful to say farewell to our beloved principal and his family, and to leave Alpenhof behind. We loved the pension with all of our heart and never minded its shortcomings. We were conditioned to farewells, but we expected this to be especially painful, since from the windows of the convent we would always be able to see the lovely outline of the Alpenhof to remind us that we lost one more home in our young life. How can we get over it when we'll be seeing the place every day of our school life? And then on top of it, we had to face a new principal and two new teachers.

But our worries and concerns soon dissipated and we loved our new home. For one thing, we were not as cold as we were in the Alpenhof. At one end of the very long hallway there was a large room, probably used formerly as a dining hall or conference room. At the opposite end were the kitchen and the bathroom facilities. Several small rooms, formerly good sized bedrooms, opened from the long hallway. Every room had a tiled stove and plenty of space.

The big room was immediately assigned as the common sleeping area for all of us. It was furnished with our trusty bunk beds (although the straw in them by this time was truly abominable); the smaller rooms were designated as classrooms. Instead of the usual school chairs and a desk for the teacher, each room was furnished with a large table and chairs around it because it had to serve as schoolroom, dining room and living room all in one. It suited us fine. These smaller rooms could be heated far better than our former rooms at the pension, and for the first time we did not have to study in coats and mittens, scarves, and one degree Celsius away from chilblains. In addition we had the luxury of a room for each grade, which was heaven. After all, up until then we lived in something resembling the environment of the Tower of Babel. There the confusion of voices would have tried the patience of a saint. At one table literature was discussed, at the next there was a dramatic struggle with Pythagoras, or the square roots, and right at the next table the names of exotic rivers and mountains were hesitantly confused and mispronounced. And the tables were placed closer than those in a smoky cafe at the Montmartre. Here at Reisach we had our own room, but it was large enough that when we had free time it could accommodate visiting friends from other grades. Ah, the peace of a soundless world of the convent after Grand Central Station.

We also accepted our new principal without much grumbling. It helped that he was not new to us. We liked his kind, gracious wife, and their little girl, who was all mischief and she captured our heart immediately.

We had our own cook now who made food much tastier, and we had more to eat. Naturally, we still saw meat on our plates on special occasions only, and fresh fruits and vegetables or milk were also rare. Mostly we had potatoes, dried beans, peas, lentils and soy beans. But our cook flavored these with herbs, or onions, or whatever she could find, and at times it was quite good. At least we did not have to face the terrible blood sausage or barley soup any more. Also the brutal schedule for studying was gone. By the time we moved to Reisach in October, 1948 most of us had caught up the years lost, and we had the luxury of a ten-month school term. Our new, leisurely schedule even included a short nap period during the afternoon. Life was good.

We did not fully understand the tremendous financial burden our parents had to endure, their need to solve the problem of our tuition in order to keep us at school. We also did not know that while our sisterly bond was getting stronger with each passing month, the time was not too far off in the future when we would have to say goodbye to each other. While we thoroughly enjoyed our school life, immigration to overseas countries suddenly became a reality. Our parents were already busy writing applications and securing affidavits. It is indeed lucky that Pandora slammed her box shot before the last monster, foreknowledge, could escape from it with the other ills of mankind. It was a good thing that we were unaware that our school years would end much sooner than we expected. "Ye shall not know the day or the hour…" We were happy and carefree, and did not know that within a year or two, we shall end up in the improbable adventure of a new life in Canada, Australia, Brazil Venezuela, or Argentina—and finally in the USA because, eventually, it too was willing to accept us, Hungarians.

My own personal and special gratitude go to the now deceased Prior of the convent at Reisach. At that time we were hungry for books and of course, there were just a very few available, at least for us. Once during confession I told him that I could actually steal (and not regret it) if I saw a book anywhere. From that time on when I went to confession, he always had a book ready for me, which he selected from the magnificent library of the convent. Thus he was guarding my soul from temptation and the sin of stealing, and took it upon himself to provide me with books. Because of the prior's generosity and caring, I remained sinless and happy with the books handed to me somewhat furtively in the confessional booth during my monthly visits there; while just as furtively I returned to him the previous book. Thus we participated in a somewhat clandestine affair, which he probably enjoyed quite a bit. The saintly brothers did not possess a great many such books that would appeal to young girls; nevertheless, he managed to find some fascinating biographies and historical books for me. One book, which stands out among those he slipped to me was the history of the Roman Empire by Felix Dahl. The kindly old prior, seated safely in the darkness of the confessional, could not have guessed that while reading this book I fell madly in love with Totila the magical, dashing Ostrogoth king. My passion was of Olympic magnitude and because there was a time warp of about fifteen hundred years, my ardent love was hopeless, unfulfilled, hence heartbreaking and tragic not to say virginal. These dark emotions were just the right combination for the romantic soul of a teenager. I never confessed to the prior my chaste and undying love for the admirable king because I sensed that he would laugh at it.

Of course if there is one thing a teenager can't stand is being laughed at. It took almost half a century more until I found the mature Totila in my second husband.

But we never saw the mythical library of the convent; it was located in the "clausura" section, where women, not even very young ones, had no permission to enter. However, when we revisited Reisach sixty-five years later, Pater Bruno, the present Prior, showed us this unbelievably magical place. The thousands of books are housed in richly carved bookshelves or cabinets, the result of the patient work of one of the brothers a century ago, who spent his entire life carving these stands. The experience was as exciting as getting the books passed to me in the semi-dark confessional booth.

About this time the school also acquired some boys. I was especially delighted because I was always yearning for a brother. Having none of my own, this seemed like an especially wonderful relationship to me. Now I had half a dozen at once. They were funny, lively and adorable, always ready for some adventure, and we loved them all. One of them, Tony Mélynádasy, wonder of wonders, possessed a camera, and as he was a gifted and avid cameraman, he took over the job of picture documentation of our school. No longer did we have to rely on hesitant drawings to show the future world where we lived and what we have done—Tony's black and white photos did the job nicely and reliably.

We also loved our new principal and his wife, although they were quite different from our former principal. Dr. Dezső Ravasz was warm, loving, but at the same time nothing seemed to disturb his calmness. He was a rock, an anchor in our thoroughly disturbed life. He established the school, ran it smoothly, welcomed us and loved us like a father. We felt secure and happy, and adored him and his wife. On the other hand, Kovács was younger, he was an electrically wired intellectual. After he sorted out the financial troubles of the school following the money reform, which almost eliminated it, and found a new home for it, he could sit back and do what he was doing best: he was teaching us. He gave the school an academic flare quite unusual for a middle- and high school. He introduced us to classical music, philosophy, aesthetics, ethics, logic and even theology.

I remember the day when he came into the classroom, calmly sat down, smiled and announced: "There is no God. There is nothing. No God, no redemption, no afterlife." We were stunned. He was dead serious, and did not seem inclined to add anything more to his astounding comment. This was blasphemy of the first order, and as a just response from a wrathful God, we expected the ceiling to come crashing down. We were confused and did not know how to react to this; after all, we were only around 17-18 years old. Could he have been affected by some strange virus and so his brain deteriorated as a result?

After what seemed like a very long and painful silence, feigning desperation he burst out in his usual staccato style: " For many a month now I taught you with the sweat of my brow, the blood of my heart. As a result of all the frustration I suffered while teaching you I developed nerves more numb than that of a baked potato—and do you know how numb that is? Dead-numb, that is how numb! And you sit here like a bunch of geese deprived of voice! How can you tolerate my atheist views? Haven't you learned a thing all this time? I expected you to seriously attack me! Can't you convince me of the opposite?"

We could. We argued with him all through the class, and afterwards during the midday meal, then continued it into late afternoon, until he finally decided that he is once again able to accept the existence of God. Yes, he taught us how to argue, how to stand up and defend our beliefs, and to ask questions. He also taught us literature—both Hungarian and German—in a way that the written word became forever after a treasure for all of us.

He was a gifted organist and when he played the organ during Holy Masses and prayer sessions in the magnificent baroque church of the convent, he sent us in a state of emotion very close to ecstasy. Our non-Catholic schoolmates would never miss a service in the Catholic Church because they did not want to be left out of the musical delight. "Don't get excited about my presence," said one of them after a tremendous musical storm on the huge, masterfully built organ. "I am not about to convert. I just came for the music."

And finally, we loved the closeness of the church. Formerly, we had to leave a cold place, march through the snow-covered long way to the cold church, freeze for an hour in the unheated edifice, then march back again through the snow into the cold Alpenhof. At times we thought we would never be warm again. However, we now lived in warm rooms and the church was at our doorstep. There was no end to the delights of this world!

Interestingly each principal different as they were, offered us just what we needed at that particular time in our development. Had Kovács preceded Ravasz, Niederaudorf could not have been the same because our needs were quite different at the start of our schooling from what they were later. Providence saw to it that we got exactly what we needed at the time when we needed it. Kovács <u>had</u> to come after Ravasz and not the other way around. The wisdom of past generations still holds in most situations: it brings only grief if you put the wagon in front of the horses and not the other way around. What needs to be in front should be at the front.

<u>Fun time, exercising, discipline</u>

Farsang, Fasching, carnival, carneval—whatever its name—is a period of fun time in Europe and South America, in areas where the population is predominantly Catholic. It is the time period starting on January 6th (Twelfth Day of Christmas) and ends on Shrove Tuesday, the day before Ash Wednesday. Beautifully clad, mysterious figures roam the streets, thousands participate in, or at least watch the parades, and craziness is in the air.

In the liturgical church calendar the carnival precedes the 40- day long Lenten period, which starts on Ash Wednesday and ends at Easter. Lenten is marked by fasting and praying, a time for quieting down, turning inward, for contemplations, meditations, pious and penitential activities and by doing good deeds.

But during the time before this forty day austerity period, during Carnival, people traditionally try to have as much fun and as much food as they can tolerate without having to have medical aid. There are many private balls and parties, but also public celebrations and parades, street balls, concerts, ballets and circus performances. During this time people enjoy masquerading in various creative and rich costumes. Since 1268 a mask is also worn. When wearing costumes and masks people cannot recognize each other's ranks and so for a while the social order is overturned to the delight of most. In Italy, especially in Venice, mask making is a highly specialized and lucrative cottage industry.

The name of this period is probably of Latin origin, and is commonly accepted to mean "carne vale;" "carne" meaning meat, and "vale" farewell. In other words: farewell to meat, and to the pleasures of the flesh because a time of fasting will follow. Historically all stored up rich food, such as meats, fats and sugar was disposed. One way of doing this was to give huge parties where these foods would be consumed on the last day of the carnival, on Shrove Tuesday, in some areas called Fat Tuesday.

Some of the best known traditions (parades, balls and masquerades) were first recorded in Italy. The carnival of Venice was for a long time the most famous carnival in the world. Interestingly enough its beginning had nothing to do with religion; it was a celebration of a military victory. In the year of 1162 A.D. Ulrico, Patriarch of Aquileia, noticed the obvious: the Republic of Venice was once again embroiled in fighting two enemies at the same time. (These were spirited times in Italy, every city-state either grabbing, or protecting territories). Ulrico decided that while the Serenissima was occupied simultaneously fighting Padua and Ferrara, his time came. His plan was to slink in unobserved through the back door (or back canal), and capture the prize of the Adriatic. He marched against the city, fought and lost. As part of the war reimbursement he had to pay the city a bull and twelve pigs. The animals arrived around Shrove Tuesday, were promptly slaughtered on the Piazza San Marco, and were roasted and eaten. People danced and sang to celebrate the victory. Carnival was born.

During the following years the celebration was repeated yearly, and gradually it fit into the religious content of the liturgical year.

The students at the school of Niederaudorf-Reisach prepared most enthusiastically for this particular celebration. Beside the costumes, masks were also fabricated, although, to tell the truth, despite the great pride in them, the handiwork somehow did not quite match the quality and the beauty of those made in Venice. Fortunately none of the students ever visited the Queen of the Adriatic; therefore, comparisons were not possible, and so the cloudless delight in the creations of costumes and masks was undiminished. Also, heaven knows, there was no need to dispose of an excess of rich food stuff on Shrove Tuesday, after all the cupboards were habitually bare, and the fasting started several years ago, nor did it ever end at Easter morning. But nonetheless, the excitement about the celebration was limitless.

Another celebration very much enjoyed in the school was St. Nicholas Day on December 6th. St. Nicholas was a real, historical person. He was a Greek bishop at Myrna in 270 A.D. Many miracles were attributed to him For example, the saving of three children from death. He had the reputation of gift-giving, often placing coins and small gifts in shoes. One of his famous and often retold good deed was about a very poor man, who was not able to provide dowry for his three daughters and so was not able to find husbands for them. Remaining unmarried in those times was a true tragedy for a girl. It often meant abject poverty, exclusion from society, often prostitution. Nicholas the bishop heard about their plight and decided to help. He prepared three bags of money, one for each of the girls. Being too modest to do it during the day when everybody could see his good deed (or possibly wanting to spare the father from the humiliating spectacle of accepting charity in public), when the darkness of night came he threw the bags through the open window into the girls' bedroom, thus saving them from a horrible fate.

His popularity grew and he soon became the patron saint of children and of students. In memory of his habit of slipping gifts during the night to people, especially to children, youngsters place their shoes in the window on the evening of the 5th in the hope that St. Nick will pass by during the night and place some candy or small toys in their shoes.

On the sixth of December in many homes and schools a terribly frightful scene is enacted: St. Nicholas appears in the purple robe of a bishop, accompanied by an angel and a devil. One carries a golden book and reads out the good deeds of the children; the other carries a black book which lists all the misdeeds committed during the past year. In the end, small gifts mostly candy and fruits are distributed to the properly impressed children.

By the time we were old enough to attend Niederaudorf-Reisach, the old fear of these otherworldly apparitions was long gone, but we still enjoyed celebrating the day. With a good measure of humor and bantering, long poems were written about every one of the girls, listing the good and the bad deeds to the amusement of all. Diri or one of the male teachers played the role of the bishop and there were always plenty of volunteers to take the part of the angel and the devil.

Voices of students:

Ballusz: In 1949 Diri agreed for us to have a ball in masks. Everybody was preparing for this great event with the proper degree of excitement. Considering our limited resources, it was amazing how creative we were and what wonderful costumes we fabricated from paper and rags.

Our "little brother" Zsolt dressed as a girl to the general amusement of all. Somebody gave Csiusz a German military uniform in the village, and Klára appeared as a toadstool. She wore a simple white dress to imitate the stem of the mushroom, and she fabricated a huge hat using a wire frame, white and red paper, and so represented the deadly amanita muscaria. In her costume she appeared rather glamorous instead of poisonous. Many used crepe paper to make a costume because it lends itself to wavy lines, flounces, ruches and ripples, and because for some reason it was just then available. Koci was a Turkish pasha, Markóczi was a baby in swaddling clothes, Panni a nurse, my sister fashioned for herself a grass skirt and I was a Spanish singer, gloriously attired in my grandmother's ball gown, which heaven only knows why we happened to have among our belongings which we took with us from Hungary. Mari created a black gown with numbers and solar symbols appliquéd on it; she was a medieval wizard. Kati was terrific as the scarecrow out of the Wizard of Oz.

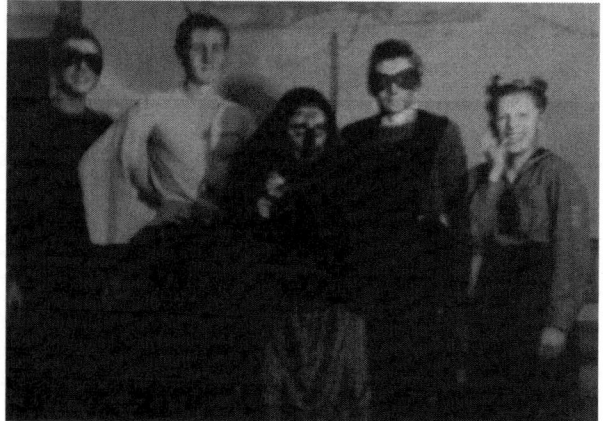

There were some clowns, and also a few Pierrots. The brother of one of our classmates had a camera and he was busy snapping pictures. Our creations are thus preserved for the future—if not for eternity.

Vica: There was a big, empty and mostly unused room above our quarters at the Kloster, and we had permission from the prior of the Kloster to use this for our carnival "ball". Everyone wore costumes and masks. This was when the faux pas of the evening occurred. Iván, dressed as a girl, hit a "boy" playfully on the head. Iván only saw that this person was kneeling on the floor working the gramophone, and assumed it was one of the boys. I shall never forget Iván's face when the kneeling person turned around—and it was Diri. Yes, the social and the age distinctions were successfully erased for that evening.

(These photos by Gábor Buza Jr.)

Markóczi: My masquerade plans changed several times. Originally I planned to be a knight. The owner of the nearby palace lent me a wonderful armor. What a terrific camouflage and nobody would have anything similar, I thought joyfully. However, it turned out that the wearing of it was less of a joy, as it was very heavy. I sadly but realistically decided against it. Next, one of the women in the village lent me a gorgeous black skirt, and I wanted to appear as Jeanne d'Arc, who always intrigued me. But in the last minute I was persuaded by Panni to attend the ball as a newborn baby, and she would be the midwife. She assured me that my eiderdown quilt would serve as the perfect swaddling cloth and we should be a sensation. That we were, only I all but died of the heat.

Jutka: from a letter *"At this time Ping-Pong fever is raging, and we are all afflicted. Zsolt brought the table tennis set from home, and our table in the classroom is fortunately large enough for the game. We spend every minute hitting the ball... The German gentleman (he really is one, I mean gentleman) who teaches us English, even asked us whether we mean to play the game during his English class, or are we willing to put up with a 45 minute pause so he could introduce us to the fascinating topic of the gerund. We had no choice but to agree to the delights of non-finite verb forms, which we don't really understand, but are full of hopes that one day we shall."*

Marika: We were taken for walks every afternoon. When the weather was nice we loved these outings. When the weather was bad—well then not so much, but we still had to go. Fresh air was important, so our teachers told us.

And then we were all infected with the volley ball fever! I do not remember who brought the ball and the net (did we even have one, or just pretended the existence of one? We had no real yard either where we could play. Although the convent had large, fenced-in yards and gardens, which we could see from our upstairs windows, but it was off limits to girls and women. Only the monks were allowed to walk around there. That did not stop us from looking for a court for our game. We played on a strip of no-man's land between the convent wall and the railroad tracks. The ground was very uneven and it was a challenge to play on it, but we enjoyed it tremendously.

Zsuzsa: Silencium! In my opinion it is the most hated Latin word. It demands total silence for long periods of time. I mean so silent that not a word could be spoken during the time when "Silencium" was enforced, which was almost all afternoon while we were supposed to study or to read. That was difficult. To voice my opinion, even when nobody is interested in it, is now and always has been the biggest problem in my life. And when I had an opinion, I also had the need to announce it instantly. How very difficult it was to keep quiet! And it still is.

Ballusz: During "silencium" time the teachers didn't supervise our room as rigorously as they did the other rooms. We were a quiet group and they knew it.

Zsuzsa: (From a letter to her mother, at age 12. Fall 1948) *"Our school is located at such a gorgeous place. There are big mountains all around us. I mean really big, like huge. Mom, I am having such a good time here and am so happy...Imagine the system in our school: if I collect twenty black points, I am flying out of the school! That would be the end of it. Having collected twelve such points, the parents are notified. When someone has nine black points, she does not get her mail for nine days; at six points for six days; at three points for three days. That must be real* *tough. But three good points can erase one black point. At this time I have one black point because of the 'silencium,' but two good points because of my behavior toward the teaching staff. Must be careful with these points..."*

Jutka, from a letter: *"I only got your letter yesterday, although it arrived the day before. If we talk during the afternoon rest periods, or during 'silencium' for a punishment our mail is withheld for a day. This time I was innocent because I slept the entire time. Isn't that funny? I think the last time I slept in the afternoon was when I was a baby. Yesterday was an exception and I slept while the others talked, and we were all punished. Well, I guess it is fair enough. We all share the same bedroom, so we also share the same punishment. Anyhow, how could the teacher tell that among the 45 girls who talked and who slept?"*

The majestic mountain Wilde Kaiser, beyond the Inn river in Austria, is in the background.

Boys in 1948-1949

Iván Zoltán, Béla Gaál, Tóni Mélynádasy, Miklós Hernády. Front: Zsolt Csaba
Missing: Laci Kardos, Kálmán Illyés

Tíbor Diószeghy with Zsolt.

In 1949-1950: (?) Gyuszi Vígh, Jenő Csaba, Zsolt Csaba, Laci Hegedűs

BOYS IN THE GIRLS' SCHOOL

The appearance of boys changed the tone of our school. In the beginning it was barely perceptible, but gradually the change was undeniable. The formerly gentle and quiet harmony turned livelier, more robust and more challenging. Even though still boys, they introduced a masculine presence. They somehow raised the moral. The positive outlook on life was more present after they joined us. The intellectual productivity increased and they added a more realistic viewpoint to our life, formerly shrouded in a veil of refined but highly unrealistic ideals. In our School Club we did not merely discuss poets, poetry or music; the boys introduced the mysteries of science and futuristic thinking and a new brand of creativity. I suppose this would defy scientific proof, but we felt that somehow their very presence enriched our scholastic life. They were worlds away from our demure lady-like behavior, but they were fun, lots of fun. Their laugh was louder than ours, their challenging questions to teachers more to the point, sometime almost bordering on impertinence. They dared to ask, to challenge, and we quickly learned that from them. They were easygoing, brotherly and we learned to be less sensitive and discovered how to really laugh at ourselves. Pranks appeared in the bedroom at the Kloster, such as was unthinkable before. We removed the planks from the lower beds and when the girls wanted to go to bed they fell to the floor, straw sack and all. Some of the girls dared to smoke a cigarette on the sly. It was a change, but it felt right. The boys provided an extra dimension which was lacking until then.

Voices of students:

Ballusz: After 1948 a few boys also attended our school at Reisach. They had sleeping quarters in the village of Niederaudorf and had to walk every day to Reisach to the Kloster for instructions and also spent the afternoon with us studying. I mostly remember Tony, who on Saturdays rearranged our classroom and provided music from his radio so we could dance. He and Zsolt had the duty to feed our little stove during the day. Tony had a special job besides keeping our room warm. We had no central bell, so it was his duty to walk up and down the hall and ring a cow bell when an instruction period ended.

Kati: from a letter written on 1949.7.9. *"...There are three of us now in the twelfth grade, Vica, Iván and I. We have a lot of fun, bordering on silliness. At times we are reminded by serious adults that soon we'll graduate and it would be high time to leave childhood behind and start behaving like adults. The admonitions do not help much. Iván is the instigator, and Vica and I follow his suggestions blindly. Lately we took time to sew together the sleeves on the coats and the top of the mittens of the girls in the lower grades. It was delightfully funny to watch them trying to struggle into their coats when the time came for the afternoon walk. It took them some time to figure out why it was impossible to stick their arms into the coat sleeves.*

Iván, by the way, is the fussiest eater I have ever known. He is so picky, it is pathological and I am sure there is name for it in the medical dictionary. The only food he actually enjoys eating is mush, cooked from corn grits. Vica and I felt that this must be fixed. We found a length of black thread, approximating the color of Betty's hair, or anything else a vivid fantasy could imagine, and while Vica was distracting him, I slipped it into a bowl. Koci was on kitchen duty and when I handed her the bowl with the yarn she did a double take, but then decided it was none of her business, and without hesitation ladled a nice portion of the corn mush into the bowl. I then placed it in front of Iván. With obvious delight he dug his spoon into the yellow mush, saw the thing at the bottom and his mind made a quick conclusion, albeit a false one.

Iván's reaction was predictable and magnificent. Not wanting to disgrace himself at the table he hurled out of his seat as if fired from a cannon, toppled several glasses of water and almost went through the closed door in his hurry to reach the toilette.

Now you must know that each day another teacher sits with us during meal time. The piquancy of the thread affair was that on that particular day Diri sat with us. He uses these occasions to teach us table etiquette and the art of polite, social conversation. At first he did not understand the sudden dramatic departure of Iván, which he certainly did not consider to be approved social behavior. Then he glanced at Iván's bowl, saw the thing and probably made another false conclusion, and suddenly he too forgot about approved and polite social behavior.

Actually Vica and I are pretty fed up with the regularly recurring lentils, and one day last week we were not going to eat it. Everybody was already finished, but the three of us still had almost full plates in front of us. Erzsi Néni, (Takáts) who has the most angelic temperament of anyone I ever knew, was eating with us that day and she was upset. She considers food left on the plate a cardinal sin, and when we argued against Esau's legumen, she simply got up, released the rest of the students then turned the key on the door. As she departed for the afternoon walk, she told us we cannot leave the room until we clean our plates. We were speechless. What did she really think, were we still just little kids to punish us in this way? It was shocking. But we did not stay angry too long; nobody could stay angry at Erzsi Néni. And Iván showed us how to clean our plates: we simply scraped the food into our trusty stove in the corner of the room."

Jutka: from a letter. *"Nobody needs to worry about the boys just enrolled in our school. They are all decent, serious-minded, trustworthy individuals, who are an asset to our school and won't ruin our reputation. They are gentlemen and we are ladies.*

Let me tell about them. We instantly loved Zsolt the youngest, who always salutes us with the old formal greeting used in Austro-Hungary to greet ladies of consequence. We love it. He is polite and helpful and lots of fun and lovable. Then there is Tony, but you know him from Laufen, so I won't describe him. You also know that we love him, and always did. We sometimes call him Kam-Kam (I don't know why) or we use the pet name 'Naso' because his nose is as big as that of Ovid. He does not mind because he knows we don't want to hurt him. The next enrollment was Miklós, and he is a story by himself.

We immediately called him Toldi because we imagined that is how Miklós Toldi looked and behaved. He is very handsome, has a face like a Greek god on a vase, but that beautiful face, just like its original on the vase, never shows any emotions. He speaks slowly, is circumspect, and apparently most things we enjoy do not interest him. He is not even interested in the girls although some of the girls would like to change that. He is terribly smart, knows all the answers, but never raises his hand and only answers when he is asked, but then he knows everything. I don't even know why he is at school. I don't think he learns anything new here. The next boy to join us is Iván. In contrast to Toldi's muscles and impressive build, he is skinny, almost puny and fragile. He has a great sense of humor, and also knows everything, especially physics. Last week he spoke to us for

Miklós Hernády with Tóni

over an hour about the atom, and all we could do is listen to him with jaws dropping to the floor. The strange part was that as he explained this miracle to us, we actually understood it. I would like to know where the boys get all this knowledge from. It is awesome. He too is by now a fixture of our school, and we do not know how we got by until now without him and the others. They are now one of us. In addition, we have two more boys coming each morning for the lessons; one of them is Tibor, our poet in residence. These two are older and their days are numbered: their immigration to somewhere is a question of weeks only.

So far I cannot report to you any blossoming love affairs because the boys not only behave like brothers, but are indeed that. This is wonderful because all my life I wished to have brothers. Or at least one.

Yesterday was May the First, and I am not sure why, but apparently this is the night when young girls and ladies are serenaded. So at midnight all our boys came from their homes in the village where they board, and gathered under our bedroom window and sang for us. They were so sweet. To stay proper and to avoid scandal, (after all, we are living in a convent!) Diri joined them. We knew that in accordance to accepted custom we were supposed to light a match to show that we heard and appreciated their songs, but of course, we had no matches. Instead we kept turning the electric light up and down in lieu of matches..."

Many nations have their own epic poetry, such as the Greek "Iliad," the Finnish "Kalevala," or the German "Song of the Nibelung." It was felt that Hungary lagged in this respect. For this reason a contest was announced in 1846 for the creation of an epic poem. The rules of the contest were that the hero must be a real, historical person, and the poem should have ethnic elements. János Arany, one of the greatest of Hungarian poets, was immediately interested, knew of a person, who would be the perfect fit for the poem, and also knew that he wanted to write it.

Miklós Toldi was a real person. He was a big man of enormous physical strength, a noble but somewhat brooding character and few words. He was the ideal hero for an epic poem and his dramatic story was Arany's entry in the contest. Arany was familiar with his hero's life story; the Toldi clan lived in the same region as Arany, and the heroic doings of the family were cherished and retold many times by the local people. Arany also added legends and adventures from long ago times and introduced other heroes bigger than life, as is expected in epic poetry. He incorporated those traditions, whose roots are almost forgotten but which nevertheless engulf the simple folk, its golden memories, its religion, dreams, pride, morality, conflicts and wisdom. The entries were judged by celebrated authors and poets. Arany won first prize and the epos was an instant success, and is cherished to this day. And...we were required to memorize many, many verses from it.

Mari: We had a rare and exciting experience when the Prior of Reisach not only permitted, but fully supported a conference for Hungarian males; they were really young men rather than boys. They were housed right above our living quarters in the convent. Our excitement was limitless and although we were rigorously guarded and protected, we did manage to have a glance or two at these wonderful, good looking guys, of course without being too obvious about it. We suspect that Piri managed more than just a covert glance because later she married one of them, and they lived happily and in harmony till the day he died many decades later. Just like in the fairy tales.

Ballusz: Having the boys for a few days above our heads was a real trial for poor Diri. He probably developed ulcers during the time, and, with the help of the staff, he guarded us so totally that we barely saw these delightful boys. However, they were resourceful. Their room was above ours. They tied their letters to a string and lowered them from their window down to ours.

On the last evening, Diri relented (probably out of gratitude and relief that it was over) and agreed to accompany us upstairs for an evening of socializing and singing together. By this time though, he managed to subdue us so much that we did not dare mingle but sat bravely and demurely at separate tables, far from the boys, while no doubt most of us had more romantic pictures dancing in our heads.

One of our former schoolmate, Kató Vereczkey, is in the photo.

Nóra: The above-mentioned conference was organized in 1949 by MDSZ, initials in Hungarian for the Hungarian Student Association for university students in Germany. Most of the participants came from München. The main subject of the conference was the situation in Hungary: the occupation by the Soviet Union, the political direction forced upon the country. Scholarly presentations included theories of Marxism, bolshevism, and the communists' takeover of Hungary. Reports were given on arrests of prominent people, Archbishop Mindszenthy among them. The future of the country weighed heavily on all. In retrospect, I wish, we could have participated in this conference. (These details became available only recently).

MEMORIES FROM REISACH:

Some students enrolled in the school for the first time in the fall of 1948 after the regular ten-month school term was already in operation, missing the short term school sessions. Perhaps they heard about the existence of the school too late; or else could not be admitted earlier because of lack of space. They too had lost two or more years of schooling, just like the rest of us. The principal of the school did as much as he could to give these students an opportunity to catch up. One way of accomplishing this was to permit these late-arrivals to complete two grades during one ten-month school year, provided they could keep a decent grade average. Another was to outline the material of the grade level for the students and to permit them to study at home, then at intervals conduct regular examinations at the school to make sure that the students were keeping up with the material. To make this home study option easier for these students, they could stay at the school during the summer vacation while the regular students were gone, and they could get help from the teachers, who of course lived year-round at Niederaudorf, and were always very willing to help. Also the principals offered vacation opportunities with many activities to children while the school at Alpenhof, and later at Reisach were not used during the summer breaks. This practice was enlarged after the move to Reisach and offered summer school for students who attended German schools during the school year. The summer school emphasized language, literature, history, art and geography, as well as folk music of Hungary. It was of great benefit to parents and students, and it also provided some much needed revenue to continue the operation of the school.

Nóra: During the summer of 1950 my sister Piri was appointed to organize the programs for the vacationing children, who stayed at Reisach to participate in the summer school. Six of us from the upper grades were also staying at the school and Piri assigned each of us a small group to supervise and to entertain. In the mornings, there were classes for them to practice the Hungarian language and to learn about the culture of our nation. In the afternoons, we did arts and crafts, played games and went on excursions.

Feri Jautz, a seventh grader, was the oldest of the group, and Piri pulled him from the group of younger kids and promoted him to be assistant to Tony, who

supervised one of the groups. This was an inspired move since Feri was so enchanted by the school's atmosphere that when September came, he enrolled as a full time student.

During their association as "supervisors," he and Tony built a friendship, which is lasting to this day. They were inseparable. Feri wrote in one of his letters: "...*Yes, in 1950 our life improved by leaps and bounds, or so it seemed to us. Tony and I were by then the proud owners of bikes. Somewhat beaten up, 'previously owned' (by more than one person), 'experienced,' or whatever term they use to describe second hand junk on the flea market to make it desirable to the buyer, but they were bikes nonetheless. We worked on them diligently, and in due time, they were once again usable. Only those who remember how it felt to sit for the first time in their very own (used) car are able to appreciate our delight with our glorious transportation. Even rain, a more or less constant condition in the alpine valleys, did not stop us. We pulled our big, black rubber capes over our coats and off we went. When the rain stopped, we unbuttoned our capes and they flapped like huge wings in the wind as we sped down the roads. One day, as we passed a Bavarian farmer, he looked at us with something like awe, and shouted in his heavy accent, 'Do komm's schon wieder die Kloster G'schpenster!' 'Here they come again, the ghosts of the convent!'"*

Nóra writes in a letter at the time *"...An excursion, followed by a camp fire, is planned for tomorrow, and even the littlest ones are joyous and full of expectations. We have seventy of these tykes at our hands, labeled hopefully as the 'future leaders of the nation.' I hope the prophecy will come true. They are cute, charming, smart, enthusiastic, and eat a lot. When they want something, they know how to get it, and also know, how to talk themselves out of some mischief or a sticky situation. So I guess they do have the attributes to become successful diplomats and statesmen..."*

Tóni's and Feri's group heading to the Tatzelwurm waterfall. Summer 1950.

Parents joining one of the weekend excursions.

A walk of Király Éva's and Nünü's group along the Inn river

A group photo of the 1950 Summer School's youngest participants.

August, 1950. Photo was taken a day before some of us left the school forever. Note the cross on top of the roof. Still there a few years after the end of WWII.

Péter: My career at Reisach started in my nebulous childhood when I was six. Like many children of that age, I do not remember too much about those times. As I try very hard to conjure up the past, only some disconnected scenes and emotional states are surfacing. My older brother Tibor was eight when he and I were sent to Reisach to participate in the summer school. I do remember that when we arrived, the children were participating in a noisy and wild "cowboys and Indians" game. We were immediately categorized as Indians and the cowboys tied us to the rain spout of the convent. I remember that it was Andrea Barcsay who rescued me from our precarious situation. Even at age ten, she was already dedicated to protect the weak and the helpless.

I remember more vividly the sad or the bad times than the good ones. The worst was the way I missed my mother. As a farewell present she gave me an orange, a fruit which I have seen for the first time. But for days I did not eat it, but kept it as a talisman, and in my great sadness I even shed some tears on it.

And I remember Father Fekete, who would not give me an eraser during our drawing class, never mind how I begged for it. "No," he insisted. "No eraser. Next time you watch more carefully how you use the precious pencil on the precious paper. We don't waste. This was my introduction to "waste not, want not."

Of course, my big brother, eight year old Tibor was there to protect me from insults and worse, and that was good. I also remember the gentleness of the older girls, our leaders, who often caressed my head as they passed by me.

I remember an excursion along the River Inn. We found what we thought was a foxhole. Dombóváry, driven by his seven year old bravado, climbed into the hole. Upon emerging again, he claimed to have stared eye-to-eye at the fox for a long time, but the fox finally broke down, averted his eyes and whimpered. This by the golden rules of chivalry was a clear victory for Dombóváry in the eye-to-eye contest. He was triumphant and we were awestruck and admired him as our hero. When you are a little kid, you are easy to impress. Since our adventure at the river Inn, we climbed into more "foxholes" at distant places on the globe than we care to remember, and were in eye-to-eye combat with worse than a fox, but we did not get any admiration for it and nobody was awestruck.

Ákos: I spent the summer of 1950 at Reisach enrolled in the summer school. Dombóváry was the gang-leader. I admired his wildness and his dedication to free the Indians in our game, although, to be quite honest, I lacked some of his bravado and I also feared the consequences. My fear was well founded because it did not take too long for the principal, Endre Román, to notice and evaluate the situation. He did not care about our shooting the Igo-Kemenes brothers, Tibor and Péter, with arrows from our bows. The brothers were not only without weapons, but in addition they were tied to the rainspout and could not escape or defend themselves. The principal was of the opinion that our behavior was not exactly in the class of chivalry. I think finally my sister Andrea interfered, but what else but interference can one expect from girls? At any rate, we received a sound spanking. Our principal also took a dim view of our other cherished occupation: we were hiding in the bushes across the convent and were shooting arrows at the passing German children. That earned us another thorough spanking.

I do not know where all the bows and arrows came from, and I do not know who imagined that these would be appropriate toys for 6-10 year old ruffians. I also do not remember whether they finally confiscated the deadly weapons, or just continued to mete out more spankings for misusing them.

(As far as we know, Péter is the only student who attended all five Hungarian schools in Germany. First, he spent a year at Reisach and when the school closed he moved on to Passau. When that school also closed he enrolled at Lindenberg which also closed. He then moved to the only refugee school still in existence: Bauschlott. Eventually Bauschlott also closed, but he still had a year to complete before graduation. As was his fate, he again enrolled in a new school which just opened: at Burg Kastl.

Eventually the refugees either returned home or immigrated somewhere on the planet and as a consequence the initial four refugee schools closed. But in 1957, a year after the Hungarian Revolution, a new Hungarian school opened at Burg Kastl, Germany. By that time the difficulties of the post war years were gone and almost forgotten. Burg Kastl was well equipped and the parents of the students were well off financially, many of them living in other countries, or on other continents. They sent their children to Burg Kastl so that they could receive not just a classical education, but also be instructed in Hungarian history, language and literature. Burg Kastl operated in the same general spirit as the four initial schools, but it served a different student body, satisfied different needs and operated in a vastly different environment than its four predecessors.

After Péter graduated at Burg Kastl, he attended the six hundred year old university of Leuven in Belgium, in the center of Europe and of international distinction. It serves 31,000 students, including foreigners from 120 countries and has always been a loadstone for intellectuals from the days when Desiderius Erasmus taught there. Péter earned his doctorate in physics there; then moved to Genf (Geneva) to do research in particle physics at CERN. CERN stands for "Centre Européen pour la Recherche Nucléaire" or European Organization for Nuclear Physics. Established in 1952, it has the world's largest laboratory for this purpose, and provides state-of-the-art research facilities to astronomers and astrophysicists. Since 1992 Hungary is also a member of CERN, and Péter had a major role in the admission process. In 1981-83 he was teaching at the University of Columbia (N.Y.) then returned to Genf to continue his research and to teach at the University there.

His brother and fellow sufferer, who was bound along with him to the rainspout at Reisach is now teaching chemistry at the University of München's medical school.

Their parents too applied for immigration permits to the USA, but were rejected on the ground that the family included a set of grandparents. The immigration officials found that this family could be a burden to the United States because they might not be able to support the grandparents, and therefore might require social help. (A good thing Andrea freed them from their potentially fatal predicament at the rainspout and from the arrows of the cowboys. The world would be poorer without these two brilliant Indians.)

Ballusz: After the Christmas break my younger sister Marika was also enrolled at Reisach. The two of us arrived together at the school just when Diri's door flew open and he barreled out of their room screaming and carrying a Christmas tree in flames. He was heading top speed to the huge stone wash basin in the hallway to douse the tree. "It seems like a lively place, burning with excitement," my sister calmly summarized her first impression of our school.

As was mentioned before, our school was built next to the church. There was a quiet little shrine near the entrance, always open, always lit up by the soft light of candles. A few of us had the habit of slipping out from our living quarters for a quick prayer in the quiet of the shrine. Klári, Koci, Vica and Mészárka used to accompany us, but their ritual of "adoration" was of a different kind. As soon as we reached the shrine the foursome disappeared behind the bushes to indulge in smoking a secret cigarette. I couldn't imagine that Diri and the teachers were unaware of the situation because the four reeked of the tobacco and in good weather the smell of smoke could be detected a mile away. My suspicion was confirmed at the St. Nicholas festivity. According to our tradition a short ditty was written about every one of the girls, and then recited either by an angel or a devil, depending whether it was a question of sin or virtue. Diri's wife insisted that she'd author the verse about Klári. It went something like this:

"In the bedroom on top of the bunk bed,
from nosy mortal eyes well concealed
like an Olympian goddess our Klári sat
her divine form enfolded in bluish mist.
No one knows whence the gossamer shroud was blown thither,
Was it a holy cloud or was it just smoke which completely hid her?"

Or something like this. She was the poet, not I.

Of course, Diri's wife indulged in pure fiction. Nobody ever smoked in the bedroom. We were too aware that we were sleeping on straw sacks, drier than gunpowder, prone to go up in flames at the mere mentioning of fire. Diri's wife could never have seen Klára or anyone else smoke in the bedroom—or indeed anywhere inside the Kloster. They always left the premises most discreetly to indulge in their sin. Was it a gentle warning to the foursome about something they guessed but did not know for sure? I suppose they were also lenient. We were nearing graduation and soon would be counted as adults, and if some of us wished to smoke, they did not see any reason in fighting it. Sixty years ago smoking was not at all the Public Enemy Nr. 1, as it is today. It was discovered only later what it could do to a body.

One year we realized too late that in addition to our own mother, we ought to celebrate Diri's wife, Erzsi *Néni* and also Mária *Néni*. It was too late to prepare anything, so a council was called to find a solution. After countless unworkable schemes were dismissed, eventually it was decided—bolstered by an old Hungarian tradition according to which it is not a sin to steal flowers—that we should do just that. We concluded that we must steal. Since the decent Bavarian farmers went to bed when the hens did, that is at sundown, we were pretty sure that we would be undetected in a nightly raid. In the cover of the conveniently dark night we snuck out of the convent to accomplish our mission.

Every house in the village boasted several lilac bushes and their fragrance intoxicated the night air. We rationalized that the owners would never miss a few branches if there were lots of it there in the first place, so we selected a house with the most lilac bushes. When we cut enough branches for two bouquets, we planned to depart the scene of crime just as quietly as we came. But as we reached the gate of the farmer's house, dark figures blocked it. Shall I say we got scared? That would be the understatement of the post-war years. It is to our credit that we did not scream. I guess this is what they mean when they say "was speechless in terror" or in our case paralyzed into a totally soundless state. All we could do is just stare like animals at night when confronted with headlights; I am sure the farmer (had he imbibed one less bottle of beer before going to bed) could have woken up from the sound of our beating heart.

But then it turned out that the menacing figures were not highwaymen, but the very German boys, who followed our every move since we settled in their village. It is to their credit that they did not betray us. As a matter of fact, they courteously accompanied us back home to the safety of our convent in true knightly fashion.

In the spring Markóczi was very ill. I don't know what ailed her, and I suspect Dr. Arnold didn't either. She was so weak, she could not walk, could not eat, and had a host of other problems. We put her in the trusty hand wagon, our "ambulance," and two girls pulled her into the village, where, after a short examination, Dr. Arnold announced that she was suffering from hunger edema. He thought she did not get enough nutrients and therefore requisitioned extra food ration cards for her. He also encouraged the drinking of goat's milk, which at that time was considered the miracle stuff good for almost everything from broken bone through dandruff to tuberculosis. Diri made inquiries, made the situation clear to a farmer who owned some goats, and after some soulful explanations on Diri's part, (he was always rather good at convincing anyone), the farmer was willing to supply the coveted milk. Tony and Zsolt were detailed to bring the milk home daily from the village. As they were nearing the Kloster, they commenced bleating loudly to announce their arrival. They sounded frightfully like real goats.

About this same time my sister Marika had an unfortunate accident. She was playing handball with her friends in the adjoining field. It was dusk and she did not see the barbed wire fence. She ran straight into it full speed and literally sliced her legs into strips. Poor kid had so much pain she could only whimper. Now we had two invalids, and neither could walk. Diri and the staff decided both needed fresh air before they got even sicker. Diri got two army cots from somewhere, placed them in the meadow, and we carried first the beddings, then the girls outdoors, where they could rest and study so they would not fall too far behind in the school work. One sunny afternoon the Kloster's total silence was pierced by the screaming of the two Márias. Diri and the boys flew out at top speed to see who is killing the girls. They almost choked laughing when they saw the scene. Apparently the cows, grazing in contentment in the next field as is expected of decent alpine cows, found a way to enter the meadow where the girls were resting. This certainly should have been the picture of the year: the two screaming girls immobilized on their cots were surrounded by the most peaceful and lackadaisical alpine cows in the valley, wondering no doubt about the strange welcome greeting, members of the human race offered.

Koci: When the weather was good, we loved to study outside. The field across our school was ideal. It had sunny spots for the sun-worshippers, and shades under the trees for the rest of us. I remember the young Carmelite brothers coming home from the fields, bone tired, and their brown habit covered with dust after a day of hard physical labor. When they were aware that in the field next to the road we were watching their progress, their embarrassment could not be hidden. They marched on with bent heads, never looking to their left where we sat in groups, but always straight down at the pavement in front of them. I guess they considered our presence a temptation of the devil, and even just glancing our way must have been a sin for them. They were so serious, so sweet and so young. We wondered about all they had to give up in order to follow their calling.

Béla: I enrolled at Reisach in 1950. Tony, Feri and I had a room in the village at the Wechselberger's, but spent most of the day at the school. Endre Román was the principal by then. We had instructions 8-14 every day and spent the afternoons studying and preparing for the following day. We enjoyed the evenings most when our principal and Father Fekete as well as some of the teachers sat around the big dining room table and we carried on great discussions. The adults brought their rich store of knowledge and their patience, and we, our youthful curiosity and idealism to  the "round table." We talked about all sorts things, such as Man's mission on earth; the reason for our existence; about the future and our place in it; about the oldest enigma of evil existing in the world which is created by an all-good and perfect God; our unusual experiences during the last few years; and the necessity and difficulty of trying to forgive those who caused our losses. We wondered what logic the Universe has, and in general, does it have any sense, and if so, must we understand it? And we asked whether it would ever be possible to comprehend the mind of God, or His plans. And then the inevitable question came up: how far will civilization evolve and what will mankind do with its spectacular accomplishments and successes? And how long can Earth with its dwindling supplies sustain mankind? Are we nearing the end of the world as we know it?

When once we talked into the night, the Principal finally closed the discussion by quoting from one of the greatest Hungarian literary works "The Tragedy of Man."

> *"It's done. The great act of creation.*
> *The maker rests. The wheel's in motion*
> *And will rotate upon its axle for*
> *A hundred million years before a single cog wears out."*

"So it is," said Father Fekete adding another often quoted line from the masterpiece: "*Oh Man! Strive on, strive on! And have faith and trust!*" He was silent for a few minutes than added with conviction, "This is really all we can do: work and believe.

And love. And one day we shall meet again at the final destination at our eternal home, and we shall all find out the truth and all the answers. Until then, a good night and a refreshing rest to you all."

Imre Madách (1823-1864) was the author of "The Tragedy of Man," a major dramatic poem of approximately 4000 lines long, the most brilliant diamond in the rich literary treasure house of Hungary. It is mandatory reading for students in Hungarian high schools, and then again at the college level. Many of its lines have become often repeated quotes, such as the two above. It is also the central piece of repertoire of the Hungarian theatres. Yet, at the beginning, it was only known in its printed form because at that time theatres did not have the technical means to arrange the stage for the 15 totally different scenes.

Madách, a nobleman of considerable wealth and having had a distinctive education, was a much suffering individual. He lost his father early and he suffered from ill health from his youth on. He participated in the failed struggle to free Hungary from the Habsburg oppression, and ended up with a prison sentence. After he was released, he was kept under constant surveillance and the proceeds of his estates were sequestered. His sister, his nephew, and his brother-in-law were beaten to death by Rumanian peasants, whose loyalty never belonged to Hungary. A year later, his younger brother died of pneumonia. He was agonizing over the failed attempt to free Hungary, and finally his marriage ended in divorce. Yet in his short life, he created enduring and uplifting literature. Reading it, or seeing it on stage, is not only a true literary experience, but offers material for philosophical contemplations as well.

As the main protagonists, Adam and Eve visit from scene to scene the most important historical times and sites. Their discussions touch the existence of good, love, art, science, greed, lusting for power and so on.

The main characters of this monumental drama are Adam, Eve, Lucifer and occasionally the voice of an invisible God. The threesome are traveling through the entire span of human history, from the caves to a future, frozen world. The goal of Lucifer is to convince Adam that life is meaningless and mankind is doomed.

Many analyst do not feel that the drama of mankind found a solution in this monumental work, but others are of a different opinion. When the three arrive at the most hopeless, most inhuman scene of the history of mankind, when it seems that Adam is ready to admit the senselessness of the world and of life, when he is ready to admit that the hopeless struggle is futile, when he is ready to give up, Eve whispers to him: "I am, oh Adam, I am with child." And having a child gives a different perspective, and Adam is ready to accept the decree of God: "Oh Man! Strive on, strive on! And have faith and trust!" And Adam is willing once again to work for the future because the new life wakens his sense of responsibility and the love of life.

Feri: I was one of those home study students, at least in the beginning of my school career. Fortunately I had an aunt, who was a teacher in a *gimnázium* in Hungary and she sent me some textbooks. With the help of the books, with the determination of my father to beat some knowledge into my often unwilling brain, and the good fortune of my being able to spend two months at the summer school at Reisach, I was able to complete three grades during a fifteen month period. This I have to thank my father, who never let up, although if I recall correctly I did not appreciate it at that time. He made me memorize a list of poems and the entire fourth song of Toldi. And yes, I could recite it today if anybody would be interested hearing it. At any rate, I passed my examinations with decent grades and by September I was enrolled at Reisach as a full time student. All that studying paid off.

The three of us (Feri, Béla and Tony) were best friends and the friendship lasts to this day. In the evenings, when we were back at our night accommodation, we requisitioned the pots and pans from the kitchen of our landlady (against her objections), and improvised impressive jazz numbers. She did not appreciate it. She claimed, it disturbed her husband's sleep. We were understanding, but tried to explain to her that we were raised on the glorious sounds of the AFN (American Forces Network) and we imbibed jazz along with mother's milk. (Naturally not true because we never heard it until we had access to AFN—and by that time we did not imbibe any mother's milk, but let her figure out that one.) We also assured her that one day we'll be very famous jazz interpreters and she'll be glad that she knew us way back when. She pretended not to understand. And they say that Germans are all such gifted musicians!

I remember that we were often homesick. By that I don't mean just missing our parents, although that too was part of it. But homesickness for us was much more: a yearning for the home we lost, for the relatives and friends, whom we might never see again. A yearning for the security which we have lost. I often dreamt about my room which I left behind, and about my things, my personal treasures. Painfully I remembered the winter evenings when the family sat together in the old, familiar living room and played board games, or worked on some project. What we felt was a complex sadness made up of many things, like a life style lost forever. John Ciardi touched on it so well when he wrote in <u>Talking Myself to Sleep</u>:

> "There was a house as sure as time
> Sure as my father's name and grave."

And then it was all gone and nothing was sure any more. But we compensated. We mourned for our grandparents, who were unbelievably far and unreachable, and we filled the horrible loss by building enduring friendships. Our schoolmates became the substitutes for our lost family. But he pain of homesickness remained then and in way is still with us today.

Excerpt from a letter from Australia: *"...I finished reading the Koncz-Hegedűs documentary—not just our part of Niederaudorf-Reisach, but the entire book, including the histories of Passau, Lindberg and Bauschlott. The biography section was the most amazing part for me; I could not stop marveling about the achievements of former students. We in Australia were less lucky and could not develop quite as freely as you; therefore, we could offer less to our new country than you, who immigrated to the USA.*

Upon our arrival in Australia around 1948-1949, all who were over eighteen years old, were required to sign a contract, according to which we were obligated for a period of two years to accept any job the government planned for us. These were exclusively menial positions or common labor assignments not requiring any skills and paying minimal wages. We cleaned, shoveled, built roads, or worked in the agriculture. We were dead tired, demoralized, could not properly acquire the language, so even after our obligatory two years of labor were completed most of us could not get a decent job for some time. For most of us further schooling was not an option. Of course by and by we too made a good living, and are very happy and grateful to have the privilege to live in our new home, but we cannot show as many brilliant achievements as you have in the US because we were so thwarted in the beginning.

I always thought that one of Hungary's recent tragedies was the enormous brain-drain toward the end of WW II, when the great westward exodus began, and highly educated, skilled and talented people left the country. A nation of a mere ten million cannot afford the loss of several hundred thousand intellectual resources. Hungary became poorer and the US richer.

In the same way I feel that the Australian nation too lost out by its very harsh policy of suppressing the new-comers, and by not utilizing and supporting their talents. Now that I read what you could and did offer in your new home, I am more than ever convinced that the American policy of supporting talent and education was more cost-effective, and the results are certainly not to be disregarded...."

THE LAST YEARS OF OUR SCHOOL

Ferenc Cserháti:
"The years of 1948-1949 were extremely difficult for the staff, and foreshadowed the end of the school. Patience was exhausted, nerves frayed and the presence of constant insecurity because of the looming financial disaster were weighing heavily on the adults. When the immigration wave started, first slowly then at increasing speed, the enrollment dwindled by mid-term and new worries surfaced. The worries were not only of a financial nature, but the loss of carefully selected, excellent teachers also was a blow to the school. From the staff the first to leave in April, 1949 were the sisters Sarolta Takáts (Sári), teacher of mathematics, physics; and Erzsébet, (Erzsi), teacher of language, literature, art history. Mária Bárány the housemother and teacher of the lower grades soon followed. About a third of the students did not return after the spring break; they waited at home for the call to board ship. Ferenc Kovács the principal tried to hold the school together. He hired new teachers, not an easy task at the time when everybody was getting ready to immigrate somewhere. He also attempted to recruit new students, which of course toward the end of the school year was quite futile. Many, whom he contacted, simply could not afford the tuition; other would-be students, like everybody else, were waiting for the call to board ship.

Ferenc Kovács was also concerned about the 'private students,' so called because due to lack of space at the school, financial or other problems, were forced to study at home on their own with the help of occasional tutors whenever they were lucky enough to find one. These students only came to the school for examinations. Their test scores were far below those of the boarding school students, and the principal felt responsible for the low performance. At the same time he did not wish the standard and reputation of the school to suffer. To improve the performance level of these students he accepted 25 of them to participate in intensive training during the summer break when the regular students left for vacation. While they could not afford to stay at the school year-round, the parents did manage to cover the cost for the short summer break. They were instructed by six teachers during this time. At the examinations they showed marked improvement in their test scores and at the same time the fees paid by these students improved the financial situation of the school.

At this time there were three official elementary schools operating in Bavaria: at Waldwerke, Plattling and Kinzing; two middle-high schools: at Reisach and at Passau-Waldwerke. 292 students were attending Hungarian schools: 127 as full time students in middle and high schools; 75 as home study students; 90 elementary students. The schools were served by twenty-nine educators.

In August of 1949 the efforts of Mrs. Ernő Lits and Mr. Gusztáv Hennyey paid off: the teachers received a regular salary from the IRO (International Refugee Organization) which in turn was supported by a USA based committee. But then unexpectedly shortly after the good news in December 1949 the IRO terminated the employment of all teachers and the hope for the continuing existence of the school was once again crushed. Yet despite the seemingly insurmountable problems, the school managed to survive almost two more years."

Voices of students:

Ballusz: During the spring break Sári *Néni* and Erzsi *Néni* left to immigrate to the UK. Diri, the teachers and six of us, who stayed at school during the break, accompanied them to the train station. Appropriately we transported their suitcases in our hand wagon. It was a sad little group saying farewell to the two sisters we loved. We knew that school won't be the same without Sári *Néni*'s biting but witty remarks and without Erzsi *Néni*'s gentleness and much appreciated tendency to close her eyes to our failings.

On the left, one of our rare photos of Erzsi *Néni*, Mária *Néni* and Sári *Néni*. On the right, farewell photo at the Oberaudorf railroad station. The Takács sisters are leaving for England. Mária *Néni*'s mother, who cooked for us at Reisach, is the small women behind the wagon, third from right. Others from left: Éva Balla, Mária Hochenburger, Erzsi *Néni*, Marika Balla,, Erzsébet Kovács, Laci Kardos, Sári *Néni* and Mária Bárány.

Ballusz: Diri hired new teachers. One of them was Béla Csikesz, young, good looking and kind. The girls in the lower grades were madly "in love" with him, and were not at all bothered by the fact that he was happily married and that he was the father of a new baby. The girls loved him, loved his wife and fought for the privilege of pushing the buggy with the baby during the afternoon walks.

With Béla Csikesz are:
Zsuzsa Petres
Judit Király
Marika Balla

Nóra: When we returned to school in the fall of 1949, we found a totally new teaching staff, headed by a new principal, Endre Roman. A large group of students did not return because their immigration was imminent. All through the school year students left to board some ship to sail away to a new, far away home. Our enrollment dwindled to a handful of students. The last year was a long series of farewells as our friends left one by one. It was truly painful. We belonged together; we were a family. We already lost so much in life and this new and prolonged loss was miserable. We did not cry during the bad times but we shed plenty of tears at all the farewells.

1950-51. The last group of students.

Names are given as in Hungarian: last name first, with proper accent marks.
We were able to identify Lahner Béla, Jautz Feri, Mayer Teréz, **Király Éva**, Király Judit, Bakcsy Emőke, Égi Éva. Mélynádasy Tóni not in the picture. He was the photographer.

As we were writing the book about our school, official information was not available to us about the last years at Reisach. It is not known whether the principals following Ferenc Kovács stopped sending reports to the School Committee, or else the reports were lost. Ferenc Cserháti's valuable essay also ended at about this point, probably because he too lacked official information about the last two years. We can report about this time only what the former students remember. Especially helpful were the contributions of Tony Meynadasy, Béla Lahner and Feri Jautz because they were present until the school closed in 1951; as a matter of fact, they were there to move the school's furnishing to Passau, and then on to Waldwerke.(Later, as enrollment dwindled even there, it fused with Lindenberg until that too closed. In the end only Bauschlott remained. It operated until 1956. And with that the chapter of the postwar refugee school's history closed.)

Béla: In the spring of 1951 it was evident that Reisach no longer could sail on its own, weakly supported by occasional chance winds. After some heartbreaking considerations, it has been decided to fuse it with the school of Passau-Waldwerke.

The principal was then Dr. Árpád Marcell, and he asked the three of us (Tony, Feri and me) to help move the school's furnishings. It took us two days. An American army truck came to our help. First we dismantled the bunk beds, and then loaded them on the truck. The next day we returned and piled all the chairs, tables, kitchen utensils and whatever else were left on the big vehicle. And this was the end of our beloved school. Tony and Feri continued to study at Passau-Waldwerke, but I had to leave in May, as we were called to Bremen to board ship.

Feri: I love your royal plural, Béla! What do you mean by saying "we" dismantled? You made me do it, by declaring that I am supposed to be an expert because, so you claimed, my father was a joiner. I tried to explain to you that someone dealing in antiques is not the same as a joiner, but you just ignored me, and let me do the dirty work. And that is the truth, as I know it.

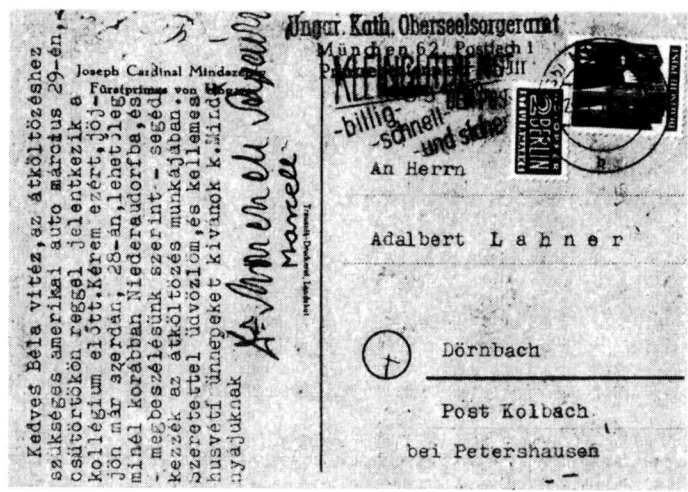

Béla Lahner saved this postcard, in which the principal asked Béla to return to school by March 28, (1951), to help with the move. We are so grateful to him and to all the other students, who shared with us their documents, photos, memories. Our bond was strengthened.

****

But we continued our rigorous schedule of studying with the same determination as before, even though we were not overly happy with our new teachers. We often felt that they were not properly prepared and they had a rigid teaching style, which often bored us. We were spoiled by the quality of teaching we had before. We must truthfully admit that after we were exposed to the teaching of Diri and his wife, or indeed to the quality of presentation of all of our teachers, nobody could have pleased us. We had the best. But we trudged on, continued to take our walks, went on excursions and continued our sport and scout activities. But our soul was no longer in it. Studying was now a job dutifully performed without excitement and without the giddy sense of discovering the world with its mysteries. We once again discovered the ancient truth: the secret of a successful educational program are not determined by rules, restrictions, plans, monetary support or incentives. The true secrets for success are the inspired, unusual and gifted teachers, whether trained for their vocation or not. The example of this truth is the long list of men and women, who could and did change the world, starting with Solomon, but including such diverse personalities as Socrates, Confucius, Aesop, Plato, Jesus, St. Paul, Anne Sullivan Macy, Andrea de Verracchio, Noah Webster, Albert Einstein or J. Piaget. This list of course does not pretend to be complete or perhaps not even fully representative, but it shows the diverse talents by which the interest of those who seek knowledge can be captured.

Jutka: Life was changing; the tone of the school was changing. Most of our friends with whom we started this unbelievable adventure in "the school in a hotel," have already left to start a new life in countries and cities, the existence of which were vague, and only dimly recalled from our geography lessons. Those who were returning after the Christmas break were waiting any minute for the call to return home because their turn to board some troop ship finally arrived. After the spring break our school's enrollment shrank to half its starting number. New teachers, new students came, but it was not the same, and we all felt the loss. At the end of the school year Vica, Iván and Kati graduated, and we cried at the final ceremony because we knew that we won't ever see them again; the farewell was final.

The teachers too had their own dramas and had to work out their own insecurities and disappointments. Up to the time when the massive immigration started around 1950 they were dedicated to teach in the spirit as if they were really preparing us for a return to Hungary some day very soon. But when teachers and students disappeared into the far continents, the structure of their illusion collapsed. They must have questioned what was the sense of it? Why did they insist on the Hungarian language, history and literature, why did they torture us with two thousand years of European history? Would it not have made more sense to intensively teach English, Portuguese and Spanish instead of Latin and German? Would it not have been more useful to teach some practical skills, which could be used in a new country? And anyhow, what is to become of all of us?

At that time neither teachers nor students realized yet the lasting impression the school made on us. Nobody guessed that in the relatively short time we spent there our teachers laid the foundation for our future successes. True, we were immersed in our Hungarian heritage, but that never prevented any of us to become loyal citizens of whichever country accepted us and offered a new home. In this way, perhaps, we could even add a little color to the existing fabric of the accepting nation. And it is also true that all the involvement with abstract ideas paid rich dividends in later years. But we did not know it at that time.

And we also did not know that the farewells were not really final. At a time when the train fare for even a short distance was beyond our means, we could not imagine that a time would come when the distance (and the expense) between continents would cause no problems, and that we would meet again, and again.

At that time the farewell seemed final and we cried. Yet, we met again, and many of us took our children back to Niederaudorf to show them the site where we grew to adulthood and where despite all odds we were very happy. In turn our children took their children to see the magical place where we lived, learned, laughed and metamorphosed from frightened children into happy, self-assured and independent adults. And the grandchildren understood that parents transfer their values to the next generation and the secret of their budding character, unbelievable as it sounds, is rooted at Niederaudorf where their grandparents absorbed the philosophy of life. The bond we created among each other never broke, and this belonging together lived on in our children, and in our grandchildren. Old age and the uneasy waiting for death ("the day and the hour are not known") does not seem frightening to us because in a way we see how our life, and our ideals continue in the next generations. In this way we'll live on, at least as long as the values are kept.

Many years later, there was an international jamboree for scouts in Canada. On the last day of the jamboree the son of a "sister," who immigrated to South America, called me. It turned out that there was a group of six Hungarian scouts, teenage boys and girls the same age as our own children, who, after the jamboree, had about a week left before they returned to their respective countries. Could they spend this week at our house, home away from home, in Aurora, Ohio, he asked. My husband and I were delighted to host them, and spent an unforgettable week with the new generation of Hungarians, who all spoke fluent Hungarian.

On the last evening, we were sitting around the supper table when I reminded my guests that they need to call the respective airlines to confirm their flight reservation back home. There was a wall phone in the dining room and my young friends, one after the other, picked up the receiver. First the two from Caracas called Viassa airlines and confirmed in rapid Spanish; then the one from San Paolo talked to Varig in Portuguese. Next was the boy from France, speaking French to Air France; the one from California called Delta, and finally the young lady from Germany confirmed with Lufthansa.

Suddenly there was a heavy silence around the dining table. After all the calls were completed, somebody remarked haltingly, trying to find the meaning of what we just witnessed and to put into words what the little scene really meant.

"Strange," he mused. "We are all Hungarians, yet a minute ago we had no idea what each of you said on the phone."

"My mother had planted a gingko tree in our yard," added the one from California. "She spoke about a poem from Goethe, which she learned at the school in Niederaudorf. He was writing about the leaf of the gingko which is one, and yet divided. Just like us."

Only the Lufthansa connection, who attended German schools, knew the poem and she recited quietly the last line: "Fühlst du nicht an meinen Liedern, daß ich eins und doppelt bin?"

"OK Smarty, translate," was the unanimous request.

"I wouldn't dare blaspheme the hallowed words of Goethe, but the meaning of the line is exactly what you just said: we are one, yet double. One, yet somewhere, somehow divided, and so we are dual."

CONCLUSION

In 2006 we had a reunion at Niederaudorf which, because of our advanced age and increasingly limited mobility, turned out to be the last for the group, at least in Europe. It was here that the idea of placing a commemorating tablet on the wall of our former school was suggested. We all felt a need, or more correctly expressed a keen desire for this. The school was important to us, but above and beyond this, we were convinced then, as we are convinced now, that our story is not only part of the saga told in a personal way of an unusual time period, but it played a significant role in the way our life turned out, and in the way we later made the significant choices. We wanted to have a permanent memento to remind people of the existence of an unusual school, and we wanted to remind future generations of the true miracle of our existence on this planet: the unbeatable spirit of mankind. The feeling ran deeply and was fed by the mysterious source of idealism and the very human wish of leaving a physical mark of some exceptional accomplishment. But in cooler, more rational moments, we were afraid that our desire touched on the sentimental, immature regions of our soul. Sentimentality is not particularly endearing at any age, and past eighty, it should be avoided at all costs. To steer clear of the ridiculous and the maudlin, we joked away the schmaltzy aspect of our eagerness, and called the tablet blasphemously "our sacred graffiti," or at times referred to it in the sentiment of the young, who like to scribble, etch, paint, carve on any patient surface something like: "Observe: we slept here."

Many years ago Father Fekete, our instructor in religion and ethics told us that mankind can be divided into two groups: those who create and those who destroy; but we are also to remember that those who do not do anything for the betterment of the world, belong to the group of destructors. Then he added that no matter where fate would place us in the future, we are always expected to act as representatives of Hungary, and beyond that, be ambassadors of a spiritual and intellectual realm which is the inheritance of everyone, and which gives content to meaningful human life everywhere on earth.

We felt that despite some limitations and obstacles, we more or less did fulfill this expectation, and wanted to have it remembered in a material form, visible to those who pass by. Beyond this, we also felt gratitude to the villages of Niederaudorf and Reisach, to the owners of the Alpenhof, the Carmelite order and the Kolping Foundation because they gave us a home and helped us to continue our education in those difficult years. The tablet then was to be a sincere thank you note as well.

We unanimously agreed to place it on the inside wall of the church of Reisach as that being the most appropriate location. This was a noble and enthusiastic decision, but to accomplish the plan was quite another matter. Anikó Radnay from Australia volunteered to set the plan into motion, but despite repeated correspondence, she did not even so much as receive an answer to her letters. The plan was then slumbering for a year or two until Zsuzsa Petres shook the plan to life once again. Fortunately for us, Zsuzsa is the type who, when starting something, will never let it slip out of her hands. A relative of hers lovingly, admiringly but rather stridently compared her to a dog: "She has the bone-complex. Like the dog, she would never let go of the bone once given to her."

Zsuzsa, like Aniko, had a formidable amount of difficulties to overcome, namely the great geographical distances between the aging former students; the establishing of the financial basis for the venture; finding the officials across the Atlantic, who could help; and finally, overcoming the most difficult hurdle: the red tape dance with German authorities. Since our life there, the Kloster of Reisach has been declared a "historical building," protected and registered, hence more or less untouchable. According to this protective law, renovations or even slight changes, such as fixing a memorial tablet on the wall, can be undertaken only with special permits from the Historical Society, and of course this is routinely denied. Anybody who ever had to obtain a special permit can appreciate the difficulties this involves. I dare say, these difficulties multiply many times in Germany where officials confess the creed hourly: "Ordnung muss sein," (things must be regulated in an orderly manner) — and where this motto is surely tattooed somewhere on their body. In correct translation this means: the petitioner arrives at the proverbial brick wall. Verboten. Not allowed, or more correctly: forbidden.

When it seemed even to Zsuzsa that the proposal must die again, she acted with great resolve. This is her account:

"It was in December 2010 when Nóra Sztáray brought to my attention an article that was published by Fr. Imre Tempfli about a Catholic priest conference, held in Kufstein, Austria. Bishop Ferenc Cserháti was the organizer of the event, and part of his lecture dealt with post war Catholic youth's religious life. He was quite knowledgeable on the subject. His research about our school was completed in 1999, and published in his Catholic circular. At the Kufstein conference he talked about the Hungarian school in nearby Niederaudorf-Reisach and suggested an outing to view the school's location. Everyone enthusiastically agreed, and later unanimously stated that a commemorating plaque would be very appropriate.

Nóra knew that for years I was intrigued by the thought of a memorial plaque and suggested I get in touch with Father Tempfli. He proved to be a valuable ally and it was with his help that a correspondence was established with Bishop Cserháti, which led to a highly successful meeting in Cleveland in 2011 where we found that his and our hopes for the plaque converged, and could be realized. So now the scene was set."

His Excellency Ferenc Cserháti, who by this time was the bishop of Hungarians in exile, and was touring the cities in the US where Hungarians lived, knew about, and sympathized with our long-ago survival struggles, and fully understood the present difficulties we were now facing in placing the tablet. As a result, His Excellency joined Zsuzsa in her efforts. With his support, she was now able to make some progress, and move some stubborn stones. The current Prior of Reisach, Pater Bruno, as well as the mayor of Oberaudorf Herr Wildgruber, became involved. They were both helpful beyond any call of duty, and without their help, and His Excellency's support, and despite Zsuzsa's "dogged" insistence, our dream would have died in its infancy. (By this time she authored something like two hundred letters, e-mails and countless transatlantic phone calls. Some of us felt that she too deserves a memorial tablet!)

At long last, the permit was granted for the tablet, but not to be placed inside the church as we originally planned, but on the outside wall of the Kloster, right under the first floor windows—our former dormitory windows. As it turned out, the newly designated site of the commemorative tablet was far better than what we first chose: it can be well seen from the road and also from the trains, which pass every half hour almost directly by this wall. Trains always slow down at this section—not so much to honor us or our tablet, but because right at that spot there is a pedestrians' crossing over the tracks. Anyone, who cares, can comfortably read the text in his seat through the window of the train.

Originally, Zsuzsa and her husband designed a bronze tablet, but on learning that it would be placed on an outside wall, rather than inside the church, the bronze was cancelled and weather-resistant granite had to be considered.

In the fall of 2011, the four of us (Zsuzsa, Nóra, Piri and I) met at my "House by the Lake" in Hungary to make final plans. By invoking the spirit of Sári Néni, our former math teacher, we jogged our brain for the formula of the Golden Section to figure out the correct and pleasing proportion of the enlarged tablet. Once this was decided, we finalized the Hungarian and German wording.

An added problem was that we wanted to include the Hungarian coat of arms, but it is so intricate that stone cutters would not accept the order of carving it into granite. But luck was with us again: after searching endless antique and souvenir shops, we finally found the one, which was perfect in size, quality of workmanship, and material. The crest, made of bronze, was then worked into the granite tablet.

Because of its great weight and size, and its potential fragility, it was decided that the tablet should be made in Hungary. The Hegedűs sisters chose the services of an excellent stonemason in Sopron. Our alumnae from all over the world contributed to the expenses, and the sisters, Piri and Nóra transported it by car from Sopron to Reisach.

As the Bard said, all is well that ends well.

May 5, 2012 was the day when in a figurative way, we put the period on the unusual saga of our school. Only six of the former students could make the long and exhausting trip to Reisach: Gabi, Nóra, Piri and Zsuzsa from the USA; Anikó from Australia; and Jutka from Hungary.

The festivities started with "pomp and circumstances:" a Holy Mass at the Reisach church, co-celebrated by His Excellency Bishop Ferenc Cserháti, the Prior Father Bruno, Father Derka and Pater Joachim. The Hungarian scouts provided the guard of honor, and hundreds attended the service: the Hungarian consul of Bavaria, Mr. Tamás Mylo; Mayor Herbert Wildgruber from Oberaudorf; local dignitaries; Germans from the surrounding villages; Hungarians from as far away as Innsbruck, Salzburg, Stuttgart. and Rosenheim; the grandson of our first principal, István Ravasz, who came from Hungary for the occasion; the daughter and granddaughter of Éva Tirczka our former school mate, now living in Brazil. Mother and daughter, (just like the grandmother was, and still is) are active scouts, and their presence in uniform emphasized the importance of the scouting organization to Hungarians.

After the mass, the procession moved outside, to the wall of the Kloster where the commemorative tablet was unveiled, and speeches were delivered. A small reception followed at the Alpenhof, and Istók's poem, the one which introduces this book, was read by Emese Rátfai from Budapest.

It was an emotional and uplifting experience. The life paths of the former students, after branching off in different directions on the planet, and were played out in alternating successes and dramas, met again at Niederaudorf. It was truly unusual that the original chronicler of our history, His Excellency Ferenc Cserháti, in his new dignity as bishop, was with us.

We knew that this was to be our last trip to Niederaudorf, but we were happy and content to know that the story was thus completed and sealed with a tablet on the wall to mark an unusual time and an unusual school. It won't be soon forgotten, and will remind people that the human spirit can be hurt, injured, beaten but not destroyed.

Our goal has been accomplished.

The guests were departing, the intermittent rain of the day was clearing and the six of us, lone representatives of the once vibrant boarding school, stood at the large glass window of the dining room at the Alpenhof, — long ago our school room and then turned back again into a dining room—and gazed at the Kaiser Mountain range as it emerged from the heavy cloud cover. And then a magnificent and vivid double rainbow appeared on the sky. "It is a message from our friends. They are with us now," whispered Anikó. She did not have to say more, we understood. One rainbow was from those who no longer can endure the ordeal  of traveling, and the other from those who already left us. "Amen," we responded, and were not ashamed of the tears.

Holy Mass at the Reisach church, co-celebrated by His Excellency Bishop Ferenc Cserháti, the Prior Father Bruno, Father Derka and Pater Joachim.

Scouts provided the guard of honor. The commemorative tablet was consecrated.

At right center: the grandson of our first principal, István Ravasz, from Hungary.

Local dignitaries; Germans from the surrounding villages. Guests.

Farewell to the Alpenhof
&
Kloster Reisach

May, 2112

Our last breakfast together in the outer room of the Alpenhof, where all of us started this journey in 1947. Mayor Wildgruber joined us.

Our offsprings often visit Niederaudorf and Reisach. On the left is Éva Tirczka's (Pillér) daughter and granddaughter. On the right is Klári Csaba's (Hidas) son and grandsons.

When we asked, if they were the ones who were peeking into our bedrooms way back in the 1940's, they only smiled.

BIOGRAPHIES

Students:
Life paths and case studies to show how some of the values received at the school were transmitted to the countries which accepted them as immigrants.

Judith Ábrahám – Nagyőszy (Mrs. Nagyőszy-Wolf)

I was born in Sopron, Hungary in October of 1930. My father, born in Transylvania, was a career army physician and was stationed at the time of their marriage in Sopron; mother was a native of Sopron and she had a large family in that town. I was an only child and having relatives so close to me (and cousins my own age to play with) meant a lot. It was quite a shock when I was told that my dad was transferred to Budapest and we will have to move. My father worked in different positions, and then in 1942 he was detailed to the Russian front where he spent a whole year. Meanwhile, mother and I were left in Budapest to fend for ourselves. Times were rough, there was food rationing and the lines were long when supplies arrived. Bombing of the capital started, and we spent increasingly more time in the air raid shelter. We tried to maintain our life as if life were normal. When Dad came back from the Russian front, he was promoted to head the large Military Hospital in Kolozsvár, in Transylvania (at the time Transylvania was part of Hungary). His promotion meant that we had to move again. Like all military children, I too hated to move because this always meant a new school, new teachers and new friends. I hated the change, but it couldn't be helped. Military families move. That is part of their life. Once a wife was overheard of saying, "There are some advantages to it. I never had to do a spring cleaning yet. When the time for it comes, I just move to another town."

Early in 1944 we heard gunfire from the east. In the beginning, it was just a faint, albeit ominous sound, but it was coming closer and closer. From the town of Torda, the number of refugees was increasing day by day. They were coming by car, by truck, by wagon, by bicycle and on foot, carrying what they could. It was a heartbreaking sight. The number of wounded brought in from the nearby battlefield also increased. The war arrived at our doorstep.

My parents decided at this point that Mom and I should move back to Budapest, and stay with mother's sister Rózsa. It would be safer for us, and my dad could devote all his time to the business of the hospital. We stayed in Budapest till the end of September when Dad came to pick us up. He also invited Rózsa *Néni* to join us, but she refused to leave her home.

We went to Léva, in northern Hungary, where we joined Dad's "hospital" which was really a long train of perhaps two hundred wagons, (cattle cars), to transport the military hospital further west, away from the front lines. The wounded were placed on cots, the medical staff, their families, and all the medical supplies were moved on the train in order to prevent that all this should fall into Russian hands. Here we stayed put for a few weeks, housed in the cattle wagons, but the Russian army was relentlessly approaching. It is hard to describe the suffering of the sick and the wounded who had to endure these barbaric conditions. Even for healthy people it was a real trial. My father agonized over the condition of the invalids, but there was little he could do about it.

Meanwhile, we had a chance to buy more supplies. We slaughtered pigs, made sausages, bought chickens and fried them, put them in large containers, and poured lard over them to preserve them. There was no refrigeration. The manager of the sugar factory in the neighboring town of Nagysurány approached my father, and made a donation of one full wagon of sugar to the hospital. He said, the Russians would take it anyway, so why not give it to the Hungarian soldiers. Individual families also bought sugar from him; I think my family bought 200 kilos, which had proven its weight in gold in the years following the end of war. We could go to the farmers and trade all kinds of food, like egg, milk, bread, etc. for the precious sugar.

All in all, we were fortunate because the cattle cars provided space, and we were able to take along more supplies, and more of our personal belongings than most people. On the other hand, to travel on a train in a war zone was a dangerous undertaking because railways were always prime targets for bombing. I guess you get a little and give a little.

We left Léva in the evening, and six hours later the occupying Russian army moved in.

1944 Christmas Eve: we reached the border city of Szenc where we crossed the border into Austria. Puli, my little dog, jumped off the train. He didn't want to leave his country; his loyal little heart wouldn't let him. It was a very sad day in more than one way.

And thus began the long journey into Austria and Germany. Our train was about 200 cattle cars long, and after days of traveling, the first order of business was to find a suitable hospital which would accept all the wounded soldiers because the condition in the wagons was truly intolerable for them. Once this has been accomplished, and all the hospital supplies unloaded at the accepting hospital, most of the turmoil settled. Now the journey started in war torn Germany with the remaining soldiers, staff and family members in the hope to find a place that would accept a train full of refugees. I do not recall how many cattle cars remained, but they were quite a few, and there is no one around anymore whom I could ask. So we just rode the rails aimlessly back and forth. Once we were even attacked, as we emerged from a tunnel; an airplane opened gunfire on us. Fortunately, no one was hurt.

In mid February, a small railroad station high up in the Hartz Mountains took pity on us, and allowed us to park on one of their side rails. We lived there till the end of March. The scenery was beautiful, but life was quite a challenge. By this time we acquired all the tricks of survival because we wanted to live. At the end of March, we moved up to the resort town of Clausthal-Zellerfeld where we experienced the end of the war.

And the challenge continued. First, the surrounding woods were teaming with deserting German soldiers, who all looked for a refuge on their way home. Then came the occupying American Forces. Later, when the victorious powers decided who gets what, this region became part of the English Zone. The hospital staff was dispersed. Some opted to return to Hungary, and some were transferred to the various DP camps. We were moved to Holzminden; there was quite a large Hungarian camp. The Army Hospital personnel from Szeged was also there. This is where I met Klári Kölcsey, whose father was also a doctor. We lived on the same floor across from each other for 2 years; then our life parted. Later we met again at the school of Niederaudorf, and even later again in Cleveland Ohio. As the old saying goes: it is a small, small world.

Two years later, the English authorities decided that there was a great need for physicians in the different refugee camps, and my father was transferred to a Polish DP Camp in Moringen. This was about 30 km north of the University town of Göttingen. At this point, we were far from any Hungarian community and this made life pretty lonesome at times. While in Moringen, I worked. I had a job as a dental assistant.

I remember the day so well, when in May my father came home and declared that he found a Hungarian school in Bavaria, and he is going to take me there because I cannot grow up quite so terribly uncultured. I was 18 years old and finished only the seventh grade. So they packed me up and we took the long train ride to Bavaria. I think I was the student who came from the longest distance. I had a hard time to adjust to the new surroundings and to the learning schedule; fortunately, the girls were friendly and we forged lifelong friendships. I managed to finish the eighth and ninth grades, and spent the summer of 1949 still studying in Reisach, but after Christmas I didn't return. We heard about the Hungarian school in Osterode, which was much closer, so I enrolled there. In January of 1951, in front of the German Schulrat, I did my Matriculation. Four of us took the exams, but we only had one book. So we made a schedule: some of us would get the book in the evening, and then put the book in front of the door, and the next person would get it at 5 in the morning, and then passed it to the next person right after school, and so on. It worked.

But the population of the camp got smaller and smaller; people were called to complete their processing to immigrate to different parts of the world. My family too was summoned to Camp Wentdorf in April, from where we departed to America on an US military transport ship. After a rough crossing, we arrived in New York on May 2nd.

My family spent a month in New York while the Internal Rescue Committee was searching to find my father a job in a hospital. Finally, he decided to accept a residency in St Louis at Peoples Hospital, the only black hospital in St. Louis. Our choice was also influenced by the fact that we already had a cousin of my mother's and her family at St. Louis. When we arrived at St. Louis, the temperature didn't drop under 100 degrees for over 2 weeks, not even at night. Only the rich people had air conditioning at that time. We were quite miserable. They found me a job within a week as a nurse's aide, so I could learn the language. After a year, I quit my job and my parents sent me to Business College. Upon graduating from there, I got a job in an office, which was not as demanding as the nurse's aide job. In 1953 I enrolled at St. Louis University Commerce School where I finished in 2 years.

I met Laci Nagyőszy at the Hungarian Church; he and his mother arrived at St. Louis about 6 months before we did. All newcomers used to gather at the church on Sundays. After the Mass, we socialized for a while, exchanged pertinent information about jobs and housing and made new friends. St. Louis had a relatively small Hungarian community, but we had eight doctors, some were in the same DP Camp as we were in Germany, and that bound us together. At the beginning it was not easy, everyone had to fend for himself; there was no government help, or support of any kind. People usually took almost any work available, bettering their situation as they learned the language.

Laci and I got married in June 1956; at the time he was a sophomore at St Louis University School of Engineering, studying to become an electrical engineer. We had some hard times in the summer after we got married. He had two jobs and I worked in a factory. In 1957 our first daughter Judy was born; then I dropped out of school, Laci continued, and also had a job as a TV service man. We didn't see each other too much. June 1959, our second daughter Esther was born, and we also celebrated the big achievement: Laci graduated as an engineer and headed for Seattle, where a job at Boeing awaited him. We thought we were so rich with the salary he made, but for the first year we were really very poor. But oh, we were so young.

Seattle and the surroundings were absolutely beautiful, but I was very homesick for my parents and friends. So after a year and a half, Laci agreed to find a job closer to Steubenville (Ohio) where my father had his medical practice. This is how we came to Cleveland and lived here ever since, Laci worked for TRW. In 1961 we had another child, a boy Les Jr., followed by another girl named Susie in 1967. We decided at this time that I would be a stay-at-home mom, and raise our children and look after the two aging mothers. After the children grew up, I sold real estate for a while. When Laci retired in 1993, so did I. Our children are all successes in their own lives; Esther is the only "mommy" with 3 children.

The grandchildren are grown too: David, born in 1988 is out on his own, working in the grocery business; Kayla, born in 1991 is in college, and Kevin, born in 1994, is finishing his senior year in high school.

Laci and I are retired now, enjoying the fruits of our labors. We traveled all over the world, seeing beautiful places, meeting interesting people. Now we kind of slowed down, but we still enjoy getting together with friends and playing a mean game of bridge, or going to discussion groups, or spend an evening in one of the theaters. We greatly enjoy our children and grandchildren, and are grateful for the good health that has been granted us.

Eva Bonyhay, Mrs. József Magyar: I was born on the Hungarian national holiday, March 15 in the year of 1928 in Kolozsvár, Transylvania; at that time it was part of Romania.

I was young at the time, but I do remember that for the Christmas holidays we all gathered at my grandparents' place. Later, on the last day of December, when at midnight we were passing into the New Year, we carefully closed all windows and doors and gathered in the "safest" room where nobody could hear us. We turned on the prohibited radio, the volume so low that it was barely audible. The adults crowded around, as if wanting to prevent with their very body the sound to escape into the street. With tears glistening in their eyes, they listened to the forbidden "Radio Budapest," when, according to tradition, the Hungarian National Anthem was broadcast at midnight. Later, my mother sat at the piano and just barely touching the keys played ever so softly the anthem of Transylvania, also forbidden. As a child, I thought that both were prayers, but I also understood that they were forbidden prayers.

My education was started in a Romanian school and continued in that language until September 14, 1940 when the balance of power again changed in Europe. In consequence, the territories, given away at Versailles in the Treaty of Trianon, were reattached to Hungary to the enormous joy of the entire reunited nation. Years later, a similar exhilarating joy was celebrated by an other nation when the Berlin Wall fell. And so Hungary remained united for a little more than four years, until the end of WW II. But, after the war ended, it was back again to the division the Treaty defined. Another light had gone out.

At any rate, after 1940, I was able to attend a Hungarian school up to the 9th grade in Transylvania. At the Kolozsvár schools, the acquisition of foreign languages was very important: French, German, Italian and Latin were required. In addition, we all spoke Romanian as well.

My stepfather, a forestry engineer, was employed by the Hungarian state, and was working away from home, high up in the snowcapped mountains. On August 23, 1944 the Romanian state capitulated to the Russians, and almost immediately the Russian army started pouring into the country. We knew, without the slightest doubt that we could not stay at Kolozsvár. Three weeks later my mother and I left our home in the hope that my stepfather would catch up with us in Budapest where we planned to wait for him at the home of our relatives. And indeed, he did arrive the third week of October. He came on a simple wagon, pulled by two small mountain horses. The wagon was packed with food, which was a true treasure, appreciated by all. After a short pause, we continued to travel toward the west, and the two little horses pulled our cart bravely through the long journey, never wanting much in the way of food, rest or warmth. We arrived in a small Bavarian village in the middle of January, 1945. Fortunately, by April, the village was occupied by American troops, and we could start feeling safe once again.

I was accepted in the German high school at Bamberg where I completed the tenth grade. My stepfather, because of his expertise, was employed to work in the forests near Bamberg. We took the train to Bamberg each morning at six, and he went off to do whatever he had to do with the trees, and I, to face whatever had to be learned at school. The Red Cross maintained a sort of waiting room near the railway station for those who were waiting for connecting trains. This is where I found shelter and where I tried to study until the time my stepfather arrived from the forest. We took the train back to our village at six in the evening. No wonder, I flunked English!

Sometimes later we heard that my aunt, a dentist, the one with whom we stayed at Budapest while waiting for my stepfather, was in the town of Pocking. We went to see her and she told us about the Hungarian school. It was then decided that I should complete the two last grades of high school at home and then travel to Niederaudorf for the examinations and finally for the graduation. Two high school teachers lived in the next village down the road and they were willing to tutor me. My stepfather agreed to teach the mathematics section

Eventually, my aunt immigrated to the USA and we left for Australia. But after some time, we lost contact to each other. I often think about the quirkiness of fate: in those chaotic times we were able to find each other, which was almost a miracle, yet, when our life continued in peace and prosperity, we lost each other forever.

Magda Hadady "Rusnya" (1931-1991)

She was born in Nagyvárad (Transylvania. After leaving Hungary, she attended Niederaudorf where she absolved the 7th, 8th and 9th grades. In October 1949, she immigrated with her parents to the USA and settled in Cleveland, Ohio. She completed her high school there and then continued her studies at the Carnegie Institute of Medical Technology. While working in the laboratories of Case Western Reserve University, she earned a B.S. degree, after which she was doing research work at the Veterans Administration Medical Center; her special interest was in neurology. She also conducted research at the "Department of Developmental Genetics and Anatomy," and at the "Bioarchitectonics Center, Case Western Reserve Union School of Medicine," all in Cleveland. The result of her group's research was published in the Journal of Neuroscience, June 1986: "Transport of Cytoskeleton Elements from Parent Axon to Regenerate Daughter Axons."

An ex-student remembers her: "Magda and I were among the first students to arrive at Niederaudorf when it opened its doors. We both had started seventh grade in Hungary and were somewhat familiar with the material, so Dr. Ravasz decided to let us complete two grades simultaneously, provided we could maintain the required grade average. This we could manage. Magda was an excellent student. I recall that she also did wonderful drawings. She seldom talked about herself, but we knew that the center of her life was her family.

On January 17, 1951 she wrote in a letter: *"Dad and I are employed and our income is enough for a quiet, peaceful life. We are gradually getting used to the idea that God willing, the United States will be our home from now on. This is good. After the long years of insecurity, this is a blessing... I don't have anybody in this new world—and I mean by it an extended family or friends of my own age. I only have my parents. The most important person in my life is my mother. I think in our life there comes a time for all of us when we realize what a marvelous treasure this relationship is."*

Another student remembers: Besides Magda, three other alumnae also earned BS degrees in medical science and worked in various laboratories. This is an interesting percentage, considering the school's total enrollment. Magda lived a frugal life and saved a considerable sum of money which she unselfishly donated to needy families in Transylvania.   1984. July 18

The Hegedűs siblings, Piroska (Mrs. Sándor Zoltán), Nóra (Mrs. Zoltán Sztáray) and Laci, (László Hegedűs.)

were born is Sopron, Hungary. Piroska in 1931, Nóra in 1933 and Laci in 1938. All three of us attended the Nieder school. Piri and

Nóra from March 1947- August 1950, finishing grades 7-11 and 6-10 respectively. Our brother Laci joined us for the school year 1949-1950 and completed fifth grade.

Our track to the West was different from most of our schoolmates. Our father worked for MAVAG, (Győri Wagon és Gépgyár), the second largest machine factory in Hungary, established in 1896 to produce vehicles of all kinds, appropriate for the times – trucks, tractors, trains, streetcars, autos, airplanes. In 1941 they added the manufacturing of fighter planes. At the end of 1944, when the Soviet army was nearing Budapest, this division of MAVAG was ordered by the German occupying forces to be transported to Germany, to continue producing planes in support of the war. The staff and workers were given a choice: they could either return to the front to fight the Russians, or go to Germany with the factory, taking their family with them. Two hundred members of this division chose the latter and left Hungary with their families, transported in cattle cars. The heavy equipment and supplies were floated on barges on the Danube all the way up to Passau.

Our family was one of those opting to go to Germany. Until then we lived in Sopron, a beautiful and peaceful medieval town near the Austrian border. Our father's job took him to Győr and Budapest. He commuted home on weekends. On New Year's Eve 1944, our mother was roasting a goose in the oven, waiting for our father to arrive for the celebration. Instead, one of his staff members rang the doorbell at eight, telling us that the train is at the station, waiting for us to board, leaving for Germany at midnight. Our father's telegram, informing us of this impending event, never arrived. Frantic packing ensued. We had no chance to say goodbye to friends and relatives. Assured that we'll be returning home within a few weeks, it looked like an adventure but when that didn't happen, we were heartbroken.

Our first stop was in a village near Linz, Austria, where we stayed for six weeks. We found accommodation in a schoolhouse; we slept on triple bunk beds. Rude awakening was the horrible food provided by the locals. Our mother, realizing what sort of life awaited us, decided to return to Sopron to pick up some provisions for us. She and Piri left our group with the permission of the authorities, knowing that they would certainly find us upon their return. It took a lot of courage on their part. They met a series of difficulties, including air raids, bombings, trains not running, walking many kilometers in the freezing weather—just to mention a few. The return trip was even more difficult, during which they had to face the theft of some of their luggage. Their awful trip was almost pointless.

Once again united, we continued our trip on the train, heading west. After days of traveling taking refuge in the forests during air raids, we arrived at Train, a small village 40 km. south of Regensburg. There part of our group eighty-five of us including men, women and children settled in a huge dance hall. There we welcomed the end of the war.

The factory planned earlier was never set up, the heavy equipment, all properties of the Hungarian factory, were strewn all over the country, locals taking possession of them, hiding them in their homes, barns. By the end of 1945 the majority of the employees returned to Hungary. From those who stayed behind with their families twenty were selected by the Allied Forces; the selected members were formerly in charge of the operation and spoke German. Our father was one of the selected ones. Their job was to repossess the factory's properties and to ship them back to Hungary under the auspices of the occupying U.S. Forces. The headquarters were set up in Augsburg and a huge hangar was provided for this purpose. This process took three years.

While the men worked at the Augsburg headquarters, their families were left in the dance hall to fend for themselves. After the war there were no accommodations available in cities because of all the damage caused by the bombings; therefore, it was not possible for the families to join the working heads of families. Our mother stayed in the dance hall with Laci, while Piroska and Nóra were sent to the boarding school in Niederaudorf.

Our grandfather joined us in 1946. He had a thriving family business back home in Sopron, a honey cake bakery, established in the early eighteenth century. He also made candles for the local churches, which was an important and honored assignment. My grandfather was as proud of his honey cakes as he was of the superior quality candles he delivered to the churches.

My grandfather was deported to Germany by the new government, under a new law, which forced those whose mother tongue was German to leave the country. His business was taken away, and he was put on a train, all the possession he was allowed to take along were placed into a small trunk. As he never lived anywhere else but in Hungary, his forced exile was truly traumatic for him, especially since he was no longer young. It was very difficult for him to adapt.

In Augsburg Grandfather joined the crew which was taking care of the rescued equipment of the Hungarian factory and lived there with my father. Thus, except for summer vacations, the family lived apart for five years, until we immigrated to the United States. This enforced separation of families in those difficult times was an added difficulty we had to endure.

In the beginning we all thought that soon we shall all return to Hungary, but because of the increasingly uncertain political situation there, and because our grandfather due to the new law could not return with us, our parents decided emigrate. Our family was sponsored by the Ardmore Presbyterian Church in Pennsylvania.

They received us with open arms. The members of the church rented and furnished a house for us with everything a six-member family needs; paid the rent for three months; found a job at the Autocar for our father; Grandfather found a job at a local bakery. Piri and Nóra planned to go to work; however, the minister of the congregation Dr. Frew told us we have to finish high school; his edict was not open for discussion. The girls babysat after school, and Laci had a paper route and mowed lawns. Our mother was taken to English classes by the ladies of the church; they also took her shopping for groceries. Eventually she acquired a job at a delicatessen, where she prepared the food. A short time later she started her own business baking delicious Hungarian cookies. Several years later she expanded and offered a "broasted chicken takeout store." We all worked. After so many years of homelessness and tough times, we could not believe that this was happening to us. The generous members of the church gave us a wonderful start. The rest was up to us to make a successful life in the United States.

("Broasting" – a revolutionary method of preparing chicken, meats and fish by combining pressure cooking and deep frying, was introduced by Flavor Fast Foods, Inc., in Rockton, Illinois. The Broaster Company, headquartered in Beloit, Wisconsin, markets and licenses the Genuine Broaster Chicken®, Broaster® Recipe Express, and Bro-Tisserie® food programs worldwide to a wide range of restaurants, supermarkets, bars, nightclubs, convenience stores, and military, institutional, and governmental foodservice operations through a network of authorized distributors.)

Piroska Hegedűs (Mrs. Sándor Zoltán): During our years at Nieder we had few opportunities to meet boys. At school we never had more than five or six boys, most of them were younger than the girls. Besides, our teachers guarded us, even on our walks. We saw boys only from the distance. Piri was an exception. She met her future husband at school. The principal arranged for the Protestants to have Bible studies because there weren't any Lutheran or Reformed churches in the area where we could attend. Agreement was made with Dr. Géza Soós, the head of Soli Deo Gloria in Munich, that he would provide experts to conduct Bible studies at our school. They came regularly. One of them was Sándor Zoltán, son of a Unitarian minister in a small village in Transylvania. He was just completing the last year of his university studies in art and architecture when he had to flee the country.. He not only held Bible studies at our school, but also talked about Hungarian folk-art, explained all the details of székely kapu – these are beautifully and intricately carved gates seen all over Transylvania. He always looked so serious and sad. We found out later that he lost his wife, and temporarily had to put his two young children, still toddlers, into an orphanage. All of these made a strong impression on Piri. She later had an opportunity to meet him at a convention in Prien, on the shore of Lake Chiemsee; here they had the opportunity to get to know each other.

When Sándor immigrated to the U.S in 1951 with his children, who were then 5 and 6 years old, he got in touch with Piri. They held their wedding the fall of the same year. The children needed a mother. Our sponsoring church members were totally involved in the preparation of the wedding, and even gave Piri a shower where she received just about everything a new couple would need. Our mother made nine beautiful and decadent cakes, in addition to a three tier wedding cake and our father decorated this with little white roses; grandfather baked a whole lot of his special cookies to be sure there would be enough for everyone. The whole congregation was invited. The newly wedded couple settled in Detroit, where Sándor worked first as a draftsman at the Albert Kahn architecture company; soon moved over to the Argonaut Realty Division of General Motors, staying with the company until retirement. He planned their buildings and eventually served as chief engineer. Piri stayed at home, raising the children. In their spare time, both of them spent more than 50 years in serving the Hungarian causes in their community.

Very early, already in 1953, they became regular participants in the International Institute of Metro Detroit's cultural and fundraising events, presenting slides, lectures and exhibits of Hungarian art, folk-art, history and culture. Over many years, they were volunteer decorators for the Detroit Historical Museum's Christmas Tree decorating project. When there was a large influx of Hungarians after the revolution of 1956, they helped in various ways – finding jobs, translating and interpreting, troubleshooting for them. They took active part in the life of the Hungarian churches, coordinating various events for the Hungarian community. Cultural exchanges with countries behind the Iron Curtain opened up in 1971. Over the years they hosted artists, singers, lecturers from Hungary and Transylvania, and organized more than 82 events for the Detroit Hungarian community, inviting the city's dignitaries and the general public for these presentations.

Meanwhile Piroska went back to school to continue her education, completing an AA degree at the Henry Ford Community College. After reading about the medicine men in the culture of the Indians she became interested in healing the natural way. She pursued that all her life in an informal way, reading books and taking correspondence courses from Clayton College of Natural Health. In 1949 she was selected by the principal of Niederaudorf to participate in a certificated course at Prien, (at Lake Chiemsee), sponsored by the U.S. Occupying Forces and conducted by the YMCA. The goal was to train future physical education instructors. This made her an advocate for lifetime physical exercise, which she herself practices. In her spare time she was an avid viewer of the U.S. Space program, videotaping hours of it for Sándor, who would view it when he came home from work.

After retirement they spent much time visiting Hungary and Transylvania, where he was born. In 2005, while they were in Sopron, Piri unexpectedly lost her husband after 53 years of marriage. She kept their home in Grosse Ile, but spends much time in our apartment in Sopron, where she often revisits her childhood memories and keeps up with world events, both home and abroad.

Nóra Hegedűs (Mrs. Zoltán Sztáray). A year and a half after arriving in the United States, I finished high school and started college. I received a tuition scholarship from Beaver College. Working during summers in a variety of jobs, first as a housemaid in a hotel, later as salesclerk at a delicatessen, another summer as a waitress I earned part of my room and board and was able to finish college in four years earning a BA degree in secondary education in 1956 with a major in Latin and a minor in English and French. It was tough.

During my college years I had a great time and lots of good experiences. I was often invited by community groups, churches, clubs, such as the Rotary Club (I was their district student in my senior year), to talk about my experiences as a refugee in Germany and the reason my family left Hungary and settled in the United States. This gave me an opportunity to talk about the Russian occupation of Hungary and how much people suffered under enforced Communism. I became a recognized speaker for Hungary in the area. I never forget how I was shaking in my boots when I had to present in front of 250 Rotarians at their Atlantic City district convention in the spring of 1956. I totally forgot my speech and spoke from my heart. The Rotarians actually got in touch with me during the Hungarian Revolution on October 1956, asking me, how they could help. By the time they sent a sizable donation, the Iron Curtain was again closed. The Red Cross in Vienna which helped the huge flood of refugees was the well-deserved recipient.

After graduation from college I was lucky to have received a grant-in-aid from the Philadelphia chapter of Delta Kappa Gamma to study French at the Middlebury College Summer Language School in Vermont. What a beautiful state! This led me later to teach French in addition to German at a junior high in California at a time when few wanted to learn Latin.

But my first job was teaching Latin at the Baldwin School in Bryn Mawr, in the suburbs of Philadelphia. One of the members of the Ardmore church arranged that for me. They looked out for us for a long time, even after we were settled. However, I didn't stay there long. As soon as I was able to get out of my contract, I went up to New York and worked as translator and interpreter for a Hungarian organization. The Kossuth Foundation was set up after the defeat of the Revolution to do research, and to feed facts and updates to organizations such as the U.N. on the Hungarian situation. There I met Zoltán Sztáray, a researcher and economist who had arrived from Paris just weeks earlier to head the organization. Two years later we got married and moved to Brussels, where he continued his research and was editor of a publication. We had the opportunity to drive to the border of Hungary near my hometown, shocked to see the watchtower with guards on the top, pointing guns at us. Then I knew that my homeland was closed for me. The move back to Europe was also healing for me. I was able to visit places I couldn't while we were refugees in Germany. One of the highlights of my year in Europe was a camping trip to Greece and Italy, seeing all the ancient sites of which I studied in college. Our daughter Zsuzsa was born in 1961 and in 1962 I returned to my original profession, spending over 40 years in the field of education—a most varied and rewarding experience.

The four years my sister and I spent at the Niederaudorf School was a determining factor in my life. At a time, when we should have been under the loving guidance and protection of our parents, we were much on our own. We became independent early, and the experience gave us courage and strength to face life whatever it may bring. I'll never forget the walk, carrying our luggage that contained even our bedding, from the little village where we lived 12 kilometers from the closest railroad station; then the transfer in Munich to the next train and the long walk to the school from the Oberaudorf train station to Niederaudorf. This 200 kilometer long trip took us a whole day. The first time our parents accompanied us, but the rest of the time we did it on our own. All this at age 14 and 15! Since then I have a lot of sympathy for hitchhikers. I even devised in my mind a vehicle that has benches all around, onto which people in similar circumstance could hop on or off. I didn't think of the economics part. The problem of liability never entered my mind..

The absence from home during our teenage years brought us close to our parents even after we got married and lived in various parts of the country. Our brother Laci stayed in the east, close to our parents, Piri lived in Michigan and after spending a year in Belgium, we moved to California. But we often visited our parents and each other. Every summer in the 60's we drove cross country, camping all the way, choosing a different route, which gave us the opportunity to get to know all the fascinating places, all the national parks between California and Pennsylvania. We did this more than a dozen times. Once we did a 21 day trip around the country with Piri and her family and we got to know the geology of the United States from Zoli, who studied it under Pál Teleki while he was a university student in Hungary. Teleki used the geology of the U.S. to illustrate most of the important geological features in the world.

In Zoli I found a perfect partner. We were independent, each working on our own jobs, yet supporting each other's work, while taking care of our daughter Zsuzsa. We agreed that I'd continue my career in education, and he his work, doing research and writing. He wrote scripts for Radio Free Europe, was an editor of a literary and political journal published in Munich, Germany; wrote several books, which were published by Püski publishing in New York, and Budapest, all in Hungarian.

In raising Zsuzsa, one of our successes was that she became totally bilingual, doing well both in English and Hungarian, to which later she added French, Spanish and Japanese. We instilled in her the love of her heritage. She embraced our past and developed into an intelligent, well educated young lady with a BA in anthropology and MA in urban planning.

My interest to be an educator started early. I decided already at Nieder that I wanted to be either a teacher or a mom with many children. I'm fortunate that I achieved the first, and was lucky to have at least one child. I wish I had more children, but it was not to be. I spent 13 years in junior high school teaching French, German, at times social studies, environmental studies, speech and reading, depending on what was needed; taught 18 years in a high school and spent 10 years teaching at a university in the School of Education.

The success of the Soviet space program gave a real boost to foreign language teaching. In 1958 Congress signed into law the National Defense Education Act, which established summer institutes for teachers to improve U.S. education in math, sciences and other areas such as foreign languages to be able to compete with the Soviets. I attended an institute in French at Princeton University in 1963 and in Latin at SUNY in Albany in 1969. In addition, I had a chance to improve my German proficiency at a summer Goethe Institute in Staufen, Germany in 1967, sponsored by the German government. At these institutes the old way of translation and grammar instruction was challenged. I totally agreed with that. These were wonderful and productive experiences which provided me with new tools. In my classes I emphasized the development of listening and speaking skills before introducing reading, writing and grammar. I consider this essential especially for English speakers learning French or German. Had they seen the written text first, their pronunciation of French would have sounded more like English. They also developed good listening skill. They had to stay alert and be on task during the class. We were able to get new tools, such as tapes, record players. Within a short time we set up a language lab, with earphones for each student. Learning for them became fun and productive.

Having been without things as I was growing up, I was disturbed by the waste and carelessness of the students, especially at lunchtime. I started a club, encouraging students to stop littering, start collecting recyclables. This was before the first Earth Day. We organized weekend activities. Students picked up trash in the surrounding area, after which they had a picnic and games. It was fun for them. In southern California smog was a big concern. I encouraged students to ride their bikes to school. We did fundraisers to pay for a fenced area for the bikes, collected tons of newspapers and aluminum cans, did tree planting and reseeding areas that were destroyed by the fire in the hills above the city. Interest was so high that we added an ecology class to the curriculum. The school yearbook gave us a two page spread with the title: Nóra's Raiders. That was at Nader's time. We organized the first Earth Day in our town. Over several years it became the most popular club, with more than 200 members and additional teachers and parents helping with supervision. These were great activities and teaching tools for the students. I often wonder if some of them became the stalwarts of the environmental movements. Our program received several recognitions, one from the Freedoms Foundation at Valley Forge.

In 1970, when I was asked to teach a 7th grade social studies class—ancient history—I had a rude awakening. I found during the very first week that the majority in that class could not read the 7th grade textbook! Students weren't answering my questions, which were based on their previous assignment. They told me, the chapter was too hard, and they couldn't read it. I didn't believe them. Until then I taught bright students in my foreign language classes which was an elective. I asked one of the students to read a few lines—I still remember his name, Adolf. Truly, he was unable to read the text. I could not believe it. I went to the office and checked the students' CTBS scores. It turned out, most of my students in that class read at 3- 4th grade level. Naturally, a 7th grade level book was too hard. I asked one of the English teachers, what is the English department doing about it? His answer was: nothing. It's too late to teach them to read. That really upset me. I went to the principal. She was also aware of the problem. I offered to do an experiment on the condition that class size be limited to 25 students. I was given free hand. The class started at the beginning of the next semester. Using appropriate and interesting material, Reader Digest Skill Builders at various levels, I grouped students according to their level, three to four in each group, and arranged for cross-age tutors, bright students, one for each group. After some training it was a delight to see them work. By the end of the semester a significant number raised their reading skills several levels. I remember one of the boys. He told me with a big smile that before the program he was convinced that he will never be able to read. He thanked me. The next year I was moved to the high school to be a reading teacher. This assignment took me back to the university to get an M.A. in education, with emphasis on reading improvement.

This experience led me to be involved at the district level. In the 70's the Hart Bill was passed in Sacramento, requiring students to pass a district devised minimum competency test in reading, writing and math. This was mandatory and they had to pass it before they could be moved from the elementary school to junior high, and from there to senior high and so eventually to graduate. I worked with a district committee on this. It boosted awareness and responsibility of the need to improve education overall, reaching back to all grade levels. I was in charge of implementing the requirement at my school, setting up proficiencies labs and tracking students who needed remediation. This became one of my jobs over several years.

I still continued teaching French and German, and occasionally Latin. Foreign language classes were electives. Fluctuation in numbers of students who signed up for it determined my teaching assignment. Luckily for the school, I had a general secondary credential, which meant that theoretically I could teach any subject. (Once I did refuse to teach one: an art class). Soon after I began teaching, the state changed to single subject credential, which meant, there weren't many of us in that category. In 1981 we lost the advisor of our school newspaper. I became one, which was another tough assignment. Luckily the newspaper had a well-trained student staff and the support of my husband, who helped me in improving the learning curve of the students. This became a great experience and a chance to pick up lots of skills, which later contributed to doing a newsletter for the local AFS (American Field Service) student exchange organization and getting a couple of my husband's books ready for publication. An added reward was: that year the renowned sci-fi author Ray Bradbury visited our school and we had a chance to talk and take pictures of him.

The 80's introduced us to technology. Early on, my school built a computer lab, using title VII monies. It was furnished with Apple IIe computers, using 7" floppies. I taught a couple of classes, both remedial readers and ESL students, where students needed additional help in the basics and we were scheduled to work in the lab to do reviews, based on their needs. The summer of 1987 I attended a Summer Technology Training Institute at UC Irvine where we were introduced to the various uses of the computer, saw the first e-mail exchange between a US school and one in Brazil, and got some inkling of the World Wide Web coming in our direction. It was exciting. As a reward, we each were given a "high tech" Apple 2C. After the training I became one of the district's technology mentors with the responsibility of holding afterschool workshops for colleagues until I retired from the district in 1991. It was tough. We all stumbled in the dark, so much new stuff was thrown at us and kept on coming. Only the ignorant thought that he or she knew it all. These were exciting times.

I did early retirement because this was the time of changes behind the Iron Curtain and I wanted to have more time to visit relatives and friends I haven't seen since 1944. Of course some of them were no longer on this earth. Since we left in 1945, I was unable to visit my hometown three kilometers from the Austrian border because my husband, who was blacklisted, begged me not to cross the border in fear of retribution. I had to honor his request during all the years. But in the fall of 1991 I crossed the border with my US passport in the company of my mother and brother. It was a very emotional experience. I was able to hug my godmother for the last time; she passed away the next year as if only waiting for me. Sadly, I missed meeting my mother-in-law for the first time because she died a few weeks before our arrival. But we made connections with cousins and other relatives and friends, which we are maintaining to this day.

I didn't stay retired for long. I hardly returned from overseas when a call came from the SB County Office of Education, asking me to take over the CLAD training (Cross-Cultural Language and Academic Development), which led to a certificate, that was required of teachers of LEP (Limited English Proficient) students – all through California. The training was for teachers of San Bernardino County. That meant quite some distances of traveling because S.B County is the largest in California. Before I retired I did complete two years of training to become a trainer, but didn't finish the third year. Always very active and always ready to embrace any new challenge I suddenly surprised myself by truly enjoying my retirement. It felt good not to have to get up so early and it was great to be free. It was a new, comfortable and pleasant lifestyle. However, I reluctantly accepted the challenging position of CLAD training. I started by revising part of the handbook and then went on the next few years doing more than a dozen workshops.

The CLAD workshop became a credit program, administered by CSUSB's (California State University, San Bernardino) Extended Education Office. I worked closely with Jan Jackson, Associate Dean; and Susan Summers, Extension Director. In 1993 they applied and received a grant to create a program to address the needs of Hispanic adults, mainly parents of school children in the district, who needed English language instruction so they could get involved in their children's schooling and become productive members of society. In Southern California this was and still is a great, ongoing need. They targeted another group: senior citizens from all walks of life, who have completed high school education and who wanted to be active in their retirement. Susan asked me to be the director who'd implement the program. This would be a part-time job, just for a year. Well, it sounded exciting and much needed. Since I was doing other smaller jobs anyway that kept me in town, I decided to go for it.

The recruiting of volunteers was successful; we selected 40 seniors for the training, meeting with them once a week. Two of my colleagues worked with 15 seniors, who were retired teachers of various subjects, and I trained 25, who never taught before. By the end of the year we ended up with more than 30 enthusiastic seniors, who completed a summer practice session under our supervision, and by fall were ready to go out in the field. I stayed with the project for 10 years, a most fulfilling experience.

Around the same time CSUSB office of education called to see if I was willing to teach a couple of classes in the spring, Reading and Writing in Secondary Schools, a class I've taught several times the last part of the 1980's after I completed my master's degree. By the fall of 1994 I was appointed full-time lecturer, teaching six or seven different classes during those years, and supervising student teachers. I remained faculty member until 1998 to my second official retirement.

On the last day in my office a friend of mine and colleague called. She just returned from Hungary. She participated in a training session in the Mátra mountains for a program called RWCT (Reading and Writing for Critical Thinking), that IRA (International Reading Association) developed for those countries that have been under Communism and needed to infuse some of the western thinking into their school curriculum. It was already in operation in several countries with much success. This program was to start in Hungary in the near future, but they just lost one member of a group of four, and they were desperate to find a proper replacement. Would I be interested? I was speechless. For me to be involved in my field in Hungary? It was like dream come true. It was to be a three-year commitment, doing 5 day workshops twice a year and do follow-up visits on school site; e.g. Budapest, Győr, Pécs, Szeged, Debrecen, Eger. After getting more details I felt I could do it. They accepted my application.

László Hegedűs. Laci's schooling was much tougher. His first grade started in Hungarian a few months before we left Sopron. Even that was interrupted by the occupying German forces, who took over the school building and the class was held in the neighboring Lutheran church. He missed school entirely until the spring of 1945. Then he continued in German in the village school where we stayed. This was not easy in a strange language in a place where he wasn't welcome by his peers. He was a refugee. During summers we tried to teach him to read and write in Hungarian. It went quite well. Occasionally he wrote to us letters in Hungarian. We still have some of them. Often it wasn't easy. He'd rather roam the fields on his bike that he at age 8-9 put together by himself from usable parts he found in the junkyards. Seeing his determination, our father with much difficulty, bought treads for his bike. After that it was even more difficult to make him sit down to do Hungarian lessons.

For the 5th grade he was enrolled at Nieder. He doesn't have fond memories of this experience either. Teachers were strict, expectation was high. Four years in German school didn't help his studies in Hungarian. One of his teachers severely punished him for not knowing his lesson. We, the older sisters, reported this to the principal. That helped. He remembers the cold in his room at Frau Bauer, where he and the older boys boarded. But he also has good memories. He enjoyed the hikes to Luegsteinsee, climbing Mt. Brünnstein, and once Frau Bauer allowed them to cook pasta, sprinkle it with sugar mixed with ground poppy seed, one of their favorite meals.

The fall of 1950 we were waiting for our turn to get on the ship to the US. None of us went to school that fall.. Laci used this time to learn English, visiting the Augsburg America House. Not long ago we visited the Lewis and Clark's winter encampments in northwestern Oregon, and Laci remembered that's where he read about it.

Upon arrival to the US, he was enrolled in seventh grade. Age wise he belonged there, but his knowledge of English was close to zero. According to second language acquisition experts, Cummins and Krashen, it takes 4-6 years of language study to achieve well at the higher academic levels. I'm still amazed that my brother and many others, whose fate was the same or similar, survived against all odds and did well in life. Laci wanted to be an engineer, in which he succeeded. He finished his 29 years of employment as senior industrial engineer with General Motors and was rehired as a consultant for seven more years. For six years he was in reserve status in the Marines, achieved the rank of sergeant, and worked also in the technical field, finishing as helicopter crew chief.

In 1960 he married Susan Bainbridge. They have three daughters and are the proud grandparents of 14 grandchildren, all living in the Newark, Delaware area.

The honey-cake mentioned above is somewhat different from the "honey-cake" known in the US, although the American version of the cake is also well known on the Old Continent. But the cakes Nóra mentions in her recollection are different and have a history of several thousand years. Archeologists found honey and honey-cake dough in the Pyramids. The Greeks, as well as the Romans prepared

elaborately decorated cakes of flour, honey, syrup, water and spices for special occasions.

Folks in Central Europe learned the skill from the Romans and its fame spread rapidly. It was known as Pain d'épice in France; Lebkuchen in Germany; and Mézeskalács in Hungary. To produce this specialty requires a fine blend of baking know-how and applied arts no less demanding in artistic talent than pottery.

The flat cakes, which were really more like giant cookies, could be displayed hanging from hooks in the wall. They were elaborately decorated with fondant flowers and with various motives; often lines of a poem were piped on them. Some of the best were heart-shaped, had a mirror pasted in the middle and a love message of the admittedly naive folksy kind such as "Look in the mirror and you'll see the one I love." It was a favorite gift to take home from the market. A girl who received a fancy honey-cake from her dream guy was no less enchanted than a modern girl receiving the solitaire—the message of the honey heart was the very same as that of the diamond.

In Europe the first such cakes were probably baked by monks for church festivities, but soon the trade passed on to lay people. For many centuries it was the main attraction at the patron festivals of churches and of markets. It was an important trade, which fathers taught to sons and was passed down from generation to generation. The honey-cake bakers soon formed their own guild and very high standards were exacted in the training of apprentices and in the production of the honey cakes. Membership into the guild was granted only to those, who could produce a masterpiece for the jury. The members of the guild were highly respected citizen, real pillars of society.

Those who made honey-cakes often managed their own bee hives, made candles from the beeswax and honey-wine (mead) from the honey. They often carved their own fancy molds in which they baked the cakes in the form of dolls, hearts, spurs, flowers, Christmas trees, and whatever else their fancy dictated. These giant cookies were the for-runners of the "gingerbread man" and the "gingerbread house."

As sugar replaced honey the wonderful old tradition was pushed in the background, although lately the interest is awakening. They are again appearing in abundance at the famous Christkindlmarkets (Christmas markets) in Austria and Germany, and many can be seen at the stands in München during the Oktoberfest. (This may be of interest: at every Christmas Chicago also stages a Christmas market, which is quite as delightful as those in Europe.) Perhaps the renaissance of the traditional honey-cake is a sign of wanting to bring back some old, precious memories.

About candles: the church liturgy requires that even in broad daylight at least two candles burn on the altar, not in order to chase away the darkness, but as a sign of joy when listening to the "good news" as written by the Evangelists.

Most of the wax was produced in the bee hives of monasteries and the monks worked the wax into candles. Up to as recently as the twentieth century all candles for the altar had to be made exclusively of beeswax. Finally in 1902 a papal sanction was given for the use of candles made of other materials also. Beeswax candles are still preferred in many churches as it symbolizes absolute purity, probably because the wax is produced by the special glands of very young virgin worker-bees, and because no additives are used. Wax candles used in the churches were considered the symbol of the purity of the Savior; the flame of the candle denoted the love and divine person of Christ. Some say it also symbolizes the mystical combination of fecundity and virginity associated with the Mother of Christ. At any rate it is a symbol of absolute purity and for a chandler to make candles for churches carried a special honor and distinction.

Klára Kölcsey (Mrs. Shelton)

The Beginning: In the spring of 1944 my father was Director of Health of the city of Szatmárnémeti in eastern Hungary and I was in the 4th grade. School ended early that year and because of the threat of bombings my dad moved us out to a vineyard in the country. The Csaba family with their children also moved to the same area for the same reason. Zsolt and Klári, my brother Pista and I hung around together during that summer. It was a great summer for me as I felt very little of the war's horrors at the time. My Dad stayed in the city where a German officer took over our apartment, but we were not there anyway so it did not matter much. During that summer we picked cherries, peaches and plums and took them into Szatmár to sell. My brother drove my dad's car, which according to Zsolt must have had special certificate on the windshield as cars were not permitted to run about freely. One time I was with him because I had an ear infection which had to be treated in town and on the way home a dog ran into the car. It hit the fender hard enough so that before Pista could stop the fender had cut a groove into the tire. My dad was naturally furious because getting a new tire was close to impossible. I have no clue what happened to the poor dog.

I do remember some good times. There was the great challenge of who could eat more plum dumplings (*szilvás gombóc*) and of course my brother won with some ridiculous achievement of 16 (?) dumplings.

During my recent phone call to Zsolt we reminisced about this szilvás gombóc contest, and about how hard it was to get gas and a permit to drive a car, and how we stood on top of the vineyard to watch [and pray] as Szatmár was getting bombed and how it burned with humongous flames.

Neither of us could remember just exactly when we left the vineyard, but I think it was somewhere around late August when my Dad got orders from the government to move and to supervise the medical staff stationed at Csór near Balaton on the west side of Hungary. This was a lucky turn for him because it allowed him (us) to leave Szatmár officially and so we were saved from the Red Army which was getting dangerously close. By the time we left people were abandoning their homes. The scene from Fiddler on the Roof was a duplicate of the way people trudged on the roads carrying their meager belongings on their backs. Grandparents, the sick or very small children were pulled in hand-wagons, provided they were fortunate enough to have wagons. My father drove his car (a four-seater and very tiny Ballila) with the official permit on the windshield. The multitude of people would part and allow us to pass, then flow back to form a mass of refugees. I always remember it like a flowing river parting around an obstacle. What I cannot comprehend is how he acquired the gas to run the car.

Everything we had was jammed into that tiny car with my baby sister and 15 year old brother. We traveled for several days before we reached Csor. On the way there we made overnight stops at the houses of generous local dignitaries at little villages. I am guessing that because my dad was a doctor such courtesy was offered to us, but then it could be that in extremely difficult times people become more generous, kind and understanding. Otherwise I cannot imagine why anyone would allow us to crash into their home. During these stays I overheard the adults discussing late into the night the rumors of the atrocities of the Nazis, the cruel experiments that were carried out on the Jews and others in those German concentration camps and the incomprehensible agony those people endured. They also whispered about the unspeakable 'final solution' in the gas chambers. These were uneasy rumors and no one could believe it to be true. It was really beyond reality that such horrors could be committed in a world believed to be civilized and done by a nation which produced Beethoven, Kant and Nietzsche.

On the other hand I also overheard the discussions about the cruelty of the Soviet soldiers in the parts of Hungary they already occupied—such as knocking out the teeth of the captured population to get at the gold, the unthinkable abuse of women both young and old, the burning of the houses to the ground, lining up the men and either making them watch their cruelty and killing them after, or just killing them outright. I suppose those who were shot at once were the lucky ones. Some of the younger men were packed up and sent to Siberian prisons. Very few returned from there and if they did they were mostly crippled for life physically and psychologically.

My dad's assignment at Csór was very fortunate as he spent many years as a doctor in that place; as a matter of fact I was born there and it felt like going home again. The villagers remembered us and welcomed us with open arms. For the next few months we lived well due to their generosity and contributions. We never received the huge boxes with our clothing my mother so carefully packed at Szatmár, but she was able to buy winter clothes for us at Csór and so be ready for the cold months. This loss of our belongings was repeated again just before Christmas when we had to leave the little we owned to run for our lives as the Russians were gathering forces around Csór.

My Dad then joined the army and they assigned him to the Military Hospital of Szeged; however the hospital was packed up and by the time he arrived there it already left Hungary, so we had to catch up with it. We carried all our worldly possessions in a couple of suitcases. When we arrived at Berlin, where we had to change trains I witnessed real terror for the first time. Up until then my parents shielded me from the reality of it all. But that day as we were waiting for our train there was an air raid. The train which was on the tracks had to leave the station with very little warning. There were people hanging off the windows, sitting on top of the cars, and several babies were handed to strangers through the windows in the hope that the parent would eventually also squeeze into the car. But the train pulled out without some parents. I shall never forget the anguished screams. At that point I finally realized it was a most dangerous world and I clung to my mother with all my might for the rest of our trip until we finally caught up with Dad's hospital.

Around January of '45 the hospital packed up again to move to safer area. We were packed into boxcars, 4-5 families in a car, living on top of bundles of linens at each end of the car. I have no recollection what sanitary conditions were available or even if we were able to wash ourselves. I know there was a lot of black-marketing and paying off the stationmasters so that our train could be moved here or there. We had traveled aimlessly back and forth between stations for a month, having no specific place to settle down. My dad and some other officials kept going up to Berlin to try to get a place to settle into. Whenever they left (I do not remember what they used for transportation), we were petrified that they might get killed by either side of the opposing armies, or by the bombings.

A couple of months before the end of the war the hospital was finally given housing in a private boys' school in Holzminden. The hospital was set up in two of the three huge buildings. Here they assigned one room to each family and we were able to use modern facilities, showers and bathrooms at the end of the hall. As I have lately learned the girl living across the hall from us was Judith Ábrahám, her father too was a doctor at this hospital. Two years later we met again because she also attended Niederaudorf. We were finally captured by the Americans. After the victorious forces decided where the borders for the occupational zones were to be we were turned over to the Brits.

We made the best of our life as much as we could, but we knew that this state would not be permanent. My brother Pista black-marketed ("*feketézett*") regularly. We were regularly given coffee, a rare treasure and an unthinkable luxury by the British occupation government. Pista carefully packaged 2-3 tablespoons of coffee into small sacks. Taking along the English cigarettes as well he proceeded to barter for some food from the farmers and villagers. He'd come home from a 20-25 mile bicycle trip with a dozen eggs, and some fruits or vegetables, cheese and on rare occasion even some meat (chicken.) One of our favorite memories of the black marketing was my toddler sister's comment when one day she saw Pista head out on his trip: "My dear Pista, *hozz nekem egy malackát*" (bring me a little piggy). We had no idea if she wanted to eat it, or play with it, but it became a treasured comment in the family.

I also remember the sacrifices of our parents and their willingness to do all kinds of work to provide for their families. Their creative resourcefulness was limitless. When we were living in a camp at Osterode in the British occupied zone the Brits actually provided for our basic needs. Every week there was a distribution of food and cleaning materials, although on a very limited basis, but it was invaluable and we appreciated it immensely. At the beginning in the years of 1945-46, my mother was the "provider," and she asked the authorities for knitting yarn. To our great surprise her request was granted, but the yarn given was limited for just one single item to be made. She agreed and declared that she needed it for a coat. She proceeded to knit a really huge coat in order to prove to the authorities that she really needed that much yarn. After the finished coat was inspected and approved by the officials she unraveled it and made sweaters for my dad, my brother, sister and me. I cannot even imagine how much work went into making the original item and then taking it apart to make more useful things for the family.

Right after the war ended my 18 month old sister Kathie had surgery for her displaced hips at the world famous Göttingen Hospital. Six months later (with 3 additional trips to change her cast) I could spend a month with her in the children's ward while she went through physical therapy. It amazes me that they allowed me to stay with her. I helped the nurses carry food and attend to the other children in the ward to pass the time, but I was only 12 years old and very lonely. But she was slowly improving. She stood firmly in her U shaped cast and even walked around her crib. After she was released from the hospital my 16 year old brother Pista carried her often in a homemade sling. We took her mushroom picking, or for a walk in the woods and meadows. She was just a little kid and we all entertained her by telling her stories, reading to her, and playing with pencil and paper. Maybe that is why she became an artist.

Then just before the Hungarian hospital was sent back to Hungary my mother had to have surgery and we were transferred to the Osterode DP camp. It was due to her unexpected surgery that we stayed in the West instead of returning home to Hungary with the others.

Shortly afterwards my Dad was assigned to be the doctor at a Polish DP camp. We were lodged in the medical wing which consisted of an exam room, hospital rooms and 3 rooms for us with bathroom facilities, which were basically private. We were in heavenly luxury. My dad, Pista and I arrived there without my mom. She was still recuperating at some other hospital from her stomach operation and she was allowed to have Kathie with her. I remember cooking 'steckrüben' (rutabagas) in a metal can for 3 weeks straight. I did not have any other ingredients and also I did not know where the pots and pans were, or even if we had any. I think I cooked the same thing every day and hard as I tried I could not keep it from burning it. My Dad and Pista were of no help. They told me they liked the "kozmás" (scorched) flavor.

It was here that we heard about the Niederaudorf-Reisach school, where I was subsequently enrolled from October 48 to April 49. To my great joy I met Zsolt and Klári again whom I did not see since we left the wine cellar in Hungary. In April of '49 I was called home from Niederaudorf because we were able to go to the USA. My dad's 5th cousin's uncle was willing to sponsor us. According to the Displaced Act of 1948 only those were granted immigration papers who could assure total financial independence. This uncle, whom we never met was willing to sign the document of assurance that we shall not be a burden to the State because he was willing to take full responsibility for us. I hope God richly rewarded him for this unselfish act. Unfortunately it took us 6 more months before we were able to leave the camp to Bremerhaven from where we finally sailed to the USA on the military transport ship USS Gen Stewart.

And here a different life started for me and I was asked by Nóra and Jutka to share the high points.

It has been very difficult to force myself to write this review of my life, as requested. I guess I gave myself all kinds of excuses of being busy etc. so that I could postpone writing it. But upon closer examination, I have to be honest with myself: I was simply afraid to see my life on a piece of paper in its nakedness for everyone to see in all its glory and its many failures. And then I took a deep breath, and remembering the promise they gave me and decided to oblige and to write. The irresistible promise was: in exchange for my humble attempts to tell about my life, I would be able to read the life story of every one of my schoolmates of long ago. The temptation was well seasoned with friendly curiosity and it was too much to resist: I do want to read about your life paths. So I will try to zip through the last 36+ years.

A small group of Hungarians arrived in the US as the first DPs (displaced Persons) in 1949. We were pretty much on our own and were quickly scattered among the American population. I, as most youngsters, worked and went to school simultaneously because education was of prime importance to us. I finished high school, went on to college intending to become a doctor, but instead got married right after graduation. Only on occasion, (I abhor dwelling on the past), do I ponder on the subject of what would have happened had I not met Tom on that fateful autumn day so long ago.

Tom was an engineer from Case, in addition a handsome ROTC man and off we went to enjoy the often so-envied Air Force life. Our time at our first station at Englin AFB Florida brought us a daughter (Muki) and two years later a son (Thomas E.IV) and they survived 23 years of military life with us. Right after we arrived in Fla. I applied at a chemical plant at Melbourne and even though I held a legitimate chemistry degree, they did not hire me because I was a female—and What Would the Boys in the Lab Do with an Attractive Female Around!?! I couldn't believe it even then and a half century later such discrimination is even more unbelievable. However, the incident set my path for the future.

I took up teaching; taught 6th grade that year (didn't know there was such a thing as a teacher's manual) and although I quit 3 times, for some reason I kept drifting back into teaching, and now I am a veteran with 19 years behind me. I have taught just about every subject, including chemistry. I am in the field of Special Ed now, and I like it. I guess I was never a "normal teacher" anyway. I always worried about the Johnnies who couldn't read, or had problems sitting still. I finally found out why and what to do about it. The remedy is never fully successful and the heartache for these kids does not go away. The frustration remains and every day I am looking for new ways to challenge, soothe and to improve their self image. I am teaching at the area high school now.

During our years in the military (23 of them), Tom had followed a goal of retiring with a pension and with a skill that is marketable. He pursued his career with zest and imagination, acquired an MB and is now an "eggzegutib." We are all very proud of him. However, I guess nobody can be completely happy. His wish is that I become a successful Real Estate agent (I am a broker with my own agency, but not successful enough) so that he can retire on the farm with his tractor and lawnmower and 15 junk cars and live happily ever after.

My saga includes being alone in strange lands like FL, CA, TX and Mass, while Tom went to Iran, Greenland, SOS or other vacation paradises. We were all ready to settle down permanently when we finally found NH. Unfortunately, the children were all grown by then. So here we are, on the farm, with mother-in-law, 4 cats, a German Shepherd, and endless problems wondering not so much how it happened, (although that is important enough) but what next?

Muki went to Portland, OR to follow in my sisters' footsteps, who is now an Art Director of Advertising for a large department store there. By the time Muki graduated in '81 she too had a responsible job in the art department and since then had three serious promotions. The latest one puts her in a supervisory position with 4 lay-out artists under her, all several years older than she is. Two years ago she married a sensitive, good natured young man and seems to be very happy. I am waiting for my first grand child, but they are not yet ready to accommodate.

Tommy managed to survive growing up too. With all the stitches and the accidents for a while I was not so sure that he'll live to voting age. He took 2 years off after high school (which he just barely passed. I am convinced they passed him not on his accomplishments but on his potential) and is now into computer engineering at the University of Lowell with a 3.2 overall average. Same kid?! Leeann, his steady girlfriend of 3 years, has a lot to do with his success. They have survived running an apartment (4 apts.) so they could live near the college and be able to support themselves. And now they too are getting married in August.

So what is next? Neither Tom nor I are quite sure. We continue to work hard, planning for a pleasant final retirement, but I often get the feeling that the road getting there was the best part of it all, but the future seems fair enough and we ought to be happy.

I wish you all a marvelous reunion at Niederaudorf, and maybe the next time I'll be able to make it too. July 18, 2007

Béla Lahner:

I was born in Budapest on April 25, 1933. When I was about one year old we moved to the town of Szekesfehervar about 40 miles southwest of Budapest, where we lived until the year of 1945. In the fall of 1944 I attended the second year of *gimnázium* (sixth grade in US schools) when drastic changes occurred in our lives. It was the last year of WWII and the Soviet Army entered Hungary around April of that year. By October the fighting front was only few miles from our town. All schools were closed and the population was preparing for the occupation by the Russians.

The Red Army occupied our city on December 23 1944, one day before Christmas. The townspeople suffered through one month of looting and raping by the occupying forces (which was a norm on the Eastern frontline of the German campaign). On January 23, 1945 our town was retaken by the Hungarian and German military, and they held it for eight days. Six German soldiers (members of a tank brigade) were billeted in one of our bedrooms. They told us that they were running out of gasoline and were ordered to withdraw from the city to regroup and return in a week or so. If we wanted to avoid further street fights and bombardments they could take us with them to the next town, from where we can return later, they said. After considerable evaluations the adult members of my family decided to take their offer. So we left our home in Hungary on January 31, 1945 at 5PM and so we too became refugees of the war.

Within 3-4 days we realized that all the towns in Hungary were full with refugees and there was really no room for newcomers, so we moved on and crossed the border to Austria and continued to Bavaria, a region of Germany. We arrived there in February of 1945. During the following 2-3 years we were shuffled from one refugee camp to another and I had few chances to go to school; in fact I did not attend classes for over two years. Finally, a friend from one of the camps, Dr. Kovács, invited me to be his private student. In 1947-48 I traveled to his home and back again by train every two weeks for recitations and new assignments.

I had known of the Hungarian Girl's Gimnázium at Niederaudorf, but boys were not allowed to attend at that time. Great was my surprise when quite unexpectedly I received a letter in 1950, stating that I was welcome to enroll in the school that coming fall. So I packed up and moved to Reisach where the school was located. There were 40-50 students, two-thirds of them girls. The girls lived at the Kloster, but boys were assigned to live in the village with local families. The "Three Big Boys," namely Tony, Feri and I shared a room and we remained friends to this day.

I was attending the eighth grade, although I should have been three grades ahead. But just like everyone else I too had lost those years due to the war. The curriculum in this school was quite intense. We took eight to ten subjects. Each subject was taught 2-3 times a week, six days a week. We learned four languages, Latin, German, English and Hungarian (literature). My group had an ancient history class, including six weeks of Greek Mythology. Father Fekete taught a class in art history and art appreciation relying completely on his past knowledge as there was no textbook available. He dictated to us the concept definitions which we wrote down and recited the next day. I still remember his first lecture on the difference between culture and civilization. He was a superb lecturer. I learned some very good study habits which were an asset in later life.

Because of the diminishing number of students due to emigration, in the spring of 1951 it was decided that the Reisach Gimnázium should be merged with the one in Passau. Before spring vacation Dr. Arpad Marcell the principal at that time asked two of the Big Boys, namely Tony and me, if we could help with the move during the vacation. We both volunteered. The move lasted two days.

The first day we loaded up an American military truck with all the cabinets and beds. When it came back the second day, we loaded chairs, dishes and small items, everything that did not belong to the Kloster were sent to Passau. I stayed at the Passau school only for two months because at the end of May my family was called to Bremen to initiate our emigration to the USA. We arrived to Kalamazoo Michigan on July 1, 1951.

In the fall of 1951 the school advisors in Kalamazoo could not decide which grade of High School I should be admitted to. I had too many subjects in my certificates, which at that time were taught at the college level in the US. Finally they decided to allow me to complete the 11th and the 12th grades simultaneously with the understanding that if I can learn the assigned subjects successfully I could graduate within one year. It was a very difficult year but with the good study habits previously acquired I did graduate in one year.

In 1952, I entered Western Michigan University and finished with a degree in physics and mathematics. Luckily in the same month I got a job with a mechanical engineering firm doing design work. About three years later the first "big" computers appeared at the colleges around us, introduced as some new toy. The academia kind of shunned them. The firm for which I worked decided to find out if we could benefit from these computers. They sent me to the University to investigate. During the two years of traveling between the University and the firm I did not yet realize that I was actually building a career in computer science. I stayed with the firm for 25 years solving engineering problems on computers. Later I joined a pharmaceutical company for 15 years putting applications in statistics on IBM computers.

I was married in 1965 to a marvelous biology teacher, we had three daughters. Later, in what seemed like a short period we were blessed with six grandchildren. Now more than sixty years later I truly enjoy thinking about that wonderful and useful year I spent in the Reisach Girls Gimnázium in the Alpine valley.

Dr. Mária Magdolna Markó (Mrs. Gajáry) Markoczi: I was born in 1931. As times changed in the postwar years so did my name. First I lost some of the accent marks from my name. At other times uncaring officials misspelled it and were loath to change their errors. The school at Niederaudorf had a handful of girls with the name of Mária, so I was named almost instantly Markóczi to distinguish me from the other Marias. (I suppose the name Mária has a built-in confusion in it—just look at the three Marias in the life of Christ!) After some turbulent years I voluntarily changed my maiden name to Gajáry for the rather brief period of my married life but after my failed marriage I voluntarily gave up my married name, at least for a short time. The light of my life is my only child, a daughter, and after a while I found it intolerable that she had a different last name. So I was back again to my ill-starred married last name, which by the way none of my students at the American high school where I taught could remember, let alone pronounce. So for years I was known simply as Dr. G.

So much about my name. This I wrote not because I plan to waste paper ("Save the forests" etc.) but because I do believe in the ageless tribal sentiments passed down to me by my ancestors, that my name is my fate and in a sense it defines who I am. It defines me as accurately as the unreadable (at least to the uninitiated) mystic lines on the palm of my hand and on my fingertips. Shakespeare said, "What's in a name? That which we call a rose, by any other name would smell as sweet." However roses, unlike humans, are mostly very much alike and they can be recognized by their generic attributes. Humans on the other hand are individuals and most of them stubbornly insist on retaining that individuality, part of which is their name. There is also an admonishment in the Bible, I forgot where, perhaps in Jeremiah. It tells us to take care of our name (did he mean reputation?) because it will accompany us our life to the end, and is worth more than a thousand treasures.

My father was a high ranking career officer in the Hungarian royal army but since the German takeover of Hungary his power was ever waning. In December, 1944 following German orders he moved the regiment he commandeered and all its equipment together with some family members of his officers into an endlessly long freight train. Nobody, absolutely nobody dared to say that we were fleeing; the Germans, who by this time had the upper hand in everything, called it officially: "temporary planned retreat for regrouping." Labeling it as anything else different from the official definition would have counted as high treason. The troops moved into the wagons just returned from fighting on the Russian front. They were exhausted, malnourished, sick and badly outfitted as far as winter clothing, boots or weapons were concerned. The official plan stated that they would be moved to a place to rest where they would also be properly equipped before sending them back to fight in a final wondrous effort which would end the war. Some, including my mother, truly believed in this promise so much so that when the train stopped at Halle, she actually went to the Hungarian Consulate there to obtain papers for our reentry into Hungary, where we would pick up life exactly where we left it.

Well this also turned out rather differently from all expectations. No sooner did we pass the border from Hungary into Germany, right then and there the Germans ordered two companies off our train. They were sent not to rest up and be outfitted for the winter, but to fight at Breslau, never mind that in the worst winter of the century they were dressed in summer rags, were bone tired and most were quite ill. My father later recalled that this was the worst nightmare he ever had, except that it was not a bad dream from which one could wake up, but it was the stark reality. He was one of those career officers who considered every single member of his regiment as his own son, and he agonized over their fate as a real father would. He suffered seeing that they were actually used as cannon fodder in a war that was already lost months ago. But he could do nothing about the hungry, ill, shivering young men, almost boys, who were entrusted into his care. Hungarian military men, no matter how high their ranks were, had no power left; previous agreements and promises were ignored.

The rest of the soldiers and the families left on the train continued the journey toward Dresden, but we stopped at Wissenfels, short before reaching the city, which was unbelievable fortunate because ten days later Dresden was practically wiped off the map due to extremely heavy bombing. We still lived in the freight cars, but my father, ever worried about my education, immediately enrolled me in the local German school. Needless to say I did not approve of this unnecessary hurry to further the improvement of my mind, but my father was not in the mood to argue; besides he was much too used to giving orders without anybody ever questioning them. I didn't learn anything during the short time I spent that in that school except to extend the arm and shout "Heil Hitler" when a teacher entered the room. There were no books, and no homework, and this suited me just fine. Cautiously and out of self-serving foresight I never let them know that I spoke German as well as they did, so they left me alone. An occasional pitying glance was sent my way—given to the foreign girl, a descendant of an obviously inferior race. (It seemed that everyone was inferior except the Aryans, or Germans. I was wondering even then: how many of them believed this? However, if they believed that contrary to evidence some groups of people are inferior, then it is only a very short mental hop to come to the conclusion that by the same token some are superior.) At any rate, the attention they gave me was more than enough as far as I was concerned. But the idyll at this excellent Aryan school did not last long. There were several Messerschmitt factories nearby, and the location was not a secret to the Allied Forces; this had predictable results. As soon as instruction would have started the air raid alarm was sounded, we were released from school and I ran as quickly as I could to the "safety" of my freight wagon "home," parked on a railway.

Gradually the fronts were closing in on us. The Russians were advancing from the east, the Allied Forces from the west. And bombs fell without ceasing from the sky. At regular intervals the Germans removed entire companies from our train and engaged them in sporadic fights here and there. In just a few weeks only the truly ill soldiers and the civilian families were left on the military train; the entire regiment was gone. After about half of our wagons were detached from the train, we were ordered to move on. We had no goals or directions; the order was simply to move away, anywhere.

By all accounts that was the coldest winter of the century and we all suffered, even though we had little stoves in the cattle cars, and whenever possible we did steal a bit of coal from the train stations when we stopped at nights. During these breaks we got off the train to walk and stretch a bit, but we had to carefully watch our steps, as the freight cars usually transporting cattle, had no toilettes…

After pointless and hopeless traveling back and forth on various rail lines we finally arrived at Mittenwald almost at the same time when it was the general feeling that we could not take another hour of this unbelievable and potentially very dangerous journey. Mittenwald was already packed with refugees and the station master refused the permission for us to leave the train. Fortunately we still had a store of supplies which was prized highly during the last months of the war. It took four men to carry the bottles of cognac, cigarettes, lard, sugar and other luxuries to the mayor. Apparently it was not at odds with the Aryan dignity to accept bribes from inferior people. Naturally it was called 'negotiations' and not bribe. My father, a high ranking military man of unbending principles wore a civilian suit for the occasion. As a career officer of the Hungarian Royal Military his sense of honor did not permit him to wear the uniform with his medals for the clandestine affair when he was getting ready to bribe an honored public servant of German officialdom. One must have a certain standard in every situation, be it ever so questionable. But the important thing was that the bribe worked and our endless voyage ended before anybody lost his mind.

A teacher gathered a few boys and girls and we met regularly at a restaurant table to learn this or that. Leave it to my father for hearing about it and of course, I was immediately enrolled. I was less than enthusiastic about this arrangement and disapproved of the unnecessary hurry to improve my mind. But at least we did not have to shout Heil Hitler at regular intervals. The Bavarians were unique in this respect anyhow. Although by definition they too are German, but they hated Hitler so passionately that if an unlucky would-be customer forgot his manners upon entering a store and greeted with Heil Hitler, he was simply ignored and could not hope to get served. The accepted greeting was *"Grüss Gott,"* the closest approximation in translation would be either "God may greet you," or "Greeting you in the name of God." But since the words to greet and to bless have ancient common root, it could also be understood as "God bless you." At any rate it has nothing to do with Hitler. If someone did not follow the accepted form of invoking God instead of Hitler in his greeting, it was his trouble and of course he learned real fast to greet properly because he did want to be served at the store.

In Bavaria the war ended in May and my father and the remaining soldiers and officers of his regiment were taken prisoners by the American Forces. We had no idea where he was. Mother and I traveled from prison to prison trying to find him. This was not easy because in those times a special permit was needed to travel from one point to another. Also at seven every evening the former air raid alarm was sounded and nobody was permitted on the streets until next morning. We had to very carefully arrange our schedule of searching for him to fit into these restrictions. Finally late in September we met a German soldier, who was just released from one of the prisons. After we showed him my father's photo he recognized him as one of the inmates in the prison where he was kept. The nuns at Mittenwald were our friends and they rejoiced with us for finally finding him. They baked a wonderful loaf of bread for us to take to him as a gift. We didn't have to go empty-handed.

As a high ranking officer of the military he was scheduled to be extradited to the Communist government of Hungary. We knew exactly what fate awaited him there, and it filled us with dread. Fortunately he became quite ill, his symptoms suggesting typhus. Promptly he was transferred to a hospital, where it was diagnosed that he suffered not from the dread disease, but "only" from malnutrition. Although his condition was life-threatening, but not infectious, he was sent back to the prison. The inevitable confusion surrounding his transfer gave him a chance to escape and he did not hesitate to take it. It was so very lucky that we could meet him before his illness. He knew where we were staying. Our family was once again united although we did not feel safe for a long time for fear that he would be tracked down.

So our refugee life commenced. My parents, my uncle and I lived in a tiny room with a washbasin and a little iron stove. We were allowed to collect twigs in the nearby forest and we could bake the potatoes on top of it for our supper. Each day was spent in agonized speculations. Will they eventually catch on that Father escaped and will they find him? Would it be better to move from place to place to avoid detection instead of sitting tight in the same place like sitting ducks? If he would be captured again and extradited, should Mother and I attempt to go back to Hungary or should we stay in Bavaria in relative safety but in pronounced poverty and misery and hopelessness?

In order to buy food to supplement what was given us on the ration cards we had to travel to München and try to barter some of our worldly goods at the black market. During these excursions we had the opportunity to buy some newspapers where we read with horror the list of names of those officers who have already been extradited from the Allied Forces prisons to Hungary and into the hands of the Communists. We cried over the fates of our close friends and were filled with dread: how long would our extraordinary luck last, and how long can my father keep hiding?

New problems were added to our life. When we left Hungary my parents brought with them all the cash money we had, which they immediately exchanged for German currency. Although money was not worth much, still it could be used to pay for the items we received on the ration cards, or for buying railway tickets, or to pay for school tuition, or for the room where we lived. Everything else was only available in exchange for some goods. Still, we were more fortunate than most refugees because we left Hungary on a military train, which was neither safe nor luxurious, but at least it was spacious enough and so we could bring with us more of our belongings than most people could. By and by we kept exchanging these items for food.

When the money reform came our life changed from bad to worse. People who had jobs earned a decent salary, the stores filled up with goods and nobody was interested in used items any more. The Economic Miracle (Wirtschftswunder) happened, but it side stepped us.

I was enrolled at Niederaudorf in 1947, and that was the best thing happening to us. Finally I could attend a school, which had extremely high standards, was accredited and accepted by the German Dept. of Education as well as by the American temporary government in Bavaria, and later by every universities worldwide where former students applied. True, we were facing difficulties, perhaps of greater magnitude than what we anticipated, but it was our school and we loved it. We not only learned a great deal about our world, but acquired a love which was bordering on passion for knowledge.

Up to the money reform the tuition caused no problems for my parents. This changed drastically. According to my mother's carefully notated "household expenses" book, after the reform they could only pay the registration fee of five DMs, but not the tuition. From then on I did not receive any allowances and the "emergency food packets" sent regularly to me before the reform also stopped. Somehow though I could attend for another year; I do not know how this was accomplished, or even to whom should I be grateful for the privilege.

However by early spring I became very ill; my ailment was diagnosed as complications from malnutrition. The local doctor called it "hunger edema," whatever that is. I became so weak that I no longer could walk. My friends wrapped me in blankets and carried me daily outside into the nearby meadow so I could get strong in the fresh air. The rumor of my illness spread in the village, and the good people of Niederaudorf were concerned. Food donations arrived daily at the school; they sent what they had, such as milk, bread, cheese, eggs, butter. Once I even received a lemon!

By the end of May I was well enough so my mother could take me home, but even then I could not manage the long walk to Oberaudorf to the train station. The girls placed me into our trusty hand wagon and pulled me the entire long way. On arriving back home in Mittenwald, my mother borrowed a cart and pulled me to our little room there. When September came I still was not strong enough to return to school to complete the twelfth grade, and my parents decided to keep me home and help me prepare for graduation as a "home student." I successfully graduated at the school of Passau.

In 1951 we immigrated to the USA at Marymount College in N.Y. I earned a BS followed by a master's degree in applied mathematics. I was employed first at Cleveland, doing research at the Union Carbide's laboratories, and then moved to Rochester N.Y. and continued research at General Dynamics Corporation. Meanwhile I realized that research is fine, but not really my vocation, so while working I again attended school and earned a doctorate in education. Since then I have been teaching math in high schools for the next 23 years. I was happy.

I married and soon had a little girl, but my marriage did not last long. My parents died within three years and I was left alone with my daughter, the light of my life. She grew up into a wonderful person, studied and earned a masters degree in medical anthropology, and has been doing research in that field for the last twenty years. She is my treasure, my support, the reason for every day of my life.

Antal (Tony) Mélynádasy: My father's name was originally Machowitsch. He changed it to Mélynádasy when I was born. My mother's name was Stefánia Alsebesi Mélynádasi Tormássy. My father, when he decided to Hungarize his foreign sounding name, took one of my mother's forenames. Later, after my parents have died, I legally changed my name to Meynadasy, taking the "l" out in order to make the pronunciation of the name easier for the English speaking people.

My parents and I lived in Székesfehérvár where after being tutored privately for the first four years of elementary school, I attended the Cisztercian Gimnázium (High School) for three years. In the Winter of 1944 we left the country. We were in the bomb-destroyed city of München, Bavaria when the American forces came in. My father was a physician and a refugee organization asked him to take on the job of a camp physician in Laufen, Obb. where there were Hungarians living in a huge former prison building. Laufen was a small border town on the River Salzach where we all lived until 1951.

Many of the Hungarian families sent their daughters to Niederaudorf and later Reisach. Jutka Petres and Zsuzsa Petres, Éva and Judith Király, Vera Hadanich all came from Laufen and this is how I came to be there also. Naturally, the boys did not stay at the dormitory; they lived in the village of Niederaudorf with families in different farm houses. One of the students, who boarded with me, was Zsolt. We walked to school at Reisach every day. I stayed at Reisach for three years. During the third year, I stayed at another farm house with Feri and Béla. We three became good friends and we still keep in touch with one-another. When the school moved to Passau it was the three of us who accompanied the truck to offload the school's furnishing.

I finished the eleventh year at Passau.

In 1951 my parents and I emigrated to the US. We arrived in NY harbor on my 20th birthday. I knew English because in the Niederaudorf-Reisach and Passau-Waldwerke schools we learned English, German, Hungarian and Latin. My father, however, could not speak very well English and at first he could not be employed as a physician. The Catholic Welfare Organization in New York sent us to Hartford, Connecticut where both my father and I got a job at St. Francis Hospital. He became an orderly and I worked at the admitting office and the mailroom. We both started our career at the bottom. I was delivering flowers to the floors and pushed the patients into their rooms while my father pushed the dead patient on the stretcher to the morgue. After he learned the language and passed the board exam, he worked at the Prospect Heights Hospital in Brooklyn, N.Y. I moved to New York with my parents and worked at the Empire State Building for Diners Club, a credit card company just starting out.

My school credentials were accepted at Hyllier College in Hartford and later at St. John's University in Brooklyn. After I graduated from the College in Brooklyn with a BA degree, I got a job as a social worker at St. Joseph's Home in Peekskill N.Y. It was a home for neglected and abandoned children from New York City. Later I received an MSW degree from Fordham University. In 1960 I married Anna Váczy (Pancsi) who came over from England. I have known her from the school in Reisach and we kept in touch through correspondence.

We got married in New York City, but moved to Peekskill, N.Y. where my wife worked as a nurse at Peekskill Hospital. Eventually, I worked as a therapist at the New State Hospital for emotionally disturbed children and adolescents. In 1966 we both retired and moved to a retirement community in Southbury, CT.

God blessed us with four lovely children and seven beautiful and talented grandchildren. Our oldest son Michael graduated from RIT in Rochester, N.Y., where he married and they have three daughters. Our son Andy did not get married and he works at a Music Publishing co. in Manhattan. Our twin daughters are both talented artists. Betty Ann graduated from West Conn. University. They have two sons who are students at the same university. Mary Jane married an Irish man and they have two daughters. She works with graphic arts and her husband is in sales. Both girls chose fine arts as their career and inherited their talents from their mother, who has become a very fine painter.

We have been back visiting Niederaudorf and Reisach many times. I have many happy memories of the school. I liked director Kovács and learned a lot from him. He used to play the organ at the church and I often pumped the air for the organ. Thanks to him, I learned to appreciate classical music. When I was at a loss what I should do with my BA degree, he was the one who suggested Social Work for me.

I didn't regret getting into that profession. The school gave me a strong base for my carrier. My marriage to Anna is my greatest happiness. We worked hard but we feel gratitude for what we learned there.   Southbury, CT 2012

Judith Petres (Mrs. Balogh)

Was born in 1933 at Hévíz, Hungary. After her parents' divorce, her mother moved with her two children to Székesfehérvár. In September 1944, Judith just started the sixth grade when the school building was converted into an emergency hospital. At the same time, the furious bombing of the city forced people to move almost permanently into their cellars for safety. This ended her schooling in Hungary. The city fell after weeks of fighting and was occupied by the Russian troops. Life turned into a nightmare. A month later, at the end of January 1945, the Hungarian military was able to drive out the Soviet troops for a short while, and this gave the townspeople a chance to escape before the city changed hands once again.

In 1947 she was among the fist students to be enrolled at Niederaudorf, and was a student there until 1951 when mother and daughters immigrated to the United States.

Judith worked at St. Luke's hospital (Cleveland) as a receptionist in the emergency room, married, had three children, and attended Kent State University where she earned a BS as well as masters degree in special education. Later she attended the University of Dayton where she earned another masters degree in administration..

She is the author of seven books. In one of these novels, THE COUNTESS AND HER DAUGHTER, although the story is fictional, she used many elements of her experiences while fleeing Hungary, and later in the book she incorporated facts about their arrival in the United States. Another book, THIS OLD HOUSE BY THE LAKE, is a humorous account of the formidable venture of moving from Germany to Hungary and rebuilding an old, abandoned house there. **Here follows her own account of her life path:**

"When in the early fall of 1950 the news came that our immigration to the United States has been approved, I left Reisach, and we moved to München to wait for the final processing of our documents. While waiting there, I obtained a position at the hospital for the refugees. (UNRA Hospital at Schwabing.) After having been trained for about a week as a laboratory assistant, I was dispatched to work in the laboratory to help do blood tests. I was also expected occasionally to draw blood from patients when they had the bad luck to be admitted at a time when I was the only person available to do this job. Later, when once again I was employed, but this time in a "real" hospital in Cleveland Ohio, I recalled with horror how little experience and training I was given before I had to do such a responsible job. I suppose, the general sentiment was that DPs don't deserve better than me.

Once, when I was working the night shift, I was called up to one of the rooms to take blood from a new admission. I laughed and cried when I realized that she was a former student at Niederaudorf—although she stayed there only for a very short time, just long enough to absolve her graduation. By this time, I was fairly brave when I had to draw blood—but not this time. I could not do that to a "sister," and so went about frantically searching for a nurse, who was willing to do the bloody work for me. The world is small indeed. Even in the most chaotic, improbable times, it is possible to run into someone least expected.

After we settled in Cleveland, I worked first in a bank, then at St. Luke's Hospital as a receptionist in the Emergency Room. I married Maksymilian Ewendt, and in quick succession had three wonderful children. In due time, we moved into our lovely, brand new house in Aurora, close to Cleveland. When my youngest child was about four years old and already in Kindergarten, I had to realize that working the night shift in the hospital, about 25 miles from our home would have to end if I did not want to die young. I did not, but I could no longer deny that I was totally exhausted. A major change was necessary. I was afraid that if I spent too much time considering my plan, I would be overwhelmed by it, so I immediately followed the sudden decision with action and enrolled at Kent State University to earn a degree in teaching.

It was a daring decision; some thought it was sheer insanity. I have not been in school for a dozen years, my language skills in English were good but probably not adequate for college work and I have never seen a multiple choice test before. A friend of ours, teaching psychology at the University of Pittsburgh, offered to administer an IQ test to see how I would handle choices in a foreign language. The result was shattering. "The test shows that you are definitely severely handicapped intellectually," he said. "According to this, you cannot be educated at all. However, we know that this is not really the case, but the fact is that you are totally unprepared to take such tests. But I am willing to coach you." I left the eleventh grade an immigration and three children ago and was obviously much older than the rest of the students, a true misfit in those years before war veterans on GI Bills started to change the age profile of universities.

The gentleman at the admitting office at Kent State University, (Ohio) whom I approached with my request, leaned back in his leather chair and smiled benevolently: "No problem, Ma'am. We can take care of this easily. And whom do you plan to enroll, a daughter or a son?" Did I really look that old? For heaven's sake, my son just started Kindergarten! After we both recovered, he from his faux pas, and I from my wounded feminine pride, I confessed that I did not graduate from high school. I thought that would be the end of it, but he offered a solution: I may take the college entrance examination and if I pass it successfully, I may attend Kent State on probation. If during the first year I can maintain the required grade average, he told me, then my status at the sophomore year would change to that of a regular student. I accepted it, but not without trepidations.

However, I passed the entrance tests, and did so well that I was offered an unusual option: I could start at the sophomore level. I thanked but did not accept the skipping of a year, for I knew I needed that freshman year to polish up my English. From my letters, which I wrote to my mother from Niederaudorf, it is quite obvious that I was not a star student. The result I achieved on the college entrance tests, despite my obvious handicaps, was not because of my own "giftedness"—far from it. The credit and the praise must go to my teachers, who taught us so well. Our beloved teachers, none of them alive now, hopefully are at a place where they can see my test scores and can accept my deepest thanks. The years spent at Kent were extremely tough, but it paid off. I so loved teaching that I would have probably done it without a salary—and in addition, my own children had a full time mother during the summers, school holidays and snow days.

Despite some grievous and pessimistic prophesies, I finished college "Cum laude." At the same time, I raised my three children, took care of a big household, was an active member of the Hungarian cultural life in Cleveland; I also owned, edited and published a monthly magazine: KÉPES MAGYAR VILÁGHIRADÓ, single handedly. The magazine, lasting seven years, was devoted partially to literature and the arts; partially it was a means of informing Hungarians, by then living on four continents, of the accomplishments of their compatriots and the outstanding events they organized.

When after twenty-five years my marriage ended in divorce, I felt that a totally different life style was needed. Divorce is never easy, and everyone deals with it in a personal manner. ("Banging your head against the thickest brick wall," was the way my second husband later defined my problem solving strategies.) I applied at the Department of Defense, and was hired within weeks to teach at one of the overseas schools in Germany.

DoDDS-E serves children (K-12) of U.S. military service members and of the Department of Defense civilian employees throughout the European command. Its headquarters are at Wiesbaden, Germany. A general Director at Arlington, Virginia oversees all agency functions. The schools are organized into three Areas, each of which is managed by an Area Director. Within each Area, the schools are organized into Districts, headed by superintendents. When I was hired, the military presence was much larger in Europe; there were 144 of such schools in operation. After the Gulf War, the military drawdown started and of course, as military-fathers left Europe, the school system also shrank. At present 82 schools are operating, serving about 33.500 students, but with the next wave of downsizing, the numbers are going to change. (For more information on this, see my book THIS OLD HOUSE BY THE LAKE, available at amazon.com)

Life was wonderful and exciting. Returning during the summers to the USA, I earned two master degrees (one at Kent State University and a second one at the University of Dayton, both in Ohio).

And then I met my second husband, Győző Balogh, and a new, infinitely rich life was unfolding for me. My husband, also of Hungarian descent and an author, shared all my interests; our marriage, as the saying goes, was made in heaven. While building our new life, we traveled as much as our time would allow. This was also the time when I started to attend the University of Gutenberg at Mainz (Germany) to work on my PhD. However, when my position was abruptly eliminated due to the drawdown after the Desert Storm, we moved to Hungary and I never earned the degree.

When DoDDS adopted the Renzulli system for special education, I was selected to design enrichment programs for six schools, and to teach special classes for the gifted. I loved the challenge and was truly in heaven. Those children were unbelievably alert, open to the world and eager to learn. It was a privilege to teach them. Some samples of how they saw the world:

After a session of math, fifth grade students were asked to express some thoughts in one or two sentences about "zero" and they came up with:

"Zero is like money. You sometimes start with something, but you always end up with nothing...

You can't hear zero, you can't smell zero. It is like a dark room where you cannot see that there is nothing...

In the number system, you cannot get any lower than zero and still make sense, unless it is about the weather...

Zero is a wimp when it comes to adding. It is also a wimp when you subtract...

Zero is like the sound of a train...

Zero cannot make up its mind what to be. You see, if you have zero, you have nothing, but if you have one of something and put a zero after it, you have suddenly ten of it. Put two zeros after your one and you have a hundred. And it is easy to get a thousand, a million or a billion, just keep adding zeros. So then is it nothing, or is it a magic something?…

Zero is to me like a person with no eyes..

I write zeros when I am frustrated…

I wish I could multiply my brother by a zero so he would turn into nothing…

Zero reminds me of the time when I didn't have an allowance…

Zero cannot be used for anything sensible, except to show that the team lost a game and didn't get any points…

If zero was a unit of money, it is what a millionaire wouldn't want, but a bum usually gets…

Zero is there in all the –ty numbers…

Zero is like a coat you place on a chair to hold a place for your friend at a show. Nobody but your coat is on the chair, but everyone knows that it is taken…"

Another time, a group of fourth graders were shown two photos of paintings and were asked to compare the two and give a response to what they perceived.

The paintings shown were:

1. **Madonna and Child**, Giotto di Bondoni (12th century pre-renaissance) and

   The Nightingale's Song at Midnight and Morning Rain, Miro (mid-20th century surrealism)

   "They are both very old. That is the similarity. They must be hundreds of years old. The Madonna looks stiff and her baby in her arm is a little man, not a baby at all. They used to do that a long time ago. The other painting looks very old too. It is maybe something the Indians did a long time ago."

2. **Les Demoiselles d'Avignon**, Pablo Picasso (20th century cubism) and

   The Feast in the House of Simon, El Greco (16th century mannerism)

   "Both are similar because people don't look like this. The one painter went crazy and put all the wrong parts on the wrong places. The other made everyone long and blue-green. Look at those necks! Maybe they are goose-people."

3. **Supreme**, Kasimir Malevich (20th century. Vivid colored geometric figures on a pale background) and

   The Minuet, Domenico Tiepolo (18th century)

   "These two paintings are similar and they are both fun. The red rectangles make me want to laugh. I love music and dancing and that is what I see in the other picture. I'd like them both in my bedroom. Then I could go to sleep laughing and wake up laughing."

4. **Man Bearing Offerings** (detail from a relief frieze in an Egyptian tomb at Mehu. Sixth dynasty, 2345 BC)
and
Bullfight, Joan Miro (20th century surrealism)

"See, these are from Egypt. They had tombs there where they put the mummies. They decorated them with pictures. You can tell that they are Egyptians because their bodies are all twisted and they always have big eyes painted on the side of their heads, but sort of looking at you. This other part shows their picture writing. I forgot what they call it…"

"Hieroglyphs…"

"Yeah, that. They wrote pictures, not letters. Maybe they didn't learn spelling. The other picture has sort of stick figures too, but they are all over the place, not neat, like the first picture where the Egyptians march in a row. Maybe a baby Egyptian drew the second picture."

5. **Rouen Cathedral**, Claude Monet (19th century impressionism)
and
The Blue Dancers, Edgar Degas (19th century impressionism)
and
View of Toledo, El Greco (16th century)

"All three paintings are blue. I don't really like blue. Sometimes it is scary, like when the sky is dark blue and a storm is coming. And I don't like blue people. These paintings are very blue. You first see blue and only a little while later do you see the painting. This is the fun part of these pictures. I wonder how the painter hid the picture under all that blue."

6. **Painting T-17-17E**, Hans Harting (20th century. Black brush strokes on blue-yellow background)
and
Informal Pastel, Jean Fautrier (20th century. Blue brush strokes on a pale background)

"They are similar because these two painters did not have to work very hard. It would take about two minutes to splash on the paint and about five minutes to clean off the brushes. I don't think they would get a good grade in our art class. Our art teacher likes it when we really work hard on our pictures."

7. **Woman Under a Tree**, Japanese, (from the eighth century)
and
The Judgment of Paris, Peter Paul Rubens (16th century. Detail: head of Venus.)

"What fat ladies! They should go on a diet. If my mother looked like that, I think she would kill herself. The pictures are similar because the ladies are very, very fat. In one picture we only see the head and the neck. Maybe the painter did not feel like showing all of her, or maybe he did not have a canvas big enough for all of her."

One of the most outstanding achievements of this time was the unbelievable space project Lynn Langford, (Mrs. McDaniel's, another teacher for the gifted) and I have done together. Totally independently from each other while working for our master degrees, we both absolved a semester at a NASA Space Center. (She in Florida, and I at Cleveland's Lewis Center.) Upon completing the course work, our instructors assured both of us that if we ever decided to teach space science in our classes, they would provide all the help we needed. A few years later, Lynn and I met for the first time at a conference in Germany. We talked about our experiences at NASA and also about the need for an aerospace program. We both wanted to start one, but only half believed that we would really get help.

However, what NASA finally gave us was far beyond our most extravagant imaginations or dreams. Its fabulous support enriched the curriculum for about a hundred thousand students, and also gave a unique, never to be forgotten experience not only for the students but also for thousands of American and German adults. From the beginning, we involved the military in our project, and they became enthusiastic partners. We could not have accomplished it without their generous help, unfailing enthusiasm, and amazing know-how. The result was spectacular.

We worked out a threefold plan—and to this day we don't understand why it went so smoothly without a single glitch, or where did we find the energy and the courage to make it happen. I don't know about Lynn, but I am sure I could not do it today. It was not an easy venture, and it filled our summer vacation, and then the entire school year following it. Both Lynn and I taught a full schedule all day, so we had to do all the planning, preparations, and make the contacts for our project in the evenings and weekends. An added problem was that Lynn was teaching at Ulm and surrounding areas, and I in the Frankfurt area. The two areas are quite a distance from each other. Anybody, who has ever tried to use a military phone in Europe, can understand the added difficulties we had in communications. Fortunately, our husbands were most generous, and did not grumble (much) about the phone bills we ran up at our homes. They felt that considering all our calls and the length of them, the phone company ought to give us a discount.

The first phase of the project consisted of a general introduction to space science in our gifted classes; however, it was not exclusive: any student showing interest could also attend our lessons. This was the easy part because we were both well trained in this, and the youngsters were truly interested.

The second phase included four special aerospace instructors, selected and sent to us by NASA. A military plane brought them to Germany with all the equipment they needed to do their demonstrations and experiments. The plane also brought the material for phase three. We scheduled the four instructors to spend 2-3 days at each of the 144 schools, where they taught several classes during their stay there. Their success was phenomenal. They did spectacular demonstrations and conducted experiments of such complexity which none of the classroom teachers could ever hope to offer to their students. The students were not willing to leave the classroom after these instructional periods, but swamped the instructors with questions. The instructors left at each school movies, books, lesson plans, and material for experiments for the continuation of the program they introduced. It was amazing to see youngsters so fired up by science.

We arranged for the instructors to have food and lodgings at these various locations, and not only hired for each a van in which to cart their equipment from school to school, but because this was their first visit to Europe, we also introduced them to German highways and the aggressive driving style used on them. At the end, we gave each a T-shirt with the printed message: "I survived the German Autobahn." These American schools were located at various points at considerable distance from each other, and coordinating the regular schedule of the schools with the timetable of the four instructors was difficult to say the least. This was the most difficult phase of the program, at least for Lynn and me, but it was also the most successful as far as the students were concerned.

The third phase, consisting of two exhibits of almost Smithsonian quality, was scheduled for the end of the school year as a closing activity. Here the military and their phenomenal skills, and their willingness to help, produced miracles. They converted a hangar at Mainz to house the first exhibit. When Lynn and I entered the formerly inhospitable dark area, we could not believe our eyes seeing the miracle they performed on it. It was not an easy task on many accounts, but first of all they had to solve the problems of electricity and transformers. Many of the movable models and hands-on exhibits were designed with electrical (110 volt) connections, and before anything else, the problem of converting them to work at 220 volts without blowing every fuse there was, had to be solved. The displays were professionally arranged, well lit, every movable part moved, and the rock from the Moon was one of the many attractions. For lack of other words: it was awesome. The students, well prepared, enjoyed it with deep understanding. Those, living close to the exhibit, often returned in the evenings with their parents for a repeat viewing; it was amusing and satisfying to witness how they explained various aspects of the exhibit to their more or less baffled parents.

At the end of two weeks, it was disassembled, taken by military convoy to Ulm in the southern part of Germany, and set up again at a warehouse for the next two weeks. We requisitioned military buses, and scheduled all children to be taken on them to one of the two "museums" during the day. In the evenings and on the weekends, the museum (at both locations) was open to the general public, both German and American, who often stood in long lines, waiting for their turn to be admitted. The success of the project was immense.

I loved my job. The principals in the schools I served were very accommodating, even those who were not totally sold on the idea of providing extra fare for the gifted. But none was as supportive as Max Leonard at my "home-school," Col. Gail Halvorsen Elementary at Rhein-Main, which was my base of operations. He was the principal every teacher dreams about: totally committed to the school, to the children, loved his teachers—and loved all the special programs. There was never any reasonable request he denied, and he had a magical way of getting for us what we wanted. This was probably because he was almost a fixture of DoDDS-E, serving as principal from the time when the overseas schools were first established. When he retired, he took part of our heart with him. My programs, especially at the "home school," were great, mostly because of his unfailing support.

I could do what our teachers at Niederaudorf-Reisach only dreamt about. I could take the students on long study trips all over Europe; I could take them to theaters and concerts, museums, special events; I could invite guest speakers from a wide variety of fields, buy any book or teaching material I needed. My students were received at the ambassadorial mansion at Bonn by that most gracious lady, Ms. Gahl Burt, wife of the US ambassador to Germany at that time; she was the former private Secretary of Mrs. Nancy Reagan. The students were deeply impressed by the wonderful ambience of the ambassadorial residence which was already decorated with pine boughs and red ribbons for the Christmas season. They loved Mrs. Burt's baby boy sitting and gurgling happily under the Christmas tree, and they were enchanted by her gracious, elegant appearance. I too was impressed. First, because she was willing to receive us despite a broken leg; second, because of her superb calmness as if not considering the very real possibility of spilled hot chocolate over her precious rugs; but mostly, by the way she treated the children, as if they too were members of the rarefied atmosphere of Washington and of the international high society. She talked to them about the importance of education, of having a goal, of doing whatever you have to do with love and dedication, to take time to live and to enjoy each phase of life for whatever it offers without rushing headlong and too prematurely into the next phase.

My students met Otto von Habsburg, son of the emperor of Austria and last king of Hungary, and discussed politics with him. A few weeks earlier we have travelled to Vienna where the students visited the imperial palace, the Burg. It was there they first saw Otto von Habsburg in the official portrait done to commemorate his father's coronation as head of the Austro-Hungarian empire. He was then a seven-year old, festive, decorative, and a deadly serious boy with an imperial frown as befitting a future king and emperor. Later, when they met him in person—and he was by then well past seventy years of age, a smiling, kind man—they were awestruck as they realized how immediate history can be. After his presentation, the children asked him questions. One boy wanted to know whether his highness thought a third world war. He smiled and told them, "We are already deep in it. Only this war is not fought with conventional weapons. It is fought with misguided principles of economics. And I am afraid, the enemy is winning."

I organized many guest speakers to visit our classes. One was a famous and sinfully expensive designer of high fashion clothes. She must have read "Sartor Resartus," or else, her mind worked very much like that of Carlyle because she voiced most emphatically the thoughts of Professor Diogenes Teufelsdrökh (at times the name spelled less elegantly as Teufelsdreck) about the Philosophy of Clothes. She told them that since more clothing than skin is visible to the world, (at least this was true around 1980), the garments we wear become our outer surface, the part of us that is visible to the world. Socially and philosophically speaking, it is more important than our skin; people know and judge us by the way we package ourselves. She abhorred the uniform garb of blue jeans and T-shirts, one of which was once the garment of farmers and laborers, and the other an undergarment, both lacking individuality and character, not to mention beauty, elegance, or taste. She was truly disturbed by the new trend of madly striving to look like everybody else. She made a deep impression on the students and later invited them to one of her fashion shows in Frankfurt, attended by the rich and the beautiful—and us.

Truly, I could offer to my students experiences few children get in schools. I had it all: terrific parents, who took the education and behavior of their children seriously; a principal who was enthusiastically supportive; wonderful people outside of the school, who were willing to give time and effort to enrich the curriculum; and of course, Europe, offering all its treasures at our doorstep. It was heaven; it was yet another "school of a different kind." If I would have to start my life all over again, I would not do anything differently. Well, not true. I would certainly try to avoid the missteps, we humans seem unable to avoid in our life.

Max Leonard retired and the new principal had a vastly different approach. Many of us found it difficult to work under the circumstances she created. For one thing, she disliked special programs; as a matter of fact, she was downright hostile to them. Within weeks, she managed to destroy what I have built up with the support of Max Leonard during the years. I even lost my classroom, and had to share an open hallway with the remedial reading class and the German language instructors. This area was actually a wide, connecting hallway between the Junior High School and the Elementary School, and the traffic was continuous and extremely disturbing. I found teaching in this drafty, noisy hallway totally unsuitable. The children felt it too, and soon many stopped coming to classes. I was unhappy and demoralized to the point that my health suffered. I was defeated, and I knew it. I also knew that I could not and should not teach under those circumstances; it was not fair to the students. There was nothing I could do about it; my only option was to leave.

By that time I already earned my second masters in school administration, and by October I asked for a transfer to the Hanau elementary school to fill the position of EPM (Educational Program Manager) and supervisor. This was a lucky break. Christine Holston, the principal at Hanau, and Joyce Christian, the assistant principal, were both terrific women, absolutely dedicated, highly trained and were blessed with a great sense of humor. The three of us got along fabulously. The school was a happy place. This was fortunate because during this time, bomb and other threats to the school were almost a weekly occurrence. There were several assaults with fatal results on some of the US military bases; therefore, we always took the threats seriously. We, and the children, got used to see armed military police watching all the entrances of the school, and the children learned to keep their coats on the back of their chair to have it handy when they had to evacuate the building in a hurry without touching anything, such as locker doors or light switches, when the alarm went on. A bomb could be wired to almost anything. While the children more or less froze outside at a safe distance from the building, the three of us accompanied the military experts who searched the huge building from basement to attic. After some repetitions, it became a routine and we were actually calm during these walk-throughs. But to tell the truth, during the first few times, we were sure that our heartbeats could be heard in the fifth village down the road. I tried to imagine what it would be like if we actually found a bomb somewhere, but at this possibility my mind usually blanked out.

Then, in 1991, the Gulf War broke out. From Hanau, being an army base, many fathers—and sometimes mothers—were immediately deployed to Desert Storm, and we had bewildered, frightened children on our hands. On that first day there was very little teaching going on, partly because about half the children were kept at home by concerned mothers whose husbands just left for the war. We mostly hugged and tried to make all those, who came to school that day, feel safe and loved. Instead of instructions, we offered "fun activities" to help them over the first shock. In her mesmerizing voice, Christine Holston told stories; we found movies, and painted murals as large as the hallway was long on which the children depicted the best days in their life. But mostly, we just loved them and wiped away the tears. It was lucky for us that the sexual abuse cases were not yet the daily topic in the news: with all the hugging and caresses, through which we tried to sooth our frightened children, we could have easily been accused of the worst.

Following the Gulf War in 1991, the US military started its massive draw-down in Europe which mostly affected Germany because a large part of the troops was stationed there. As the bases closed, so did the schools, and the number of students decreased to less than a third the very first year the trimming started.

As the plan for the draw-down was implemented, the school at Hanau (K-6) shrank from 1400 students to less than 700 in just a few months. And it kept on shrinking… It was obvious that the smaller school did not need three persons in administration, and since I was the newcomer, my job was the first to be eliminated. Our future, which we took for granted, became very insecure and we had to make truly difficult decisions. In the end, for reasons we thought were rational, (at least at the time), we decided to stay in Europe. I'll never know if the decision was a good one. Perhaps if there existed a parallel universe where our alter egos would have made a different decision and in the end we could compare notes, then we could find the answer to this painful question.

For another year I still hung on—once again as a classroom teacher,—but the situation became everyday more stressful, and when my husband retired from his job at the end of the year, so did I.

My three children are happily married to wonderful partners, and are engaged successfully in meaningful jobs and are active participants in community affairs. I am extremely proud of them and also of my four grown grandchildren, who are reaching their thirties. None of them is married and so I will probably never know the joy of being a great-grand-mother. My family is my absolute pride and I give thanks everyday for the High Power to have given me the joy to see what each of these ten individuals achieved in their life.

We then moved to Hungary for several important reasons. There we remodeled and enlarged an old dwelling. I wrote five books, which enjoyed a degree of pleasurable success, and were very happy for another decade and a half. And then he died and I believe the world stopped spinning for a while.

After his death, I could not immediately decide to move back to the US. But meanwhile, time did not stand still, and I have now reached the age when it is beyond me to make such an enormous move. Zalaszabar in Hungary is my final home—just a few miles from the resort town where I was born. The circle closed, and I am back where I started. I fight off my inevitable loneliness the best I can. I keep busy, write for Hungarian literary magazines, work with the youth in our village, help out occasionally at a convent which houses elderly nuns (yes, there are some people around, who are even older than I am. Now isn't that incredible?) I have a few true friends, keep in touch with family and stateside friends through the magic of Skype or the e-mail, and I love the region where I live. I am truly rich, and am grateful for these gifts. To quote John Ciardi: "Life is good. At least not bad. It does. Or it will have to do."

Zalaszabar, 2011.

Zsuzsa Petres (Mrs. Szappanos)

Before I start translating my autobiography from Hungarian to English, I need to state that I had serious problems with the task. First, I discovered that the translation process from Hungarian is very difficult because the moods, the slight variations and the emotional content of the very precise words and expressions are so unique in Hungarian that it is almost impossible to transpose the same meanings and feelings into another language. What appears meaningful, even beautiful in Hungarian, comes through as stilted and artificial in another language, or else many words are needed to explain the intent of the word or sentence. While working on my autobiography, I realized the absolute truth of the statement: "lost in translation."

Second, all my memories have already been disclosed in the previously written book, in which these were related through the eyes of a very young person; the quotations used were from childish letters written to our mother at that time. Rewriting it after a sobering three score and four years later presents not only an obvious change in the way I now see events of the past, but it is a most troublesome task to remain objective and informative without burdening the reader…

In 1931 our newly married parents arrived at Hévizszentandrás (now Héviz), where my father was appointed physician to serve the surrounding villages as well as the bustling resort community of the largest thermal lake in Europe, Héviz. Three years later, succeeding my sister, I was born at Keszthely on June 8, 1936. After my parents separated in 1939, the three of us moved briefly to Dunaföldvár, joining my aunt's family; then in 1941, we transferred to Székesfehérvár.

Most of my childhood memories date from this lovely town. This is where I began first grade at the Catholic Externat School, now called Szent Imre Elemi Iskola (Saint Emeric Catholic Elementary School) where I received my first Holy Communion in the second grade. In 1944, I was enrolled in the third grade, but could not attend for long because the German army occupied all available space in our town, including school buildings.

However, while it lasted, it was a very pleasant time for us. We spent winter mornings in school, which we liked; then, in the afternoons, we took off for sledding on a nearby hill, or went ice skating. The evenings were spent listening to stories, or playing board games. During summers we went swimming at a place called Rozsáskert with several pools, which lived up to its name as there were rosebushes everywhere! The rest of our time was spent playing with our many friends in our sheltered courtyard, safely surrounded by buildings. We had a sand pile, parallel bars to swing and play on; there were swings, and walks where we could ride our rollers, and we had, among others, a wonderful huge chestnut tree which we could climb. We spent endless hours building chestnut furniture for make-believe small dolls. In midsummer, our father drove us to Diás to be with our grandparents for part of the vacation where we spent glorious weeks by Lake Balaton. Life was good for us kids. But the war was not far away.

Then on December 23, 1944, after eight weeks of fierce fighting, the Russian army invaded our city. During this time, because of the constant air raids and bombings, we were forced to take refuge in the cellar (not basement!) and share it with dozens of strangers who hoped that the massive, arched cellar walls of the ancient building offered protection from explosions.

We slept and lived on bunks on which the luckier ones, including us, placed mattresses. A small wood burning stove had to be shared by everyone for warming up food. It certainly did not give out much heat.

After a month long Russian siege, our forces were able to recapture the city for a short period and during this time my mother decided that we had to leave town. So on the last day in January 1945 we packed up the most important personal items (as there was no possibility to take along real luggage). Due to a very fortunate circumstance, we were able to get transportation to a border town, from where a truck took us into a camp near Linz, Austria. Maybe it was a special gift of compensation to be transferred to a picturesque countryside where a Hungarian camp under the auspices of the Szent László Rohamtüzérség helped us survive the next weeks. The beauty of the area helped to overshadow the horrors of the last weeks. I don't think anyone realized then, that we would never return home again, and that our homes were lost forever.

And so our new life began. The camp was rather poorly equipped for the great influx of Hungarian refugees, and there was a great need for food. Everyone was destitute, and our provisions lacked almost everything. As money had little value then, many resorted to a new kind of shopping, namely bartering and black-marketing. Whatever belongings people had, they took to the local farmers. Family heirlooms, lace, fur, and jewelry were traded for vegetables, fruit, milk, and eggs, or whatever food was offered in exchange. By this time the locals were spoiled by the rich offerings of the refugees, and they turned choosy. Not every piece of jewelry was considered worth the eggs, which they preferred to hold back for better merchandise. As I look back on these times, I realize it had to be extremely humiliating for my mother and sister to resort to this type of "trading." After repeated failures and shameful experiences, they eventually gave up on their futile attempts. Later, when there was nothing left to trade, people were practically begging, and many times were cursed at and chased away. But, I decided to try my luck and so joined the marketing corps. I was then a mere 9-year-old, small for my age, and often they took pity on me. Sometimes I was the only one who was able to get something edible. Victoriously I carried my treasures home, and was immensely proud and pleased with myself at my success. In the early spring we also went out into the fields to pick sorrel to make it into sauce or soup, searched for wild berries, or for nettle, which was a substitute for spinach in our diet.

After a few weeks of staying at the camp, my father, who at the time was in Bavaria, discovered where we were and sent a horse-drawn carriage and two Hungarian soldiers to escort us. The plan was to join him at the military hospital, where he was chief of staff. The war was not quite over and the border between Bavaria and Austria was still open for travel.

On this trip I got critically ill with pneumonia and due to the seriousness of my condition, the trip ended here. I was placed in a hospital in a small Bavarian town called Laufen where we stayed until we immigrated to the United States. The kind nuns who ran the hospital not only accepted me as a patient, but also provided shelter for my mother and my sister.

Laufen was not meant to be our final destination, but circumstances forced us to stay there. It was in this town where I met Király Éva, Király Judit, Mélynádassy Toni and Szabó Dóri whom I met later at the Hungarian school at Reisach. Their families were among the Hungarians, living in the town and our parents knew each other well. After I arrived at the school, it was a comfort to see familiar faces so far away from our parents.

The years 1946-1947 were just a big haze in my life. During this time I was ailing again. My father was by then in Salzburg, Austria, practicing at an UNRA hospital. When he found out about my condition, he made arrangements for me to be taken to Salzburg, and from there we traveled to Telfes, Tyrol where he was just appointed physician at a Polish orphanage. I spent six glorious weeks with him in a beautiful alpine setting. I returned to Laufen much healthier and stronger.

In 1948, I could finally enroll at the Reisach Girls' School where I finished two full years crammed into one. This change in my young life was huge, as it was the first time that I was separated for a long time from my mother. The only circumstance easing the pain was that my sister was already at the school, and she assumed the "little mother" role. This was also the place where I was inducted to scouting. Scouting to this date is an integral part of not only my life, but that of my husband's also. Even in our golden years we are staunch supporters of this organization. Our four children were also members, and partially because of this, they speak, read and write fluent Hungarian.

The years spent in Reisach were memorable for many reasons. Besides a very rigid and regulated teaching schedule, we were also given a lot of opportunities for excursions in the lovely alpine environment. The scenery was breathtaking, and taking walks or mountain climbing was a joy for all of us. I remember a particular climbing experience that turned into a strangely fun time. Of course, no one had good comfortable shoes, not to mention climbing boots. When we reached the summit, I realized I had horribly painful blisters on my feet and could not walk anymore. As it turned out, I was not the only one; so another girl and I were left behind and stayed at an alpine hut for the night. The place was totally empty except for the two of us and we did not sleep a wink but spent the night trying out all the empty beds. Next morning we limped back to school in our bare feet much to the delight of the villagers. But we would not have missed this outing for anything. There was also a small lake nearby and a cold river where we swam. There were lots of evening walks, singing, and volleyball playing. What we lacked was decent food and were forever hungry and cold in the winter months. Our parents, in my case our mother, sacrificed practically every morsel they were able to spare and sent us parcels with supplements. Eventually my mother paid for her heroic efforts with her health, which was almost a disaster when our immigration procedures started to the USA. For a while we were fearful that on account of her frail health we would be rejected by the physician who examined us.

In 1949 I started the seventh grade at Reisach School, but by November my sister and I returned to Laufen. By now there were a lot of changes in our school as a number of the teachers immigrated to various countries, including our principal with his family. We had also started our own immigration procedures so it was more feasible to stay close to home in case the call for the final part of the process came. I enrolled midterm in a German school at the 7th grade level and stayed until July 13, 1950. I continued mountain climbing with a local youth group. As I think back, I realize that times were so different then. Young girls were safe, and felt no fear in taking part in these excursions. I still remember one particular climb, starting early in the dawn as the sun was rising. Mass was said on the summit. The altar was made of rocks and decorated with alpine roses and the wind was blowing... We all sat very quietly on the moist grass and felt closer to God than ever before. What a lovely memory!

Then, due to yet another fortunate circumstance, I was able to enroll in the fall of 1950 in the Ursuline nuns' all girls school at Salzburg. My memories of this time are very fond, even though getting to school was difficult. Every morning, with my special permit, I had to walk across a bridge over the River Salzach, which was the border between Austria and Bavaria; then catch the train to Salzburg. In the fall, this was not a problem, but as the cold weather arrived, far too early, we were shivering outside on the open platform of an overcrowded train, huddled together with the other students. We were practically frozen by the time we arrived in Salzburg. It was a miracle that dressed in our flimsy winter coats and paper thin shoes which were soaked in the snow, we did not get sick. But after arriving at the school and partaking in the compulsory early Mass, the nuns silently ushered us into the kitchen for some hot chocolate and wonderful, buttered hard rolls.

The scenery of Salzburg was gorgeous and the city was rich in musical history. Often our entire art class was taken outside with pencils and drawing pads to draw the city's lovely buildings. The Ursuline nuns left a lasting impression on me with their quiet, reserved, exemplary but strict attitude. I was in touch with the school till about a couple of years ago.

Finally, the much anticipated immigration procedure started to escalate, so right after the Christmas holiday I did not return to school but rather our family of three moved to Munich. We stayed at an IRO camp (I believe the acronym stood for International Refugee Organization) where the very strict final processing and testing took place.

On January 21, 1951 we all boarded the troop carrier General Blatchford in Bremerhaven and embarked on a rather stormy Atlantic crossing. After a miserable 10 days, we finally arrived in New York Harbor and social workers helped us board a train to Cleveland.

All this was not as easy as it seems, and the beginning was hard on all three of us. Only my sister spoke English, and I suffered greatly after being literally dropped into high school in the 10th grade. This school fortunately had a class for young immigrants who needed help in English, so by the end of that year I knew enough to finish the school year. It was very awkward to be around American students because they looked down on us due to the language barrier. I think this was the most difficult time in my life, but I managed to graduate in January 1954. My mother also met her new husband, who was a wonderful person, and much loved by all of us.

During this time, I joined Hungarian scouting and also a Hungarian girls' club. Unfortunately I was not able to spend as much time with them as I would have liked because I also had to work part-time after school. Our family of three did everything to get settled and be established in this new environment. In particular, it was our mother who had the most difficult time, as the job she was given should have been done by a man. Finally, she was able to obtain work in a very nice place where she was truly appreciated and treated with respect.

After high school, I worked at BF Goodrich Chemical Company as their bookkeeper. This was a very nice and sought-after position at the time. It was also at this time that I met my husband who just returned after a two-year tour of duty in Korea. Steve enrolled at Fenn College (now Cleveland State) and eventually got a bachelor's degree in electrical engineering. We got married in 1955 and had our first baby the following year. Since then, our family has grown to four children and as of this moment, nine grandchildren! For a time I was a stay-at-home mom, but eventually I assumed holiday part-time jobs, and when our two older children enrolled in Lake Catholic High School, I was able to secure the position of main office secretary at the same school. In the meantime, I continued with scouting. First as a scout wife, then scout mom, then was appointed organizing staff chairperson for our troop. I also volunteered at the Hungarian Radio and Television Station WNBN in doing programs. I volunteered for everything under the sun, and it kept me busy. I guess my strong points always were my perseverance, my compliance, and my willingness to do hard work. I never shied away from anything that had to be done. I accepted hardships with hardly any complaints, knowing, that everyone had his share of troubles, and in this respect my life was no different from the life of others. Yet, I had plenty of good examples and role models to follow.

Eventually I completed a comprehensive course in travel-agenting and for 13 years was able to see different countries and islands due to the generosity of my firm. My memories of these trips are priceless When my husband retired, I left the travel field and dedicated my life to my family, children, grandchildren. Both my husband and I kept up our work as "scout elders" and both of us are active volunteer members of the Hungarian Heritage Society and Museum in Cleveland.

The person who left the deepest impression on me was my mother. She was always my shining example, my guiding light. She was widowed in 1984 and after that my husband and I took care of her. When she became frail, she lived with us for a scant year until she passed away in 2007 in our home. When she passed her ninetieth birthday, she started to develop a dread of ever having to move into a home for the elderly, which of course we never considered, not for a moment. Gradually she found her peace, and was able to believe that she will stay till the end in the surrounding in which she felt comfortable. It gave me a tremendous peace of mind that we could take care of her in our home, surrounded by the family she loved, to the very last minute of her long and remarkable life.

Now that the grandkids are grown, I spend my time gardening, reading, listening to classical music, and communicating with our friends of 65 years.

Jutka: The following was left out of my sister's story, probably because she was too ill at the time to care about anything except surviving from hour to hour. But this part of our story shows another incredibly sad aspect of the war years, a fate of being separated from family members, shared by thousands:

Our father, through some mysterious channel, discovered that we were staying near Linz in Austria at a camp. This accomplishment was nothing short of a modern day miracle. He was at that time chief of staff of a Hungarian military, so-called "moving" hospital in Bavaria, taking care of the wounded. Knowing that he could offer us a measure of safety at his mobile hospital, he sent a horse drawn wagon to the camp in Austria with a pair of Hungarian soldiers to accompany us to Bavaria and to his hospital. Fortunately, at this time, the border between Bavaria and Austria was still open for travel.

Our horse was tired and ill nourished, so were our two soldiers, but we made our way west, although very slowly, taking many days for the long journey. We had to save the strength of the failing horse and could not burden it with too much weight to pull, so mostly we walked the many miles. But we were grateful because at least we did not have to carry our belongings, and we could take turns sitting on the wagon for periodic rests during our long march.

According to our information and calculations, we expected to be almost caught up with my father when unknown to us, his unit,—hospital and all,—was ordered to turn back to Austria. So this was the situation: he was heading back east while we were still going west, ultimately missing each other. It would have been pure slapstick, if it were not so tragic, so frustrating, so frightening and so close to death,—because on this long and difficult trip my sister became critically ill with pneumonia. In a time when medications, let alone penicillin, were not available, her condition was frightening as bedded on the wagon she was fighting for her breath, burning with fever, no longer recognizing anyone. My mother and I, walking on either side of her, prayed to every saint we knew. She needed to be hospitalized as soon as we could find a hospital, which would take her. We eventually found one in the small Bavarian border town, Laufen. Here, our gentle and well bred mother suddenly proved that she could be as aggressive as a tiger when her cub is in danger. When the nuns hesitated to accept my very sick sister, Mother wouldn't take "no" for an answer. And this she announced in a loud and clear voice pitched to almost a scream. She baffled me because I have never seen her in this way; the nuns, who were in charge of the hospital, too were speechless. As a result, they admitted my sister, and even gave us temporary shelter so our mother could be close to her very ill child. I could never figure out whether they were scared of her holy rage so foreign to them, or they simply admired her royal imperative, born out of frustration and raw fear.

Our soldiers took off with the horse, heaven only knows to what destination and our futile travel terminated. By the time my sister would have been well enough to continue the journey, we were horseless; besides, the war then was over and the border between the two countries were shut down, putting a formidable obstacle between my father in Austria and us in Bavaria.

At Laufen we had an amusing experience. When my mother heard that toward the last days of the war the American troops already reached the town limit of Laufen, she went to the hospital ward and gathered up my sister, blanket and all, and then took refuge with us in the fruit cellar. There we huddled in a corner, shaking with fright. Too well we remembered the horrors of the Russian occupation in our town in Hungary. Finally a nun found us and wanted to know what exactly were we doing in the fruit cellar.

- We are hiding from the enemy—my mother replied.
- What enemy? The innocent and saintly woman asked.
- Well, the Americans.
- Oh, that! The enemy, consisting of a single tank, is stationed at the town square, and the two soldiers, who took the town, are standing on top of their monstrous vehicle and are distributing candy and gum to the kids—she reassured us. Apparently, thank God, there is a difference.

About a year later, at the end of 1946, my father managed to pull strings most people did not even know existed, and so could obtain a passport to Austria for my sister, who was ailing again. They spent six wonderful weeks together in the Alps where he was appointed physician in a hospital to care for sick Polish refugee children, but I have not been able to see him for the next twenty-five years. Years later he ended up in Argentina and we in the USA. War has a way of reshuffling people on the globe, separating people and inflicting yet another class of pain on humanity.

Anna Mária (Anikó) Radnay (Mrs. Kent)

My father attended the LUDOVIKA Military Academy in Budapest and in 1931 graduated as Lieutenant in the Royal Hungarian Army. His first posting was to the 13th division of the infantry in Budapest.

Here, my father met and married my mother Ilona Latkóczy; she was member of an aristocratic family with recorded history from the 15th century. I was born on March 21 in 1935 at Sátoraljaújhely in Northern Hungary where my father was stationed at the time. In 1939, my father was promoted to the rank of Captain and his posting was at Kőszeg in Western Hungary. Here he was appointed Adjutant to Colonel József Finta, who was the principal of the military high school at Kőszeg. While still at Kőszeg, our life-style changed drastically. My father was sent to the Russian war front, and soon after his departure, the German army occupied Kőszeg.

They established their headquarters in the Dominican school where I was a third grader. Having lost our school building, a new location for instructions was found, but because of the changed circumstances and inadequate accommodations which many of us had to share, school time was reduced to late afternoons and even so, we did not meet every day.

In December 1944, my father was sent home from the Russian front as he was severely ill with dysentery. On his way home, he was stranded in Budapest for the month when the city was under siege by the Russians. It was fortunate that he met there his former Commandant, Field Marshal Finta, who told my father that a retreat to the West was being planned for his unit, and that he would be passing through Kőszeg. My father then asked Finta if he would allow his wife and three daughters to join the convoy. Luckily, our mother still had her small Opel Olympia, enabling us to join. On the morning of March 27th 1945, Field Marshal Finta telephoned my mother telling her that if she could be ready with her three little girls by next morning at 08:00 she would be welcome to join. The convoy started from the military high school right on time, and later that morning we crossed the Austrian border.

After several days of perilous traveling we arrived at Handlab in Bavaria on April 3rd, 1945. Accommodation was provided at the Grubmüller Gasthaus in the big hall, converted into a dormitory for the Hungarian refugees. Soon after this, the American army occupied Handlab and confiscated our little car.

At the end of the war (May 1945,) the proprietors of the Grubmüller Gasthaus offered my mother a room at their premises. In exchange, my mother had to work as a housekeeper and kitchen maid. Here, in the one small room, we all slept, lived, cooked, and did the washing until we could emigrate five years later. During this time my father was transported from the hospital (Auerbach) to the Heilbronn camp as a prisoner of war of the American Forces. Of course we had no idea about his whereabouts and worried endlessly about him. At the beginning of 1946, the Americans extradited several trainloads of war prisoners to Hungary. As the train stopped at the Austro-Hungarian border, my father had the presence of mind and the good luck to be able to slip off the train unnoticed. Eventually, the Red Cross helped him to locate us, and it was to our immense joy when, totally unexpected, he appeared at the door of our little room.

While we were at Handlab, our education was again disrupted because we were not accepted into the local Bavarian school. Late in 1946, my parents heard that a Hungarian high school, a *gimnázium*, was opening at Niederaudorf. My parents applied and were delighted when I was accepted. When in January 1947, accompanied by my father, I arrived at Niederaudorf, I was the very first student in the school. I was then almost twelve years old, enrolled in the fifth grade, and was immediately given the pet name "Anikó."

By June 1947, during the first shortened school term, I completed one grade, and by December during the second term, I absolved yet another grade. After this, I had to stay out of school from January 1948 to the middle of March 1948 in order to look after my two younger siblings while my mother gave birth to another sister.

While I was at home helping my mother, I received a very affectionate farewell letter from the principal of the school, Dr. Dezső Ravasz, informing me that he would no longer be at Niederaudorf when I returned for the new school year because he and his family had chosen to return to Hungary. He was very popular with all the students and I especially liked him and his family, so on my return to Niederaudorf in March 1948 I was not very happy to find a new principal. As far as I was concerned, the new principal, Mr. Kovács and his family, were not as caring as Dr. Dezső Ravasz and his family. Consequently, I was quite pleased when I was told by my parents that my days in Niederaudorf had come to an end.

The reason for this abrupt termination of my education was the money reform. In June 1948, Germany changed its currency from the Reichsmark to the Deutschmark. It seemed strange to us that suddenly everything was available in the shops but many people, especially the refugees, had no money to buy any of the wonderful things. My father had made a reasonable income from his black market activities, and from it was able to pay my school fees, but after the money reform, the black-market collapsed. He was allocated a very low unemployment benefit, not nearly enough to live on, and our financial struggle for survival began. This was when I learned that I would not be able to return to the Alpenhof.

Later in September 1948, my two younger sisters and I were able to commence schooling in a German school at Iggensbach, the next village down the road. The State School was a 2 km walk from our one room home in Handlab.

In 1949 some countries opened their doors for immigration. So in January 1950, my parents decided that it was time to relocate from Germany where we were still only displaced persons without any hope for a better future. Australia was accepting couples even with dependent children, and my parents applied.

We sailed out from Bremerhaven on August 24, 1950 on a Norwegian troop transport ship, and arrived a month later in the early hours of 24th September ,1950 at Fremantle, the harbor city of Perth in Western Australia. During this long journey the ship was clearly short of staff, so my mother and I applied to be Kindergarten attendants. We were paid with cartons of cigarettes which we were able to sell to the immigrant passengers and because of it, we could start our new life with a little bit of cash.

After our arrival, we were located in army barracks at Northam, a small town 50 km from Perth. Here, my sisters and I attended the local school but since we did not speak English well, we learned very little.

For a few months we stayed at this camp and then the Australian government started to implement the terms of the two year contract, signed by all immigrants 18 years and older, (excepting mothers with very young children). This required everybody to accept the work which the Australian officials allocated to them. Expertise in any field, former education and training were not considered; men were assigned as laborers, women usually as cleaning help. My father was placed with a pipe manufacturing company in Perth, so we had to move to that city.

After we arrived in Perth, my mother tried to find employment for herself, but this was far from easy because she still had to care for 3 year old Agnes, my youngest sister. She then heard that the nuns in the Sacred Heart Convent in

Highgate (Perth) needed a cleaning woman and she gladly accepted the position. I thought at the time how sad it was that my mother was to become a cleaning lady, so terribly different from the comfortable and pampered childhood in the safety of a loving, privileged, aristocratic family. It never fails to amaze me how our mothers, including ours, were able and willing to do endless sacrifices in providing for their children and promoting their education. When I asked her how she did it, her simple answer was "Love makes it easy."

At any rate, my mother was content with the arrangement because the nuns let her keep Agnes at her side during working hours, and so one of her biggest problems was solved. Soon after this, my mother and the nuns made an agreement that henceforth she would work without a salary, and in return, the Convent would accept the three older girls at the boarding school of their "sister convent" in Narrogin, 150 km from Perth. My mother was very pleased with this arrangement because she was convinced that this would be the best and quickest way for her three girls, for Mary, Helen and me, to learn to speak English.

Our Mother was correct about the improvement of our language skills because in December 1951, when we returned to Perth, our English was quite good. So much so, that being a confident 16 year old, I sought employment during the school holidays. I was accepted for the very first job for which I applied, which was in a large department store in Perth. I was employed as a sales assistant and was very proud to bring home my first pay check. I was happy that my salary helped to support the family.

In October 1952, I met a Hungarian man, László Jarosek and married him in January 1954. We had three children, Stephen, born in 1955, Frank in 1957, and a daughter Annette, in 1962.

As "New Australians" we were not readily accepted by the local Australians, and so at times we felt lonely and rootless. My husband Laci and I were not well off financially, but fortunately Laci soon found work as a service engineer with the telephone company and I was employed as a theatre manager at a new drive-in theatre which just opened. Now, with our combined income, we could finally establish a comfortable living. The timing of our work schedule was also favorable since I was at home with the children during the day and when I left for work in the evenings, Laci was home and acted as a wonderful father. He did all the home duties in the evenings, cared for our three children and helped with their studies and homework.

Unfortunately, Laci became ill and eventually, in January 1972, he was diagnosed with cancer. He died in July of that year.

With three children at home, I could not continue working in the evenings at the theatre. As a solution, I completed a course in insurance-underwriting, and then joined an insurance company as an underwriter. I could now care for my three school age children and earn enough to cover our needs. I worked for this same company for 20 years, and only left, when the company was sold in 1992.

In 1976, I married again. My new husband was Dr. Kenneth Kent, Veterinary Surgeon. Six years later he died, also of cancer. There were no children from this marriage.

The next 12 years were spent in bleak loneliness, and then, in 1993, I met Charles White, a professional Mechanical Engineer who was a widower. Charles asked me to marry him, but, since I had already lost two husbands, I refused the marriage, I did not want to lose a third man. We enjoy a committed partnership and a great relationship. He is a wonderful companion. Charles is still working in his profession and I manage his office affairs.

In summary,

In spite of all the highs and lows in my life, the determining factor of my youth as well as the source of my most cherished memories were the 15 months I was fortunate to spend at Niederaudorf. I enjoyed the times with the first headmaster, Dr. Dezső Ravasz and his wife Margit néni, and liked the Wallers, who owned the pension.

In my later years, life has been very good to me. My children are grown and settled, and the many reunions we have with former classmates at the Alpenhof and elsewhere are important to me; these meetings always fill me with joy and sort of recharge me. I appreciate the unconditional sisterly love from all the ex-students, now living in different parts of the world.

I must not overlook mentioning the hospitality provided by the Schmid family, the current owners of the Alpenhof, during the times we had our reunions at Niederaudorf. Frau Schmid, daughter of Mr. & Mrs. Waller has always welcomed us lovingly for our reunions in their wonderful Alpenhof, where our school found its first home.

August, 2012.

Dóra Szabó (Mrs. Badzey)

I was born in 1937 at Gyula, but my parents soon moved to Szatmárnémeti. During an air raid our house had a direct hit, totally destroying it. We fled Hungary in the early spring of 1945 during the last days before all of Hungary fell under Russian occupation. Trains were no longer operating; my parents, my uncle, and I walked the long distance to Austria on foot. Unfortunately, I badly injured my foot, and simply could not walk on. Acquaintances of my parents passed us on the road in a car, which, because of lack of gasoline, was pulled by horses. They offered to take me along. As we moved somewhat faster in the horse-drawn car, then my parents on foot, our friends agreed to wait for the walking party at a certain town. However, we drove into a major air raid, and had to move on. In the chaotic, panicky scramble, we were not able to be at the appointed place to meet my parents, and we had to continue our journey to Salzburg. Four long weeks have gone by and I was devastated because I feared I'd never see my parents again. I was only eight years old and was with people, who were practically strangers to me. I was scared. Meanwhile, my parents were frantically looking for me. My uncle left them in order to search for me in a different direction from where my parents did. It was he, who eventually found us, but by that time he had no idea where my parents were. Then miraculously, on my father's birthday, we were finally united again. My mother often told me that this experience revealed to her the degree of anguish the parents of Jesus must have suffered when they too lost their child at the Temple. Up until then, it was just another verse in the Bible. Without wasting time, and much relieved, we continued our march from Austria to Bavaria because our aim was to reach a region which according to our calculations would be occupied by American forces. By that time my parents knew enough about the other occupation techniques of the other members of the Allied Forces, and they knew that our best chance was with the Americans. In the nick of time, practically hours before the border was closed, we crossed the bridge over the River Salzach to safe Bavaria, in the small city of Laufen. There were already about 3000 Hungarian refugees there who came with the same purpose in mind.

According to my father's notes, we moved from Laufen to Oberaudorf in October of 1948, most probably because that way I could enroll in the Hungarian School which was located in the Carmelite Kloster in the neighboring village of Reisach.

In Hungary I had completed only the first grade before we had to flee. After we had finally settled in Bavaria and I had learned German, I should have been in the fourth grade, but I was permitted to enroll in the third grade only. The following year, I could finish fourth grade in the village grammar school of Laufen.

The Hungarian Gimnázium in Reisach gave me the opportunity to study in my native language again and to finish the fifth and sixth grades in one year. Thus, I had finally caught up the lost years.

As I remember, I was very happy to be a boarder because that had always been my dream.

My mother accepted the position of "janitor and cook's helper" in order to pay the tuition and make my dream a reality. I saw her working many hours. She was cooking, cleaning, and scrubbing the long corridor from which the individual cells opened. These cells were our classrooms and the large room at the end of the corridor was the dorm where all of us girls slept.

Unfortunately, my stay as a boarder was short lived because my poor mother simply could not continue the hard work. In spite of this, I remained a student but not a boarder.

Of course, that meant that I had to walk the route from Oberaudorf to Reisach in sunshine, showers, and snow. I did not mind it too much because the walk took me through meadows covered with flowers, and in the winter snow crunched under my boots. Then the trees and bushes were clothed in soft white cloaks and even the fence posts wore little white caps. In the fall, I often saw serious storms when black clouds massed behind Brünnstein Mountain. Lightning flashed in the darkness and the wind drove the autumn leaves angrily before me. Ever since then, I have loved all the different faces of nature, but since fate brought us to Southern California, I have not had much opportunity to enjoy the playful changes of seasons.

Even though I only spent one year at the Hungarian School in Reisach, the opportunity awakened in me the love of my native language and an enduring interest in my country's history and literature. The years may have dimmed some memories, but I will never forget those teachers who persevered in enlightening us during those impressionable years. They have my lasting gratitude.

We immigrated to the USA in 1951 where our first home was Bridgeport, Connecticut. Life there was extremely difficult and we were pretty lost. I kept in touch with Mária Barany our former teacher and housemother, and she advised us to move out to California where opportunities were much better than in Connecticut. We did so, and never regretted it, even though the beginning there was tough, but not hopeless.

My parents worked in rich homes at Beverly Hills and Bell Air as cook and valet respectively. My mother was soon able to graduate from her cooking pots, and was employed at the same insurance company where Mária Barany also worked.

For my father it was more difficult to advance because he found the English language extremely difficult to master. In the beginning he only had miserable and badly paid jobs. His friends suggested that he ought to attempt the bar examination. In Hungary he was an attorney, and also the president of the Department of the Public Law Prosecutors and the Bar Association. However, he knew that his English was not good enough, and also knew that the Hungarian and the US legal systems are so different that it wasn't a question of passing the bar examinations, but rather starting from square one. Eventually, he completed a course and a training period in Engineering Drafting, and finally was able to get a decent job.

Meanwhile, I enrolled at the local high school, and this was rough going in the beginning because of my halting English. However, by the time I graduated and entered college, I was awarded a four year stipend, thus easing for my parents the burden of my educational expenses. At Mount St. Mary's College I earned a BS degree in English and Spanish, and a minor in Theater Arts. After graduation I was teaching at a Catholic High School, but I was keenly interested in drama; therefore, I enrolled at the University of Southern California where I earned a masters degree in Theatre Arts. I married Jenő Badzey, who just finished serving in the US Air Force and was consequently employed by McDonnell-Douglas where he worked until he retired.

For a while I was a stay-at-home-mom but was involved with the "Right to Life League of Southern California." I was also a volunteer teacher in the chapter "Christian Family Life Education" of the Los Angeles diocese. Our children were growing up and they did not need me home all day, so I went back to the Catholic high school to teach English, Spanish, German and on occasion religion, Hungarian, and drama.

The children grew to adulthood, completed their university studies and got married. Their interests are as widely divergent as their temperaments. We have a computer scientist, a space flight engineer, a ballerina, a manager in the film industry, an economist, an author and a physicist, who received his PhD at Boston in 2005. Four of our sons are married and so far they gifted us with two grandchildren. My children's Hungarian language skills are rather poor; however, they have a keen interest in their heritage. It was their wish that we visit Hungary time and time again. On these occasions, we are their happy and willing cicerones. These trips are big family occasions; so far three of our daughters-in-law also joined us and we conduct the group to galleries, museums, and to all the wonderful sightseeing spots of that beautiful country.

After we retired, we moved to La Quinta; it is a pretty little town between Palm Springs and Indio, located in the California Desert. We enjoy our retirement, are involved with volunteer work, and if needed, we are always happy to help out our children whenever they need us. We give thanks to the Lord for each day. He lets us live in peace and health and are especially grateful for the children and grandchildren we have.

Éva Tirczka, (Mrs. Piller)

I was born in 1932 at Budapest. My parents were Lóránt Tirczka, mechanical engineer and Ilona Orosz. My husband, Gedeon Piller, started his education at Késmárk in a German school (*gymnasium*), continued at the University of Budapest and completed it at Graz, Austria. He is now a retired engineer. We have three children and eight grandchildren and they live on three different continents.

I enrolled at Niederaudorf during the second school term in 1947, was attending the 8th grade, started the 9th, but then I had to leave school because my parents were planning to leave Germany. After the "Währungsreform," when the Reichsmark turned into Deutschmark, my father made the big decision: we took the 60 DMs per head given to everybody for a new start, and slipped across the border to France,—without papers, of course, because that is the way it was done in those days. We travelled to Paris and settled in the Vitry-sur-Seine arrondissement. My father had a job-offering, but after considering it carefully, he decided against staying in Europe. The war had left such a holy fear in all of us that all we wanted was to remove ourselves as far as we could from Europe. The IRO (International Refugees Organization) helped us to immigrate to Brazil. In October 1949 we left Paris and stayed for a while in Bagnoli (Italy) in a refugee camp. From there, we were transferred to Naples and sailed on the good ship Protea to Brazil. On November 11, 1949, on a hot, tropical spring day, we reached Rio de Janeiro. The ship turned into the Guanbara Bay, and there, on top of the Sugarloaf, Christ was waiting for us with open arms.

After we settled, we found that there were no possibilities for adults to continue their education (It took many more years before the government re-thought its policy). Not that we could have enrolled in any school any time soon, as we spoke very little Portuguese. My father, being an engineer, found employment immediately, but we were a family of six, and his salary alone was not enough to make ends meet. I too started to work to help out.

And so the years passed. I got married. Then I got divorced. Then I married again. And doing so, I had to leave my beloved Rio de Janeiro because my new husband, Gedeon, was from San Paulo. Actually this is his one single fault; I mean his being from "Paulo". Otherwise, he is perfect, a true life-mate in the noblest sense of the word. In good times and bad, it is reassuring to hold unto his strong hand. In this world of today, when it is so difficult for a couple to want the same things, when unlimited and diverse possibilities offer themselves, this can make an easy job of tearing up the bond between two people. But somehow, we always wanted the same things, and pulled in the same direction. For better or worse, we always managed to pull the cart of marriage safely through the many pitfalls one encounters during a long life, and so we could keep our small family safe and intact.

But the time came when I finally mastered the new language, and the government mastered the old biases, and finally opened the gates of the high schools and universities to adults. My children were already of school age when I managed to graduate in a Brazilian high school and could then attend college. I did not choose a major, but instead. I elected subjects which interested me, and which could give me the necessary background while helping my children in their school work, or when teaching my scout groups. Today's youth is interested in a great many things and they also know a great many things. Being uninformed while working with them just would not do. I could not stand there with less to say than the ass of Balaam; I had some catching up to do.

I was always interested and involved in the scout organization, but in Brazil this interest grew into a vocation. Scouting was the best or perhaps only way to introduce Hungarian children, or the children already born in Brazil of Hungarian parents, to the rich cultural heritage of Hungary, and to practicing the language of their parents. I would say that not counting the raising of three terrific children, creating a safe and happy home with the man I love, my greatest lifework was my involvement with scouting.

My mother died at the age of 66 of a brain hemorrhage, and three years later my father followed her. He had cancer, but I believe he just died of grief, he missed her that much. My parents' generation did not have an easy time in life. They endured losing the war, their homes, their country, their social status, their careers, and had to overcome improbable difficulties. They could not live long enough to witness the breakdown of Communism in their beloved country, or the successes, which their children eventually achieved. They are the anonymous victims of the Second World War.

And their children did achieve successes. My husband and I built a marvelous suburban home, swimming pool and all, and we moved in with three children, four cats, two dogs, a housekeeper, a part time servant and a full time mother. The children, the grandchildren, and by now even the great-grandchildren grew up loved and safe, and they earned college degrees and became successful and happy adults. But many of the parents, worn out before their time, died before they could witness the happy end. And that was their final tragedy.

Naturally all three of our children were scouts, and I spent a great deal of my time to organize, to teach, to oversee all levels of scouting. In 1970, as the South American Area Scout Director, I organized a major camping event lasting ten days. It was in those years that the new highways connecting the South American states were completed, and finally it was possible to travel from one country to the next on roads without the danger of dislocating one's organs. The camp was a great event because thanks to the new roads, for the first time scouts living far away could also attend. There were altogether 270 Hungarian scouts attending. Two buses brought the "Argentineans" from Buenos Aires on the 2000 km road—the trip lasted 40 hours! It was an uplifting sight to see them all together—the kind of sight which can mist the eyes.

Since I had so many wonderful and happy memories from Niederaudorf, I wanted to give the same great experience to our own children. Aside from this wish, we also wanted our children to speak the Hungarian language perfectly and at a high level, (this was accomplished), and wished for them to spend a few years in Europe to absorb the western culture. (This too was accomplished.) As they reached high school age, we sent them back, one after the other, to Germany. By that time the four original schools no longer existed; however, in 1958, Burg Kastl, a Hungarian boarding school, opened its doors. It was the "heir apparent" to the first four schools, and it was operating in the same spirit and having the same values and goals as the predecessors, and we happily enrolled our children there. After the initial adjusting problems, our children were happy in the school. Their language skills improved, and their knowledge of the world was expanded. They spent the Easter and Christmas vacations with relatives in Hungary, and the family ties were greatly strengthened by this. Almost everyone who left Hungary after the war, literally and psychologically, left all relatives behind. This often caused a sense of loneliness, a pain, similar to homesickness; the loss, causing a sense of disconnectedness. The refugees were detached from the loving safety net of the extended family. In our case, this did not happen. Because our children visited so frequently the relatives in Hungary, they never felt what other children did: "We are alone. Everybody has family gatherings, but we have nobody." At other holidays, their classmates, living in different countries in Europe, invited our children to spend the days in their home. This way our three "Brazilians" visited many countries in Europe and their horizons were further expanded.

While they were gone, I joined the working force once again. I spoke three languages; a skill highly valued in Brazil, and therefore easily found a secretarial position with various international concerns: Honeywell, Volkswagen and Mahle-Leve. In the end, I was promoted to the rank of Director's Secretary—an enviable, somewhat glamorous and well paid job; at least it was so before the advent of the computer.

But the economic situation in Brazil turned from bad to worse, and that put an end to our children's European adventure; they had to return home to Brazil. But the experiment was highly successful, although there was a small price to be paid for it: our children lost an entire school year. It was unavoidable, not because they were less qualified than their Brazilian schoolmates, but because the differentiated school year: in Brazil school starts in February and ends in November. The children left Burg Kastl in mid-June, and of course they could not enroll midterm in Brazil. But the compensation for the lost year was invaluable. At the airport of Rio de Janeiro we picked up mature, intelligent, world-travelled, disciplined and accomplished ladies and a gentleman, with exquisite manners. We were enchanted.

A few words about our new home, Brazil. We love it. The people here are friendly, accepting and respect European newcomers because of their high level of education. Instead of having considered us as some miserable flotsam washed up at their shores, they sorted us into a high status, and felt that we were enriching their country.

Sao Paulo has a subtropical climate so that one can swim outdoors during eight months of the year. The winters are unpleasant because the houses are not equipped to face the cold weather. The wind blows in through the doors just as it pleases, and the single panes of window glasses are not adequate to keep the cold outside. July and August are especially uncomfortable. We then try to wear every piece of warm clothing we have, and shamelessly envy the lucky ones who had the foresight to build a wood burning fireplace into their living room. Fortunately, the winter is very short. So much for Sao Paulo. Northern Brazil is totally tropical and the heat there is ferocious. Southern Brazil is temperate, and they can grow wheat and produce outstanding wine.

When we arrived here after WW II, it was very easy for Hungarians to find employment because at that time professionals with university education and special skills were rather rare; Hungarians had more job offerings than they needed. Brazil experienced an economic boom starting in the fifties, which lasted for about thirty years. But gradually from 1980 the general prosperity diminished, and inflation increased at an ever more rapid and alarming pace. It was difficult to make ends meet, and to manage life toward the end of the month was incredibly difficult in most households. Many plans were born and just as many died. Every elected government fought against the economic disaster, but they were not able to change the course. In 1994, in only a twelve month period, the inflation reached 5000%! At the end of the year, a new start was attempted, new faces appeared on the scene who promised new plans. Miraculously, the promises actually turned into deeds and somehow they managed to save the situation, which is at this writing, more or less normal. However, it is also true that there always was, and is to this day, an immense social imbalance. There is a large class of super rich people, with unimaginable wealth, then a much smaller group of well-to-do, rich people. The middle class is small, taking home medium to smallish salaries. But then there is a huge, a very huge group of have-nots. We also have 22 million persons, who cannot read, and we have 200,000 Indians, who lack everything.

Then after two terms, the reigning government, defined as right wing and elitist, was ousted by the Labor Party, and its leader, "Lula" (Luiz Inacio Lula da Silva) was elected president. He was not only a strange candidate with six elementary grades as his highest achievement in education, but he sported red flags and red stars during his campaign. Although he won with a 52% majority, we Hungarians, who hate everything red, and are especially repulsed by the red star, naturally did not vote for him. But we accepted that if 52% of the nation was not happy what the previous government produced, than obviously a change was necessary. But in Brazil, things don't always turn out as they would elsewhere. In contrary to what most people expected, the country did not adopt Communism. Lula quieted down. He stopped wearing a red tie and the red star from his lapel also disappeared. A new hope was born. However the Partido Trabalhista (Labor Party) introduced a horrible new disease: corruption. The result is not a happy scene.

We, older people, try to survive by living frugally and scaling down our wishes and expectations. Fortunately our son, Gedeon, has a very good and secure position, and he plans to stay put here in Sao Paulo with his wife and two children, but my daughters live abroad. Kinga is married to a Brazilian, whose one desire was to get away from the insecurity of Brazil, and she of course followed her husband. They now live in Westport, Connecticut. Emese married a former school mate from Burg Kastl, and now lives in Wörth, Bavaria with their four children. It is not the way I planned our future, but they are happy, have a meaningful life, and that is more important than the pain of this awful distance.

My parents and the teachers at Niederaudorf instilled in me two basic rules. First I was taught to always be ready to do some service, to give time and effort where it is needed. I was told many times that whatever talent I was given, it was with the understanding that it would be shared with the community, or with those who lacked such gifts. The second teaching was about the love of my Hungarian heritage, some would say, a feeling of patriotism. I am not sure that this is a politically correct word to use. Ever since the Second World War, patriotism was confused with nationalism, and the latter acquired a very bad, unacceptable connotation. Because it is difficult to distinguish between the two, people tend to avoid both terms. I understand under patriotism a love of a country, its culture and a special place, the memory of which we shall always carry in our heart, regardless where fate would sweep us on the planet. It is similar to the love of the old, lost family home and the longing for it, which will always cause a keen pain, some call homesickness. This disease is the painful longing to see the old house again, the sycamore trees, the oak door and the knocker hanging from the lion's head, all of which might not even be there anymore. I loved that place as I loved the entire country. What is it then? Patriotism, nationalism, or sentimental nostalgia? I am a good Brazilian citizen. I like living here and would never consider leaving. But at the same time, I also value my heritage, the culture, the old country, and what it stands for. I never felt that my being Brazilian made me less Hungarian, or the other way around. Just like a parent may love two children at the same time, the same way I too can love and serve two countries without being disloyal to either.

In this spirit through my long life I was always deeply involved with the scouting movement because I considered it the best means to transfer the Hungarian culture to the youngsters. I have gone through the ranks from first being a girl scout through becoming leader of smaller groups, until I was holding the leading position of the scout organization in Brazil. I have written two handbooks for girl scouts, and lately my most important work concentrates on training new leaders. Music is an important part of a culture, and I worked out a program to teach it to our scouts. The program introduces the earliest songs, based on the ancient pentatonic scale, and takes the youngsters all the way to the classical Hungarian music. Often we exchange the singing at the evening camp fire to viewing a Hungarian opera on a CD. So far we have seen *Bánk Bán, Hunyadi,* Háry *János, Kékszakállú herceg.* I also wrote for the scouts a short introduction to the Hungarian National Gallery as a handbook for those who plan to visit Budapest in the near future.

But scouting is not the only work I have done (and still do) for the community. The Hungarians established at Sao Paulo a university, and I am currently its dean. I also do volunteer work at the Hungarian library, and for fifteen years I was the

Director of the Hungarian House, a cultural center. Eventually I was elected president of the House.

However, time has gone by so swiftly, and I am mostly retired now. But I still write. For one thing, I wrote a short, but adequate Hungarian history book in Portuguese so that youngsters, who do not speak Hungarian, are able to learn about the country of their ancestors. At the same time, I have written a short book of Brazilian history in Hungarian because ever more Hungarians are coming from "the old country" to visit relatives here, and they would like to know more about Brazil, naturally in their own language. This book also lists the names of Hungarian travelers, immigrants, or adventurers, who visited or stayed in Brazil as early as 1519. More information can be found about this at www.ahungara.org.br

This work gave us the idea to compile all the names of people who settled in Brazil from 1890. There seems to be a need for it because many people are searching for lost members of family, or friends. Even as I am writing this, we are diligently working on this project.   Written at Sao Paulo, 2006

Iván N. Zoltán (1929-2000)

Iván attended the 12th grade at Reisach in 1949 and successfully absolved the graduation examinations. In 2000 he was happily anticipating the school reunion at Niederaudorf, when unexpectedly his dormant illness flared up, and a few weeks before his planned transatlantic trip "the one of the black robes" came to fetch him. Two letters written by him tell the story of his life, his feelings about the school, and the classmates:

To: Nóra Sztáray—Date: Wed, 19 Aug, 1998.
"Dear Nóra,

You may have hidden masochistic tendencies to want to hear my story. Be as it may; now you have it.

Although my life is on the quiet side, it does require time when relating from "Nieder" onward. That was in the 40s. My life in 1949 was beautiful, charming, exhilarating, and devastating at the same time. Shall not tell of the exquisite sufferings while I contemplated the bleak future in those years. I assume we all had to live through that.

The 50s were spent in New Jersey and was devoted to the development of new roots. Completed the BS degree in engineering (electrical) in 1955, was married, was a research associate for a year at Rutgers U., joined RCA for 15 years, and our children, Nick and Liz, were born.

The 60s was the decade to reap the benefits of the work Olga, my wife, and I put forth in the last decade. Settled in a nice house, obtained 3 advanced degrees between us, raised our children, made some friends (some of them are our yearly traveling companions to this date) and we were able to be of some assistance to our extended family. These were busy, vigorous, productive years. Vacations were devoted to seeing and enjoying with our kids the National Parks, starting with the western, Californian parks, and moving toward the east with the passing years.

The 70s, although we prospered, were stressful as we lost all but one of our parents. It was the decade when I became a government employee and became involved with increasingly restrictive projects in the competition between the two halves of the divided World. I was so very certain of the future; there could be no change and the country of my birth shall forever be closed to me.

The 80s were filled with the activities of our children. Their schooling, our little girl's marriage, the birth of the grandchildren. This decade was the time of maturing. By now we became the seniors of our extended families. Significant were the two meetings with the former schoolmates in Cleveland and in Niederaudorf. Our existence continued in a quiet, satisfactory manner. I moved away from the military and became employed by the FAA. The only pain, a reminder of our vulnerability, was the passing of my mother and brother within the same day. Suddenly I became the only one remaining of the Zoltán clan.

The 90s brought drastic changes in history and in my life. When Olga retired, we moved to Washington to be closer to both of our children who lived in the Baltimore area. However, our little girl moved to California to show the faults in our planning. My son and his wife are still here, so we are not alone. I retired in 97 after a year long bout with some illness. Cannot say what it was, only that it was most unpleasant. Since then, things have improved greatly, enabling me to contact remnants of my family in Hungary. To date, I was able to locate one cousin and the children of another cousin. We are making progress! Also, I now have a cousin, a contemporary, a kindred soul from the distant, destroyed past. Amazing what may cause anguish!

Well, my dear, here it is. My story. Hope it was short enough, and do remember that you requested it!"

To: Kati Pettendy — December 26, 1999

"Katám:

The big thing hereabout is the meeting scheduled for next spring. I, being the oldest among you, I should,—no, I must attend,—as I very much would like to see all of you at least once more. Why? Well my friend that is not easily answered! It took me about fifty years to think of the reasons while I remained ambivalent about it. A couple things happened to clear my mind: First, I found one of my cousins and the wife and two grown sons of the other. The second was an eye-to-eye confrontation with the one of the black robes. The first reason gave me the desire to keep and hold all that was and is dear. The second gave me a wonderful release from inhibitions. As long as I do not hurt others with what I do or say, I now go ahead and do or say it. It simplified my rules of behavior. Were I to summarize what the school meant to me, how I think of all the girls and boys, now it would go something like this:

I shared your school's world which was remote from reality before returning to the outside world to face its cruelty. We were discards of the world; we shared a mean fate. Lived in an insane world that had nothing for us but hate. We studied without a clear goal, seeking a place all along where we could say: This is it, here I belong! I remember you all as children from a long time ago; realized now that I loved you then, a love I dared not show.

Studied conjugation and declension, was hungry all the while, memorized long Latin verses without knowing why. Looked for knowledge to lead me to my rightful place, where I could stand straight and look the world in the face. Then all I could do, with my many doubts and fears, was to show toughness instead of courage—with loving tears. An attitude of tough became my norm. As such, I could not show care, be tender, it would not fit the form.

Later, when I was married, when she gave me a son, I gained strength, knew how to find our place in the sun. With the gift of my little girl, there was no more doubt; I was strong. Knew right from wrong, what life was about. Heard that you all achieved more, nurtured a larger brood. Took care of parents, siblings, even descendants once removed. Knew that we built a place for us as well as for them. Today I can admit and show: I love you all now, the same as then. Or something like this.

I would include Diri in my affections. See what age and a close call can do to some? Before this, I would never admit having such thoughts unless reclining upon the rack! Neither the desire to express myself, nor the courage to appear the fool would have induced me to do so. They say: We are what we eat. But I believe: we are what we survived…"

Our Teachers:

Mária Adelsberger was the mystery-woman of Niederaudorf, who only had a present. She appeared in our school as if she had no past and then disappeared nobody knows where. Nobody can guess whether she had a future. Only smoke has the talent to disappear so totally. She never talked about herself and nobody knew if she had any family. All we knew about her was that before the war she taught Latin and Greek at the Nagyvárad Gimnázium for boys. She was the strictest, but one of the most effective of the teachers. As we slowly learned to appreciate her delightful dry humor, we gradually lost our fear and developed a true liking for her. She mostly taught Latin, German and English at Niederaudorf, but her knowledge was so multifaceted that when in addition she was assigned some other subject to teach, she was just as good and thorough. Someone seems to have heard that she returned to Hungary and, taking the veil, joined a convent. This is not likely because at that time all convents were just being eliminated by the Communists in Hungary and the nuns were sent home.

Mária Bárány (1923-2007), teacher and housemother at Niederaudorf and Reisach, was born in Erdély (Transylvania). She attended the University there, earning a teaching degree, her major being languages (Latin and French). In addition to the languages of her major and of Hungarian, she also spoke German and Romanian.

The most cherished and emotionally packed memory of her youth was Friday, September 6, 1940, when dressed in the formal Hungarian court dress, and with flowers in her arms, she was greeting the returning Hungarian army at Nagyvárad. She was part of the heady moment, when after twenty years of foreign rule, Erdély (Transylvania) once again was made part of Hungary.

The euphoria did not last long because in less than four years she and her mother had to flee to escape the invading Russian troops.

Almost as soon as she arrived in Germany, she started teaching wherever she found children in need of instruction. She taught for short periods of time in makeshift schools in the camps of Piding, Dachau and Taglachin until finally she ended up at Niederaudorf to teach Hungarian grammar and literature to the lower grades, and to fill the responsible job of being housemother to 45 girls not much younger than she was. She fulfilled the position splendidly, and was the darling of the girls. Her quiet and sweet disposition, her modesty, her caring and the support always generously given when help was needed or problems had to be solved, earned the love and respect of all. When a student was seriously ill, she was known to sit up like a real mother all night, never leaving the patient alone.

In 1949, she immigrated with her mother to the United States, where she worked as an office employee until her retirement. After her mother's death, she lived alone, and during the last years of her life, friends from Nagyvárad, but by then US citizens, took care of her.

Besides Mária Bárány, several of the students of Niederaudorf came from the region "Erdély," or as is better known in the English-speaking world: Transylvania. This region, as a result of the peace treaty after World War I, was annexed to Romania. Some explanation is needed here to explain the seething problems, continuous unrests and abject misery in that unhappy, volatile area.

After the First World War in 1920, the infamous Treaty of Trianon was designed in Versailles. As a result, besides fining Hungary to pay war reparations, 75% of the country was divided among Hungary's neighbors. This number is so staggering that it is almost hard to believe. The pre-treaty area of 93,073 square miles shrunk to a mere 36,939. The prewar population counted a little over twenty million people, but after the dismemberment of the country almost 2/3 of them woke up to find themselves as hated and despised "minority" in another country. Five of the most populous Hungarian cities were also annexed to the countries which received parts of Hungary; Kolozsvár (to Romania) being one of them. And while the population thus annexed endured untold hardships, the "truncated" country of Hungary also suffered immense difficulties. Gone were some of the parts which provided essential natural resource. The debt of the country rose to astronomical heights. Inflation was staggering.

One of the principal beneficiaries of the territorial division was Romania. It entered the war as ally of the (original) Triple Alliance: Germany, Austro-Hungary and Italy; but then changed its mind and joined the Entente: France, the Soviet Union and Great Britain and attacked the army of its former ally (Austro-Hungary) from the rear. Afterward, this act was richly rewarded in the Treaty of Trianon by allocating to it generous portions of Hungary.

At that time, those who engineered this unjust and impossible Treaty tried to convince the world that it was in the interest of righteousness and justice and a means of securing long-lasting peace in the eastern and southern part of Europe in the hope of avoiding another world war. But this was obviously not the real reason and the years following the implementation of the Treaty showed a very different result and a degree of inhumanity, which was totally new and never experienced in that region before. These areas turned into an unhappy, broiling kettle of hatred, injustice and endless misery. Almost immediately, the dictators of the successor states fabricated laws and regulations to make life all but impossible for the ethnic Hungarians. Unchecked nationalism flourished, history was being roughly revised to fit the claims and plans of the successors, personal and church properties were confiscated, life became a never ending tragedy for the Hungarians living in these areas. Many historians believe that the Treaty and the subsequent problems caused by it were the reason for the outbreak of the Second World War. It certainly was one of the reasons Hungary joined the Triple Alliance; although its freedom of choice were severely handicapped by geographical, historical, political and economic constrictions.

At any rate, the Treaty most certainly influenced Hungary's political stance at the outbreak of WWII. Over and over again, history showed that hundreds of miles away in a posh meeting room, the drawing of artificial borderlines for a nation never produce anything but continuous disaster and human drama.

When Transylvania was returned to Hungary in 1940, there was a brief time of peace and contentment lasting four years that is from 1940 until the end of the war. But after the war, everything changed back to the prewar situation to comply with the shameful and thoroughly inhuman Treaty of Trianon. Unfortunately, the situation has not eased in the intervening seventy years since.

Nor was it considered inhuman from only the Hungarian point of view. The United States never ratified the Treaty. President Wilson had said: "The proposal of the dismemberment of Hungary is absurd…," and years later Churchill remarked: "Ancient poets and theologians could not imagine such suffering, which Trianon brought to the nation of Hungary…"

Kálmán Csia (1911-2009), Protestant minister and one of the founders of the Niederaudorf School was born June 26, 1911 in Hungary (Transylvania). He was born into a family of 10 brothers and sisters on a large farm in the Carpathian Mountains. Among his siblings, he alone followed the vocation of his father and grandfather, both Protestant ministers. The others followed the father's advice and went into law, medicine and pharmacology.

During the last months of WWII, he was fleeing from Hungary with his wife and young son, always just 10-15 kilometers ahead of the Red Amy. As soon as they arrived in Germany, he started to serve in various refugee camps, sometimes walking 50 kilometers to reach a congregation. In 1946 he was transferred to München where he was in contact with the Allied Forces, and could obtain considerable help for the Hungarian refugees. In München, he also made contacts with various Hungarian groups, whose aim was to establish accredited refugee schools for Hungarian children. Using his former contacts with the Allied Forces, he was able to get support, and indeed, a few months later, the doors of the Niederaudorf School were opened to forty teenage girls. He appeared every Saturday at Niederaudorf to provide religious instructions and services to the Protestant students, and to prepare them for confirmation.

After losing all of his inheritance and most of his family members in the two world wars, and as the congregations in the refugee camps dwindled almost to nothing due to immigration to countries all over the globe, he came to the Land of Opportunity with a small wooden crate labeled: "Mattawan, Michigan." There, a kind old farmer, Alexander Szakács and his wife, met them at the railroad and provided shelter to Kálmán, his wife Zsuzsanna (who died in 1995) and his surviving son Kálmán Jr.

As "personal wealth," he only had a degree in divinity and the knowledge of five languages, none of which was English. Kálmán and his wife found work in a paper plant during weekdays and served a small congregation of Hungarians at a Reformed Church in Kalamazoo the rest of the time. Like his sponsors, Mr. and Mrs. Szakács, Kálmán and his wife would for the rest of their life keep their doors open to refugees, some of whom were total strangers, others were relatives; but in the end, they all became one big family. He went on to minister in Milwaukee, East Chicago and Ligonier PA, where he administered the Bethlen Home for the Aged, which at the time was a fraternal charity organization. His wife was doing the cooking and supervised the nursing of the elderly; he drove patients to doctors, gave final solace and in his old car, drove the groceries up the icy hill in the winter. He traveled on weekends to raise money to feed the guests, to provide them with medical care, and to eventually convert the rickety old wooden house on a hill into a full-service facility. After 15 years of putting in limitless hours to keep the Home running, financed alone by his 40-hour salary and by donations, Kálmán and Zsuzsanna retired in 1976 to their beloved cottage on Donnell Lake in Cass County. There, they became known for hosting parties featuring his wife's fresh raspberry cake and homemade wine.

After Kálmán Csia's wife died, their son, with the full understanding and support of his wife Becky, moved to Kalamazoo to stay with his father, and so enable Kálmán to continue living independently for another nine years on the shore of his beloved "golden lake." He died June 5, 2009 at Park Place Assisted Living where he found a loving and caring family among the staff for the last five of his nearly 98 years.

Géza Fekete OFM (Order of Friars Minor, Franciscan Order.) Father Fekete was also one of the founders of the school at Niederaudorf and was later one of the commuting teachers of the school. He was born in 1913 at Kisvárda, Hungary, and completed his elementary and high school there. After graduation, he entered the Franciscan order, studied philosophy and theology, and was ordained in 1936. He was first active at Veszprém, then was transferred to be secretary to Joseph Mindszenthy. **The Venerable Joseph Mindszenthy (1892-1975) was later Cardinal of the Catholic Church, archbishop of Esztergom, the seat of the Catholic Church in Hungary. His Excellency opposed Communism, and spoke out against the Soviet persecution of his country. He was arrested, tortured and convicted to life for "treason." During the Revolution of 1956, he was rescued by the Freedom Fighters, and transferred to the US Embassy in Budapest for his safety. He lived there for many years until finally the government decided that they (the government) would be better off without a martyr at their hands and finally made him leave Hungary. He died in exile.**

During the war, Father Fekete joined the armed forces of Hungary and was active as field chaplain at the battlefronts in the Soviet Republic. After the decisive battle of Stalingrad in the brutal cold of the Russian winter, he too started the long march back towards Hungary. Wounded and very ill, he was eventually picked up by a Hungarian military hospital, also retreating, and was treated there. As the fighting front reached Hungary, the medical staff placed all the sick and wounded into freight wagons and moved them west into Germany.

There Father Fekete and the other invalids were taken prisoners of war by the American Forces. After he was released, he joined the work of several Hungarian organizations which tried to solve the problems of the refugees. Father Fekete offered spiritual assistance in the camps and also taught religion and some other subjects in an abandoned freight car on a no longer used railroad track, known as the "Wagon School." It is believed that this was the first attempt to establish some sort of instruction for older refugee children.

It was at this "Wagon School" where he met the dedicated Ravasz couple, also teaching there, and together they worked out their shared dream of a real school, which was shortly thereafter established at Niederaudorf. Father Fekete also organized the establishment of a Hungarian refugee hospital at Landshut, and was a leading participant in the Hungarian Red Cross. They organized the collection and distribution of medications through the CARITAS, and published a Hungarian Catholic newspaper under the most primitive conditions imaginable. He argued with authorities and successfully demonstrated against the practice of drafting young Hungarian refugee boys into the French Foreign Legion. After 1956, he cared for hundreds of university students who fled from Hungary after the tragic defeat of the Hungarian Revolution. He died in Erlkamm, Germany and is buried there.

Béla Lahner, a former upper grade student at Reisach remembers this remarkable man:

"Father Fekete taught several other subjects beside Religion, and did it with admirable expertise. He never used a book, simply knew everything. His brain was a wonder; he was a real genius. There were very few questions he could not answer.

He traveled to Reisach 2-3 times a week from München and his arrivals were so much on time that one could set the clocks according to his appearances. He always walked fast, although he had a strange gait, as if one of his legs wouldn't want to coordinate with the other. He had unusually long fingernails, giving his hands an almost feminine appearance. The younger students cracked quite a few, admittedly not too funny jokes about his hands.

One evening when he stayed overnight at the school, we were talking about the war and the fatal losses of the German army at Stalingrad, in operation Uranus, which many feel was the turning point of the war. 'I know,' he said quietly. 'I was there.'

He then related the story to us. After it was obvious that the German losses were immense, and that they could not possibly match the one million Red Army soldiers, they tried to save what was left of the German army. Still fighting while retreating, the remaining regiments fled back to the west. It was never called defeat, but to the last it was always worded proudly, insincerely and euphemistically: 'Planned retreat in order to reorganize for the attack.'

Father Fekete too walked toward home, painfully struggling with the small group of surviving Hungarian soldiers of his company. They trudged in total exhaustion through the endless miles in temperatures of minus 30 degrees. He encouraged the soldiers to move on, and saw to it that no one sat down because that would have meant certain death in those temperatures and in their condition.

But even his astounding energy reserve was finally exhausted, and he fell headlong into a ditch totally giving up the struggle. But he didn't die. It seemed to him that a stench woke him. He was not sure what it was, but later thought that a huge truck stopped near his rapidly cooling body and the smelly, but warm exhaust of it brought him back to life. No matter how it happened, he was saved. He was convinced that God woke him from his near death because He had some plans for him. This gave him an unexpected and powerful strength to continue that terrible march out of the arctic hell toward home.

But he had to pay for this trip: one leg and both his hands were frozen, and even after several surgeries and treatments, the one leg and both hands were numb and did not respond to stimulus. This is why it was so important for him to keep his nails long. Due to a total lack of sensation in the fingers, while trimming his nails, he could easily cut into the damaged tissue, causing even more problems than he already had. Even picking up a pencil or trying to write caused severe problems, as indeed every other task for which hands were needed was most difficult and often painful.

We have known him for a long time before this memorable evening, but we never guessed at the problems he had. He never complained, was always loving, patient and upbeat. I am a Protestant, but I was deeply impressed by him and I think he was one of the most influential persons in my life."

Ferenc Kovács, (Kovach) principal and his wife Erzsébet Thököly (Erzsi *Néni*).

Our beloved Diri and his wife had both passed away; so, instead of biographies, we let two of their children remember their remarkable parents:

Tamás (Tom) Kovach, the youngest son:

I love both of my parents very much and remember so many wonderful things about them. Mama was the heart of our family. Like most siblings, we did not always get along peacefully, but she brought the warring Kovach children together in peace. She made each of us feel special, starting with the lullabies she composed for us, individually; every one of her children had a special, personal lullaby. For our birthdays, she made a special cake for us. It was not the number of candles on them that was special, but the way she made the cake: one layer for each year up to 21. As we grew older, baking the layers often took all night. She made wonderful meals while singing sad Hungarians songs, but on occasions we saw her crying in the kitchen. I guess, she was suffering from a special brand of painful homesickness, which we, born in the US, did not fully understand.

She always made a ginger bread house for St Nicholas Day (again staying up all night long), and had it ready and decorated by morning and placed the goodies in our shoes. We sang and prayed around the advent wreath each night, and each day she added more decoration to the house, until by and by it looked like a Christmas fairyland. With this slow process she taught us the meaning of Advent: the waiting and preparing, the getting ready.

Christmas was her favorite holiday. The whole family gathered at our house for Christmas no matter how far away the children had moved. Sometimes there were 17 of us. She decorated the Christmas tree days earlier, slowly, a little at a time, just as she did the house. But by tradition she left the last touches for the 24th to be completed. This is when the Christmas bell, the "angel hair" and the star were placed on the tree. Christmas was quite the crescendo. When the bell rang, (one of the few things which survived the war years), we sang "Mennyből az Angyal" and Jingle bells, which she translated into Hungarian as "Csingi-ling." Then we prayed, wished each other happy Christmas, and dove into the presents.

Only once did she go back to Hungary, in 1980, but all along she missed her former country dearly. Having gone there myself, I now understand why.

She was both highly intelligent, yet very simple in her compassion and her unconditional love. We joked and said, she was so pure that she had seven children by Virgin Birth. She was very proud to be Hungarian and to be a born Thököly. When she died, the heart and soul of the family died with her. We just did not come together like we did while she was with us, and when we did arrange family reunions, it was not the same any more. We miss her smile and contagious laugh which was hauntingly melodic, bubbling up from the depth of her soul. I still miss all the wonderful things which were part of my life with her, but am fortunate to have enjoyed it while it lasted. Some very wise man said at one time that it is better to have loved, even if at the end loss must be suffered, than never grieving but living without love.

Papa was always busy with his work; he even took his work papers out into the woods on family picnics. He taught me the relative sizes of the planets when I was four, and hooked me on astronomy. He was strict and sometimes aloof, but he mellowed as he got older. The real change came when he had to accept retirement and at the same time he had to also face his personal tragedy: Mama was dying of leukemia. He loved her dearly. I had traveled back home to help him after Mother died, and he asked me to stay on, since he had no experience caring for himself. Mother had always done that. I did stay and watched him age. In 2000, when I went to see Hungary for the first time, I asked Papa to come along, but he refused.

However, in 2001, he quite suddenly announced that he wanted to go home in October, "but not too late," he added enigmatically. I was not sure whether he meant the season, or his own life, which was nearing its end. We bought tickets and despite 9/11 and the anthrax scare, we flew "home." I knew something was happening to him. I could not put my finger on what it was, but he was far too happy to go home, and this enthusiasm was out of line with his character. He met his long lost sister Mária in Dorog, and reunited with Pauli, his brother, who had moved home a few years earlier. After this trip, he rapidly got worse and died the next year. Papa accomplished many wonderful feats in his life, but I am so glad that toward the end, he chose to relax and enjoy the kind of life for which he never had time before.

László (Laci) Kovach, one of his other sons:
The memories of my parents are easier told by beginning with memories of my father. In our Hungarian home away from Hungary, we were raised to speak both Magyar and English. We called our father Papa and our mother Mama.

To frame the impressions about Papa, I'll begin as an adult, and then go back to earlier years.

When I went to college, I enrolled in one of my father's classes, and it was a memorable experience. The classes were held in the large auditorium, located in what was then a new building on the University of Oklahoma campus. Papa was 'on stage' at the head of the classroom. He always spoke without a microphone; his voice boomed and was clearly audible from any seat. He had an amazing command of current events, and could relate them brilliantly with the various topics which he covered in his "Introduction to Philosophy" class. I was deeply impressed by him, and quite proud of his intellect; he could in all fairness be only described as an absolute, pure genius.

While on the auditorium stage, there was an occasion when he began his class in the following manner. He raised his arm dramatically—high over his head. A momentary pause and then— "If I can crook my little finger" he began, "then I know that there is a God!" From this catchy opening he began to give one of the classic proofs for the existence of God, how logically everything has a cause, and if you go back through the chain of events, you have to come logically to something that had no cause, no beginning. This Something had to be powerful enough to create all that we know today, and this First Cause, this Something we call God. He would then answer all of the usual objections about the existence of God, the problem of pain, the existence of evil in the world, and so on. From this sort of strong grounding, even during the darkest times in my life, I never once doubted God's existence.

Now imagine this sort of a dynamic intellectual, living under the same roof with you! It would be formidable enough for an adult, but think of how a child would feel!

Flashing back to the years of my youth, I recall that Sunday dinners were a time of great intellectually stimulating discussions. Mama would prepare a tasty multi-course Magyar meal and Papa would talk about some philosophical topic. Our dinners were not just social occasions, but always meant some theological or philosophical discussion. At a young age, there were times when I would 'hide' under an end table, and listen to the adults discussing world events, post Second Vatican Council events, or some philosophical question. The discussions might include one of my father's favorite topics: "Can there be action at a distance?" (Descartes), or else the philosophy of beauty, another favorite topic of his. My father always knew both sides of an issue. He could articulate the opposition clearly and then demonstrate why that perspective was flawed when objectively viewed. Syllogisms, inductive and deductive reasoning, or the history of some school of thought—these were the routine fares served up by Papa at the dinner table!

It seemed like my father was always studying, preparing, outlining a speech, preparing a lecture, an article, or a book. His study was a sanctuary for him, and off limits to us. We never dared to enter for just any frivolous reason. In fact, it was safer not to enter at all, unless invited. That same voice that boomed in a lecture hall, would resonate like a great eruption in the smaller dimensions of a mere room in our home. To the young, it could be quite a startling experience.

To limit Papa to 'just' his intellectual genius would be to paint a very imperfect picture. Because Papa was also an artist, a musician, a composer as well. His art is on display in one of Hungary's museums, his music was played in the DP camps after WWII. His brilliant books and essays appeared in print. One had to wonder, how ONE person could be gifted in so many ways.

Like all of us mortals, our parents, as amazing as they were, had their unique weaknesses. When anyone hearing all the theological and philosophical discussions at our dinner table, it would be natural for him to presume that perfect justice and great peace would reign at our home. Not necessarily so. For example, there were times when Papa would punish me for something he thought I'd done, but in fact had not. To put it in simple terms: I was innocent, but had been punished, and naturally I was seething with the injustice of it. Papa would always learn about, or else figure out the situation later. Never openly admitting his error, he would call me into his study, into that great 'sacred hall' one would not enter otherwise. Papa would reach into his desk drawer, quietly and mysteriously. Then, he would pull out a favorite treat, a Zero brand candy bar. In those days people did not just toss candy into the shopping carts as they do today, so this was indeed a treasured gift. So as time went by, it became clear that Papa's "I'm sorry" was this special treat. There was always a gentle smile that went with this and ... well, to say the word 'memorable', doesn't do justice to the ways he handled us, the way he solved problems.

I learned over time that while Papa was able to lecture and give great talks, he was in fact quite shy. What most of us call 'small talk' or some light banter about the weather or other trivia were not Papa's social gifts. But for him to sit in silence in company was painful and awkward. As long as he was with a student or a fellow professor, as long as there was some intellectual or theological topic at hand, Papa was enthusiastically partaking in the discussion. But if the discussion was reduced to nothing more than banality, he quickly lost interest. Gossip was boring to him, and it was likely that if the discussion was not serious enough, he would leave for his study, hardly caring for social graces.

After Mama died, and he later retired from teaching, Papa became visibly and sadly, lonely; he lost his partner, his best company. From then on, there were not enough discussions, no challenges. While over time he improved some in the art of chit-chat, this was not an area which he ever mastered.

Our mother didn't have an MA or a PhD, but nevertheless, she was a college graduate and had a keen intellect in her own right. And Mama was gifted on so many levels. If father was an intellect, a painter and a musician, then Mama was the poet, the singer and the gentle teacher. Mama taught us our catechism, and she did it brilliantly. We were not limited to the usual things found in the Baltimore Catechism, but were also blessed with the thoughts of intellectual giants past and present. We learned about proofs for God's existence not just from Papa, but from Mama as well. We would be shown the sort of witty and wise insights that Archbishop Fulton Sheen's writings offered for the everyday person, who are not versed in advanced philosophy. For example, she taught us how to reply to those who thought we Catholics worshipped statues or images. In Sheen-like fashion, she pointed out that many people keep photos of family on their walls, desks and in their wallets, but they do not worship them. In like fashion, the statues and images of the saints, the Lord or the Blessed Mother in the churches or homes are not idolized, but help us focus our prayers and tap on the great spiritual inspirations which they provide.

Mother was given a very modest budget to run the household. But somehow she managed to save money and with it buy furniture, art, dishes or other nice items. Mama would also help us learn via the 'incentive plan.' I can recall that if I learned a certain song well, I'd be given a nickel. Wow, 5 cents, all mine! 11 of those learning sessions (which might take weeks or months) would yield me a box of Lego building blocks. So in this simple fashion, we learned to earn, to save. We enjoyed the fruits of our labor with a deep satisfaction, which is not something experienced by those, who are merely handed some gift by their parents.

Mama made fabulous meals, and she knew well what the 'favorite' dish of each of her 5 living children was. For our birthday or name day (the feast day of our patron saint) or, if we needed cheering up because of illness or what have you, we could count on one or more of our favorite foods or desserts on the table. I'm still not quite sure how Mama managed all that because one of her arms was badly crippled by polio. Yet she cooked, cleaned, carried her children and cared for them better than so many others, who have full use of all their limbs.

A deep faith and daily prayer was the center of her life, which she further enriched by lots of reading and of course music and singing. Music was always there, be it classical, which both my parents loved, or the soulful ballads and tunes of Harry Belafonte, or the sound track from Fiddler on the Roof, or selections from many other wonderful contemporary music.

Our mother was active on campus. In the tumultuous days following the Second Vatican Council, she showed up to battle either pro-Communist speakers, or the modernists and heretics coming up like mushrooms after a good rain. Once a Communist speaker viciously mocked her heavy accent in front a large assembly of people, but she boldly retorted that his was truly the typical Communist way of *"ad hominum"*: personal attack. The Communist speaker was momentarily speechless, perhaps confused by her calm as well as by her unbending attitude. Using the silence to her advantage, she calmly explained that since he couldn't offer any valid counter-arguments, he resorted to a personal attack. She described to the crowd the attacker's obvious tactics: he tried to belittle her, making her look ridiculous while hoping others would discount her arguments for that superficial reason only. It was marvelous to see her emerge from the argument as the winner. She could always brilliantly defend the truth, be it political, intellectual or spiritual. She could do so at times with warmth and wit, but she could whip at the opponent as ferociously as an angered snake. It was his choice, whether he dared cross her path the wrong way, or chose to stay on the safe side.

I can still recall some of the wonderful Christmas celebrations, and the long Advent preparations. We'd read selections from the Prophets, like the Book of Isaiah. We prayed the Rosary and said morning and night prayers too. After years of preparation in catechism, she then pointed me toward reading the Bible myself. This was a marvelous teaching method, at least in my case. As a youth and young teen, I read The Word of God for myself. I recall seeing how this or that Christian teaching was clearly supported by the Scripture.

Mama taught us about living fully, and about suffering uncomplainingly. She taught us not to look at pain and tribulations as evil in just another disguise, but as part—even a necessary part—of life. She talked about how to unite our suffering with that of Christ, the same as His Saints did; and how suffering, when accepted with prayers, would no longer be meaningless. Suffering can be redemptive, an experience which not only reforms us, but teaches us the ultimate lesson, although admittedly not always an easy one to understand: the full surrender to God, which is our ultimate goal. This truth is not a meaningless effusion or a mystery of any sort, she taught us. Once we fully understand and accept this, we no longer dread pain because we understand its purpose and its nature. This teaching made suffering take on a new dimension.

The poetry, wisdom, and drama of it all found fertile soil not only in her children, but in the souls of so many others this spiritual giant touched. Years before I watched my mother and father die at the end of long and painful illnesses, I already have been exposed to the philosophical and religious meaning of suffering. When inevitable misfortunes happened in my life, I was ready for them. Mama's teaching brought a sense of hope to what otherwise would have been a very difficult time in my life. My parents' uncomplaining, almost blissful, acceptance of pain, not just of the physical kind, but also the emotional trauma of saying farewells, gave validity to their teaching.

The firm foundation provided by both of my parents was identical to the very foundation of the Church they loved so dearly. No matter how terrible and dark some things might seem in my life, the support of Faith was always there at hand to comfort and console. She taught us to consider our brother and sister, whom we never met in this life because they died before we were born, our 'prayer partners' in heaven. That too was a comforting thought.

Over the years, I've met the very rich, and the very poor. I've known personally or via study the lives of the 'rich and the famous'. I've learned that money, power, prestige, sex, drugs or intoxicants are false gods which create more problems than they claim to solve. I've seen 'happy' rich couples whose togetherness crumbled because their life was founded on the world's so-called truths, rather than on the Eternal Truth. While no believer ever lives up to that high calling in this life, it is the only peace, the only joy, the only hope that is worth to live for.

A brief recap such as this can do no true justice to either my father or mother. But I hope the glimpses into their lives will bless and encourage others to seek the solution which they both found in their faith. This was the essence of both of them and I'm grateful for having had such unusual parents.

László A. J. Kovach

Several times Kovács **Erzsi *Néni***'s connection to Imre Thököly was indicated. She was a direct descendant of this remarkable charming and dedicated man. Imre Thököly was born Sept. 25, 1657, Késmárk, Slovakia—died Sept. 13, 1705, İzmit, Ottoman Empire [now in Turkey). He was a Hungarian patriot, a leader of the Hungarian Protestants in their struggle against the Austrian Habsburg rule, this being a recurring theme in Hungarian history. The main issue was the religious rights of Hungarian Protestants against the unbending will of the Catholic Austrian emperor.

The son of a rich Protestant family, he lost his parents while still a child. His father was executed for his a role in the Hungarian magnates' conspiracy against the Habsburg emperor Leopold I (1670). Because of the ongoing unrest at his birthplace in Upper Hungary (now Slovakia), where Protestants and Imperialists were constantly in arms against each other, young Thököly took refuge in Transylvania at his kinsman's court, the Prince of Transylvania. Here he came in contact with refugees of his home, who had great hopes that this high-born, highly gifted youth, a fellow sufferer, whose immense estates were confiscated by the Austrian emperor, would be the answer to the continuing problems, which all but devastated Upper Hungary.

At age twenty-five in 1682, he married Ilona Zrínyi, widow of Ferenc Rákóczy I. and became involved in a life long struggle against Austrian domination. He led the Hungarian Protestant Resistance movement against the continuing repressive Habsburg policies. In 1680 he was elected commander in chief of the malcontents. Making use of the Austrian emperor's preoccupation with hostile France, and backed by the Turks and the ruling Prince of Transylvania, Thököly overran much of Upper Hungary and forced the Austrian emperor **Leopold** to restore Hungarian liberties (Treaty of Sopron, 1681). He soon resumed hostilities against the emperor, allying himself with the Turks. At the two Diets he held, the estates, although impressed by him, showed a want of confidence. They feared that Thököly might sacrifice the nation's precarious independence by relying on the Turkish alliance. It was clear to most that at the time Turkey was bent on expansion. His life path was one long succession of spectacular victories and tragic defeats. Ultimately his rebellion was crushed, his fortresses captured; he was taken in chains to Belgrade, and his wife taken in custody to Vienna. His fortunes briefly revived in 1690 when he was installed by the Turks as Prince of Transylvania and he defeated the imperial (Austrian) forces at Zernest (August 1690). After the Treaty of Carlowitz (1699), Ottoman influence was significantly diminished, and he was forced to spend his remaining years with his wife in exile in Turkey.

Tamás, the youngest son of Ferenc Kovács and Erzsébet (Erzsi) Thököly remarked: "An interesting fact of my life is, that on my mother's side I am the seventh child of a mother who was seventh among her siblings, and am seven generation removed from Imre Thököly."

Dr. Dezső Ravasz, first principal at Niederaudorf. 1901-1964

He was born in 1901, the fifth of seven children. His father was the teacher-principal of the local school. After graduation from high school, he earned a teaching degree in history and geography and started teaching at the local high school. He earned the PhD in 1924, and in the same year married Margit Matolcsy, the noted interpreter of Hungarian folk songs. He was then appointed as principal at the Bethlen Gábor Protestant Gimnázium. He was drafted in 1944, and was almost immediately sent to the Russian front to fight. Toward the end of the war, his unit was ordered to move to Germany "to regroup" and to fight there against the approaching Red Army. Eventually, he was taken prisoner by the American Forces.

After he was released in 1946, he was reunited with his family and they found shelter in an abandoned cattle wagon on a side track of the Rosenheim railway station (Germany). Immediately, he and his wife gathered Hungarian refugee children and started a teaching program in the wagon.

Soon he joined the organization "*Magyar Jóléti Bizottság*," an attempt to serve the welfare of Hungarian refugees. There he met other dedicated persons, such as Kálmán Csia, the Protestant pastor; and Father Fekete, a Catholic priest, who were just as concerned about the children growing up without schooling as he was. Under the aegis and with the support of the various organizations, the involvement of CARITAS and the RED CROSS, they established the boarding school for Hungarian refugee girls at Niederaudorf, where he functioned as teacher and principal.

A year later, he decided to return with his family to Hungary, where, after some initial difficulties, he obtained the position of principal of the Madách High School at Salgótarján. He worked there until he retired. Dr. László Herold was appointed principal at the Salgótarján school (in Hungary) after Dr. Ravasz retired. He remembers Dr. Ravasz:

"I do not know who could do justice in remembering a man of so many talents, so many interests, such spiritual depths, and such an all encompassing love of mankind, especially of children. Perhaps only a poet could.

I first met Dr. Ravasz when, very young, insecure, scared and very confused, I arrived for an interview with him at Madách High School where I hoped to obtain a teaching position. Within minutes I felt at ease. I was facing a man across a spacious desk who was obviously a master of human relations. I realized too late that totally forgetting polite behavior, I overstayed my time. But I just could not leave him and apparently he also had no intentions of terminating the interview. He wanted to know all about me, about my goals, my background, my philosophy. In exchange, he revealed quite a bit of himself. I did not, not even for a moment, feel that I was being cross-examined.

I was hired. During all the years we worked together, I was strengthened in my first impression of him. Dr. Ravasz was exactly how he showed himself that very first day: a thoroughly good, caring person, absolutely professional, in possession of an admirably large body of knowledge and who never deviated from his standard of excellence and never stopped improving himself and everything else that was connected to the school.

He had extremely high standards, and did not tolerate any sort of slackness. Totally dedicated, he expected everyone who wished to work at his school to be just as dedicated, and never would tolerate a colleague, who considered teaching as just another job. His overwhelming love for children was touching. He treated everyone with respect and kindness, and was always open to listen to problems, or opposing views. He was totally open to suggestions, which he often incorporated into the school's program. He created an unbelievable tranquil atmosphere in the school at a time when the nation no longer knew what tranquility was; we felt that we were a tightly bound unit, all working together for the same goals on a very safe island.

His knowledge in fields other than his specialty was phenomenal. The conferences after the obligatory class observations were intellectual experiences, and true sources of learning and professional development for the teacher involved.

He was always bursting with energy, always busy improving and adding to the curriculum. During those difficult political times after he returned from Germany, when schools were bombarded with conflicting, unacceptable ideologies, and were often targets for political manipulations, he was unshakable and guided his small community with diplomatic finesse, avoiding catastrophes, which were happening daily in other schools. He created a peaceful island of safety and of excellence in the broiling waters of revenge, hatred, suspicion and political reforms—and he did this despite all the forces wanting to destroy it. He was operating from a high level of spiritual platform, where love and the development of the intellectual and spiritual potentials of young people took precedence above all. We felt blessed and privileged, having such a principal in those evil times.

I had the good fortune to be the homeroom teacher of Istók, son of Dr. Ravasz, for a period of four years. During this time it became evermore clear to me that nothing, absolutely nothing is of more consequence in the development of a young person, than the home, which raises him. Special programs, individualized care, behavior modification programs, remedial instructions are only providing a band-aid over the problems, but do not solve them. They merely attempt to patch up the neglect which children suffered in their homes. Children grow up very fast, and once they pass a certain phase in their development, and enter into a new phase, it is almost impossible to provide, as an afterthought, the care withheld from them in their earlier stages. It is sad but hard fact that institutions or their complex and expensive programs cannot fix what the family neglected. Only a good family background can provide the magic power, which ensures the scholastic success and spiritual growth of growing children. Istók was a shining example of what a student can achieve, who has the good luck of coming from a caring, goal-oriented family.

Istók graduated from high school and to the immense delight of his proud parents, was accepted at the University of Eötvös Lóránd, the Hungarian equivalent of Harvard, or Yale. This was the fateful year of 1956, when the memorable, almost unbelievable Hungarian Revolution ended in failure and tragedy. The euphoria was buried in a blood bath. In the aftermath of revenge and senseless hatred, there was a horrible massacre at Salgótarján. Istók died of gunshot wounds in the arms of his father.

It was a senseless mass killing and the town was in shock. Parents, spouses, children, entire families broke down because there were few people who did not suffer the loss of a loved one. Dr. Ravasz was one of the parents mourning a child and he was totally devastated.

He tried to find solace and relief in hard work and drove himself ever more. His days at the school routinely started before seven in the morning, and he seldom left before 7-8 in the evening. But his soul was no longer in it. Overnight, he turned into an old man, not only lost in a world he did not understand, but also losing his will to live on in it. He started avoiding people and increasingly excused himself from participating in events. Only his love for children lasted till the very end. Eventually he retired, but his sadness and loneliness only deepened as he faced the bleak empty days which he shared with his beloved wife. Three years after his retirement, at age 63 he died."

INDEX

A

Ábrahám, Judith (Nagyőszy), 3, 173, 192
Adelsberger, Mária, 21, 30, 33, 34, 56, 63, 69, 73, 100, 234
Adenauer, Konrad, 88
Aeneas, 31, 32
Allied Forces, 8, 88, 128, 131, 179, 198, 199, 200, 225, 236
Almássy, László, 110
Arany, János, 32, 147
Argentina, 15, 136, 220
Asbóth, Gyula, 47
Ash Wednesday, 138
Australia, 29, 58, 76, 100, 136, 160, 167, 169, 178, 222

B

Baden-Powell, Lord Robert, 109, 110
Balla, Éva (Zahoray), x, 3, 95, 96
Bárány, Márta, 3, 71, 125, 127, 161, 234, 235
Barcsay, Ákos, 3, 153
Bauschlott, 154, 160, 161, 164
Bavaria, 13, 17, 44, 79, 86, 91, 92, 93, 117, 126, 134, 161, 169, 175, 195, 200, 201, 202, 216, 217, 219, 220, 221, 224, 225, 230
Bayerbach, 17
black pudding, 65
blood sausage, 64, 65, 68, 136
Bodnár, Gábor, 110, 111, 114
Bond, James, 9
Bonyhay. Éva (Magyar), 3, 176
Brandenburg, 84
Brazil, 15, 136, 169, 186, 227, 228, 229, 230, 231, 232
Bridges, Robert, 74
Brueghel, 110
Brünnstein, 56, 78, 79, 115, 188, 225
Burg Kastl, 154, 229, 230
Burt, Gahl, 211
Buza, Mária, x, 3, 91, 112, 116
Byron, 15

C

Canada, 29, 136, 166
Cantrell, Christina, 2
Carlyle, 211
Carmelite, 134, 148, 157, 167, 225
carneval, 138
carnival, 138, 139, 141
Catilina, Lucius, 33
Cecey, Éva, 112, 114, 116
CERN, 154
Chiemsee, 45, 86, 87, 181, 182
Christian, Joyce, 62, 212, 226, 243
Ciardi, John, 159, 214
Cicero, 33, 72
Circe, 30
clausura, 48, 137
Clinton, Hillary Rodham, 46
Cole, Tyler, 87
Csaba, Zsolt, 3, 190
Cserháti, Ferenc, x, 1, 13, 22, 25, 41, 71, 117, 119, 125, 131, 161, 163, 168, 169, 171
Csia, Kálmán, 10, 22, 24, 42, 48, 236, 237, 245
Czihy, Kati, 96

D

Dachau, 14, 16, 234
Dahl, Felix, 136
Dax, Anna (Winkler), 3
Derka, father, 169, 171
Diószeghy, Tibor, 44, 95, 96
Displaced Persons Act, 7
DoDDS, 87, 206, 210
dogma, 44

E

Eisenhower, Dwight D., 88
Emerson, Waldo, 15
ermine, 21
ersatz, 65, 68, 71
European Recovery Act, 132

F

Farsang, 138
Fasching, 138
Finkey, Lilla, 3
Fischer, Tibor, v
fondant, 70, 71, 189
Frank, Anne, v
Frost, Robert, 106

G

Germany, i, iii, vi, x, 1, 7, 13, 14, 22, 25, 30, 47, 57, 65, 68, 70, 87, 88, 93, 110, 122, 128, 132, 154, 166, 168, 174, 176, 179, 180, 182, 183, 184, 189, 195, 198, 204, 205, 206, 209, 210, 211, 213, 222, 227, 229, 234, 235, 236, 237, 238, 245, 246
Goethe, Johann Wolfgang, 32, 122, 166, 184
graduation examinations, 102, 119, 120, 232
Gruber, Éva, 3
Gulf War, 206, 213

H

Habsburg, Otto von, 211
Hadady, Magda, 3, 178
Halvorsen Elementary, 210
Hanau, 212, 213
Hannibal, 34
Hautzig, Esther, v
Hefty, Laci, 91
Hegedűs, Nóra (Sztáray), 2, 3, 160
Hegedűs, Piroska (Zoltán), ix, 3
Hennyey, Gusztáv, 161
Heron, 124
Heuss, Theodore, 88
Höchster, Erhard, 88
Hölderlin, Friedrich, 35
Holston, Christine, 212, 213
Homer, 29, 31
Homo Erectus, 67
Homo Sapiens, 67
honey cakes, 180, 189
Horthy, Miklós, 93, 110
Hungarian refugees, x, 25, 215, 221, 225, 236, 245

Hungary, v, vi, x, 5, 7, 8, 10, 13, 14, 15, 16, 17, 29, 34, 42, 45, 46, 47, 49, 55, 57, 62, 70, 79, 80, 86, 91, 93, 95, 96, 97, 101, 102, 103, 106, 109, 110, 116, 119, 122, 125, 126, 127, 128, 134, 140, 146, 147, 149, 154, 158, 160, 165, 167, 169, 173, 174, 177, 178, 179, 180, 182, 183, 187, 189, 190, 191, 193, 195, 197, 198, 200, 203, 204, 206, 211, 213, 214, 220, 221, 224, 225, 226, 228, 229, 233, 234, 235, 236, 237, 238, 239, 240, 241, 244, 245
Hypatia, 33

I

Igo-Kemenes, Péter, 3, 153
Inn river, 13, 79, 91, 117, 153
Irányi, László, 71

J

Jancsó, Miklós, 110
Jautz, Feri, 3, 149, 163
Joachim, father, 169, 171
Jókai, Mór, 70
Juhász, Klára, 3, 58, 126

K

Kaiser Mountains, 78
Kálózdy, Nándor, 119
Kearsley, Loranna, 87
Keller, Dr. Anton, 119
Kennedy, John F., 9
Kertész, Imre, v
Khayyam, Omar, 106
Knudsen, Gene and Debra, 2
Kölcsey, Klári (Shelton), 3, 175, 190
Kolping, Adolph Foundation, 131, 134, 135, 167
Koncz, Lajos, x, 2, 160
Kossuth, Lajos, 123, 183
Kótay, Zoltán, 44
Kovach, Francis, 127, 128, 129
Kovach, László, 240, 244
Kovach, Tamás, 239
Kovács, Erzsébet, 95, 97, 98, 244
Kovács, Ferenc, 2, 24, 36, 42, 43, 44, 45, 63, 75, 84, 86, 95, 96, 104, 112, 125, 127, 131, 137, 138, 161, 163, 196, 203, 222, 239, 245

Kovács, Joseph, 128
Kovács, Margit, 42
Kővári, Lajos, 111
Kozányi, Kati (Fodor), 3
Králik, László, 109
Kristó-Nagy, Kati, 3, 99, 107, 111, 112, 114, 116
Kufstein, 13, 79, 91

L

Lahner, Béla, 3, 163, 195, 238
Lang, Dr. Karl, 119
Laufen, 14, 102, 146, 202, 216, 217, 219, 220, 225
Leonard, Max, 210, 212
Leonardo da Vinci, 9, 21, 22
Leowey, Klára, 79
Lindenberg, 154, 163
Lits, Ernő, 161
Ludwig II of Bavaria, 86, 87, 134

M

Madách, Imre, 158, 245, 246
Madame Butterfly, 97
Marcell, Dr. Árpád, 164, 196
Markó, Mária.Magdolna (Gajáry), 3, 112, 197
Marshall Plan, 132
Marshall PLan, 132
Marshall, George, 132
Matolcsy, Margit, 10, 37, 80, 97, 245
Matthew the Evangelist, 66, 67, 88
Mécs. László, 96
Mélynádassy, Antal, 3, 137, 202, 216
Mészáros, Éva (Katafias), 3
Meynadasy, Antal, vi, ix, 3, 163
Millet, Jean-Francois, 67
Mittenwald, 16, 17, 32, 100, 199, 200, 201
money reform in Germany, x, 35, 75, 101, 104, 107, 131, 137, 201, 222
Mt. Blanc, 84
München, x, 1, 10, 18, 22, 23, 25, 41, 44, 45, 66, 71, 84, 97, 125, 131, 134, 154, 189, 200, 202, 204, 236, 238
Munich, 17, 18, 22, 45, 181, 183, 184, 217
Mylo, Tamás, 169

N

NASA, 9, 209
Neuschwanstein, 86, 87
Niederaudorf, vi, ix, 1, 3, 4, 8, 13, 14, 15, 17, 18, 20, 21, 22, 23, 26, 29, 41, 42, 45, 48, 49, 55, 57, 67, 68, 72, 79, 85, 93, 95, 97, 102, 107, 110, 111, 112, 114, 117, 118, 119, 123, 126, 127, 128, 131, 134, 138, 140, 145, 149, 160, 165, 166, 167, 169, 170, 175, 177, 178, 180, 182, 183, 192, 195, 196, 197, 201, 202, 203, 204, 205, 221, 224, 227, 228, 231, 232, 233, 234, 235, 236, 237, 245
Niederaudorf-Reisach, x, 9, 10, 49, 95, 139, 193, 202, 211
Nymphenburg, 84

O

Oberammergau, 86, 88
Odysseus, 29, 30, 31
Ordódy, Mrs. Sándor, 10, 18, 22
Organisationsentwurf, 119
Osterman, M., 118
Osterode, 175, 192, 193

P

Passau, 10, 15, 17, 22, 97, 119, 123, 154, 160, 161, 163, 164, 179, 196, 201, 202
Passau-Waldwerke, 164
Passion Play, 86, 88
Penelope, 30, 31
Perth, Australia, 222, 223
Petres, Judith (Balogh), ii, xi, 3, 4, 202, 203
Petres, Zsuzsa (Szappanos), 2, 3, 167, 202, 214
Pettendy, Kati, 3, 112, 233
Piding, 126, 234
Plattling, 161
Pocking, 177
Pythagoras, 37, 72, 124, 135

Q

Queen Victoria, 34, 35

R

Radnay, Anikó (Kent), 3, 167, 220

Ravasz, Dr. Dezső, vi, ix, 2, 10, 17, 19, 20, 22, 25, 29, 34, 36, 37, 39, 41, 55, 71, 72, 99, 111, 117, 119, 123, 125, 126, 127, 131, 137, 138, 178, 221, 222, 224, 237, 245, 246, 247
Reagan, Mrs. Nancy, 211
Red Cross, 10, 18, 25, 177, 182, 221, 238
Reisach, x, 3, 35, 41, 44, 48, 50, 69, 71, 74, 75, 76, 92, 97, 101, 103, 105, 114, 115, 127, 131, 134, 135, 136, 137, 140, 145, 147, 149, 152, 153, 154, 157, 158, 160, 161, 163, 164, 167, 168, 169, 171, 175, 196, 197, 202, 203, 204, 216, 217, 225, 232, 234, 238
Rembrandt, 133
Rome, 30, 31
Rónay, Tamás, 111
Rosenheim, 22, 86, 113, 117, 119, 169, 245
Rózsa, Sándor, 79
Rozsály, Ferenc, 10, 13, 18, 22, 131
Rubens, 133, 208

S

Salgótarján, 127, 245, 247
Sao Paulo, Brazil, 229, 230, 231, 232
Sartor Resartus, 211
Schulrat, 117, 175
scouting, 46, 100, 109, 110, 111, 114, 116, 169, 216, 218, 228, 231
Sforza, Lodovico, 21
Shrove Tuesday, 138, 139
Silva, Luiz Inacio Lula, 230
Sinkovits, Imre, 110
Socrates, 124, 165
Soli Deo Gloria, 44, 45, 46, 47, 147, 181
Soós, Géza, 45, 46, 47, 181
Soviet Union, v, 5, 6, 7, 10, 47, 51, 85, 103, 110, 128, 132, 179, 184, 191, 195, 203, 235, 237
St. Augustine, 51
St. István, 122
St. Theresa of Avila, 51
Stalingrad, 237, 238
Stoll, Dr. Gábor, 131
Strada, Ferenc, 38
Szablya, Helen, v
Szabó, Dóra (Badzey), vi, 3, 216, 224
Szaloncukor, salonzuckerl, szalonczukkedli, 70
Széchenyi, István, x, 123
Szerb, Antal, 110

Szkladányi, Ágnes (Vanjek), 3
Sztáray, Zoltán, 183
Szücs, Marika, 3
Szűcs, Marika, 112

T

Tag der Jugend, 113, 117
Takáts, Erzsébet, 97, 146
Takáts, Sarolta (Sári), 38, 96, 161
Teleki, Blanka, 79
Teleki, count Pál, 25, 110, 112, 183
Thököly, Erzsébet, 128, 239, 245
Thököly, Imre, 244, 245
Thun-Hohenstein, count Leo von, 119
Tintoretto, 133
Tirczka, Éva (Piller), 3, 32, 68, 78, 111, 116, 169, 227
Toldi, Miklós, 32, 146, 147, 159
Totila, 136
Train, 179
Troy, 30
Truman, Harry S., 7

U

U.S. Air Force Base Rhein Main, 87
Ulrico, 139
United States, 22, 128, 132, 154, 178, 180, 182, 183, 203, 204, 216, 234, 236
Uranus military operation, 238
Urfahrn, 134

V

Váczy, Anna (Mrs. Méynadasy), 3, 96, 203
Venezuela, 15, 107, 114, 136
Venice, 138, 139
Virgil, 31
Vörösmarty, Mihály, 122

W

Wagner, Richard, 86
Währungsreform, 37, 92, 131, 132, 133, 227
Waldwerke, 161, 163, 164
Wallenberg, Roul, 47
Waller, Simon, 13, 25, 64, 104, 131, 133, 224
Weiss, Helga, v

Wendelstein, 78
Wesselényi, Miklós, 79
Wirtschaftswunder, 132, 133

Y

Youth Day, 113, 117

Z

Zoltán, Iván, 3, 96, 232
Zoltán, Sándor, 42, 181, 233

Made in the USA
Middletown, DE
09 May 2015